Reference Guide to English

Reference Guide to English

A Handbook of English as a Second Language

SECOND EDITION

Alice Maclin

Dekalb Community College

Holt, Rinehart and Winston
New York Chicago San Francisco Philadelphia
Montreal Toronto London Sydney
Tokyo Mexico City Rio de Janeiro Madrid

To My Husband

Library of Congress Cataloging-in-Publication Data

Maclin, Alice.
  Reference guide to English.

  Includes index.
  1. English language—Text-books for foreign
speakers.   2. English language—Grammar—1950-   —
Handbooks, manuals, etc.   I. Title.
PE1128.M3254   1987   428.2′4   86-14809
ISBN 0-03-004193-7

CBS COLLEGE PUBLISHING
Holt, Rinehart and Winston
The Dryden Press
Saunders College Publishing

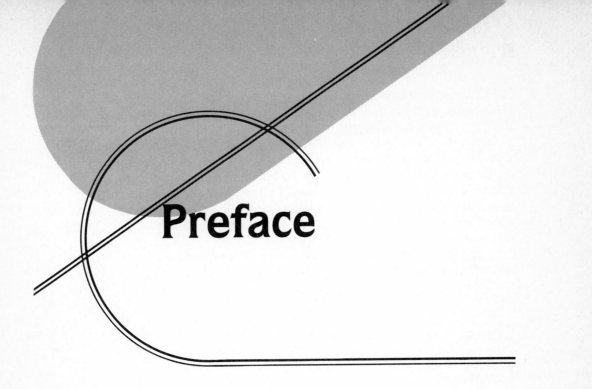

Preface

This second edition of *Reference Guide to English* explains many features of written English that trouble nonnative writers. With the addition of exercises and a key, this new edition enables students to locate and correct many of their own problems. Alphabetical organization and cross-references help students locate the facts needed. Many differences in British and United States usage are mentioned. Since students have been learning languages not their own for thousands of years, obviously they can learn by many different methods. This book is intended to supplement other texts, no matter what their theoretical bases or methods.

The extensive index includes grammatical terms not used in the text but cross-referenced to those that are used. Words of special difficulty are indexed, but individual words in long lists and tables are not.

The grammatical terminology chosen is mixed, based on experience in the classroom with students from many different parts of the world. Most students coming from outside the United States are already familiar with many of the terms of traditional grammar and with many of the concepts of the newer grammars. Students who have spent more of their time in the United States often have the most difficult time learning to write well because their fluency in the spoken language makes them impatient of the time and patience needed to produce good writing. Simple explanations and clear examples can help them see the differences between what they hear and what they must write.

The author thanks many friends and colleagues who gave advice and encouragement in the preparation of the first edition, but especially the late David DeCamp of the University of Texas, Austin, and Zenobia T. Liles, formerly of DeKalb Community College. Special thanks for classroom testing of this edition go to colleagues at DeKalb Community College: Eleanor Smith and Charleise T. Young, and to Jane Chisholm at the Georgia Institute of Technology. Additional thanks go to the reviewers of this edition: Kyle Perkins, Southern Illinois University; Frank Pialorsi, University of Arizona; Barbara Radin, Hostos Community College; Jean Zukowski-Faust, Northern Arizona University; and to Lucy Rosenthal and Jeanette Ninas Johnson of Holt, Rinehart and Winston.

Special appreciation is given to students of many national origins, backgrounds, and aspirations who have helped the author gain insight into the difficulties of learning English.

A.M.

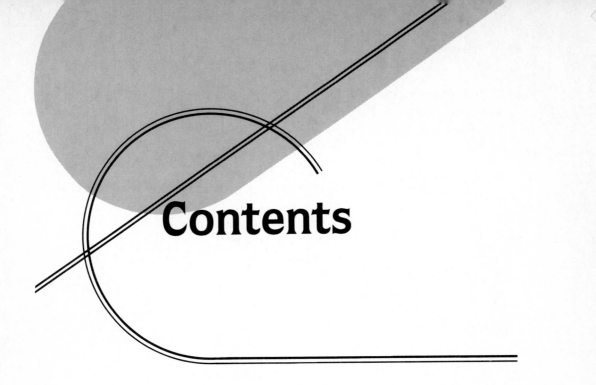

Contents

Abbreviations

Abbreviations are used differently according to the subject matter and the purpose of your writing. Formal academic writing, scientific writing, and business writing have different usages. You can find lists of abbreviations in all dictionaries and in handbooks for secretaries.

Formal Academic Writing (Humanities)

Avoid most abbreviations in formal writing for the humanities. Write out in full the following kinds of words even if you know an abbreviation for them:

1. Proper names and titles: William, not Wm.; Mister, not Mr.
2. Street, Road, Boulevard, and other geographical terms: Street, not St.
3. Cities, states, provinces, and countries: Los Angeles, not L.A.; Ontario, not Ont.; EXCEPTION: use Washington, *D.C.* (See below under "Business Writing" for addresses and postal abbreviations.)
4. Months and days of the week: February, not Feb.; Sunday, not Sun.
5. Units of measure: ounces, not oz.; hours, not hrs.

1

6. References to volumes, chapters, and pages when these references are part of the composition: page for p.; volume for vol. In references and bibliographies, however, follow the standard forms for accepted abbreviations.

7. Do not use an ampersand (&) in place of *and* unless a business firm uses it in its name.

Some abbreviations are acceptable in formal academic writing, but not all authorities agree on their forms and usage.

1   Use abbreviations from Latin with care, even the ones that are now considered English words and do not need to be underlined or set in italic type. Use the English words that mean the same when you can, as you are less likely to make mistakes with them.

c. or ca.: *circa,* about, to indicate a date that is not known for certain (c. 1290 or 1295?)
i.e.: *id est,* that is
inter alia: among other things
e.g.: *exempli gratia,* for example
etc.: *et cetera,* and so forth. Avoid this form; never use *and* immediately before *etc.*
v. or vs.: *versus,* against
v.z.: *videlicet*—that is or namely, to introduce examples or lists.

2   Use abbreviations with times and dates.
A.M. and P.M. for *ante meridiem* and *post meridiem* to mean before noon and afternoon only if you also use numbers to show exact time.

Incorrect: The plane arrived in the A.M.

Correct: The plane arrived at 11:23 A.M.

A.D.: Latin *anno Domini* for *in the year of our Lord;* in formal writing put A.D. before the date, as in A.D. 1791.
B.C.: before Christ; put B.C. after the date, as in 431 B.C.
C.E. and B.C.E. are sometimes used instead of A.D. and B.C. C.E. means Common Era, as in 1791 C.E. B.C.E. means Before Common Era, as in 431 B.C.E.

3   Use all capital letters (sometimes called solid caps) for abbreviations for most government agencies, international organizations, and other well-known groups. Periods are usually not used, especially if the abbreviation stands for the first letters of the words that make the name. (An abbreviation made from the first letters of words is called an acronym.)

GOP: Grand Old Party, a political party (the Republican Party)
IRS: Internal Revenue Service (government agency)
OPEC: Organization of Petroleum Exporting Countries (international organization)
TVA: Tennessee Valley Authority (public utility company)
UNESCO: United Nations Educational, Scientific, and Cultural Organization
WHO: World Health Organization (United Nations agency)

4   Use abbreviations for titles before and after proper names if your style sheet allows them. Periods are usually used with abbreviations of titles in the United States although they are often left out in British usage. Put a comma before a title that follows a name.

Arlene Simpson, *Ph.D.*
Dr. James H. Wester, *Jr.*
St. Anne (Saint Anne)
Laney Sanderson, *Esq.*
Mr. and *Mrs.* Paul Jorgenson

Do not put the same title both before and after a name.

Incorrect: *Dr.* Agnes J. Hodges, *M.D.*
Correct: Agnes J. Hodges, *M.D.*
Correct: *Dr.* Agnes J. Hodges

Jr. for *Junior* and *Sr.* for *Senior* are often used to identify a father and son who have the same name. They can be used with *Mr.*:

Mr. Martin Williams, Sr. (father or, occasionally, grandfather)
Mr. Martin Williams, Jr. (son or, occasionally, grandson)

Sometimes a father, son, and grandson all have the same name. While all three are living, the grandson is identified by *III*.

Mr. Martin Williams III

Esq. for *Esquire* is a term of courtesy used after a man's name chiefly in Great Britain. Do not use any other title before the name if you use *Esq.* after it. Except for use by some lawyers, *Esq.* is almost never used in the United States.

Paul Reynolds, Esq.

NOTE: Titles are not used in signatures on letters, applications, checks, and legal documents. Do not use *Mrs.* with the first name only.

   5 When the last word in a sentence is an abbreviation that is followed by a period, do not add another period; use only one period at the end of the sentence:

My doctor is Agnes J. Hodges, M.D.
Ken's lawyer is Paul Hopkins, Jr.

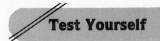

Test Yourself

Make corrections that are needed in the following sentences.

1. Confucius was a famous Chinese scholar who was born c. 551 b.c.

2. When the plane from London arrived yesterday a.m., Mr. Emerson Smith was not on

   board, but his wife, Mrs. Harriet, was on the plane.

3. Dermatitis is a skin inflammation that is often caused by chemicals in plants, foods,

   fabrics, dyes, and etc.

4. *Who* is an agency of the U.N. that issues travel documents that show inoculations a traveler has had against communicable diseases: e.g., against cholera and yellow fever.

5. The period in Europ. history known as the Middle Ages is often dated from the fall of the Roman Emp. in 476 a.d. to the 15th cent.

6. John Jas. Audubon won fame for his paintings of Amer. birds. Although he was born in what is now Haiti and educated in France, he came to the U. S. to the family estate near Philadelphia, Penna. From 1808 to 1820 he lived in Ky. and later traveled up and down the Miss. River. For a while he lived in New Orleans, La. His paintings of birds were published in sev. diff. parts in Gr. Brit. between 1827 and 1838.

Scientific and Technical Writing

Since different disciplines have different accepted styles, you need to consult the style sheet of the academic field you are writing in. Ask your instructor or a librarian to help you find the style sheet you need. Botany, biology, and zoology use the same style manual, but different manuals or style sheets are published for chemistry, geology, linguistics, mathematics, physics, and psychology. In general, more abbreviations are used in scientific and technical writing than in the humanities, and footnotes and bibliographies are also different.

The following kinds of abbreviations are usually used in scientific and technical writing:

1   Units of measure: time, linear measure, area, volume, capacity, weight, temperature, and circular measure. Periods are usually not used.

10 km, ft^2 or sq ft, in^3, cc or cm^3, qt, pt, lbs, and so forth
10°C or 10°F (ten degrees, Celsius or Fahrenheit)
a 90° angle (a ninety-degree angle)
15,000 rpm (revolutions per minute)
55 mph (miles per hour)

When alternate abbreviations exist, such as cc and cm^3, use the same form all the time.

2   In most scientific and technical papers, abbreviate and do not underline the names of periodicals.

J. Am. Chem. Soc. for *Journal of the American Chemical Society*
Botan. Rev. for *Botanical Review*

3   Use an ampersand (&) in place of *and* in titles.

Arch. Biochem. & Biophys. for *Archives of Biochemistry and Biophysics*

4   When dates are abbreviated as numbers, usage in the United States puts the month first, but British usage puts the day first.

1-12-85 means
U. S.: January 12, 1985
1-12-85
British: 1*st* December, 1985

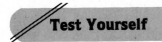

Test Yourself

Make corrections that are needed in the following sentences to put them in scientific style.

1.   Absolute zero is minus 273.16 degrees on the Celsius scale or minus 459.69 degrees

    Fahrenheit.

2.   One hectare equals 10,000 m², but one acre equals only 4047 square meters.

Business Writing

In writing the body of a letter, follow the rules for formal academic writing (humanities) above. For addresses on letters and envelopes in very formal correspondence, follow the rules for formal academic writing. For addresses in everyday business correspondence, follow the policy of the business or institution. United States government agencies follow a guide published by the Government Printing Office (GPO).

   1   You may abbreviate numbers used as street names: 1st, 2nd, 3rd, 4th, 5th, 6th, 7th, 8th, 9th, and 10th. Do not put a period after these abbreviations:

101st Street   37th Avenue

But, if local usage writes a name out in full, follow local usage:

Fifth Avenue   Tenth Street

   2   Geographical locations may be abbreviated in addresses.

Ave. for Avenue   Dr. for Drive
Bldg. for Building   Pl. for Place
Blvd. for Boulevard   Rd. for Road
Ct. for Court   St. for Street

   3   North, South, East, and West as adjectives may be abbreviated to the first letter. Do not abbreviate the name of a street.

1021 N. 101st St.   **but**   1021 North Ave.

   4   Some cities use a location after the street.

1021 N. 101st St., *N.E.* (northeast)

5 The zip code or zone number is a geographical abbreviation. Be sure to put it in all addresses in countries that use it. In the United States the zip code uses five numbers; some countries use numbers and letters. Do not put a comma between the end of the address and the zip code.

383 Madison Avenue
New York, N.Y. 10017

200 Euston Road
London NW1 2DB

6 Abbreviations for U. S. states and possessions are either traditional or postal. Traditional abbreviations are usually followed by a period. Postal abbreviations have two capital letters with no space between them and are not followed by a period. Use traditional abbreviations for Canadian addresses.

Abbreviations of U. S. States and Possessions and Canadian Provinces

	Traditional	*Postal*
Alabama	Ala.	AL
Alaska	Alaska	AK
Alberta	Alta.	
Arizona	Ariz.	AZ
Arkansas	Ark.	AR
British Columbia	B.C.	
California	Calif. or Cal.	CA
Colorado	Colo.	CO
Connecticut	Conn.	CT
Delaware	Del.	DE
District of Columbia	D.C.	DC
Florida	Fla.	FL
Georgia	Ga.	GA
Guam	Guam	GU
Hawaii	Hawaii	HI
Idaho	Idaho	ID
Illinois	Ill.	IL
Indiana	Ind.	IN
Iowa	Ia.	IA
Kansas	Kans.	KS
Kentucky	Ky.	KY
Louisiana	La.	LA
Maine	Me.	ME
Manitoba	Man.	
Maryland	Md.	MD
Massachusetts	Mass.	MA
Michigan	Mich.	MI
Minnesota	Minn.	MN
Mississippi	Miss.	MS
Missouri	Mo.	MO
Montana	Mont.	MT
Nebraska	Nebr., Neb.	NB

Abbreviations of U. S. States and Possessions and Canadian Provinces (*continued*)

	Traditional	*Postal*
Nevada	Nev.	NV
New Brunswick	N.B.	
Newfoundland	Nfld.	
New Hampshire	N.H.	NH
New Jersey	N.J.	NJ
New Mexico	N. Mex., N.M.	NM
New York	N.Y.	NY
North Carolina	N.C.	NC
North Dakota	N. Dak., N.D.	ND
Nova Scotia	N.S.	
Ohio	Ohio	OH
Oklahoma	Okla.	OK
Ontario	Ont.	
Oregon	Oreg., Ore.	OR
Pennsylvania	Penn., Penna.	PA
Prince Edward Island	P.E.I.	
Puerto Rico	P.R.	PR
Quebec	Que.	
Rhode Island	R.I.	RI
Saskatchewan	Sask.	
South Carolina	S.C.	SC
South Dakota	S. Dak., S.D.	SD
Tennessee	Tenn.	TN
Texas	Texas	TX
Utah	Utah	UT
Vermont	Vt.	VT
Virginia	Va.	VA
Virgin Islands	V.I.	VI
Washington	Wash.	WA
West Virginia	W. Va.	WV
Wisconsin	Wis., Wisc.	WI
Wyoming	Wyo.	WY

Test Yourself

Make corrections that are necessary in the following sentences for correct business style.

1. Because we have closed our plant in Penna., we will ship the parts you ordered from our plant in Mass.

2. Our sales representative in the Virgin Is. will call on Mr. Harrison in his new office in the Equitable Bldg.

3. Write the following address in the correct form for mailing. Use your own name and address for the return.

    Wilson, Peter J. — office in Atlanta, Georgia — 1015 East Grand Boulevard — zip: 30308

Absolutes

An absolute (also called a nominative absolute) is a phrase made of a noun or pronoun and an *-ing* or past participle. An absolute modifies the whole clause to which it is related. It does not modify one single word in the independent clause. Use a comma to separate an absolute from the independent clause it modifies.   (see **Clauses**)

Absolute	*Independent Clause*
noun participle	
The *door having been locked* with two bolts,	we felt safe for the night.
noun participle	
No more *money being* available,	the committee voted to keep last year's budget.
noun participle	
Her *head* almost *hidden* by a very large hat	the old woman waited on the corner

The absolute may follow the independent clause.

Independent Clause	*Absolute*
We felt safe for the night,	the *door having been locked* with two bolts.
The committee voted to keep last year's budget,	no more *money being* available.
The old woman waited on the corner,	her *head* almost *hidden* by a very large hat.

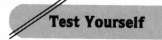

Test Yourself

Combine the following pairs of sentences so that one of them is an absolute.

1. Every evening Jim watched television. His dog sat on the floor at his feet.
2. Two hours passed. I tried to call my mother again.
3. The rain stopped. We walked from the library to the car.
4. The wind died. The roof stopped leaking.

Abstract and Concrete

Abstract and *concrete* are terms used to show the difference between ideas that exist only in the mind (abstract) from things that can be touched, tasted, smelled, heard, or seen (concrete). Concrete things are *tangible;* that is, they are directly perceived by the senses. Abstractions are *intangible;* they cannot be directly perceived by the senses. Clear writing develops ideas that are abstract by suggesting concrete examples.

An Abstract Idea	A Concrete Example
friendship	what my friend Ed does to help me
beauty	Miss Universe
	a Ferrari
	a rainbow
	Michelangelo's sculpture *David*
	the Alps
education	my experience in the first grade
motherhood	how my mother helps me

If an idea is more general, it is on a *higher* level of abstraction. If it is more specific, it is on a *lower* level of abstraction.

		Level of Abstraction		
higher		⟵————————⟶		lower
beauty	beauty in nature	mountains	the Alps	the Matterhorn
family relationships	my family	my parents	my mother	something my mother does
education	my education	my primary school	my first grade	how my first-grade teacher taught us arithmetic
health	child health	childhood diseases	measles	my case of the measles

See **Generalization** and **Outlining.**

Abstract nouns in English are often uncountable. (see **Countable and Uncountable Nouns**)

Test Yourself

Underline the word that is the most abstract or general in each group.

1. nod, dance, jump, move, shudder

2. shirt, trousers, skirt, hat, clothing

3. weather, lightning, thunder, snow, rain

4. car, wheel, transportation, vehicle, bicycle

5. dog, paw, animal, cat, rabbit

6. correspondence, letter, stamp, stationery, envelope

Active Verbs, see **Passive**

Adjective/Adverb Choice

Adjectives and adverbs function differently in the sentence. Adjectives modify nouns, but adverbs can modify verbs, adjectives, other adverbs, participles, and whole clauses.

Many adverbs of manner end in *-ly*. (Adverbs of manner tell **how** something is done.) Adjectives have a number of different endings.   (see **Word Formation, suffixes**)   A few words have the same form for both adjective and adverb uses.   (see **Adverbs, forms**)

Do not use an adverb as the complement of a linking verb (the most common linking verbs are *be, feel, taste, appear, seem,* and *become*).

Subject	Linking Verb	Predicate Adjective Modifies Subject
The *food*	smelled tasted appeared	good. (not *well*)
He	felt	*happy* about his schedule.
The *horse*	seemed	*strong.*
As he practiced, *he*	became	*quick* at shooting goals.

Good and *well* have different meanings after linking verbs. *Well* means "in good physical health."

The little *boy* is *well.* (not sick)
The little *boy* is *good.* (well-behaved)

To modify the verb, use an adverb.

The old man could not *hear well.* (*Well* modifies *hear,* not *man.*)
The blind man *easily felt* his way with his cane. (*Without difficulty,* the way he walked along, feeling with his cane)
The blind man felt *easy* about walking with his cane. (His mind was *easy, not afraid.* Felt in this sentence means *had a mental condition.*)

Test Yourself

Correct the errors in the following sentences. One or more sentences may be correct.

1. The full moon appears brightly in the autumn sky.

2. Weight lifters seem strongly enough to lift a car.

3. The new puppies are very lively.

4. These problems are too hardly for the students to solve.

5. The children from the kindergarten class behaved good at the party.

Adjectives

Use adjectives to make writing more specific and concrete. Words, phrases, and clauses can be used as adjectives. This section tells about single-word adjectives.   (see **Clauses, Modifiers, Prepositions, Infinitives, Gerunds,** and **Participles**)

Some modifying words cannot be used with all nouns: *much/many, few/little, some,* and *several,* for example. (see **Countable and Uncountable Nouns** and **Determiners**)

Form of Adjectives

In English, adjectives before plural nouns have the same form as adjectives before singular nouns. Do not add an *-s* to words that are used as adjectives before plural nouns.

Singular	*Plural*
a re*d* car	the re*d* cars
a war*m* coa*t*	some war*m* coa*ts*
a six-year-ol*d* child	three six-year-ol*d* children
an informativ*e* lecture	informativ*e* lecture*s*

Do not put an *-s* on a word that modifies a noun, whether the modifier comes before the noun or after the verb.

Professor Johnson gave informativ*e* lecture*s*. (before the noun)
Professor Johnson's lecture*s* were informativ*e*. (after the verb)
The children had ne*w* penci*l* boxes. (before the noun)
Flower po*ts* full of re*d* blossom*s* brightened the porch. (before the noun)
Some ancient ruins show primitiv*e* buildin*g* method*s*. (before the noun)
Some ancient ruins show methods of building that are primitive. (after the verb)

NOTE: A few nouns that already end in *-s* can be used to modify other nouns. These nouns keep the *-s*. The *-s* on these words does not show that the noun is plural.

Peter has opened a ne*w* saving*s* account.
Did you hear the new*s* broadcast?
Our club is having a tenni*s* tournament.

NOTE: Do not be confused by the changes in pronoun forms. Possessive pronouns take their number from the word they stand for (antecedent).

	antecedent	possessive pronoun	noun	
Singular:	Patricia found	her	book.	(*her* refers to a singular word,
			books.	Patricia)

Plural: The girls found   their   book.   (*their* refers to a plural word,
                                                books.   girls)

This, that, these, and *those* take their number from the word they modify when they are used as adjectives.

Patricia found this book. (singular noun)
                that
Patricia found these books. (plural noun)
                those

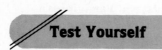

Test Yourself

Correct the adjective forms and errors in word order in the following sentences wherever necessary.

1. Imaginatives stories set in outer space or in the future are called science fiction.

2. Clevers writers of science fiction have wide knowledge of recent technologicals advances.

3. These writers put imaginatives details in their unusual stories.

4. They give us unnaturals characters with stranges abilities.

5. Some science fictions characters look like human beings.

6. The powers mentals of this characters are different from ours, however.

7. The emotions of characters in science fiction may also be differents from those of human beings.

8. A character male may have strongers feelings for her planet than for her family.

9. A female may be more concerned about his machines than about his children.

10. Science fiction introduces the reader into stranges and differents worlds.

Word Order of Adjectives

Adjectives come between a determiner and the noun that they modify. Predeterminers and determiners are not included in the table below. (see **Determiners**) Although a long string of modifiers is possible, you will rarely use more than three or four before one noun. You can put additional modifiers in a prepositional phrase after the noun. You can put *very* immediately before adjectives that can be compared (gradable adjectives), and you can put *enough* immediately after them.   (see **Modifiers**)

Some speakers of English may not follow the order in the chart exactly, but you will not be wrong if you follow it.

Word Order of Adjectives before a Noun

General Description, Opinion	Size, Shape Condition, Age Temperature	Color	Origin	Noun Modifier (see next page)	Type	Noun
fine	small, round			maple	writing	table
fresh	new	white				paint
famous	old		English		country	house
expensive	new				private	school
	tall, thin, young			basketball		player
good					home	cooking
	large, juicy				McDonald's	hamburger
	ragged, worn-out	red		golf		shirt
	hot, steamy, 100°			summer		day
interesting	new		Canadian		historical	novel

Coordinate Adjectives

Two or more adjectives that come from the same group are called coordinate adjectives. When you put two or more coordinate adjectives before the same noun, put a comma or *and* between them.

The speaker was a *tall and thin and young* basketball player.
The speaker was a *tall, thin, young* basketball player.
July twenty-first was a very *hot and humid* day.
July twenty-first was a very *hot, humid* day.
Our friends took us to a *famous and expensive* restaurant.
Our friends took us to a *famous, expensive* restaurant.
A *large and juicy* McDonald's hamburger is delicious.
A *large, juicy* McDonald's hamburger is delicious.

In the sentence above, *McDonald's* is a type, not a possessive form. The hamburger does not belong to a person named McDonald. A personal possessive form that shows who buys the hamburger is a determiner that comes before the first adjective   (see **Determiners**):

John's large, juicy McDonald's hamburger is delicious.

Noun Modifiers

You can use nouns to modify other nouns. A noun can change the meaning of the noun that follows it. If you use more than one noun as a modifier, put the nouns that modify in the order shown:

Word Order of Noun Modifiers

Material	Power	Place/Purpose	Noun
steel		typing	table
	gasoline	lawn	mower
plastic		sewer	pipes
	electric		refrigerator
stainless steel		garbage	compacter

Word Order of All Premodifiers

Prede-terminer	Deter-miner	Ordinal Number	Cardinal Number	Adjectives	Noun Modifiers	Head Noun
all	the	first	five	new	steel	beams
a few of	Margaret's	last	dozen			roses
both	the	first	two	old	oak	trees

NOTE: Put a smaller number before a larger one: *three or four,* never *four or three.*

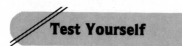

Test Yourself

Put adjectives in the correct order before the noun.

1. races — ancient, foot, Greek

2. racing — horse, modern, professional

3. matches — doubles, interscholastic, tennis

4. contest — beauty, Miss Universe, this year's

5. cars — low-slung, powerful, racing, four or three

Adjectives can be used as predicate adjectives after linking verbs to modify the subject or as objective complements after certain transitive active verbs to modify direct objects.   (see **Complements** and **Objective Complements**)

Word Order of Adjectives Following the Verb

Subject	Linking Verb	Predicate Adjective
Ernest	is	handsome.
The carpenters	are	skillful.
The air	seems	heavy.
The runner	felt	faint.
This pillow	feels	comfortable.
The sky	is growing	dark.

Transitive Verb	Direct Object	Objective Complement
Many girls *found*	Greg	handsome.
His father *thought*	him	foolish.
Our teacher *does* not *consider*	us	stupid.
The news *made*	us	happy.

A-word Modifiers

A few words that begin with *a-* are formed from a preposition that is no longer used in modern English, *a-*, + another word. The *a-* means *on, in,* or *at.* These modifiers can follow a noun or a linking verb or be used like a participle, but they cannot go directly before the noun they modify. Think of *a*-word modifiers as one-word prepositional phrases. Not all adjectives and adverbs that begin with *a-* are like these special *a*-words.

	Alike			*Identical*
Correct:	The twins look *alike.*		*Correct:*	The twins look *identical.*
Incorrect:	*The alike* twins are here.	**but**	*Correct:*	The *identical* twins are here.

	Alive			*Living*
Correct:	The man was *alive* then.		*Correct:*	The man was *living* then.
Incorrect:	The *alive* man was rescued.	**but**	*Correct:*	The *living* man was rescued.

A-words often show a temporary state rather than a permanent one.

Our team was *ahead* during the first half, but we lost in the last ten minutes. *Ahead* at the beginning, we lost later.
The child was *asleep* earlier, but she is *awake* now. Her mother found her *awake.*

Some words that mean the opposite of *a*-words also follow the words they modify.

afraid/unafraid   apart/together   away/here
ahead/behind   asleep/awake   alike/unlike

The angry parents tried to keep the lovers *apart,* but their friends brought them *together.*

Some additional *a*-words that come after the word or words they modify:

ablaze   abroad   alone   astride   ajar   atop   aware

A-words can modify as adjectives and as adverbs depending on the meaning of the sentence.

The trip *abroad* was very interesting. (adjective modifying *trip*)
Several students went *abroad* last summer. (adverb modifying *went*)
A door *ajar* is an invitation to burglars. (adjective modifying *door*)
The door was left *ajar*. (adverb modifying *was left*)

A-words are compared with *more* and *most,* never with -*er* and -*est.*

NOTE: Most adjectives beginning with *a-* can go in front of the nouns they modify.

The *alert* watchdog barked at the intruder.
She is an *able* doctor.
Active children are often noisy.

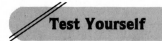

Test Yourself

Find the errors in the following sentences and rewrite them in correct form. Change the grammatical construction (word order) of the sentence, or use a synonym for the *a*-word such as *separated* for *apart* or *similar* for *alike*. Find synonyms in a dictionary or thesaurus. One or more sentences may be correct.

1. An ablaze building can burn to the ground in less than an hour.
2. Asleep people often die in fires.
3. Smoke alarms save many lives by warning people who are not awake.
4. Aware of the dangers of fires, authorities in many towns and cities now require buildings to have smoke alarms to alert people to the danger of fires.
5. An ajar door can allow dangerous smoke to fill a house quickly.
6. Alone elderly people, babies, and small children are especially likely to be trapped in a smoke-filled area.
7. Active campaigns to educate the public about fire hazards can alert people to the dangers.
8. Several apart smoke detectors give the most protection; at least one smoke detector should be near every bedroom.

Comparison of Adjectives

Adjectives that can be compared are sometimes called *gradable* adjectives. Comparative forms of adjectives show differences (contrasts) between two things or groups. Superlative forms show differences in three or more things or groups.

    With one-syllable adjectives, add -*er* for the comparative and -*est* for the superlative. Most adverbs forms are made in the same way. Use *than,* never *from,* after a comparative form. Use *the* before a superlative form.

Adjective	*Comparative*	*Superlative*
few	fewer (than)	the fewest (of all)
young	younger (than)	the youngest (of all)
tall	taller (than)	the tallest (of all)
fast	faster (than)	the fastest (of all)

Paul is a *fast* runner.

Paul is a *faster* runner than Eric. (shows how Paul and Eric are different)

Paul is the *fastest* runner in our class. (shows how Paul is different from more than one other person)

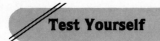

Test Yourself

Choose the correct form. Underline any other words that help you make the correct choice.

_____ 1. The (tall, taller, tallest) mountains in the world are in Asia.

_____ 2. These mountains, the Himalayas, are (tall, taller, tallest) than any others in the world.

_____ 3. Mount Everest on the border of Nepal and Tibet is the (tall, taller, tallest) of all; in Tibet it is called Chomolungma and, in Nepal, Sagarmatha.

_____ 4. Almost as (tall, taller, tallest) as Mount Everest is Mount Dapsang, also called Godwin-Austen or K-2, in Kashmir.

_____ 5. (Tall, Taller, Tallest) mountains in other parts of the world.

_____ 6. rise from plains or plateaus that are at (low, lower, lowest) altitudes than the highlands of Nepal, Tibet, Sikkim, and Kashmir.

_____ 7. As a result of rising from a lower altitude, peaks in other parts of the world do not rise so (high, higher, highest) as those in Tibet.

More and Most

Many words of two syllables and all words of more than two syllables make the comparative form with *more* and the superlative form with *most*. Two-syllable adjectives ending in *-ful* or *-re* usually take *more* and *most*. Two-syllable adjectives ending in *-er* or *-y* usually add *-er* and *-est*.

	Comparative	*Superlative*
beautiful	more beautiful (than)	the most beautiful (of all)
doubtful	more doubtful (than)	the most doubtful (of all)
industrious	more industrious (than)	the most industrious (of all)

but

pretty	prettier	prettiest
tender	tenderer	tenderest

For the opposite meaning use *less* and *the least*.

beautiful	less beautiful (than)	the least beautiful (of all)
industrious	less industrious	the least industrious (of all)

Use *more* and *the most* before past participles (*-en* verb forms).

tired	more tired (than)	the most tired (of all)
bent	more bent (than)	the most bent (of all)

Use *more* or *the most* with *like*.

Martha looks *more like* her mother than Shirley does.
Louis is *the most like* his father of all the children in the family.

NEVER use *more* before an adjective or adverb that already has the *-er* ending or *the most* before an adjective or adverb that already has the *-est* ending.

Incorrect: Sara ran *more* faster than Pat.

Correct: Sara ran fast*er* than Pat.

If you need the opposite meaning of a one-syllable word and of many longer words, use a different word instead of *less* or *least*. Use an *antonym,* a word with an opposite meaning, if you can.

young/younger/youngest—old/older/oldest
tall/taller/tallest—short/shorter/shortest
beautiful/more beautiful/most beautiful—ugly/uglier/ugliest

John is *shorter* than Pat.   **not**   John is *less tall than* Pat.

(For rules for spelling comparative and superlative forms, see **Spelling**.)

Test Yourself

Choose the correct form. Underline any other words that help you choose.

_____ 1.   Some of the (more famous, most famous, famouser, famousest) mountains

_____ 2.   are not the (high, higher, highest).

_____ 3. Mount Vesuvius is one of the (more, most) well-known volcanoes in the

Mediterranean region, but it is not very

_____ 4. (high, higher, highest) at all.

_____ 5. Mount Fuji in Japan is sometimes said to be the (more beautiful, most

beautiful, beautifuler, beautifulest) in the world.

_____ 6. Mount Kilimanjaro in Tanzania is an extinct volcano like Mount Fuji, but it

rises even (high, higher, highest).

_____ 7. At some time in the past the top of Mount Kilimanjaro must have been

blown off, leaving a (flat, flatter, more flatter, flattest, most flattest) top

than that of Mount Fuji.

Irregular Comparisons
Some very common adjectives have irregular forms.

Adjective	Comparative	Superlative
good	better (than)	the best (of all)
bad	worse (than)	the worst (of all)
little	less (than)	the least (of all)
much	more (than)	the most (of all)
many	more (than)	the most (of all)
far	farther (than)	the farthest (of all)
	further (than)	the furthest (of all)

Use _the_ before superlatives. (see **Articles**)
A few words add _-most_ as an ending to show a superlative meaning.

innermost	outermost
foremost	uppermost
furthermost	utmost

NOTE: _Most_ can be used alone to mean _very_: The guide was _most_ helpful.
    Use _little/less/least_ and _much/more/many_ with uncountable (mass) nouns; use _few/fewer/fewest_ and _many/more/most_ with countable nouns. For the difference between _few_ and _a few_ and between _little_ and _a little_, see **Confusing Choices**. For differences in usage and examples of sentences with _little, much, few,_ and _many,_ see **Countable and Uncountable Nouns**.

Double Comparisons

One comparison may depend on another: the first clause states a cause and the second clause states a result. Put a comma between the clauses that make a double comparison.

Cause	*Result*
The *better* our social life is,	the *less* we study.
The *fatter* the cattle are,	the *happier* the farmer is.
The *more* it rains,	the *more* it floods.

Illogical Comparisons

Be careful to compare two things that are the same.

Incorrect: The *books* for chemistry cost more than *history*.

Correct: The *books* for chemistry cost more than the *books* for history.
The *books* for chemistry cost more than *those* for history.

Books must be compared to *books* or to a pronoun that stands for books, such as *those*. The pronoun must be singular if it stands for a singular noun: *This* or *that* for *book* but *these* or *those* for *books*.

Incorrect: The *population* of Japan has a greater density than *Canada*.

Correct: The *population* of Japan has a greater density than the *population* of Canada.

or

The *population* of Japan has a greater density than *that* of Canada.

Japan's population has a greater density than *Canada's*.

You must compare *population* to *population*. In the third correct example, *population* may be left out but understood.

Grammatical Constructions in Comparisons

Use the same construction for both parts of the comparison. Use an operator if you need to repeat a verb. (see **Operators**)

Awkward: The population of Japan has a greater density than Canada's population (does or has).

Improved: Japan's population has a greater density than Canada's (population).

You can leave out the noun in the second part of the comparison after a possessive if the meaning of the sentence is clear without it.

Incorrect: *Boxers* train differently from *football*.

You cannot compare *boxers* (people) to *football* (a game).

Correct: *Boxers* train differently from football *players*.
Athletes who box train differently from *athletes* who play football.

Athletes who box train differently from *those* who play football.
An athlete who boxes trains differently from *one* who plays football.

Pronouns in Comparisons

When you use a pronoun in the second part of the comparison, use

1. *the one* to replace a singular countable noun.
2. *that* to replace a singular countable noun that does not refer to a person and is modified by a prepositional phrase.
3. *that* to replace an uncountable noun.
4. *those* or *the ones* to replace plural countable nouns.

The *book* for chemistry costs more than *the one* for history. (singular, uncountable)
The *population of Japan* has a greater density than *that of Canada*. (singular, followed by a prepositional phrase)
Some people think that the *beauty* of the mountains is greater than *that* of the desert. (uncountable)
Children who go to school every day usually learn faster than *those (the ones)* who are often absent. (countable, plural)
People who live in the arctic need warmer clothes than *those* who live in the tropics. (plural)

Use a subject pronoun in the second part of the comparison if you use a personal pronoun that can be followed by a verb.

David liked that movie as much as *we* (did).
Martha liked it as much as *he* (did).

Comparison of Absolutes

Do not compare things or ideas that are either true or not true. You cannot be *more asleep* or *more awake,* for example. People are either *present* or *absent,* or *dead* or *alive.* To show a state near an absolute state, use *nearly, barely,* or *almost.*

The dog that was hit by a car is *barely alive.*
After studying all night, Tom felt *nearly dead.*

Although you will sometimes see the rule broken, accurate writers do not compare absolutes such as *unique, perfect, possible, impossible, horizontal, perpendicular, round, square,* and *fatal.*

Incorrect: The photographer's work was more impossible than mine.

Correct: The photographer's work was difficult; mine was nearly impossible.

Incorrect: The accident was completely fatal.

Correct: The accident was fatal.
The accident was nearly fatal.
The accident was almost fatal.

Comparison of Equals

Use the *as . . . as* construction to show that two things or groups are similar.

Barbara is *as* tall *as* Carol (is).

The *as . . . as* construction can mean that Barbara and Carol are the same height, or it can mean that Barbara is *at least as tall as* Carol (no shorter than Carol). Barbara could be taller than Carol. You may need to give the reader more information.

Barbara is *as tall as* Carol; in fact, they are the same height.
Martin is *as tall as* Tim; in fact, Martin is taller.

You can also use the *as . . . as* or *so . . . as* construction in the negative to show differences.

Leonard is *not so tall as* Arthur.

Repetition of the Verb after Comparisons

Follow the rules for operators in verb repetition. (see **Operators**) You do not have to repeat or use an operator substitute for a verb that does not change in tense or number. *Be, have, do,* or a modal that is used in the first part of the sentence can be repeated. Replace all other verbs with a form of *do.*

Barbara and Carol *are* taller than Anne *is*. (You must use *is* because the number changes from plural to singular.)
Peter *will run* as fast tomorrow as Paul *did* yesterday. (You must use *did* because the tense changes.)
Dogwood trees *do* not grow as tall as pine trees (*do*). (You may repeat *do* or leave it out.)
Horses are larger than ponies (are).
Cars can move faster than bicycles (can).

Comparisons with *Different*

Always use *from* after *different,* not *than.*

The format of a business letter is different *from* that of a personal letter.
The kind of mathematical knowledge required for business is different *from* that required for engineering.

Test Yourself

Correct the comparisons that are incorrect in the following sentences. Some sentences may be correct.

1. Television broadcasts of World Cup football matches are watched by more people than any other sport.

2. People in every country hope their national team will do more better than other teams.

3. Players chosen for their national team are best in the country.

4. These players are greatest heroes.

5. From a younger age, boys hope to be chosen some day to play for their country.

6. Each country's team hopes to do better than its neighbor.

7. The better a national team does in World Cup matches, the happier the people in the

   country are.

8. The style of play in one country may be a different style than that in another country.

9. The training required for members of championship football teams is as difficult as

   those required for long-distance runners.

10. The team that wins the World Cup brings greater honor to its country.

The + Adjective: Adjectives Used as Nouns

Use *the* followed by an adjective alone like a noun phrase. (Possessive forms can replace *the*.) The meaning is *people who are sick, old,* and so forth (a generalization).

the sick	the rich	the innocent	our young
the old	the poor	the foolish	the world's hungry
the young	the hungry	the successful	your rich
the strong	the frightened	the middle-aged	our poor

Comparative and superlative forms can be used. These forms can be modified. They take plural verbs.

The wise accomplish more than *the foolish.*
The very young are likely to catch contagious diseases.
The youngest and *the oldest* are the most likely to be ill.

Use this construction with *the* to refer to national groups. If the word does not already end in a *-ch, -s,* or *-sh* sound, add an *-s* to the adjective form.
Use plural verbs with these forms.
Words that end in a *-ch, -s,* or *-sh* sound:

The Chine*s*e are helpful.
   Engli*sh*
   Fren*ch*
   Swi*ss*

Words that do not end in a *-ch, -s,* or *-sh* sound:

The American*s* are helpful.
   Greek*s*
   Pakistani*s*

A few adjectives can be used with *the* to show abstract ideas, *the thing that is*. . . . Use singular verbs with these forms.

The unknown is often feared.
We do *the difficult* tomorrow; *the impossible* takes longer. (advertising slogan)

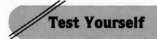
Test Yourself

Replace phrases and clauses in the following sentences with *the* + adjective wherever you can.

1. People who are well-off and comfortable can help people who are less fortunate.

2. People who are elderly often need special care.

3. People who are middle-aged often have to care for their elderly parents.

4. Young and strong people should help those who are less fortunate.

5. People who are rich can help provide for people who are hungry.

6. Weak people sometimes need help from strong people.

Adverbs That Modify Adjectives

Put adverbs before the adjectives that they modify. (see **Adverbs**) EXCEPTION: *enough* when it is an adverb.

	Adverb	Adjective	Adverb
He gave us	remarkably	clear directions.	
The movie was a	very	exciting one.	
She was	rather	quiet.	
The test was	unusually	difficult.	
The test was		difficult	enough.
The movie was		exciting	enough.

NOTE: Another adverb cannot come before an adjective if *enough* follows it.

Adjectives after the Impersonal *It Is*

Adjectives can be used after *it is* to introduce the true subject of a clause.

	Infinitive Phrase
It is good	to see you.
dangerous	to speed.
impossible	to go now.
difficult	to find the answer.

	Noun Clause
It is certain	that he will win.
clear	that she cheated.

Avoid the *it is* construction in writing by using the idea in the infinitive phrase or in the clause as the subject of the sentence. (see **It, Impersonal Use**)

Sentences with *It Is* Taken Out
Seeing [to see] you is a pleasure.
Speeding [to speed] is dangerous.
Going [to go] now is impossible.
Finding [to find] the answer is difficult.
That he will win [his winning] is certain.
That she cheated [her cheating] is known.

Phrases and Clauses That Complete Adjectives

Some adjectives following linking verbs (such as *be, feel, seem, appear*) can be followed by phrases or clauses that complete the meaning of the adjective. When the sentence is completed by a clause, *that* can be left out if it is not the subject of the completing clause.

Adjective Alone:	The runner is *certain.*
Prepositional Phrase:	The runner is *certain of success.*
Infinitive Phrase:	The runner is *certain to succeed.*
Clause:	The runner is *certain (that) he will succeed.*
Inverted Word Order:	*Certain of success,* the runner will enter the race.
	Certain to succeed, the runner will enter the race.
	Certain (that) he will succeed, the runner will enter the race.

Deciding which preposition must follow an adjective and which construction you can use after it can be difficult. A few adjectives must be followed by a prepositional phrase or a clause. Look the adjective up in a dictionary written for non-native users of English if you are not sure how to use it.   (see also **Participles as adjectives**)

Adjective Constructions That Follow the Verb
Accustomed, contrary, and *probable* almost always have complements, but all the other adjectives can be used without complements in their most common meanings.
Adjective followed by a prepositional phrase

The new student is afraid *of thieves.* (person)
                                high *places.* (thing)
                                having an accident. (*-ing* form)

Some Adjective Constructions That Follow the Verb

Adjective	Preposition	Followed by Person/Thing/-ing Form		Infinitive Phrase—Omit Preposition	that Clause—Omit Preposition	who(ever) or what(ever) Clause—After Preposition
		Person/Thing	-ing Form			
able	to			✓		✓
accustomed	of	✓	✓			✓
afraid	with	✓	✓	✓		✓
angry	about	✓	✓			✓
						✓
aware	of	✓	✓		✓	✓
capable	of		✓			✓
careful	about	✓	✓	✓	✓	✓
	with					✓
also with -ing form without a preposition						
certain	about, of	✓	✓	✓	✓	✓
close	to, by	✓	✓			✓
confident	of	✓	✓			✓
conscious	of	✓	✓	✓	✓	✓
contrary	to	✓	✓			✓
critical	of	✓	✓	✓		✓
difficult		✓	✓			✓
disappointed	about, at	✓	✓	✓	✓	✓
disappointing	with, in	✓	✓	✓	✓	✓
doubtful	about	✓	✓	✓		✓
easy	on, with	✓	✓	✓		✓
equal	to	✓	✓			✓
essential	to	✓	✓			✓
evident	to	✓	✓			✓
experienced	in	✓	✓			✓
expert	at	✓	✓			✓
	with	✓				✓
famous	for	✓	✓		✓	✓
full	of		✓			✓
glad	about	✓	✓	✓		✓

Adjective	Preposition
good (successful)	at
(kind)	to
(helpful)	for
harmful	to, for
honest	about
ignorant	of
important	for *(only after it is)*
impossible	in *(only after it is)*
interested	in
interesting	to *(only after it is)*
likely	
necessary	for
obvious	to *(only after it is)*
positive	of, about
possible	*(only after it is)*
prepared	for
probable	*(only after it is)*
proud	of
qualified	for
ready	for
right	about
sensitive	to, about
separate	from
serious	about
shocked	at
similar	to
subject	to
successful	in
sufficient	for
suitable	for
sure	at, by
surprised	of, about
uncertain	
unlikely	about *(only after it is)*
wrong	about

Adjective followed by an infinitive phrase—leave out the preposition.   (see **Infinitive/-ing Choice**)

The new student is afraid *to ask*.

Adjective followed by a noun clause

The new student is afraid *that he will lose his money*. (*that* clause—leave out the preposition)
The new student is afraid *of what may happen*. (*what* or *who* clause following the preposition—other **WH**-words are also sometimes possible after prepositions)

If the meaning of the adjective allows it, an adjective can be used in the construction *too* + adjective + infinitive phrase or *so* + adjective + *that* clause:

The reasons are *too obvious to mention*. . . . *so obvious* (*that*) *we will not mention them*.
The men were *too proud to ask for help*. . . . *so proud* (*that*) *they would not ask for help*.

Test Yourself

Put the correct preposition in the blank to the left of the sentence. Choose your answer from the following list: about, at, in, for, of, to, with

_____ 1. Many parts of the world are famous _____ their mountains.

_____ 2. Mountain climbers can be more confident _____ success if they hire local

guides.

_____ 3. Guides experienced _____ local conditions help inexperienced climbers.

_____ 4. Climbers ignorant _____ local conditions may get into trouble.

_____ 5. Good equipment is necessary _____ success.

_____ 6. Mountain climbing is a sport full _____ danger.

_____ 7. Climbers who are not accustomed _____ local conditions may have diffi-

culties.

_____ 8. Equipment must be suitable _____ local conditions.

_____ 9. Guides and clients must be ready _____ any emergency

_____ 10. and prepared _____ sudden changes in the weather.

_____ 11. Being wrong _____ the weather could lead to disaster on a mountain.

_____ 12. Experienced guides are often shocked _____ the lack of preparation of

some novice climbers.

_____ 13. Good guides are expert _____ equipment as well as

_____ 14. _____ knowledge of the mountain.

_____ 15. Good climbers enjoy facing dangers but are always aware _____ them.

Adverbs

Adverbs modify or change the meaning of other words. Words that modify a verb, an adjective, another adverb, a participle, a phrase, a clause, or even a whole sentence are called adverbs. Adverbs can be classified according to form, meaning, and function. Only certain adverbs can be used with certain tenses. (see **Tense**)
Some adverbs cannot be used with certain verbs. (see **Stative Verbs**)

Word Order of Adverbs

Verbs can be put only in certain places in a sentence. You can put an adverb in the middle of a clause or at the beginning or end of the clause. Frequency adverbs are most often put in the middle, but in a special place in the middle. You can put an adverb between the subject and main verb, or after a form of *be; do not put an adverb between the main verb and its object.* In a verb phrase of several words, put the adverb after the auxiliary or modal and before the main verb.

Adverb, Beginning Position	Subject	Modal or Auxiliary	Adverb, Middle Position	Main Verb	Adverb, End Position
Sometimes	a cat	can		run	fast
	a cat	can	sometimes	run	fast
	a cat	can		run	fast sometimes.

When a form of *be* is the only verb in the clause, an adverb follows it.

Diana *is always* friendly.
Larry and Tim *are never* friendly.
The Pendletons *were often* friendly.

Subject	Modal or Auxiliary	Adverb, Middle Position	Main Verb	Direct Object
Diana		*often*	found	the Pendletons helpful.
She	can	*often*	visit	them.
They	are	*frequently*	helping	her.

Do not put an adverb between the main verb and a direct object.

Incorrect: Diana found *often* the Pendletons helpful.

Incorrect: She can visit *often* them.

Incorrect: They are helping *frequently* her.

Put *still, just, ever, never, almost, hardly,* and *quite* in the middle position. Very rarely, *never* comes at the beginning for emphasis in an inverted clause.

Miller has *just* missed his bus.
He will *never* oversleep again.
Never again will he trust his sister to wake him up early.

Never and *again* are sometimes separated.

Never will he trust his sister to wake him up early *again*.

Adverb, Beginning Position	Subject	Modal or Auxiliary	Adverb, Middle Position	Main Verb	End Position
	Miller	has	*just*	missed his bus.	
	He	will	*never*	oversleep	*(again)*.
			(again)		
Never again		will he		trust his sister to wake him.	

Do not use *no* for *not*.

Time adverbs usually come at the end of the clause. They do not usually come in the middle. Do not confuse time and frequency adverbs. Time adverbs answer the question *when?* Frequency adverbs answer the question *how often?* Put more specific time adverbs before more general ones. Time adverbs are often prepositional phrases made with *at, by, in, for,* or *since*.   (see **Prepositions, time**)

Roberta's mother will arrive   *next week.*
                                 at ten o'clock Saturday.
                                 at ten o'clock Saturday, December 15.

Word Order for Several Adverbs in the Same Clause

Adverbs of *frequency* answer the question *how often?* (*always, never, seldom, frequently*)
Adverbs of *manner* answer the question *how?* (*easily, with difficulty, by plane, on foot*)
Adverbs of *place* answer the question *where?* (*here, there, in China, at home*)
Adverbs of *time* answer the question *when?* (*now, then, yesterday, tomorrow, in 1906, on May 7, at 10:00 A.M.*)

(Adverbs of frequency, manner, place, and time are discussed in detail below. This section deals only with their word order in the sentence.)

Put frequency adverbs in the middle position. Put time adverbs at the beginning or end. Put manner, place, and time adverbs in that order if they are together at the end of the sentence. If you have several adverbs, you may move the time adverb(s) to the beginning of the sentence. You may move other adverbs to the beginning of the sentence for emphasis unless *be* is the main verb   (see above, p. no. 29).

Adverb, Beginning Position	Subject	Modal or Auxiliary	Adverb, Middle Position	Main Verb	Manner	Adverb, End Position Place	Time
(*Last week*)	Roberta			arrived	*by plane*	in Toronto	(*last week*).
(*In his life*)	Arthur	has	*never*	traveled	*by ship*	to Hong Kong	(*in his life*).
(*Tomorrow*)	Dale	will	(*easily*)	pass	(*easily*) with difficulty.		(*tomorrow*).

NOTE: A single-word adverb of manner can come in the middle position, especially if other words follow the verb. If the verb does not have a complement or another adverb following it, the single-word adverb of manner is likely to follow the verb because of the rhythm of the sentence. Do not put an adverb of manner that is a phrase in the middle position.

> Dale will pass *easily.*
> Dale will pass *easily* tomorrow.
> Dale will *easily* pass the test.
> Dale will pass the test *with difficulty.*
> *Awkward:* Dale will *with difficulty* pass the test.

With *place* as well as *time,* put more specific information before more general information. (The day of the week is considered more specific than the date.)

They arrived in Montreal, Canada, on Friday, September 26, 1980.
Joseph was born in Mercy Hospital, San Francisco, California, on June 3, 1985.   (note commas: see **Punctuation, comma**)

Word Order of Adverbs That Modify Adjectives and Participles
Put adverbs that modify adjectives and participles directly before the words they modify.

Joy and Lee are *very* happy. (*very* modifies *happy*)
Why are you *so* angry when we were *only* late? (*so* modifies *angry* and *only* modifies *late*)
The couple who were celebrating their anniversary had been *happily* married for fifty years.
  (*happily* modifies *married*)

 **Test Yourself**

Cross out the adverbs (word, phrase, or clause) that are incorrect in form or place or both and rewrite the sentence correctly on another sheet of paper.

1. The homes of certain creatures have often special names.
2. These places are no called *homes*, but nests, dens, lairs, or burrows.
3. When a bird or an insect builds carefully a place where it can lay and protect its eggs, that place is called a *nest;* the same word may for the homes of animals and people be used.
4. A fox or rabbit may enlarge cleverly a hole underground to use as its *burrow.*
5. A *lair* is a hidden shelter above or below the ground where an animal rests and hides safely its food; *lair* may also refer to the home of people who have something to hide, such as thieves.
6. An area where rabbits breed may be called a *warren;* because rabbits multiply rapidly and overpopulate often their environment, crowded areas in cities are called sometimes *warrens* also.
7. A *den* is the home of a wild animal, usually a largely one such as a bear or a lion; because these animals steal their food, people associate easily *den* with robbers and thieves: we may speak of "a robber's den" or "a den of thieves."
8. Dogs live often in houses, but never homes of wild animals are called houses.
9. Mother animals will with great fierceness defend their young.
10. Mothers leave to hunt food as soon as the babies can be by themselves left alone in the nest.
11. Among many birds the fathers during the day hunt for food and help the mothers feed the young that are still in the nest.
12. Animals such as horses and antelopes have no home or houses but give birth to young that are able to take care of themselves and run as soon as they are born alongside their mothers.

Formation of Adverbs

Many single-word adverbs are formed by adding *-ly* to another word, usually an adjective: *soft* becomes *softly*, *bright* becomes *brightly*, and *honest* becomes *honestly*.

Learn the spelling rules that change other words to adverb forms.

1   If the base word ends in *-l*, add *-ly*.

careful, carefully
helpful, helpfully

2   If the base word ends in *-y*, change *y* to *i* and add *-ly*.

happy, happily
day, daily

3   If the base word ends in *-e*, drop the *e* and add *-ly*.

| *true*, truly | able, ably | gentle, gently |
| due, duly | suitable, suitably | simple, simply |

Exceptions: wise, wisely, sole, solely

4   If the base word ends in *-ic*, add *-ally*.

| *economic*, economically | automatic, automatically |
| historic, historically | scientific, scientifically |

speci*fic*, specifi*cally*   cri*tic*, criti*cally*
pub*lic*, publi*cly* (irregular)   ba*sic*, basi*cally*

Some words have the same form whether they are used as adjectives or adverbs. Other -*ly* words cannot be used as adverbs.

1   Words referring to time ending in -*ly* can be adjectives or adverbs:

early   monthly
hourly   weekly
daily   early

2   Certain words ending in -*ly* are adjectives, never adverbs:

courtly (manners)   heavenly (music)   lonely (people)
deadly (weapons)   leisurely (pace)   lovely (day)
earthly (comfort)   lively (party)   worldly (wisdom)

and others formed from words referring to people:

brotherly, sisterly, motherly, fatherly
kingly, queenly, princely
friendly, scholarly, saintly

3   Other irregular forms can be adjectives or adverbs:

high	adjective:	She has a *high* position.
	adverb:	She threw the ball *high* in the air.
	highly means	
	greatly:	She was *highly* regarded.
fast	adjective:	You had a *fast* trip.
	adverb:	You must have been driving *fast*.
hard	adjective:	He had to make a *hard* choice.
	adverb:	He worked *hard*.
	hardly means	
	not or *almost*	
	not:	He was *hardly* able to choose.
late	adjective:	She has a *late* appointment.
	adverb:	She arrived *late*.
	lately means	
	recently:	She has not seen the doctor *lately*.
likely	adjective:	Paula is a *likely* candidate for the job.
	adverb:	The bus will [*very*] *likely* leave on time. (Many writers modify *likely* by a word such as *very, more,* or *most* when using it as an adverb.)
	like is a preposition:	Paula looks *like* her sister. (similar to)
	or a verb:	Paula *likes* her sister.
low	adjective:	The roof is *low*.
	adverb:	The branch of the tree hung *low* over the porch.
	lowly means *not*	
	a high position:	The messenger disliked his *lowly* job.

straight	adjective:	The *straight* road led to the farmhouse. (without curves)
	adverb:	The road led *straight* to the farmhouse. (directly)
deep	adjective:	Keep away from *deep* water.
	adverb:	The treasure was buried *deep* in the earth.
	deeply refers to emotions:	I am *deeply* sorry about your accident.
		The reader was *deeply* involved in the story.
near	adjective:	The end of the job is *near*.
	adverb:	The dog was afraid to come *near*.
	nearly means almost:	We *nearly* had an accident.

See also **Adjectives, a-word modifiers**.

Test Yourself

Choose the correct form and put it in the blank to the left of the sentence:

deep, deeply, hard, hardly, late, lately, like, likely, low, lowly, near, nearly

_____ 1. People who are not accustomed to snow and ice are often surprised by how fast a _____ snow can fall, even up to several feet.

_____ 2. Anyone caught in a blizzard without warm clothing is _____ to suffer from frostbite or even freeze to death.

_____ 3. _____ temperatures that have dropped quickly can cause more damage to living things than the same temperatures that have dropped gradually.

_____ 4. Shallow bodies of water freeze more quickly than _____ ones.

_____ 5. Branches of trees often hang _____ because of the weight of the ice and snow on them.

_____ 6. When the temperature drops suddenly below freezing, especially if it is the first freeze in the fall, plants find it _____ to adjust to the sudden change.

Comparison of Adverbs

The adverbs that can be compared are called *gradable.* They can be modified by *very, so,* and *too* and can be compared by adding *-er* or *-est* suffixes or by putting *more* or *most* before them.   (see **Adjectives, comparison of**).

Adverbs that can be compared include those that answer the questions

how often?—adverbs of frequency (*seldom, often, rarely, frequently*)
when?—adverbs of relative time (*early, soon, late, recently*)
where?—adverbs of place (*near, far, close, distant*)
how?—adverbs of manner (*badly, cleanly, carelessly, poorly, skillfully, slowly, well*)

Absolutes cannot be compared in their common uses. You obviously cannot say *more always, most never,* or *more ten o'clock.* (see below for more about these classes of adverbs)

Put *-er* or *-est* at the end of a word of one syllable, following spelling rules for suffixes. (Some two-syllable adverbs have the *er/est* ending.)   (see **Spelling**).

fast, fast*er,* fast*est*
slow, slow*er,* slow*est*
late, lat*er,* lat*est*
early, earl*ier,* earl*iest*

Irregular adverb forms are closely related to irregular adjective forms.

	Comparative	*Superlative*
well	better (than)	the best (of all)
badly	worse (than)	the worst (of all)
far	farther (than)	the farthest (of all)
	further (than)	the furthest (of all)

Comparison in the Sentence

1 To show differences, use the comparative and superlative forms: *-er, -est, more,* or *most*

$$\text{carefully.}$$
The new artist prepares her work *carelessly.*
$$well.$$

$$\textit{more carelessly than}$$
The new artist prepares her work *more carefully than* the other one (does hers).
$$\textit{better than}$$

The new artist prepares her work *the best* (of all).

or

Use *not* + $\overset{so}{\underset{as}{}}$ + base adverb + *as:*

$$well$$
The new artist does *not* prepare her work $\overset{so}{\underset{as}{}}$ *carefully as* the other one (does hers).
$$carelessly$$

NOTE: Some writers prefer *so* in negative sentences.

2   To show likeness, use *as* + base adverb + *as:*

carefully

The new artist prepares her work *as carelessly as* the other one (does hers).

well

NOTE: A form of *be, have,* or *do* or a modal can be repeated after *so* or *as.* You must replace other verbs with a form of *do.*   (See **Operators;** also see **Adjectives, comparison of,** for a more detailed discussion of the meaning of the *so/as . . . as* construction.)

Some adverbs can modify adjectives and other adverbs in the comparative and superlative degree.

Modifier	*Adjective*	*Adverb*
much	more careful (than)	more carefully (than)
very much	better (than)	better (than)
far	worse (than)	worse (than)
no (*any* in questions)	easier (than)	more easily (than)
a little	happier (than)	more happily (than)

Comparatives: The cook is (*very*) *much more careful* now. (adjective)

The cook does her work (*very*) *much more carefully.* (adverb)

There is *no more careful a* worker than the cook. (adjective)

Is there *any* worker *more careful* than the cook? (adjective)

The cook works *no more carefully* than her helper (does). (adverb)

The cook is *a little more careful* now. (adjective)

The cook works *a little more carefully* now. (adverb)

Superlatives with Very:

The new clerk works the *very best.*

The new clerk is the *very best* worker.

earliest

best

worst

the very + first

last

farthest

closest

Do not use *very* before *most* except when the *most* is a pronoun:

This is the *very most* we can do. (meaning *this is the very best offer we can make*)

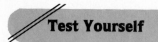

Test Yourself

Correct the comparative forms that are wrong.

1.   Many living things can move more fast than human beings.

2.   Birds move the most fast of all living things, for some of them can move at speeds as high as 175 miles per hour.

3. For a short distance a rabbit can outrun a greyhound, but a greyhound runs fast longer than a rabbit runs fast.

4. Insects are less swift than other creatures; the very most high speed of a housefly, for example, is about five miles per hour.

5. The most speedy land animals can move faster than the most speedy water animals; sailfish and barracuda can move at about thirty miles per hours, but cheetah have been clocked at more than sixty-five miles per hour.

6. The most tiny of all birds, the hummingbird, is one of the most fast, flying at over sixty miles per hour.

7. Extremely large animals such as elephants and whales find moving at very high speeds more difficult than smaller animals find it.

Adverbs of Frequency

Adverbs of frequency answer the question *how often?* (See above, "Word Order of Adverbs," for more about their position in the sentence.) Usually put single-word adverbs of frequency in the middle position and put phrases of frequency in the end position. Put *scarcely ever* in the middle position. Some common adverbs of frequency are

Affirmative	*Negative*
always	never
usually	rarely
frequently	seldom
often	scarcely ever, hardly ever
sometimes	occasionally
generally	
many times	
every day/week/month	
twice/three times a day/week/month	

          often
The driver must *always* work on Wednesdays.
          never

The driver must *scarcely ever* work on Wednesdays.

                   every week.
The driver must work on Wednesdays   *many times.*
                   twice a month.

Do not use *no, not,* or *never* in the same clause with a negative adverb of frequency. (see **Negation**)

Adverbs of Relative Time

Adverbs of relative time can be used with all tenses as meaning permits, but they are used especially with the continuous/progressive tenses. Put them in the middle position in the clause. The most common adverbs of relative time are *just, still, already* (*yet* in negative), *lately, recently,* and *soon.*

tense	
Present Continuous/ Progressive:	A student was *recently* looking for that book.
Past:	He *recently* found it.
Present Perfect:	He has *just* found it.
Future Continuous/ Progressive:	He will *soon* be using it in his computer class.
Past Perfect:	When he bought the book, it had *recently* been revised.
Past:	He *soon* decided he needed a different one, however.

Adverbs of Manner

Adverbs of manner answer the question *how?* or *how well?* Usually put them at the end of the clause or in the middle position in the perfect tenses. Putting them at the beginning of the sentence gives them strong emphasis. Do not put these adverbs between the main verb and the direct object.

Correct:	The robber searched the room *carefully.* (*very carefully*)
Correct:	He *carefully* searched the room.
Correct, Emphatic:	*Carefully* he searched the room.
Incorrect:	He searched *carefully* the room.

Do not confuse the adverb construction with the adjective after *be* or after another linking verb.   (see **Adjective constructions that follow the verb,** and **Predicate Complements**)

predicate
adjective
He is *careful* to search the room.

Many adverbs of manner are closely related to adjective and noun forms of the same base word. The endings (suffixes) show whether the word is an adverb, an adjective, or a noun.   (see **Word Formation, suffixes**)

do the work?

How did he

explain the problem?

He did it . . .

Single-Word Adverb	*Prepositional Phrase* with + *Noun*	*Prepositional Phrase:* in a(n) (Adjective) way or manner
badly	—	in a bad manner
carefully	with care	in a careful manner
carelessly	with carelessness	in a careless manner
clearly	with clarity	in a clear manner
—	with difficulty	in a difficult manner
foolishly	—	in a foolish manner
gradually	—	in a gradual manner

hesitantly	with hesitance	in a hesitant manner
quickly	—	—
wisely	with wisdom	in a wise manner
well	—	—

Using *in a manner that was* + adjective is also possible, but avoid this construction because it is wordy. Avoid using two or three words if one will do. The single-word adverb is usually the best choice.

Put adverbs of manner that are closely connected in meaning with the subject of the clause directly after the subject instead of after the verb. These adverbs correspond to predicate adjectives.

adverb of
subject   manner
The boy *kindly* helped the old woman.

Meaning: It   was   predicate adjective *kind* of the boy to help the old woman.

adverb of
manner
The boy helped the old woman *kindly*.

Meaning: The boy helped the old woman *in a kind manner*.

Some additional adverbs that correspond to predicate adjectives are *angrily, bravely, cruelly, faithfully* (and others in *-fully*), *foolishly, pleasantly*.

Adverbs of Place

Adverbs of place answer the question *where?* Like adverbs of time (below), they can be a single word or a phrase. Put them before or after the main clause. Put more specific information before more general information.

We have just moved *to a new house in the city*.
My brothers were born *in Montreal, Canada*.
You will find the book *in the upper right-hand corner of the bookcase in my bedroom*.

Learn the correct preposition to show different kinds of place. (see **Prepositions, space and movement**)

Adverbs of Time

Adverbs of time answer the question *when?* They can be a single word, a phrase, or a dependent clause. Put them before or after the main clause. Put more specific information before more general information.

My youngest sister was born at 3:15 A.M., March 23, 1987.

Use *at* before clock time, *on* before a day or date, and *in* before a month used alone, a year, or a century. Use commas to separate several items if you do not use prepositions.

My youngest sister was born *at* 3:15 A.M.
                              on March 23.
                              in 1987.
My youngest sister was born at 3:15 A.M., March 23, 1987.
Many surprising events took place *in* the 1960s.
Industrialization in England began *in* the eighteenth century.

See **Prepositions, time**.

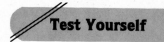

Test Yourself

Correct the adverbs that are wrong or in the wrong order in the following sentences.

1. The speeds of wild animals and birds often are difficult to measure and can hardly
    never be measured exactly.

2. New timing devices similar to radar guns that measure the speed of cars on roads and
    highways may help scientists more accurately measure.

3. These new instruments only recently have been developed.

4. Many scientists study the behavior of animals in Africa in game parks.

5. As many species of animals have become extinct, many human beings have become in
    the latter part of the twentieth century more concerned about preserving wild
    animals.

6. Yellowstone was the first natural region in the United States to become a national park
    with protection for wild animals and natural features; the park was established in
    1872, March 1, by an act of Congress.

7. Many countries in the world have now national parks where ordinary people can
    observe and study easily wild animals, birds, and other creatures; and scientists can in
    their native habitats study them.

Dependent Clauses of Time   (see **Clauses, adverb**)

Put a comma after a dependent clause at the beginning of the sentence, but do not put a comma between an independent clause and a dependent adverbial clause that comes at the end of the sentence.   (see **Punctuation, comma**)

At the Beginning: *When the industrial revolution in England began,* it brought many changes.

At the End: The industrial revolution in England brought many changes *when it began.*

Adverbs That Emphasize

Adverbs that emphasize are *only* and *even.* In writing, put *only* and *even* directly before the word they modify. Where you put them makes a great change in the meaning of the clause.

Only I (no one else) told Ed to come last week.
I *only* told Ed to come last week. (told, not commanded)
I told *only* Ed (no one but Ed) to come last week.
I told Ed *only* to come last week. (to come, not to do anything else.)
I told Ed to come *only* last week. (Before an adverb of time, *only* means either *as recently as* or
   at no other time.)

Adverbs That Modify the Whole Clause

Adverbs that modify the whole clause usually come at the beginning or at the end of the clause or directly after the subject.

1   Adverbs that express the writer's attitude:

briefly	certainly	in fairness
of course	perhaps	objectively

The solution, *certainly,* cannot be found in new laws.
Let us *briefly* consider the next piece of evidence.

2   Adverbs (conjunctive) that join ideas within the sentence or with ideas in other sentences or paragraphs   (see **Clauses, connectors** and **Interrupters** for their arrangement according to meaning):

also	therefore	however	too
as well	furthermore	consequently	subsequently
besides	in addition to	nevertheless	as a result

Do not confuse conjunctive adverbs with coordinating conjunctions.   (see **Comma Splices**)

Therefore, we must conclude that the result is correct.
We, *therefore,* must conclude that the result is correct.
We must, *therefore,* conclude that the result is correct.
We must conclude, *therefore,* that the result is correct.
We must conclude that the result is correct, *therefore.*

(Although authorities do not agree about comma rules, you will not be wrong if you separate interrupters from the rest of the clause by commas.)

Adverbs That Introduce Dependent Clauses

Adverbs that introduce dependent clauses but that also refer to a noun or pronoun used earlier in the sentence (the time *when,* the place *where*) are sometimes called relative adverbs. In this book these words are discussed as subordinating conjunctions. (see **Conjunctions**)

Agreement of pronoun and antecedent,   see **Pronoun, reference**

Agreement of Subject and Verb

The subject and main verb of a clause must agree in number. Use a singular verb with a singular noun or pronoun or with an uncountable (mass) noun. Use a plural verb with a plural noun or pronoun. Countable nouns that indicate more than one person or thing are plural in English. Even though many people do not follow some of these rules in speaking, you must follow them in formal writing.

Regular English nouns add an *-s* to show a change from singular to plural.   (see **Number**)

	Singular	*Plural*	*Singular*	*Plural*
Regular:	star	stars	dog	dogs
	girl	girls	basket	baskets
Irregular:	man	men	child	children

In the present tense forms, most verbs add an *-s* to the simple (infinitive) form in the third person singular only. The only verb that shows a difference between singular and plural in the past tense is *be* (*was* and *were*).

Singular (*-s* on verb in present tense; no *-s* on noun)	*Plural* (*-s* on noun; no *-s* on verb)
That star shines brightly tonight.	Those stars shine brightly every night.
That star *is* shining brightly tonight. (irregular)	Those stars are shining brightly tonight. (irregular)

Use the same form of the modal for singular and plural.   (see **Modals**)

Singular	*Plural*
He can go.	They can go.
He should come now.	They should come now.

In writing you will use the simple present tense more than you use it in speaking. Do not forget the *-s* on the singular verb form in the present tense.

1   Find the true subject of the clause and be sure the verb agrees with it.

a   Prepositional phrases that come between the subject and verb do not usually affect the subject-verb agreement. The noun closest to the verb is not always the subject of the clause.

```
             plural     prepositional  plural
             subject      phrase        verb
```
Correct: Several *sections* of this music *are* difficult to learn.

```
            singular    prepositional  singular
            subject       phrase        verb
```
Correct: The *print* in these books   *is*   easy to read.

```
            singular       prepositional      singular
            subject          phrase             verb
```
Correct: *This* *man* along with his sons always *catches* the largest fish.

NOTE: *along with* means something added to *man;* the meaning is similar to *this man and his sons.* But only *this man and his sons* takes a plural verb. *Along with* is a preposition.

```
            plural                    plural
        compound subject               verb
```
This *man and his sons* always *catch* the largest fish.

More prepositions like *along with* are

together with	except	with
as well as	but (meaning *except*)	
in addition to	no less than	

subject	prepositional phrase	verb
All the boys	except John but John	*are* going.
Martha	as well as her sisters together with her sisters in addition to her sisters	*is* going.
The *construction*	of these buildings of this building	*is* sound.
The *reasons*	for his change in plans	*are clear.*
The *reason*	for his change in plans	*is* clear.

b   Dependent clauses do not affect subject-verb agreement

subject	dependent clause	verb
A *person*	who has good friends	*enjoys* life more.
A *child*	who lives on a farm	*learns* about animals.

c   Predicate nouns or pronouns do not affect subject-verb agreement. The noun or pronoun that comes before a linking verb is its subject. (see **Linking Verbs**)

```
            subject                 verb
```
The most difficult *part* of biology courses *is* the labs.

```
   subject verb
```
The *labs* *are* the most difficult part of biology courses.

d Choose between *there is* and *there are* and similar expressions by finding the true subject after the verb. (*It is* never changes to *it are*.) See the explanation on p. 24–25).

	verb	subject
There	*are*	several *bananas* on the table.
There	*is*	no *reason* for you to do that.
Here	*are*	the *books* you asked me to get.
Here	*are*	three maple *trees*.

A prepositional phrase in the place of *there* or *here* does not affect the verb form.

prepositional phrase	verb	subject
On the table	*are* several	*bananas*.
In front of the building	*are* three maple	trees.

Avoid too much use of phrases such as *it is, there is,* and *there are* in formal writing. Use the true subject at the beginning of the sentence.

Correct: There are several bananas on the table.

Improved: Several bananas are on the table.

EXCEPTION: Use *it* in statements about the weather and time.

It is too hot to work today.
It rained yesterday, but *it* isn't raining today.
It is ten o'clock already.

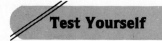

Test Yourself

A. Find the subject and the verb in each clause in the following sentences. Underline each subject once and each verb twice. Cross out incorrect verb forms and write the correct form above the incorrect one. Then copy the correct form in the blank to the left of the sentence.

_____ 1. Lightning along with heavy rains cause much damage in some parts of the world.

_____ 2. A hurricane as well as the high tides accompanying it always result in some damage to property.

_____ 3. Although not completely accurate, weather forecasting of developing storms allow people to take measures to protect themselves and their property.

_____ 4.   Storms that have been sighted ahead of their arrival does less damage than

those that arrive unexpectedly.

_____ 5.   For many people the most frightening part of thunderstorms are lightning

and thunder, not the heavy rains.

_____ 6.   There is certain times of the year that are more likely to be stormy.

_____ 7.   In the spring and the fall as the sun cross the equator stormy weather is

more likely to occur.

_____ 8.   In many parts of the world the biggest danger from the weather come

from floods.

_____ 9.   There is dangers in many areas because people build in places that are

known floodplains.

_____ 10.   There is no part of the world—tropical, temperate, or arctic—that never

face danger from bad weather conditions.

   2   After _or_ or _nor_ the verb agrees with the subject closest to it.

Not John _nor_ Harold _nor Allen works_ there.
Either the boys _or_ their _sister has promised_ to come.
The chairman _or_ the committee _members decide_ on their next meeting time.
Neither the students _nor_ the _teacher wants_ to make up the class they missed.

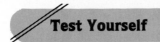

Test Yourself

B. In each clause underline the subject once and the verb twice. Cross out every incorrect verb form. Put the correct form in the blank to the left of the sentence.

_____ 1.   Either the wind or the lightning have knocked down a large branch from the

tree in our backyard.

_____ 2.   Neither the city road crew nor the residents of the neighborhood has been

able to remove the tree that has fallen across the road.

_____ 3. Either our dogs or your cat have dug a hole under the fence.

3 Always use singular verbs in certain constructions:

a with nouns that have *a, an, one, another, each,* or *every* before them and with certain pronouns:

anybody	anyone	anything
everybody	everyone	everything
each	one	another
nobody	nothing	no one
somebody	someone	something
either	neither	

Everyone needs food, clothing, and shelter. *Each person does.*

b with **uncountable** (**mass**) nouns. (see **Countable and Uncountable Nouns**)

Gold was discovered in Brazil.   This *water is* clean.   *Molasses flavors* beans.
The *money is* in the bank.   Your *advice helps* us.   The *news is* good today.

c with a few special nouns that end in *-s:*

Diseases such as *measles, mumps, appendicitis,* and many others ending in *-itis:*
Measles is a serious disease. *Appendicitis is* an inflammation of the appendix.
Subjects of study ending in *ics: Economics is* a difficult course.
Games ending in *-s: Chess (checkers, draughts, tennis) is* interesting.

Certain geographical names:

The Thames is a river in England.   *The United States is* a large country.

d with quantities and numbers thought of as a unit:

Twenty *dollars is* not enough.   Five hundred *miles is* too far to drive in one day.
Ten *pounds* of potatoes *is* often sold in one bag.

e with the title of a book or article that is the subject even when the words in the title are plural.

Modern Stories has good stories.   "Today's Heroes" *is* a magazine article.

f with *-ing* forms (gerunds) used as the subject; a plural direct object does not affect subject-verb agreement.

subject	object of gerund	verb	
Designing	bridges	*takes*	great skill.
Picking	apples	*is*	hard work.

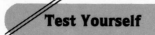 **Test Yourself**

C. In each clause underline the subject once and the verb twice. Cross out incorrect verb forms and write the correct form above them. Copy the correct form in the blank to the left of the sentence.

_____ 1. Every child in the schools learn about the heroes of the country and how they are honored.

_____ 2. *Profiles in Courage* are the name of a book by John F. Kennedy about brave people; reading it teaches us about heroes.

_____ 3. The Confederate States of America were no longer an independent country after 1865, but brave Confederate soldiers are honored by monuments throughout the southern part of the United States.

_____ 4. Remembering to honor soldiers who died for their beliefs are the concern of many patriotic organizations.

_____ 5. A medical researcher who has helped conquer diseases are also important.

_____ 6. Nobel prizes, started by the inventor of dynamite, is given for peace, not for war, and for outstanding research in physics, chemistry, medicine, and literature.

_____ 7. Teaching children about the heroes of their country and training them to be good citizens is important to all societies.

_____ 8. The advice to study history to learn about mistakes from earlier times are wise.

4   Use a plural verb with two or more nouns or pronouns joined by *and*. Do not confuse prepositions with the same meaning as *and*. See Rule 1a above.

compound subject   verb
My *shoes* and tennis *racket*   *are* in the car.
The *moon and stars*   *were* not visible last night.
Grass and flowers   *grow* fast in the summer.

Sometimes two nouns refer to the same person. If they do, use a singular verb.

subject   verb
The *secretary and treasurer was* Betty.

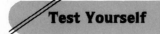

Test Yourself

D. In each clause underline the subject once and the verb twice. Cross out incorrect verb forms and write the correct form above them. Copy the correct form in the blank to the left of the sentence. Some sentences may be correct.

_____ 1. Snow, rain, and sun affects people's lives.

_____ 2. Snow and ice causes dangerous driving conditions.

_____ 3. Heavy snowfall in addition to ice on the roads make especially dangerous

conditions.

_____ 4. Cold weather and rain seems to cause illness even though doctors say germs

and viruses are the real cause.

_____ 5. Hats and loose, light-weight clothing is worn in hot, sunny climates.

_____ 6. The kind of clothing worn in hot climates are much less expensive than that

worn in cold climates.

_____ 7. Heating costs in cold climates are very high.

_____ 8. The cost of living, therefore, are less expensive in hot climates.

5   Choose between a singular and a plural verb in certain constructions according-ing to the meaning of the whole sentence.

a   Some words such as *some, all, half, more,* and *most* can be used in a phrase with singular or plural meanings.

Singular: Some (*half, all, more, most, a lot*) of the food *has* been eaten.

Plural: Some (*half, all, more, most, a lot*) of the students *have* registered.

Look at the object following the preposition *of.* If a singular or an uncountable (mass) noun follows *of,* the verb is singular. If a countable plural noun follows *of,* the verb is plural.   (see **Countable and Uncountable Nouns**)   This construction is an ex-ception to Rule 1a. The object of the preposition does affect the choice of the verb after the words listed above.

Singular: All the pie *was* eaten. (one pie—singular)
            All *the rice was* eaten. (uncountable or mass—singular)
Plural: All the pies *were* eaten. (more than one pie)

b   Collective nouns stand for groups of more than one member. These groups are usually people or animals. Most collective nouns have both singular and plural forms: *team* and *teams.* The plural form always takes a plural verb. But the singular form may take a singular verb or a plural verb. Use singular verbs with most singular collective nouns if the group is acting as a unit, but use a plural verb if the members of the group are acting separately and individually.

singular   singular
 noun verb

Our *team* *is* winning the game. (unit)

 singular plural
  noun   verb

The *team* *have found* jobs for the summer in different places, so they will not be able to practice together again until fall. (individuals)

 plural   plural
  noun   verb

The *members* of the team *are* playing in the tournament next week.

British usage and U. S. usage do not always agree. For example, in British usage, *government* may be thought of as the people who rule *or* as an institution. In U. S. usage, *government* is thought of as an institution only.

  singular plural
   noun   verb

British: The *government* *are* resigning. (members of the government)

  singular singular
   noun   verb

U. S.: The *government* *is* losing control of the situation. (institution)

Many specific collective nouns exist, especially for groups of animals and birds.

herd of animals, cattle, etc. flock of birds, chickens, etc. swarm of insects, bees, etc.
covey of quail   pride of lions   school of fish

Some collective nouns are used often.

band	class	flock	orchestra
choir	club	group	team
chorus	company	herd	youth (can be singular, plural, or uncountable)

The school *band/chorus/orchestra is* practicing today.

Certain collective nouns always take plural verbs. (*-woman* or *-man* can be added to *clergy* and *police* to make a singular form.)

cattle	people	vermin
clergy	police	

The *cattle are* in the pasture.
Many *people are* willing to help the elderly.

Test Yourself

E. In each clause underline the subject once and the verb twice. Cross out incorrect forms and write the correct forms above them. Copy the correct forms in the blank to the left of the sentence.

_____ 1. Today problems of enough food for everyone on earth seems overwhelming in some areas.

_____ 2. Poor distribution of foodstuffs, not production, are the main obstacle to getting enough food to everyone.

_____ 3. Agricultural technologies to solve problems of hunger exists at the present time.

_____ 4. Much food that we eat today were impossible for our ancestors to get.

_____ 5. All of the fresh fruits and vegetables was preserved by drying or smoking in earlier times.

_____ 6. Most of the process of canning and preserving food by keeping it away from air were invented in the early 1800s in France.

_____ 7. All of our modern transportation bring us fresh food from distant areas where it is in season.

_____ 8. Many people today has fresh food all year long.

_____ 9. Cattle is slaughtered a thousand miles from the place where the meat will be sold because frozen beef can be transported quickly and cheaply by truck or rail.

_____ 10. A team working together make our modern diet possible.

6   All rules for subject-verb agreement apply to subject and verbs in dependent clauses.

               prepositional
   subject   phrase   verb
If *either* of the brothers *wins* the race their mother will be happy.

               prepositional
   subject   phrase   verb
After *one* of those girls *has finished* with her book, let someone else use it.

In many dependent clauses, the relative pronoun is the subject of its own clause. Look at the antecedent of the relative pronoun in order to decide whether to use a singular verb or a plural verb. (The relative pronouns that can be used as subjects are *who, which,* and *that.* (see **Pronouns, relative**)

        singular   singular
        antecedent   verb

The   *man* *who* always *catches* the largest fish lives across the street.

        plural   plural
        antecedent   verb

The   *men* *who* always *catch* the largest fish live across the street

     compound subject: plural
     plural antecedent   verb

Karen, Mary, and Susan, who are going to college this fall, need to find an apartment near the campus.

        singular   singular
        antecedent   verb

The *student who has* finished the work has left.

                             singular   singular
                             antecedent   is

The library has two sections: the reference *room, which is* on the first floor, and the

     compound subject: plural
     plural antecedent   verb

reading room and stacks, which are on the second floor.

When *that* is the subject of the clause you can never leave it out unless you reduce the construction from a clause to a participial phrase.

        singular   singular
        antecedent   verb

The   *test* *(that is)* being given tomorrow is difficult.

        plural   plural
        antecedent   verb

The   *tests* *(that are)* being given tomorrow are difficult.

The word the subject stands for can be the object of a preposition.

                                plural   plural
               preposition   antecedent verb

This is an important decision   *like*   many *others that are* changing the educational institutions of our country.

              singular   singular
        preposition antecedent   verb

They rode   *with*   a *friend who has* a new car.

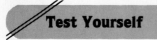

Test Yourself

F. Underline the dependent clause or clauses. Find the subject of the dependent clause and the word it stands for (its antecedent). Is the antecedent singular or plural? Choose the correct verb form and write it in the blank to the left of the sentence.

_____ 1.   The minerals that (has, have) been found on the ocean bed will be mined by

new methods.

_____ 2.   Divers who (works, work) underwater for long periods of time must be

highly trained.

_____ 3.   New machinery that (operates, operate) underwater must be developed.

_____ 4.   A country that (develops, develop) the technology to work on the sea bed

must invest large sums of money in the enterprise.

_____ 5.   Some engineers who (has, have) studied the problems compare them to

those faced by the programs of space exploration.

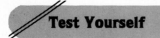

Test Yourself

G. Combined Exercise on Agreement of Subject and Verb
If the sentence is correct, put *C* in the blank. If the sentence is incorrect, cross out the error and put the correct form in the blank.

_____ 1.   Human beings has always had close contact with animals.

_____ 2.   People and animals have often competed for space and food.

_____ 3.   As human beings have developed high technologies, some animal life have been unable to compete for food and living space.

_____ 4.   Human settlement along with natural changes caused by floods and earth-quakes has changed the environment.

_____ 5.   Neither animals nor people have always been helped by changes.

_____ 6.   Some animal activity such as overgrazing by sheep and cattle have caused deserts to spread in some parts of the world.

_____ 7. Overgrazing, however, have usually been encouraged or at least allowed by human herders.

_____ 8. Knowledge of ecological principles have not always determined land-use policies.

_____ 9. Some of the suffering in the world come from human ignorance.

_____ 10. Scientists who understand ecological problems may give advice that are not taken.

_____ 11. The Dust Bowl in the United States in the 1930s are an example of a disaster to the environment.

_____ 12. Conservation practices followed by farmers at the present time are responsible for keeping soil from blowing away.

_____ 13. Changes in climate is sometimes the cause of soil erosion.

_____ 14. There is no methods to tell for certain what future climate changes will occur.

_____ 15. Unsound farming practices and changes in climate are two factors in reducing the productivity of land.

Alphabetizing

You need to understand alphabetizing in order to look up information in library card catalogs, encyclopedias, dictionaries, telephone directories, book indexes, and filing systems. You may also need to know how to put your own lists in alphabetical order for bibliographies and for filing systems.

Two methods of alphabetizing are used. You need to understand both of them.

The Dictionary Method

The dictionary method follows alphabetical order exactly. Look at each letter in order.

Jones, *David*	*Da* comes before *D.E.* in the next entry
Jones, *D.E.*	*D.E.* comes before *Do* in the next entry
Jones, *Donald F.*	*F.* comes before *W* in Warren in the next entry
Jones, *Donald Warren*	*a* in Don*a*ld comes before *n* in Don*n*er in the next entry
Jones, *Donner*	

The Directory Method

The directory method follows alphabetical order in units. Look at each word or initial. Each unit of the name is considered before going to the next unit. A shorter unit always comes before a longer one if both begin with the same letter or letters.

First Unit	Second Unit	Third Unit
Jones,	*D.*	E.
Jones,	*David*	
Jones,	*Donald*	F.
Jones,	*Donald*	Warren
Jones,	*Donner*	

D. comes before *David* because it is shorter. The rest of the list is the same as the dictionary method.

Uses of the Two Methods

As a general rule, shorter lists such as bibliographies use the dictionary method, but longer lists such as telephone directories and encyclopedias use the directory method. Some books use one system for the index and the other system for bibliographies.

Special Problems with Names

Alphabetize and look up names by the last name or family name.

1   Prefixes from foreign languages are not always treated the same in English as in the original. People who make lists try to treat the name in the way the person who bears the name would treat it, but some well-known people have had their names changed into English words. English spelling of many foreign names is very inconsistent.

A, a, al: usually put under *A,* but not always.
  Alhambra, The (palace in southern Spain): put under *A;* (English article added)
  Alhazen (Arab mathematician): put under *A.*

but

  Thomas à *Kempis* is put under *K.*

d', de, D', and *De:* usually put under *D,* especially if capitalized, but usage varies.
  The name of *Descartes,* the philosopher, is spelled as one word in modern English, but his philosophy is called *Cartesian.*
  De Gaulle, Charles: put under *D.*
  de la Mare, Walter: put under *D* (sometimes a capital letter).

but

  de *Falla,* Manuel: put under *F.*
  de *La* Fontaine, Jean: put under *L.*

El: sometimes put under *E* and sometimes under the next word.
  *E*l Capitan (mountain in California): put under *E.*

but

  El *C*id: put under *C.*
  El *G*reco: put under *G.*

L', La, Las, Le, and *Los:* usually put under *L.*
  La Fontaine, Jean de: put under *L.*
  Las Casas, Bartolomé de: put under *L.*
  Los Angeles, City of: put under *L.*

M' and *Mc:* sometimes alphabetized exactly following each letter of the word and sometimes listed as though spelled *Mac.*
  *M'*Clure is sometimes listed as though spelled *Mac*Clure.

but not

*M'*Lady Beauty Salon: *M'* stands for *my* in this phrase.
Mac (names beginning with *Mac* followed by a capital letter): sometimes alphabetized exactly following each letter of the word (both the dictionary and the directory method) and sometimes listed in a separate section before or after the general *M* listing (in some filing systems).

O': always put under *O.*

Van, van, van den, van der, and *von:* usually put under *V,* but sometimes under the family name.
  *Van*denberg: spelled as an English word; put under *V.*
  van der *W*aals: spelled as a Dutch word; put under *W.*
  Jan van der Meer von Delft is known in English as Jan *V*ermeer: put under *V.*

2   The order of names is not the same in all languages. If you cannot tell which name is the family name, look for a comma. If there is no comma, the given name or names are first. If there is a comma, the family name is first.

Warren *J*ones: *J*ones is the family name; put under *J.*
*J*ones, Warren: *J*ones is the family name; put under *J.*

EXCEPTION: English usage follows the usage of Chinese and some other Oriental languages by leaving out the comma in names in those languages.

*M*ao Ze Dong (Chinese); put under *M*
*P*ark Chung Hee (Korean); put under *P*

but

Masayoshi *O*hira (Japanese); put under *O*

3   Hyphenated last names are usually alphabetized under the first letter of the first part of the hyphenated name.

Helen *S*tephenson-Rice: put under *S.*

Titles

Alphabetize and look up titles of books and chapters in books, magazines and newspapers, articles in magazines and newspapers, short stories, plays, movies, and music by the first word in the title after *A, An,* or *The.*

The Dangerous Journey	(leave out *The*)
comes before	(*a* in *Dangerous* comes before *o* in *Domino*)
A Domino Theory	(leave out *A*)

Special Problems

1   Alphabetize numbers as they would be put if they were spelled out: consider *40* as *forty*.

Fort*u*ne, X.J.	*u* before *y* in forty in the next entry
45 Tower Place	consider forty-*five*, and *five* is before *four* in the next entry
For*ty*-*four* Bells Cafe	*t* in Forty comes before *u* in For*u*m in the next entry
For*u*m Agency	

2   Do not consider apostrophes.

John's Grill
Johns, G. W.   (dictionary method)

Johns, G. W.
John's Grill   (directory method)

3   Abbreviations are usually alphabetized as they would be put if they were spelled out except for *Mrs.* Titles such as *Dr., Mr., Mrs., Sir,* or *Capt.* are usually left out, but are sometimes included if two names are otherwise alike.

"*Mr.* Maxwell's Rescue": put as *Mister*.
Mt. Everest: put as *Mount*.
"*Mrs.* Robinson's Problem": put as *Mrs*.
St. Anne's Church: put as *Saint*.
Scott, *Rev.* Alfred J.: *Rev.* comes before *Sir*.
Scott, *Sir* Alfred J.: *A* comes before *M*.
Scott, Dr. *Marvin*: disregard title when names are different.

4   Filing systems are often set up for special purposes. They may follow special classifications that are useful to a particular business or organization.

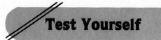 **Test Yourself**

1.   Put the following names in alphabetical order according to the last (family) name. Put a comma between the last name and other names when you put the last name before the others. If two family names are exactly the same, look at the other names to decide which one should come first on your list.

Susan Arnold	Marvin Moore	Arnold Hampstead
Ernest Brown	Mary Anthony	Peter Smith
Anne Nelson	Abner Smith	Margaret Dempsey
Paul Arnett	Annabelle Smith	Roseanna Nelsen

2.   Put the following items in alphabetical order by author's last name. Be sure to copy all punctuation accurately.

Jerome H. Paul, Jr., "The Importance of Being"
Paulding Smith, *The Ten*

P. T. Smith, *Beside the Waterfall*
Many Mansions by Gerald Prentiss
A Look at the Moon by Aaron Aronson
"Interpreting the Facts" by Gerald Prentiss
"Musical Visions" by Peter Albee
A Point in Space by Gerald Prentiss
Aaron Aronson, *The New Majority*
"Talking Back" by Martha Mitchell

3. Using the list in exercise 2 above, alphabetize the titles only. Do not consider articles that are the first word in the title when you alphabetize. Copy punctuation accurately, but do not consider it in alphabetizing.

Appositives

An appositive is a noun, pronoun, or noun clause that comes directly after another noun and gives more information about it. Set appositives off from the rest of the sentence by commas if they are not necessary to identify the noun that they follow. If they identify the noun that they follow, do not use commas to set them off from the rest of the sentence.   (see **Punctuation, comma**)

	noun		appositive	
His	brother		*John*	left yesterday.
That	dog,	the large	*collie,*	barked at us.
Two books,		both	*encyclopedias,*	are missing.

                                                noun   appositive
We cannot find either of the missing *books,* the *encyclopedias.*

If you use a pronoun as an appositive, use the subject or object form, depending on the way the word the pronoun stands for (the antecedent) is used in the clause.

          subject   appositive–antecedent
          antecedent   is subject
Only two   *students* from our team,   *Beverly* and *I,*   have a chance to win
   the race.

                    object of   appositive—antecedent is
                    preposition   object of preposition
The news brought hope to the *family, my parents, my brothers,* and *me.*

                    direct   appositive—antecedent
                    object   is object
The coach gave the distance *runners—Paul, Henry,* and *me*—clear directions before the
   start of the race.

Test Yourself

Put commas as needed in the following sentences. One or more sentences may be correct.

1. The planet earth has been compared to a huge spaceship or to a large blue marble when viewed from space.
2. Jupiter the largest of the planets has an atmosphere composed of gases that are poisonous to human beings.
3. Many people can identify Mars a planet that is distinct because of its red color.
4. The planets Jupiter, Mars, and Venus move differently in the sky from Sirius a star.
5. The star Sirius is the brightest star to the human eye.
6. Our galaxy the Milky Way is one of millions of galaxies in the universe.

Articles

A and *an* are indefinite articles that can be used only before singular countable nouns; *the,* the definite article, can be used before uncountable (mass) nouns and singular and plural nouns. No article, often called the zero article, identifies certain indefinite and general meanings of nouns. Articles are determiners and come before the nouns they modify. Except with ordinals such as *the first, second, third,* or *the last,* and *the one,* articles do not come directly before pronouns.   (see **Determiners**)

Indefinite Articles: *A* or *an*

A or *an* comes before a singular countable noun Choose according to pronunciation, not spelling. Put *a* before a word beginning with a consonant sound but put *an* before a vowel sound. *H* and *u* at the beginning of a word may have the sound of a consonant or the sound of a vowel. *Y* always has the sound of a consonant at the beginning of a word.

Sound of a Consonant	*Sound of a Vowel*
a happy day	an honest man
a helping hand	an honor
a uniform	an urgent matter
a unanimous decision	an uncle
a yellow rose	
a year	

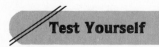

Test Yourself

A. Put *a* or *an* before each of the following words according to the sound that begins the word.

1. _____ apple   6. _____ escape   11. _____ honored guest

2. _____ university   7. _____ lucky escape   12. _____ invitation

3. _____ tree   8. _____ uncle   13. _____ jaw

4. _____ apple tree   9. _____ history test   14. _____ operation

5. _____ windy day   10. _____ ounce   15. _____ yearly review

Use *a(n)*

    1   before an unidentified singular countable noun that is one example of its class, but the number *one* is not being emphasized.

A black dog is standing in the road.
(The emphasis is not on the number.)

One black dog is standing in the road.
(The emphasis is on the number, *one*.)

    2   before an unidentified singular countable noun that is representative of its class, as in a definition—particularly in informal usage.

A dog is a domestic animal.

    3   before a singular predicate noun after a form of *be* if no other determiner is used.

Mrs. Seckson *is a* good friend.
Man O'War *was a* famous racehorse.

    4   with uncountable nouns to mean *a kind of*, or with *kind of*, or *certain*.

This man has *an honesty* that we all appreciate.
A greater unity is needed.
Literature of other countries gives us *an insight* into other cultures.

    5   before *few* and *little* to mean *some but not many* (see **Confusing Choices, few, a few**) Plural forms for *a(n)* are the zero article and *some*. (see below, pp. 61–64)

The Definite Article: The

The can be used with all nouns. Use *the* to identify a noun that shows
    1   reference backward to a noun already mentioned.

A dog has been barking all day and here is *the* dog now, standing outside the gate.

    2   reference forward to an identification soon to be made, often by modifiers following the noun.

The man *at the door* wants to speak to you.
The dog *that has been barking* all day has finally stopped barking.
All students should know something about *the* history *of their own countries*.

Use *the* before superlatives and ordinal numbers. Put additional phrase and clause modifiers after the noun.

This is *the best* cake *I have ever eaten.*
China has *the largest* population *of all countries in the world.*
Mt. Everest is *the highest* mountain *in the world.*
Charles Lindbergh was *the first* person *to fly the Atlantic alone.*

NOTE: Ordinal numbers used alone may have no article.

She was first in her class.
Our team is third in the standings.

3 context known to both writer and reader.

Here comes *the* teacher. (one teacher known to the class)
Turn on *the* light in *the* kitchen. (only one light in one kitchen)
Have you been to *the* mountains recently? (mountains nearby that are known to everyone)
They prefer to live in *the* city. (Differences between living in the country or suburbs and living in the city are known to both writer and reader.)

4 identification of a class, especially in a generalization. This usage is formal and is very common in scientific and technical writing. The definite article is followed by either a singular noun:

The child is the hope of the future.
The nuclear threat is frightening.
The honeybee is the only insect that produces food for human beings.

or an adjective form: (For the use of the definite article followed by an adjective, see **Adjectives, the + adjective**)

The elderly are often lonely.
The handicapped need access to public buildings.

5 the beginning of a phrase containing an appositive (see **Appositives**):

This is my friend, *the* one I was telling you about.
Do this experiment first, *the* experiment on page

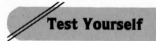
Test Yourself

B. Put *a*, *an*, or *the* in the blank in the sentence, and then copy it in the blank to the left.

_____ 1. Many people associate log cabins with _____ United States.

_____ 2. Log cabins were brought to North America by _____ settlers who came from Scandinavia and Germany.

_____ 3. _____ early log cabins were houses that required labor but no money to build.

_____ 4.   _____ colonists who had lived in forests in Europe already had

_____ 5.   _____ skill to build shelters out of logs.

_____ 6.   _____ first log cabin in America was built by Swedish settlers in Delaware in 1638.

_____ 7.   _____ different group of colonists from Britain, known as

_____ 8.   _____ Scotch-Irish, learned these skills and used them as they moved

_____ 9.   westward to _____ frontier.

_____ 10.   Indians in _____ eastern part of North America also began to build log cabins.

_____ 11.   One tribe of Indians that learned to build log cabins was _____ Cherokee.

_____ 12.   Because not all pioneers lived in log cabins, _____ idea developed about them.

_____ 13.   Politicians who had been born in log cabins were proud of _____ fact that they came from humble origins.

_____ 14.   Being born in _____ log cabin was important to Abraham Lincoln's political campaigns.

_____ 15.   Abraham Lincoln was one of _____ most famous and important of all

_____ 16.   Presidents of _____ United States.

_____ 17.   Only _____ few politicians have been able to use this idea, however.

_____ 18.   _____ few log cabins that still exist today are carefully preserved

_____ 19.   so that future generations can see how _____ pioneers lived.

_____ 20.   Visitors to Norway and Sweden can see examples of Scandinavian log cabins in parks there that have preserved _____ old ways of life.

The Zero Article
Use no article (the zero article)
1   to refer to all members of a class (with a plural noun):

Bees are insects. (all bees)
Mary likes *dogs*. (all dogs)
Water is necessary for *plants* and *animals*. (all plants and animals)

2   to distinguish one class or abstract quality from another:

Dogs, not *squirrels*, are domestic animals.
Mary likes *dogs*, not *cats*.
Men, not *women*, are boxers.
Honesty is more important for a bank employee than *beauty*.

3   to refer to an indefinite number but not always to all members of a class:

Leaves are beginning to fall. (many)
Engineers make good salaries. (many)
The edge of the field was marked by *trees*. (indefinite number)

(see Confusing Choices for *an only, only a,* and *the only,* p. 120)
4   with plural nouns after *be:*

Most of my friends are *students*.
His sisters are *teachers*.

5   with institutions and practices felt to be unique:

School begins Monday. (a particular Monday known to writer and reader)
Breakfast will be late tomorrow. (there will be only one breakfast tomorrow)
People are angry with *Congress*. (there is only one Congress in the country)

but

People are angry with *the* state legislature. (one of many but known to writer and reader)
People are angry with *the* city council. (one of many but known to writer and reader)

6   with abstract nouns in generalizations, particularly in formal writing.

Discovery of a lump or change in a mole should alert the patient to seek medical attention.
Increase in sales can be shown to be the result of *changes* in *advertising*.

Many abstract nouns have both countable and uncountable forms. In general, use uncountable forms with no article in formal writing.

7   with set phrases, usually pairs, such as

man and wife	heaven and hell
father and son	wind and rain
brother and sister	snow and sleet
lock and key	go (come) home
sun, moon, and stars	

8   with set prepositional phrases, such as

at war	in danger	on guard
at peace	in need	on purpose
at ease	in tears	on fire
at rest	in reply	on sale
at sea	in love	on vacation

at lunch	in difficulty	on time
		on duty
		on land (and sea)

by accident	out of control
by design	out of danger
by heart	out of date
by surprise	out of doors
by chance	out of order
by mistake	out of stock
by bus, plane, car	out of turn

You can find set phrases in dictionaries. Look up the object word if you are not sure of its use: *war, peace, danger,* and so on. Dictionaries written for nonnative speakers give more information about set phrases than other dictionaries do.

9   with nouns used in headlines in newspapers, captions in books, signs, labels, and the like.

PRISONER FREED
ENTRANCE TO PARKING
BEWARE OF DOG

Test Yourself

C. Look at Exercise B on pages 60–61, "Modifiers of Nouns." How many articles are in the passage? Explain why so few articles are used and the reasons for the articles that are used.

D. Cross out articles that are unnecessary in the following sentences:

The people everywhere in the world might say, "When the strangers do not understand the customs that we follow, they are confused and do not understand what is happening." The good manners are different in the different parts of the world. In many places, for example, accepting the gifts or anything important with the left hand shows the bad manners and even the rudeness. People with the good manners accept the important things with the both hands or at least with the right hand. Using the left hand to accept the important things shows not only the discourtesy but also shows that the person who is accepting thinks the thing being given is worthless. In the Europe and the North America, however, the people do not follow this custom and give and receive with either hand without thinking about the meaning of what they are doing.

Some

Use *some* for an indefinite amount with uncountable and plural nouns.

He wants *some rice.* (uncountable)
She is getting *some instruction* in music now. (uncountable)
The lecturer gave us *some* good *advice.* (uncountable)
You can find *some articles* about television shows in today's newspaper. (plural)

Any

Use *any* in place of *some* in questions and negatives   (see **Confusing choices, any, some; Negation;** and **Questions**).

He doesn't want *any* rice.
She isn't taking *any* instruction in music now.
Mrs. Johnson didn't give us *any* good advice.
You cannot find *any* information about television shows in today's newspaper.

NOTE: *Any* may also be used in the sense of "it doesn't matter which."

Any of the suits on this rack will fit you.
He has enough money to buy *any* car he wants.
Any doctor can tell you what long hours he works.

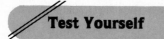

Test Yourself

E. Put *some* or *any* in the blank in the sentence and then copy it in the blank to the left.

_____ 1. Mary and Paul need to do _____ experiments in the chemistry lab this afternoon.

_____ 2. They have not done _____ lab work this week.

_____ 3. They have been studying for _____ difficult tests in math and history.

_____ 4. They will appreciate _____ help they can get to catch up on their work.

_____ 5. Their lab instructor will give them _____ help today.

Articles with Proper Nouns

Do not use an article with

1 common nouns used as terms of address and therefore capitalized.

Thank you, *Mother*.
The patient is ready, *Doctor*.

2 other proper nouns except as noted below.

Use *a(n)*

1 when using a proper noun to indicate the characteristics of the person named.

He is *a Hercules*. (very strong)
She is *a Florence Nightingale*. (a kind nurse)

2 to mean "a certain person whose name is."

A *Dr. Jones* called this morning.
A *Mr. Johnson* is looking for you.

Use *the* in the following cases:

1 for a family name in the plural

The Hendersons have moved.
The Smiths came this evening.

NOTE: Do not use an apostrophe in plural family names that are not possessive.

2 to distinguish two people who have the same name

The *George Brown* who teaches here is not the *George Brown* you knew in college.

3 when the article is accepted as part of a geographical name

| *Countries:* | the Netherlands | the United States or the U.S. |
| | the Philippines | the Soviet Union or the U.S.S.R. |

Seas and Oceans:	the Black Sea	the Pacific (Ocean)
	the Red Sea	the Atlantic (Ocean)
	the Indian Ocean	the Baltic (Sea)
	the North Sea	the Mediterranean (Sea)

Ocean or *Sea* is always part of the name in the list on the left, but you may leave it out in the list on the right. Do not use *the* with names of individual lakes, but *the Great Lakes* means collectively Lake Superior, Lake Huron, Lake Michigan, Lake Erie, and Lake Ontario.

| *Rivers:* | the Amazon | the Mississippi |
| | the Ganges | the Nile |

Mountain Ranges:	the Alps
	the Andes
	the Rockies *or* the Rocky Mountains
	the Himalayas *or* the Himalaya Mountains

Most individual peaks do not have *the* in their name, but *the Matterhorn* does.

4 when the article is accepted as part of any kind of proper name.

Ships:　　　　the *Arizona*　　　　the *Graf Spee*
　　　　　　　the *Queen Elizabeth* II　　the *Norway*

Newspapers:　　*The Times*　　　　*The Times of India*
　　　　　　　The New York Times　　but *Time* (magazine)

Deserts:　　　the Kalahari (Desert)　　the Sahara

NOTE: Names of ships and newspapers are printed in italics. Show this in writing or typing by underlining.

Hotels:　　　　The Hilton　　The Sheraton
　　　　　　　The Cloisters　　The Marriott

College and Universities:　　the University of Michigan
　　　　　　　　　　　　the University of Southern California

When the identifying name of a college or university is first, do not use *the*.

Harvard University　　　Northern Arizona University
Indiana University　　　North Georgia College
Concordia College　　　Western Michigan University

Other Organizations　　the United Nations　　the Museum of Natural History
and Institutions:　　　the National Gallery　　the Rose Bowl

but

Central Park　　　　Carnegie Hall
Soldiers' Field　　　Memorial Stadium

You cannot tell about many proper names except by learning the usage in each case: for example, the Grand Canyon, but Grand Coulee Dam.

Test Yourself

F. Put an article in the blank in the sentence if it is needed. If no article is needed, put *0*. Copy the correct answer in the blank to the left.

_____   1.   Because Terri's father is a foreign diplomat in the service of his country,

　　　　　　　the family has lived in many parts of _____ world.

_____   2.   Terri was born in _____ Great Britain.

_____   3.   Since then the family has lived in _____ Philippines,

_____   4.   _____ Saudi Arabia,

_____ 5. _____ Republic of China,

_____ 6. _____ Canada, and

_____ 7. _____ Brazil.

_____ 8. Most of the time the family took vacations in the country where they

were living, but sometimes they took special trips to famous places in

_____ Europe or

_____ 9. in _____ Middle East.

_____ 10. In many years of traveling they crossed _____ Atlantic Ocean many times.

_____ 11. They also flew over famous places such as _____ Alps,

_____ 12. _____ Rio de Janeiro, and

_____ 13. _____ Mississippi River. Now Terri is ready to enter a university.

_____ 14. _____ Should she accept a place at _____ Harvard University to study

sociology or

_____ 15. should she go to _____ University of Michigan to study linguistics?

Aspect, see **Finite Verbs**

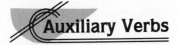

Auxiliary Verbs

The auxiliary verbs combine with main verbs to make all the tenses except the present and the past. _Be, have,_ and _do_ operate in special ways in clauses in the same ways that modals operate.   (see **Operators**)

Most forms of the auxiliaries can be contracted with a noun or pronoun (_he's_) and/or with _not_ (he _isn't_).   (see **Contractions)**

_Be_ (_am, is, are, was, were_) may be the main verb in the clause, or as an auxiliary it may combine with the present participle (_-ing_ form) or past participle (_en_ form) of another verb.   (see **Be**)

Be

Be is the most irregular verb in English. Since it is used more than any other verb, both as the main verb in a clause and as an auxiliary in forming tenses and the passive voice, you must learn all of its parts and how to use them.

Principal Parts of *Be*

	Present Singular	*Past Singular*	*Past Participle*	*Present Participle*
Infinitive (to) *be*	I *am* happy. You *are* happy. He/she/it *is* happy.	I *was* happy. You *were* happy. He/she/it *was* happy.	*been*	*being*
	Plural We/you/they *are* happy.	*Plural* We/you/they *were* happy.		

Be usually has a noun or adjective as a predicate complement following it, such as the word *happy* (adjective) in these examples, or a word, phrase, or clause showing place.

Be in Other Tenses

Present Perfect, Singular
I *have been* happy.
You *have been* happy.
He/she/it *has been* happy.

Plural
We/you/they *have been* happy.

Future, Singular
I *will* (shall) *be* happy.
You *will* (shall) *be* happy.
He/she/it *will* (shall) *be* happy.

Plural
We/you/they *will* (shall) *be* happy.

Past Perfect, Singular
I *had been* happy.
You *had been* happy.
He/she/it *had been* happy.

Plural
We/you/they *had been* happy.

Future Perfect, Singular
I *will* (shall) *have been* happy.
You *will* (shall) *have been* happy.
He/she/it *will* (shall) *have been* happy.

Plural
We/you/they *will* (shall) *be* happy.

NOTE: The distinction between *shall* and *will* for emphasis (I/we *shall* and you/he/she/it/they *will* in nonemphatic use, but you/he/she/it/they *shall* in emphatic use) is not generally observed in the United States. *Will* and *shall* are often but not always interchangeable.   (see **Modals**, 198)

    Be as a main verb is not usually used in a progressive tense unless it is used in the sense of "behaving."   (see **Stative Verbs**) Make the progressive tenses with the same forms of *be* you use when it is a main verb + *being*.

Present Progressive Continuous, Singular
I *am being* difficult. (behaving in a difficult
   manner)
You *are being* difficult.
He/she/it *is being* difficult.

Plural
We/you/they *are being* difficult.

Past Progressive Continuous, Singular
I *was being* difficult.

You *were being* difficult.
He/she/it *was being* difficult.

Plural
We/you/they *were being* difficult.

Be as an Auxiliary Verb

Use the correct form of *be* in verb phrases to make all tenses except the simple present, past, and future.   (see **Tense**)   Use forms of *be* with the past participle of another verb to make the passive voice.   (see **Passive Verbs**)

Present Passive, Singular
I *am* prepared.
You *are* prepared.
He/she/it *is* prepared.

Plural
We/you/they *are* prepared.

Past Passive, Singular
I *was* prepared.
You *were* prepared.
He/she/it *was* prepared.

Plural
We/you/they *were* prepared.

Future Passive, Singular
I/you/he/she/it will *be* prepared.

Plural
We/you/they will *be* prepared.

70   Be

Test Yourself

A. Put the correct form of *be* in the following sentences. Then copy the form in the blank to the left.

_____ 1. Silk _____ a natural animal fiber.

_____ 2. Making silk cloth _____ an industry in China for nearly five thousand years.

_____ 3. According to an old Chinese legend, a young empress _____ the one who first thought of unwinding the strands of fiber from the cocoon of a silkworm.

_____ 4. Since that day thousands of years ago, the Chinese _____ making silk thread into fine cloth.

_____ 5. The secrets of making silk used _____ known only to the Chinese.

_____ 6. Those who tried to steal the secrets _____ put to death.

_____ 7. Finally some travelers smuggled some eggs of *bombyx mori*, the silk moth, out of China and the secrets of silk making _____ known in Europe.

_____ 8. Silkworm caterpillars _____ such greedy eaters that they eat their own weight in mulberry leaves every day.

_____ 9. Strands from silkworms _____ very strong.

_____ 10. A thread of silk _____ two-thirds as strong as a steel wire of the same size.

_____ 11. One thread may _____ one thousand feet long.

_____ 12. Reeled silk thread _____ made from strands wound off the cocoon.

_____ 13. Silk fabric can _____ dyed brilliant colors.

_____ 14.   Today although many other countries raise silkworms and produce silk

products, China _____ still a major center of sericulture (the making of raw

silk).

Meanings of *Be* as a Main Verb

1   As a linking verb, *be* joins a subject to a predicate adjective that describes the subject or to a predicate noun or pronoun that restates the subject or gives additional information about it.   (see **Predicate complements**)

	predicate		predicate
subject	noun		adjective
Martha is a	student.	Alfred is	tall.

A pronoun that follows *be* should be the subject form.   (see **Pronouns**)

	predicate
subject	nominative
It	is I (he, she, we, they)

Many people use *it is me/him/her/them*, however, especially in speech, or avoid the construction because they think subject forms sound too formal.

2   *Be* can mean *exist*.

I think; therefore, I *am*. (exist)
The only difference between the hats *is* their colors.

3   *Be* can mean to *live, stay,* or *arrive* in a specific place. In this meaning it is usually followed by an adverb.

He *is* here. (single-word adverb)
He *is* in Chicago. (prepositional phrase, adverbial)
They *are* at work. (prepositional phrase, adverbial)

4   When it is followed by the infinitive of another verb, *be* has a future meaning of intention, obligation, or permission.

She *is to finish* her work before she leaves.
Charles *is* not *to go* out tomorrow.

5   *Be* can mean *go* or *come* to *visit*. (often with *by* or *in*)

We have *been to* Japan several times.
Has the manager *been* here today? **or** *been in* or *been by*

6   Use *be* to show age. Never use *have*.

The child *is* ten years old.
How old *are* these children?
Sarah *will be* twenty-one next Monday.

7 Never leave out *be* when it is the main verb in the clause. Although in many other languages you can leave out *be*, in English you must have a subject and finite verb form to have a complete sentence. (*You* can be left out of commands;   see **Commands**)

Where *are* the books? The books *are* on the table.
What *is* this? This *is* a pine tree.
This shirt *is* too expensive; it *is* seventy-five dollars.

NOTE: A plural noun that follows *be* as a main verb often has no article before it, especially if no modifier follows that noun.

plural noun

These people are   apprentice electricians.
plainclothes police.
Germans.
visitors.

Test Yourself

B. Use a form of *be* for the meaning shown in parentheses.

_____ 1. The children _____ to go to the circus tomorrow afternoon. (future intention)

_____ 2. Now that John _____ six years old, he should enjoy the circus. (age)

_____ 3. The older children _____ to the circus only once before. (visit)

_____ 4. They _____ at the circus when it came here two years ago. (visit)

_____ 5. Since we _____ in a small town now, we have fewer chances to go to the circus. (live)

_____ 6. Now that Sally _____ thirteen, she thinks she may be too old to go to the circus. (age)

_____ 7. But Sally _____ to go along anyhow to help with the young children, and she will enjoy the horses when she gets there. (obligation)

Bracket, see **Punctuation, brackets**

Capitalization

1   Use a capital letter to begin every sentence. Do not use a figure to begin a sentence, but write the figure in words or put it in a different place in the sentence.

Incorrect: 7 people came.

Correct: Seven people came.

Incorrect: $10,000 is missing.

Correct: Ten thousand dollars is missing. **or** The missing amount is $10,000.

Incorrect: 60 percent of all traffic accidents involve drivers who have been drinking.

Correct: Sixty percent of all traffic accidents involve drivers who have been drinking.

or

Drivers who have been drinking are involved in 60 percent of all accidents.

2   Use a capital letter to begin a direct quotation that begins in the middle of the sentence as well as one that starts at the beginning of the sentence.   (see **Direct Speech**)

Beginning: "Come as quickly as you can," he said.

Middle:	He said, "*C*ome as quickly as you can."
	They asked, "*W*here can we get something to eat?"
	The bus driver said, "*Y*ou must have exact change."

If the words that show who is speaking (dialogue guide) come in the middle of a sentence of the direct quotation, do not put a capital letter at the beginning of the part of the direct quotation that continues in the same sentence.

Continuing	"Come," he said, "*a*s quickly as you can."
Quotation:	"Where," they asked, "*c*an we get something to eat?"
	"I cannot make change," the bus driver said; "*y*ou must have exact change."

Capitalize the first word at the beginning of the continuing quotation if a new sentence begins.

"Come," he said. "*W*e can go now."
"Where can we get something to eat?" they asked. "*W*e are hungry."
"I cannot make change," the bus driver said. "*Y*ou must have exact change."

Do not use a capital letter to begin an indirect quotation. (In an indirect quotation, the speaker's words are reported but not repeated exactly;   see **Reported Speech**)

He told us *t*o come as quickly as possible.
They asked *w*here they could get something to eat.
The bus driver said *t*hat he could not make exact change.

3 Capitalize the pronoun *I* but not *me, my, myself,* or *mine.*

The book *I* found in *my* desk is not *mine.*

4 Capitalize proper nouns and words formed from proper names. Capitalize people and their titles. Use periods after titles that are abbreviations. Do not use periods after titles that are not abbreviations. Use commas between names and titles that follow names.   (see **Abbreviations**)

Dr. Marian Harvey

> **or**

Marian Harvey, M.D.

> **or**

Marian Harvey, Ph.D.

Mr. John Smith or John Smith, M.A.
Mrs. Arthur Moore
Ms. Jane Brown
Miss Anne Martin (NOTE: no period after *Miss*)
Sir Henry Thornton
Governor Johnston
Aunt Mary and Uncle George
Professor Jones

Major Cummings
Alexander the Great (NOTE: *the* is not capitalized)
the Elizabethan Age
a Christian civilization
Buddhist philosophy

Capitalize titles when they refer to specific people, but not when they refer to one person in a larger class.

He is a *p*rofessor at the university. (one of many professors)
She is a *m*ajor in the army. (one of many majors in the army)

Capitalize titles of relationship when a specific person is being spoken to or is referred to by title.

Aren't you listening, *M*other?
Has *F*ather come home yet?

Do not capitalize titles of relationship when a personal pronoun comes before them.

Have you seen *my* aunt?
The man you spoke to is *his* uncle.
I wrote a letter to *my* mother yesterday.

Capitalize geographical names and words formed from them.

Paris, France	French culture
Bombay, India	Indian food
Accra, Ghana	Afro-Americans
Montreal, Canada	Canadian students
Asia	Asian studies
the United States	the U.S. government
the United Kingdom	British traditions

NOTE: *The* is rarely capitalized before geographical names, but capitalize it in The Hague, the capital of the Netherlands.

Capitalize titles of books, magazines, articles, short stories, compositions, plays, movies, television shows, and music, but do not capitalize articles, conjunctions, or prepositions unless they are the first word of the title. For rules about underlining (italics) and quotation marks, see **Titles**.

The Advanced Learner's Dictionary (a book)
A Dictionary of Musical Terms (a book)
"A New Look at Old Age" (an article)
"Learning by Doing" (an article)
"Ten Minutes to Doomsday" (an article)
The Marriage of Figaro (an opera)
The New York Times (a newspaper)
Time (a magazine)

Capitalize names of particular college courses but not the name of the discipline unless it is a language.

He is taking *H*istory 101
Many colleges require students to take courses in *A*merican history.

American is capitalized because it comes from *America,* but history is not capitalized because it is not the name of a specific course.

She is writing a paper for her *w*orld *l*iterature course.
Arthur is taking *C*hemistry III this quarter.
Have you registered for *M*ath 205?

Capitalize names of the deity, religions, and religious bodies.

Christian/Christianity	the First Baptist Church
Jewish/Judaism	Mormon
Islamic/Islam	St. John's Lutheran Church
Hindu/Hinduism	Protestant
God (but *g*ods if plural)	Allah

Capitalize dates, months, days of the week, holidays, historic periods, and events.

January, February, and so on	Easter
Sunday, Monday, and so on	Passover
New Year's Day	the Middle Ages
Thanksgiving	the Civil War

Do not capitalize names of the seasons: *s*pring, *s*ummer, *a*utumn, *f*all, *w*inter.

Capitalize names of the planets, stars, and constellations.

Jupiter	Venus	Gemini
Mars	Saturn	Orion
Sirius	the Pleiades	Mercury

Do not capitalize *e*arth, *m*oon, or *s*un.

5   Capitalize the first letter of a line of poetry.

*W*hen lilacs last in the dooryard bloom'd,
*A*nd the great star early droop'd in the western sky in the night,
I mourn'd, and yet shall mourn with ever-returning spring.
                                            —*Walt Whitman*

6   Capitalize the first word of every point of an outline, a list, or the legend (explanation of the symbols) of a map.

Products of North America
  I. Plant Products
    A. Food
       1. Grain
       2. Vegetables
       3. Fruit
    B. Nonfood
       1. Lumber
       2. Cotton
       3. Tobacco

II. Mineral products
    A. Metals
        1. Iron
        2. Copper
        3. Silver
        4. Gold
    B. Fuels
        1. Petroleum
        2. Coal

7 Capitalize *north, south, east,* and *west* and compound words made from them when they refer to recognized specific regions or are part of a proper name. Do not capitalize *north, south, east,* and *west* and compound words made from them when they mean directions.

They are attending school in the *S*outh.
The *N*ortheast has severe storm warnings tonight.
Miss Collins is an expert on the *M*iddle *E*ast.
Mr. and Mrs. Adams go *s*outh every winter to avoid the cold weather.
Canada is *n*orth of the United States and Mexico is *s*outh of it.
*N*orth Dakota and *S*outh Dakota are *w*est of Minnesota.
The copying machines are along the *n*orth wall of the library.
When you come to the next corner, turn left and drive *e*ast for two miles.

NOTE: Put *north* and *south* first in compound single words: *northeast, northwest, southeast,* and *southwest.* Compass terms may have two words such as *east by northeast.*

The wind is out of the *northeast.*
Many people like the dry climate of the *Southwest.*

8 Treatment of prefixes with proper names is not consistent. Look in a dictionary to be sure when to use capital letters and hyphens.

antichrist	anti-Semite
transatlantic	post-World War II
subarctic	Postimpressionism
Precambrian	post-Pleistocene
pre-Christian	pro-American
Pre-Raphaelite	premedical
pre-Socratic	pre-engineering

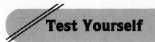

Test Yourself

Put capital letters where they are needed in the following sentences. Cross out incorrect letters and put capital letters above them.

1. alexander graham bell is remembered today mainly for inventing the telephone

    although he himself wanted to be remembered for his work with the deaf.

2. bell was born in edinburgh, scotland, in 1847, the son of a teacher of the deaf, and attended elementary and secondary schools and university there.

3. later bell moved south to london and worked with his father teaching the deaf to talk.

4. after bell's older and younger brothers both died of tuberculosis, doctors warned his family that his life was threatened by the same disease.

5. the bell family moved across the atlantic ocean to brantford, ontario, canada, to find a more healthful climate.

6. after alexander graham bell recovered his health, he moved to boston to teach teachers of the deaf; he also became a professor at boston university.

7. helped by thomas a. watson, who ran an electrical shop, bell carried on electrical experiments at night.

8. in the spring of 1876, bell's telephone carried its first inteiligible sentence.

9. on march 10 of that year, watson heard bell say, "mr. watson, come here; i want you," from another room; the message had been transmitted over a wire when bell spilled the acid from a battery on his clothing.

10. bell did not take an active part in developing the telephone business, but spent the remaining forty-five years of his life working for the deaf and experimenting with other uses of electricity.

11. because exploration of the earth was one of bell's many interests, he served as president of the national geographic society from 1898 to 1903.

12. although he became a citizen of the united states in 1882, bell chose to spend the last years of his life in canada and died at his home in nova scotia in 1922.

Case: see **Possessives and Pronouns, subject, object, and possessive forms.**

Clauses

A clause is a group of words that has a subject-verb combination in it. The verb must be a main or finite verb form. The *-ing* or the infinitive forms cannot be the main verb without an auxiliary.

Incorrect: The girl *to run* down the street (fragment)

Incorrect: The girl *running* down the street. (fragment)

Correct: The girl *is running* down the street.
The girl *runs* down the street.

Embedded clause is a term sometimes used for subordinate parts of the sentence that do not always have subject-main verb combinations.   (see **Subordinating and Reducing**)   Here, however, *clause* means a group of words that has a subject and a main verb.

Independent Clauses

Independent clauses (also called main clauses) can be punctuated as separate sentences. They may be long or short. Each independent or main clause has one subject-verb combination in it.

Running down the street chasing the bus to school, *Greg shouted* loudly after it to stop and pick him up.

There is only one subject-main verb combination in the sentence above: *Greg shouted.* Other words in this sentence that are verb forms are *running, chasing,* and *to stop* and *pick up.* None of these forms can be the main verb in the sentence, however.   (see **Finite Verbs**)

Independent Clause: *Greg ran* down the street.

Independent Clause: *Greg chased* the bus down the street.

Independent Clause: *Greg shouted* at the bus driver to stop for him.

Independent Clause: *Greg will be* late to work.

Independent Clause: The next *bus will stop* to pick Greg up.

The sentences above are independent clauses. They have a subject and a verb. They do not have a subordinating conjunction or relative pronoun that would make them dependent.

Dependent Clauses

Dependent clauses (also called subordinate clauses) cannot be punctuated as complete sentences except in direct quotations and in some transitional uses.

1   A dependent clause must be attached to an independent clause. More than one dependent clause can be attached to the same independent clause.

<pre>
                                    independent
        dependent clause   clause   dependent clause
</pre>
When the alarm *clock rang,*   the *boy saw*   that *it was*   time to get up.

A dependent clause may come in the middle of an independent clause.

<pre>
    independent
      clause
</pre>
The boy got up.

<pre>
          dependent clause
</pre>
The boy *who was sleeping* got up.

2   A dependent clause may be marked or unmarked. If it is marked, the first word in the clause is a *relative pronoun* or a *subordinating conjunction*. In an unmarked clause, *that, which,* or *who(m)* is left out. The only markers that can be left out are *that, which,* and *who(m),* and they can be left out only in certain constructions as explained under adjective clauses and noun clauses. WH-words can be used to introduce dependent clauses.   (see **WH-Words**)

<pre>
          marker
</pre>
This is the story *that* she read.
This is the story she read. (unmarked: *that* is left out)

<pre>
          marker
</pre>
They said *that* they were going.
They said they were going. (unmarked: *that* is left out)

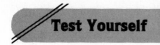

Test Yourself

A. Mark each subject and main verb by underlining. Mark the beginning and end of each clause with a straight line. Then write *ind* or *dep* over each clause. How many clauses are in each sentence? Mark the number of clauses in the margin to the left.

1.   Mary ran up the steps that lead to her classroom.

2.   Because Mary was late, she ran up the steps.

3.   Late to class, Mary ran up the steps.

4.   As Mary ran up the steps, she realized that she would be late to class.

5.   Mary worried that she would be late to class.

6.   Mary had to get off the bus far from the classroom building, but she ran as fast as she

     could to get to class on time.

7. She dropped her books when she ran up the steps.

8. Mary got off the bus and ran to the classroom building.

9. She got off the bus far from her class; because she was running so fast to get to class on time, she fell while running up the steps.

> **3** A dependent clause acts in the sentence as an adjective, an adverb, or a noun.

Adjective Clauses

Like a single-word adjective, an adjective clause modifies a noun or pronoun.

                          dependent
                          clause
                          (adjective)
This is the story *that she read.*
(*that she read* modifies *story*—it tells which story)

                          dependent
                          clause
                          (adjective)
John is the boy *who remembered.*
(*who remembered* modifies *boy*—it tells which boy)

An adjective clause in English usually comes immediately after the noun or pronoun it modifies. In the following sentence, *that we liked very much* modifies *bears.*

The story about the bears *that we liked very much* is in this book. (We liked the bears.)

To make *that we liked very much* modify *story,* put it directly after *story.*

The story *that we liked very much* about the bears is in this book. (We liked the story.)

The marker for an adjective clause is sometimes called a relative pronoun.
If *where* means *the place in which,* it can introduce an adjective clause. Adjective clauses introduced by *where* usually follow directly after the noun they modify. Adjective clauses cannot move in the sentence in the way adverb clauses can.

Paris, where Jean and Bob first met each other, is a place they would like to visit again.
People often want to visit the places where they were born and spent their childhoods.

Test Yourself

B. Underline the adjective clauses in the following sentences. Put a circle around the relative pronoun (clause marker).

1. Baseball and cricket are games that are played in many parts of the world.

2.   Both games have a batter and someone who throws a ball toward the batter, who runs when he hits the ball.

3.   Other rules, which have to do with the number of players, their positions, and the scoring, are very different.

4.   Men and boys who are British or who live in parts of the world that were once part of the British Empire are likely to play cricket.

5.   Baseball was invented in the United States, where it is very popular.

6.   Baseball is also very popular in Mexico and in the Spanish-speaking countries that are in and around the Caribbean.

7.   In the English-speaking islands of the Caribbean, however, cricket is a game that is very popular.

8.   The English-speaking Caribbean nations have produced cricket players who are among the finest in the world.

9.   Spanish-speaking Caribbean countries have produced some of the world's finest baseball players, who play on major-league teams in the United States and Canada.

10.   The Japanese, who have their own baseball league, are also very enthusiastic about the game.

11.   Other countries in Asia that belong to the Commonwealth have cricket teams, not baseball teams.

Reduced Adjective Clauses

If a form of *be* follows the relative pronoun in an adjective clause, the clause can often be reduced to make the sentence less wordy. Take out the relative pronoun and the form of *be* that follows it. Be sure to use the correct form of the participle. If the meaning is active, use the *-ing* form. If the meaning is passive, use the past participle (*-en* form).

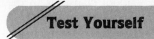

Test Yourself

C. Put the correct present or past participle form in the blank in the sentence. Then copy it in the blank to the left.

_____ 1. Diseases (that have been) _____ by a doctor can often be cured quickly if the patient follows instructions. (diagnose)

_____ 2. Patients (who are) _____ worse after they take their medicine should be sure they have followed instructions exactly. (feel)

_____ 3. Medicine (that is) _____ to the patient must be taken according to instructions. (give)

_____ 4. A nurse or family member who is _____ medicine to someone else must be careful not to make an error. (give)

_____ 5. Sometimes two different drugs (that are) _____ at the same time react with each other and cause harmful side effects. (take)

_____ 6. Patients (who are) _____ other medicines must always tell their doctors about them. (take)

_____ 7. Doctors (who are) _____ drugs need to know the patient's total medical history. (prescribe)

_____ 8. Sometimes patients (who are) _____ nonprescription drugs can have harmful side effects when they mix their own medicine with what the doctor gives them. (take)

_____ 9. Patients (who are) _____ their doctor's instructions carefully are likely to get well faster. (follow)

_____ 10. Patients (who have) _____ from a serious illness often follow their doctor's directions better than before. (recover)

Adverb Clauses

Like a single-word adverb, an adverb clause tells when (time), where (place), how (manner), why (cause), and to what extent (degree). (see **Adverbs**) An adverb clause can also show concession, condition, contrast, and purpose.

independent clause   dependent clause
We had already gone   when a message came.

In normal word order, the adverb clause follows the independent clause as in the sentences above. If the adverb clause comes first in the sentence, however, the adverb clause is followed by a comma.

dependent clause   independent clause
When a message came,   we had already gone.

The marker for an adverb clause is sometimes called a subordinating conjunction or a relative adverb. If you leave out the marker you change the adverb clause into an independent clause and change the basic structure of the sentence. (see **Sentence Structure**)

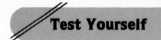

Test Yourself

D. Underline every adverb clause. Rewrite each sentence on a separate sheet. If the adverb clause comes at the beginning of the sentence, move it to the end. Do not separate it from the rest of the sentence by a comma. If the adverb clause is at the end of the sentence, move it to the beginning and put a comma between it and the rest of the sentence. (British usage does not put a comma here.) When you move a clause, you may need to change the nouns and pronouns so that nouns come at the beginning.

1. When businesses expand beyond a few workers, the work is divided into separate units.
2. As the business grows, production and marketing are separated.
3. Finance may become a separate unit because many employees are needed to keep accounts, bill customers, collect bills owed to the company, pay taxes, and arrange for credit.
4. A separate marketing division will advertise, take orders, and sell the product as the business develops.
5. Large businesses have their own research and development divisions so that they can develop new products and improve old ones without sharing their secrets with the competition.

Noun Clauses

A noun clause can replace a single-word noun, a pronoun, or a noun phrase as subject of the sentence:

noun phrase   noun clause
His speech is difficult to understand. *Whatever he says* is difficult to understand.

as direct object of the verb:

        noun   noun clause
She knew *the truth.* She knew *what he had really said.*

            noun clause   noun clause
She knew *how she could find what she needed.* (the italic first noun clause is the object of *knew;* the second one is the object of *find*)

as object of a preposition or following a two-word verb:

pronoun   noun clause
They voted for *her*.   *They voted for who(m)ever they liked* best.
(Use who*m*ever in formal writing.)

as predicate nominative (sometimes called subject complement) after *to be* or another linking verb:

noun clause
His belief is *that things will improve.*
noun clause
It seems   *that things are improving.*

A noun clause is necessary to the basic structure of its sentence and cannot be left out.

Words that can introduce noun clauses:
1 *that* (can be left out in a noun clause used as direct object and after "it is + adjective . . .")

direct object
He said   *(that) he was coming.*
It is strange *(that) he is coming.*

That can never be left out if it is the subject of the clause it introduces.
2 WH-words: *who, whose, whom, what, which, why, how, when, whether* (and *if* when it means *whether*). Most of these words also have a form which adds *-ever: whoever, whatever, whichever,* and so on. Noun clauses beginning with WH-words are usually indirect questions.   (see **Reported Speech**)

noun clause
He knows   *who broke the window.*
They do not know   *what to do.*

Test Yourself

E. Underline each noun clause in the following sentences. Over the clause mark how it is used, as subject, direct object, predicate nominative, or object of a preposition.

1. What some people say is confusing.

2. Some people confuse others because they do not think about what they are going to

    say before speaking.

3. Friends know who these people are and how they usually act.

4. Friends know, therefore, that their actions are more important than their words.

5. Strangers, however, may be insulted by what such people say.

6. Thinking ahead before speaking is what everyone should do.

Combined Exercises on Adjective, Adverb, and Noun Clauses

F. 1. In the exercises on independent and dependent clauses on page 80, mark each dependent clause as adjective, adverb, or noun.

2. In the following passage, underline every dependent clause and mark *adjective*, *adverb*, or *noun* over it.

(1) Barter is a direct way of doing business that exists only informally in highly developed societies. (2) In barter, whatever one has of value—goods and/or labor—is exchanged directly with someone else for that person's goods or labor. (3) When people barter, money is not exchanged. (4) Governments do not like a barter system because such a system makes collecting taxes difficult. (5) In fact barter systems are growing in many countries so that people can avoid taxes and governmental control of their activities. (6) In primitive societies that do not use money, barter is a necessity.

Connecting Words That Join Clauses

Two independent clauses can be joined in two ways.

1 Two independent clauses can be joined by a comma and a coordinating conjunction (*and, but, or, for, nor, yet, so*).

Independent Clause	Coordinating Conjunction	Independent Clause
The alarm clock rang,	*and*	Mark got up.
The alarm clock rang,	*so*	Mark got up.
The alarm clock rang,	*but*	Mark did not get up.
The alarm clock rang,	*yet*	Mark did not get up.
Mark got up,	*for*	the alarm clock rang.

2 Two independent clauses can be joined by a semicolon. An interrupter may be added to the second clause to show more clearly the relation between the ideas in the two clauses. (Single-word interrupters are often called conjunctive adverbs.)

Independent Clause	Independent Clause
The alarm clock rang;	the boy got up.
The alarm clock rang;	*therefore,* the boy got up.

The alarm clock rang;   *consequently,* the boy got up.
The alarm clock rang;   *as a result,* the boy got up.
The alarm clock rang;   *nevertheless,* the boy stayed in bed.
The alarm clock rang;   *however,* the boy stayed in bed.

Interrupters are movable; they may be put in the beginning, in the middle, or at the end of the clause. They must be separated from the rest of their own clause by a comma or commas.   (see **Interrupters**)

The alarm clock rang; the boy, therefore, got up.
                       the boy got up, therefore.

The Meaning of Connectors

Cause in the Second Clause
Coordinating Conjunction:

I carried an umbrella,   *for* it was raining

Effect or **result** in the Second Clause
Coordinating conjunction:

It was raining,   *so* I carried an umbrella.

Interrupters:

It was raining;   *therefore,* I carried an umbrella.
It was raining;   *consequently,* I carried an umbrella.
It was raining;   *as a result,* I carried an umbrella.
It was raining;   *thus* I carried an umbrella.
It was raining;   *accordingly,* I carried an umbrella.

Contrast in the Second Clause
Coordinating conjunction:

One of her eyes is blue,   *but* her other eye is green.
One of her eyes is blue,   *yet* her other eye is green.

Interrupters:

One of her eyes is blue;   *however,* her other eye is green.
One of her eyes is blue;   *on the other hand,* her other eye is green.
One of her eyes is blue;   *nevertheless,* her other eye is green.
One of her eyes is blue;   *even so,* her other eye is green.
One of her eyes is blue;   *by/in contrast,* her other eye is green.

Addition of More Facts or Ideas to the Facts or Ideas Stated in the First Clause
Coordinating conjunction:

He was rich,   *and* his brother was rich.

Interrupters:

He was rich;   *also* his whole family was rich.
He was rich;   *furthermore,* his whole family was rich.
He was rich;   *in addition,* his whole family was rich.
He was rich;   *moreover,* his whole family was rich.
He was rich;   *in fact,* his whole family was rich.
He was rich;   his whole family was rich *too.*

NOTE: *Too* usually comes in the middle or at the end of a clause. Words of four letters or fewer are not usually set off by commas.

Addition in Order

for another thing
second(ly)
third(ly)
finally
at last, last

He was rich; *for one thing,* he owned three cars. *For another thing,* he always wore the most expensive clothes.

An **Illustration** or **Example** in the Second Independent Clause
Interrupters:

He seemed very rich;   *for example,* he owned three cars.
He seemed very rich;   *to illustrate,* he owned three cars.
He seemed very rich;   *in fact,* he owned three cars.
He seemed very rich;   *for instance,* he owned three cars.
He seemed very rich;   *for one thing,* he owned three cars.

Choice or **Alternatives** Stated in Two Independent Clauses
Coordinating conjunction:

You must pay a fine,   *or* you must go to jail.
He did not pay a fine,   *nor* did he go to jail. (negative alternative)

Interrupters:

You must pay a fine;   *otherwise,* you must go to jail.
You must pay a fine;   *if not,* you must go to jail.

Emphasis in the Second Clause
Interrupters:

She was a beautiful girl;   *indeed,* she was the most beautiful girl I have ever seen.
She was a beautiful girl;   *in fact,* she was the most beautiful girl I have ever seen.

Repetition and **Explanation** in the Second Clause
Interrupters:

He seemed very rich to us;   *in other words,* he appeared very wealthy.
He seemed very rich to us;   *that is,* he appeared very wealthy.

Addition and alternatives are both possible. When both addition and alternatives are possible, *and/or* can be used, especially in scientific and legal writing.

The checks in this joint account must be signed by Harold Lawson *and/or* they must be signed by Jane Lawson.

Concession in the Second Clause   (see **Concession** for more examples)
Coordinating conjunctions:

The car was speeding,   *but* the police officer did not stop it.
The car was speeding,   *yet* the police officer did not stop it.

Interrupters:

The car was speeding;   *nevertheless,* the police officer did not stop it.
The car was speeding;   *still,* the police officer did not stop it.

Test Yourself

Connecting Words

Three Blind Mice
Three blind mice, three blind mice,
See how they run, see how they run!
They all ran after the farmer's wife;
She cut off their tails with a carving knife.
Did you ever see such a sight in your life
As three blind mice?

—traditional song

G. Write sentences based on "Three Blind Mice" using coordinating conjunctions and/or interrupters to show the following ideas:

1. cause (coordinating conjunction)
2. effect (a coordinating conjunction)
3. effect (an interrupter)
4. choice or alternative (coordinating conjunction)
5. emphasis (interrupter)
6. illustration or example (interrupter)
7. contrast (coordinating conjunction)
8. contrast (interrupter)

Subordinating Conjunctions
The idea in an independent clause may be modified or further explained by a dependent clause.   (see **Subordinating and Reducing**)   An **adverb** dependent clause can be introduced by a subordinating conjunction. A subordinating conjunction is different in several ways from a coordinating conjunction. (Sometimes certain subordinating conjunctions are called relative adverbs.)

1 A clause that begins with a subordinating conjunction cannot be punctuated as a separate sentence. If it is a separate sentence, it is incorrect.

independent clause	independent clause
The alarm clock rang.	Mark got up.
Mark cooked breakfast.	Mark ate breakfast.

dependent clause	independent clause
When the alarm clock rang,	Mark got up.
After Mark cooked breakfast,	he ate it.

Incorrect: When the alarm clock rang. (fragment)

Incorrect: After Mark cooked breakfast. (fragment)

2 Some subordinating conjunctions can also be prepositions. Look at the sentence to see how it is constructed. Then decide what kind of verb forms and punctuation you need. (see **Prepositions**)

prepositional phrase
Since my arrival here, I have made many friends.

dependent clause
Since I arrived here, I have made many friends.

The preposition form of *because* is *because of.* Do not confuse these forms. A preposition must be followed by a noun, pronoun, or noun-form such as the *-ing* form.

Because the alarm *clock rang,* Mark got up.
Because of the *ringing* of the alarm clock, Mark got up.

Not all subordinating conjunctions can also be prepositions.

Incorrect: *If* lack of protein, the body does not develop well.

Correct: *If* the body lacks protein, it does not develop well.

Common Subordinating Conjunctions

†after	because	in order that	†till
although	†before	once	†until
	-*er* (comparative adjective + *than*)		
as	even though	rather than	when, whenever
as far as (other adjectives or adverbs can replace *far*)	except that	†since	where, wherever
as if	how	so that	while
as though	if	sooner than	
	in case	though	

The words preceded by a dagger (†) can be prepositions. The other words on the list cannot be prepositions.

Formal Forms: in as much as, whereas, whereby, whereupon

The following words can be used as absolutes with or without *that*. They usually come at the beginning of the sentence.   (see **Absolutes**)

admitting (that)   presuming (that)
assuming (that)   providing (that)
considering (that)   seeing (that)
given (that)   supposing (that)
granted (that)
granting (that)

Admitting we have made mistakes, we can try to do better in the future.
Admitting that we have made mistakes, we can try to do better in the future.
Granted xy equals *yz,* then *ax* equals *ay.*
Granted that xy equals *yz,* then *ax* equals *ay.*

When you are combining two ideas in the same sentence to show the relationship between them, never use both a subordinating and a coordinating conjunction in the same sentence to express the same meaning.

Incorrect: *Although* the sun was very hot, *but* the plants did not die.

Correct: *Although* the sun was very hot, the plants did not die.

Correct: The sun was very hot, *but* the plants did not die.

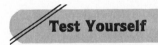

Test Yourself

H. Correct the following sentences by crossing out incorrect connecting words. Write two correct versions of each sentence on a separate sheet.

1. Even though baseball is played in many countries in the world, but association football (soccer) is played in even more countries.
2. Because soccer is probably the world's most popular game, so more people watch the World Cup on television than any other sporting event.
3. Although long-distance running, especially the marathon, has become very popular, but the marathon is not as easy for spectators to watch as stadium sports are.
4. Though the spectators do not have places to sit while they watch road races, yet they do not have to pay admission charges to stand by the road.
5. Granted that many countries have special sports that are not popular in other places, yet some form of individual combat and some kind of running are popular worldwide.

Colloquialisms

A colloquialism is a word or phrase that is used in speech but not in formal writing. Sometimes words begin as slang, become colloquialisms, and after some time become acceptable as standard English. British usage and American usage are not always the same. When you are not sure about usage of a word, look it up in a standard dictionary. Some dictionaries use the label *informal* or *slang* and others use the label *colloquial.*

Colloquialisms or informal usage can be grammatical structures or words.

Colloquial Structure:	*What* did you do that *for?*
Formal:	*Why* did you do that?
Colloquial Structure:	Alison remembers *who* she saw yesterday. (*who/whom* distinction)
Formal:	Alison remembers *whom* she saw yesterday.
Colloquial Structure:	Harry *can't* remember where he left his books. (contractions)
Formal:	Harry *cannot* remember where he left his books.
Words:	*cop* (informal) for *police officer* *kid* for *child* *a shrinking violet* for *a person who is shy or timid*

Short forms of words for complete forms:

exam for *examination*
gonna for *going to*
math for *mathematics*
tech for *technical* or *technology*
wanna for *want to*
hafta for *have to*

Test Yourself

Change the usage in the following sentences from colloquial or informal to formal.

1. When I was a kid, I didn't study so hard for my exams.

2. Since I wasn't too good at math, I didn't wanna study for math tests at all because I thought I would flunk them anyway.

3. I thought I wasn't ever gonna be smart enough to pass anyway.

4.   What did I think that for?

5.   I thought I was dumb because I hadn't ever studied hard enough to learn anything.

6.   Now I've learned who to ask to get help with stuff I don't understand.

Colon, see **Punctuation, colon**
Comma, see **Punctuation, comma**

Comma Splices

A comma splice or a comma fault is a serious error in connecting two independent clauses. Do not connect independent clauses by a comma alone without a coordinating conjunction (*and, but, or, nor, for, yet,* and *so*).

<table>
<tr><td></td><td align="center">independent clause</td><td align="center">independent clause</td></tr>
<tr><td>*Incorrect:*</td><td colspan="2">Robert has never been to New York, he has been to Los Angeles, however.</td></tr>
</table>

Do not be confused by *however*. Putting *however* between the two clauses does not correct the sentence because *however* is not a coordinating conjunction. A word like *however,* which is called an interrupter or a conjunctive adverb, cannot join independent clauses unless you also use a semicolon. Some other words like *however* are *also, too, then, therefore, furthermore, thus,* and *for example*.   (see **Interrupters**)   These words are movable in the clause.   (see **Adverbs, Word Order,** p. 41)

<table>
<tr><td></td><td align="center">independent clause</td><td align="center">independent clause</td></tr>
<tr><td>*Incorrect:*</td><td colspan="2">Robert has never been to New York, however, he has been to Los Angeles.</td></tr>
</table>

Correct a comma splice in one of four ways:

1   Put a semicolon between two independent clauses.

<table>
<tr><td></td><td align="center">independent clause</td><td align="center">independent clause</td></tr>
<tr><td>*Correct:*</td><td colspan="2">Robert has never been to New York; he has been to Los Angeles, however.</td></tr>
</table>

2   Put a comma and a coordinating conjunction between independent clauses.

<table>
<tr><td></td><td align="center">independent clause</td><td align="center">independent clause</td></tr>
<tr><td>*Correct:*</td><td colspan="2">Robert has never been to New York, but he has been to Los Angeles.</td></tr>
</table>

In a series of independent clauses, put a coordinating conjunction between the last two clauses.

<table>
<tr><td align="center">independent clause</td><td align="center">independent clause</td></tr>
<tr><td colspan="2">Robert has never been to New York, he has never been to Chicago,</td></tr>
</table>

<table>
<tr><td align="center">coordinating
conjunction</td><td align="center">independent clause</td></tr>
<tr><td>and</td><td>he has never been to St. Louis.</td></tr>
</table>

3 Put a period and a capital letter between independent clauses, making them separate sentences.

	independent clause
Correct:	Robert has never been to New York.

	independent clause
	He has been to Los Angeles, however.

4 Make one of the independent clauses into a dependent clause or into another subordinate construction.   (see **Clauses** and **Subordinating and Reducing**)

	dependent clause	independent clause
Correct:	Although Robert has never been to New York,	he has been to Los Angeles.

	participial phrase	independent clause
Correct:	Never having been to New York,	Robert has often been to Los Angeles.

A *run-on sentence* is exactly like a comma splice except that the comma is left out: there is no punctuation at all between independent clauses.   (see **Run-on Sentences**)

	independent clause	independent clause
Incorrect:	Robert has never been to New York however,	he has been to Los Angeles.

or

	independent clause	independent clause
Incorrect:	Robert has never been to New York	he has been to Los Angeles, however.

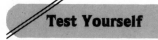
Test Yourself

Circle the incorrect comma in the following sentences and put in correct punctuation. Some sentences are correct.   (see **Punctuation, comma** for correct uses of commas)

1. In 1986 a very severe hurricane struck the island of Ignatius, it caused great damage to buildings and crops.

2. No one was killed, however, many people were injured by objects blown through the air by the high winds.

3. When the wind was at hurricane force, even small objects became deadly missiles.

4. High tides came at the same time the hurricane struck, as a result, some buildings near the ocean front were undermined and dangerously near collapse.

5. After the water pipes burst, water became unsafe to drink, contaminated ground water had entered the water system.

6. As a result of the storm, some people lost all their belongings.

7. Food deliveries were interrupted for several days, food was shipped in from neighboring islands to help in the emergency.

8. Because of the damage in many parts of the island, the government has decided to start an early-warning system for storms.

9. An early-warning system will soon be developed, then residents of Ignatius will be able to protect themselves and their property against damage from high winds, rain, and high tides.

10. They will have a warning far enough in advance so that they can put up storm shutters to protect their windows, they will cut the coconuts and dead branches off palm trees to keep them from becoming dangerous flying missiles in high winds.

11. Early warnings make the protection of life and property easier, residents of Ignatius will be able to prepare for storms and take shelter from them in the future.

 Commands

Use the imperative form of the verb for impersonal commands. (This is the same form as the simple verb form or bare infinitive.) *You* is understood as the subject and rarely stated, but a proper name is often used. Use a comma or commas to separate this name from the rest of the sentence.
Use adverbs to show time in commands.

Be quiet	now.
	for ten minutes.
Mail these letters	at once.
	this afternoon.
Julia, *finish* problem five	tomorrow morning.
	before you attempt problem six.

Use *do* for emphasis.

Do be quiet.
Do mail these letters.

Use *do not* or *don't* (less emphatic) for negation (prohibition).

Do not (*don't*) mail these letters now.
Do not (*don't*) attempt problem six before you finish problem five.

Many commands in English do not use the imperative form of the verb. Polite requests, especially, use questions and statements that are interpreted as commands. Commands using only the imperative are impersonal. They are usually used in speaking to groups and in writing. In conversation use *please* to soften the force of an imperative verb.
     You can choose from many different ways to make a command or request.

Impersonal: (Please) open the door (please).

More Polite: (Please) will you open the door (please).

More Polite: (Please) would you open the door (please).

Extremely Polite
(a command, not   (Please would you   like to open   the door (please).
a request for   mind opening
information):

Polite Command: You can be opening the door while I . . .

Polite Negative   Must you open the door now? (means Please don't)
Command:

Let + a personal object and the bare infinitive can show permission or a polite command.

     them
Let him go in now.
     Sara
       us

Let us often contracts to *let's* in speech except after *to*.

Let's go in now.
They know *to let us* go in first.

NOTE: *Allow* and *permit* are followed by a personal object + *to*. In this construction, *allow* and *permit* are more formal than *let*.

Allow }
Permit } me *to* help you.

Test Yourself

1. You are asking a stranger the way to the bus stop. Give three different ways of making the request that would be appropriate.

2. You are trying to get off a crowded bus and must ask several people to step aside. Give three different ways of making the request that would be appropriate.

3. A close friend has helped you do some shopping. Give three ways you could ask for help carrying a heavy package into your place.

Comparisons, see **Adjectives, Comparison of**

Complements

A complement is a word that is necessary to complete the meaning of a verb. In normal word order a complement follows the verb.

	linking verb	predicate adjective		
Barbara	is	friendly.		

	transitive verb	indirect object	direct object	
Barbara	gave	Charles	the ball.	

	transitive verb		direct object	objective complement adjective
Barbara	found		the work	difficult.

	transitive verb		direct object	objective complement noun
The committee	elected		Barbara	chairperson.

A linking verb must be followed by a predicate adjective, a predicate noun, a pronoun, or an adverbial complement.   (see **Be**)   A transitive verb in its active form must be followed by a direct object.   (see **Passive Verbs**)   Some transitive verbs can also be followed by indirect objects, and others can be followed by objective complements. Intransitive verbs are not followed by predicate adjectives or nouns or by direct objects. Some intransitive verbs must be followed by adverbial modifiers.

Depending on the verb and its meaning, a transitive verb may be followed by different combinations of complements.

		direct object only	
George found a		kite.	

	indirect object	direct object	
George found	us	a kite.	

direct object   objective complement
George found   the biology course   difficult.

Depending on the meaning of the sentence, the same word may be a transitive or linking verb.

transitive direct object   linking   predicate adjective
Arthur   grew   roses.   Arthur   grew   fat.

Depending on the meaning of the sentence, the same word may be an intransitive or a transitive verb.

intransitive   transitive direct object
The car   ran   well. Ben   ran   his car   into a telephone pole.

See **Indirect Objects, Predicate Complements, Sentence Patterns.**

Test Yourself

In the following sentences, identify the word that is underlined as a complement. Put predicate adjective, predicate noun, direct object, indirect object, or objective complement in the blank to the left.

_____ 1.   More people speak <u>Chinese</u> than any other language.

_____ 2.   The most popular second language in the world is <u>English</u>.

_____ 3.   Many students find English <u>difficult</u>.

_____ 4.   If a student's first language has a <u>structure</u> similar to that of English, however, English may be easier to learn.

_____ 5.   Learning a language that is <u>similar</u> to one's first language may sometimes be easier than learning a language that is very different.

_____ 6.   Words that are similar to but not the same as those in the first language, however, may cause <u>confusion</u>.

Compound Structures and Sentences, see **Coordinating Conjunctions.**

Concession

Concession is the admission that although something is true or accepted, another part of the problem or another viewpoint exists. This part may be unexpected. (see **Clauses,** and **Interrupters**)

Interrupters	*Subordinating Conjunctions*	*Prepositions*
after all	although	in spite of
all the same	though	despite
at any rate	even though	
however		
in any case	*Coordinating Conjunctions*	
in spite of that	but	
nevertheless	yet	
still		

Your payment is late;
{
interrupter
however
all the same,
in spite of that,
nevertheless,
still,
}
no penalty will be added because of the holiday yesterday.

subordinating conjunction
{
Although
Even though
Though
}
it is very cloudy today, it may not rain at all.

preposition
In spite of the clouds, it may not rain at all.

coordinating conjunction
It is cloudy,   *yet*   it may not rain at all.

Test Yourself

Combine the following sets of sentences to show concession. Use each connecting word shown in parentheses in a different sentence. (Write two sentences for each item.) Be sure your punctuation is correct.

1. The rains came at the right time. The crops failed because of the insects. (although, but)

2. Last year farmers planted more rice than ever before. Dry weather caused a poor crop. (even though, though)

3. Farmers have bad years sometimes. Most farmers want to stay on the land rather than move to a city. (yet, nevertheless)

4. Some young people leave the farm because they see little future for small farmers. A few plan to stay and farm like their parents. (in spite of that, still)

5. Problems of weather, debt, and falling prices make farming difficult. Some farmers say they will never leave their land. (although, however)

Conditional Sentences

Clauses after *if* show whether the writer or speaker thinks that the stated result is possible (real), or that the result is impossible or unlikely (unreal or contrary to fact). Use *would* in the result clause when the result is unreal or contrary to fact.

Real (Possible) Conditions

Use the present, present perfect, or past tense after *if* or *unless*. Use the present, past, future, or a command in the result clause. The result clause may come first.

Condition	*Result*
present tense	future tense
If you *brush* you teeth every day,	you *will have* fewer cavities.
If you *drive* carefully,	you *will have* fewer accidents.

Unless means *if you do not.*

If you *do not brush* your teeth,
Unless you brush your teeth,   →   you *will have* many cavities

If you *do not drive* carefully,
Unless you drive carefully,   →   you *will have* an accident.

After an *if* clause in the present tense, the verb in the result clause can be present also, or it can be a command.

Present	*Present*
If you *help* me now,	you *are* a true friend.
If you *cannot solve* the problem,	you may ask for help.

	Command
If you *understand* this problem,	*show* me how to do it.
If anyone *calls* today,	*tell* me at once.

Past	*Past*
If children *had* nutritious food,	they *were* healthy.
If they *showed* him the way,	he *found* the right office.
If the salesman *called* yesterday,	you *forgot* to tell me.

Future

If they *had* nutritious food,
If they *did* not *have* nutritious food
Unless they had nutritious food   }   they *will be* healthy.
they *will not be* healthy.

If they *did* not *show* him the way,
Unless they *showed* him the way,   }   he *will* not *find* the right office.

Generalization and truths can be expressed by *if, when,* or *whenever.*

If (when) gasoline is ignited,   it *explodes.* (*will explode* is also possible)
If (when) you understand the problem, you *can (will) get* the right answer to it.
Whenever (if) it rains here,   we *have* a flood.

NOTE: A scientific law is more likely to be stated: *Gasoline will explode when it is ignited.*

If + *should* or *happen to* means that a result is possible.
If it *should* rain tomorrow, be sure to close the windows.
If you *happen to* see John, he can show you the new schedule.

Test Yourself

A. Cross out incorrect verb forms and write the correct form in the blank to the left. Change the sentences so that all are real (possible) conditions.

_____ 1. If bad weather comes, many activities would be affected.

_____ 2. Many people would lose property and perhaps would even be injured if a tornado strikes.

_____ 3. Unless people in the path of severe storms take shelter, they might have been injured.

_____ 4. Hurricanes would cause great damage to windows if people responsible for buildings do not cover the glass with shutters.

_____ 5. Unless people would prepare for the big storm that came last year, their property would probably be damaged.

Unreal or Contrary-to-Fact Conditions

Use *would* in the result clause to show an unreal condition.

Result That Does Not Happen in the Present or Future

Use *if* + the past tense and *would* in the result clause to show that the result is impossible or unlikely to happen in the future.   (see **Modals, Would**)

Condition (past tense)	*Result* (would + main verb)

If you *brushed* your teeth carefully, you *would have* fewer cavities. (*Meaning:* You do not brush your teeth; you will not have fewer cavities.)
If you *drove* carefully, you *would* not *have* so many accidents. (*Meaning:* You do not drive carefully, and you do have many accidents.)
If you *helped* me, you *would be* a true friend. (*Meaning:* I do not think that you will help me; therefore you are not a true friend.)

Use *were* in place of *was* in unreal conditions.   (see **Subjunctive**)

If I *were* (never *was*) you, I *would* never do that.
If the truth *were* known, public opinion *would* change.
If wishes *were* horses, all beggars *would* ride. (English proverb)

Even though you will sometimes hear *was* following *if* in conversation, use *were* in formal writing.

Would can be used after *if* when it means *be willing to*.

If you *would* stop talking for a minute, I *would* be able to finish this lesson. (*Meaning:* You are not willing to stop talking, and I will not be able to finish this lesson.)

If Martha *would* save her money, she *would* be able to go home for summer vacation. (*Meaning:* Martha is not willing to save, and she will not be able to go home for summer vacation.)

NOTE: *Unless* is not usually used in unreal (contrary-to-fact) conditions.

Conditional	*Result*
(past tense)	(would + verb)

If you *did* not *brush* your teeth carefully, you *would have* many cavities. (*Meaning:* You do brush your teeth carefully, and, therefore, you do not have many cavities.)

If you *did* not *drive* carefully, you *would have* many accidents. (Meaning: You drive carefully, and, therefore, you do not have many accidents.)

Result That Did Not Happen in the Past

Use *if* + the past perfect tense and use *would have* + past participle in the result clause to show things that did not happen.

Conditional	*Result*
(past perfect tense)	(would have + past participle)

If you *had brushed* your teeth carefully, you *would have had* fewer cavities. (*Meaning:* You did not brush your teeth carefully at some time in the past, and you had some cavities as a result.)

If you *had* not *driven* so carefully, the accident *would have been* much worse. (*Meaning:* Because you drove very carefully, the accident was not too bad.)

Inverted word order in conditions: You can leave out *if* and put *had, were,* or *should* first in the clause. (This is a formal style, used in writing more than in speech.)

Had you brushed your teeth more carefully, you would not have had so many cavities.
Had you driven more carefully, you would not have had an accident.
Were the truth known, public opinion would change.
Should it rain tomorrow, the meeting will be held in the auditorium.

Punctuation: Punctuate *if* clauses like other dependent clauses. Put a comma after an *if* clause at the beginning of the sentence, as in all the examples above. When the *if* clause follows the result clause, do not separate it from the rest of the sentence by a comma. *If* clauses usually come at the beginning of the sentence.   (see **Punctuation, comma**)

You will have fewer cavities if you brush your teeth carefully.
You would have had fewer cavities if you had brushed your teeth carefully.

Other words that can introduce conditional clauses must be followed by the same verb forms as *if*. (*That* can be left out when it is not the subject of the clause it begins.)

in case (that)	suppose/supposing (that)
in the event (that)	on condition (that)
provided/providing (that)	whether or not
so/as long as	

In case our team wins, it will be the new champion.
In the event the plane arrives late, we will miss our connection.
Provided (*that*) you buy the groceries, I will cook dinner.
So long as he does not bother me, I will not bother him.
Supposing (*that*) he had been found guilty, he would have gone to prison.
On condition (*that*) she comes to every meeting, she has permission to attend the seminar.
Whether or not it rains, the game will be played as scheduled.

Test Yourself

B. Fill in the blanks and complete the sentences correctly for the situation.

1. Why don't you try to finish the lab assignment as soon as possible? If I _____ (be) you, I _____ (finish) it right away.

2. Today's assignment is very difficult. Some students never ask for help. If these students _____ (ask) for help, someone _____ (explain) the principles to them.

3. If friends _____ (help) each other study, they all _____ (do) better work.

4. Next year's classes will be even harder. Unless friends _____ (help) each other, some students _____ (have) difficulty passing their courses.

5. In case the weather _____ (be) bad, the field trip _____ (be) canceled.

6. Should it rain tomorrow, a notice _____ (post) to tell what work _____ (require) to replace the field trip.

7. Everyone who took the final examination passed Biology 221. But if as many students had failed as did last year, think how disappointed many of this year's students _____ (be).

8. In the past some students avoided taking math courses. Now, however, they realize

   that they must take them if they _____ (plan) to study computer programming.

9. If students _____ (be) interested in science, medicine, engineering, or business,

   they _____ (find) knowledge of computers necessary for their careers.

10. If students _____ (have) problems with their classes or in deciding on their courses

    of study, both friends and faculty members _____ (be) ready to help them.

NOTE: Certain meanings of *if* are not conditional.
Even if can mean although.

Even if he has lost all his money, he is still cheerful.

If can replace *whether* in informal style.

We are unsure *if* (whether or not) he will come.

Shortened clauses with *if*: *If so* and *if not* can replace complete clauses if the subject
and verb of the shortened clause is the same as the subject and verb of the clause that
comes before it.

It may rain today. *If so* (if it rains), you will need your umbrella.
You must pay your library fines. *If not* (if you do not), you will not be allowed to graduate.

Test Yourself

Conditional Sentences, Short Forms

C. Replace one of the clauses in the following sentences with a shortened form. Cross out
the clause being replaced and write the short form in the blank to the left.

_____ 1. Both drivers and pedestrians must obey traffic laws; if they do not obey
these laws, they may be fined.

_____ 2. Mary usually does her grocery shopping on Wednesday. If she does not do it
then, she shops on Thursday.

_____ 3. Mary thinks it may rain today. If it rains today, she will have to wait until
tomorrow to do her grocery shopping.

Conditional Sentences, Combined

D. Correct the following sentences wherever necessary.

1. If bad weather comes, many activities would be affected.

2. Many homeowners would lose property and perhaps would even be injured if a tornado strikes.

3. Unless people in the path of severe storms take shelter, they might have been injured.

4. Hurricanes would cause great damage to windows if homeowners do not cover the glass with shutters.

5. Unless people prepared for the big storm that came last year, their property would probably be damaged.

Confusing Choices

Diction as it is used in composition means choosing the correct word. The choices listed below are problems of diction, spelling, and grammar that often cause confusion. Not all possible meanings are given for every word, but only the meanings or uses that are often confused.

Accept, Except

Accept is a verb that means *receive* or *approve; except* is a preposition that means that everything following it is left out of the statement.

I *accept* (*receive*) your apology.
Your application has been *accepted*. (*approved*)
All applications have been processed *except* those received today. (Those received today are *not included.*)
Everyone will go *except* Bob. (Bob is *not included.*)

According to, Accordingly

According to means *on the authority of* (someone); *accordingly* at the beginning of a clause means *as a result* or at the end of a clause it means *in a suitable manner.*

According to the weather forecast, it will rain tonight. (*on the authority of*)
It may rain tonight. *Accordingly,* you may need your umbrella. (*as a result*)
It may rain tonight. You should dress *accordingly.* (*in a suitable manner*)

Advice, Advise

Advice is an uncountable noun that means a *suggestion* as to how someone should act or think; *advise* is a verb meaning to *suggest, give an opinion,* or *recommend.*

The guide's *advice* to wait was helpful. (noun)
The guide *advised* us to wait. (verb)

Affect, Effect

Affect is a verb that means *to change* or *influence; effect* may be a verb that means *to cause* or *bring about,* or it may be a noun that means *the result.*

Lack of sleep *affects* my work. (verb)
The protests *effected* a change in the bus route. (verb)
The *effect* of the protests was a change in the bus route. (noun)

After, Afterward, Afterwards, Later

After is a preposition that must be followed by a noun or pronoun or subordinating conjunction that must be followed by a subject and verb. *After* means *later than something; afterward* or *afterwards* are adverbs that mean *later. Afterward, after-wards,* and *later* can be used in the same way. Do not use *after* as an adverb by itself.

Charles came *after* me. (preposition)
Charles came *after* I did. (conjunction)
Charles came first, and I came *afterward*(*s*) (*later*). (adverb)
Afterward(*s*) (*later*) I came. (adverb)

Ago, Before, Earlier (see also **For, Since**)

Ago, before, and *since* show the relation of one point in time to another. Use *ago* in connection with past time to mean *a point in time before now.* Use *before* to show action or time *prior to* another action or time. Use *earlier* to show time before something that has already happened or will happen. Use *for* to introduce a period of time, never a point in time. *Now* is not a reference of *before* and *earlier* unless it is so stated.

Christine moved to Portland ten years *ago.* (before now)
Before Christine *moved* to Portland (past tense shows past reference of *before*) she *had lived* in San Francisco. (past perfect tense shows a time prior to the time of *moved*) Christine *will wait* six months *before* she *goes* back to San Francisco to visit her mother. (After a future

tense, *before* + *present* tense shows *future* action)   (see **Tense, present**) *Earlier* (before a time already stated) she *had lived* in Los Angeles.

In 1870 Charles' great grandfather moved to Kansas. *Before* that, he *had come* to the United States from Sweden. Earlier, even *before* coming to the United States, he *had worked* for a photographer in Sweden. *Later* in Kansas he *took* pictures of settlers who *began* to farm there. Charles *learned* about his great grandfather three years *ago* (*before now*) when one of his aunts *wrote* down the history of their family.

All, All of, Whole

(For uses and word order of *all* and *all of,* see **Determiners.**) Do not use *all of* if *all* is acceptable. Use *whole* as an adjective between the article and the noun to mean *complete, not divided,* or *entire,* and after the noun to mean *in one piece.* Use *all* to mean the *total,* divided or undivded. (If *the* comes before the noun, put *all* before *the.*)

All students who drive must have parking stickers.
Bill ate *all the* cake, *all four pieces.*
Bill ate *the whole* cake, *all of* it. (*total*)
Bill ate the biscuit *whole.* (*undivided, in one piece*)

NOTE: Use *all of* before pronouns: *all of it, all of us, all of you, all of them.*

All Ready, Already

All ready means *completely prepared; already* means *by now* or *by a certain time.*

The bus is *all ready* to go. (*prepared*)
The bus has *already* gone. (*by now*)
Yesterday the bus had *already* gone before I came. (*by then*)

All Right

Always spell *all right* as two words, never as *alright.*

The children got the answers *all right.* (*correct*)
The parking attendant told us that it would be *all right* to leave our car in the driveway. (*permitted*)

All Together, Altogether

All together means *everything or everyone in one place or group; altogether* means *completely.*

The class went *all together* to the mountains on the same bus. (*in one group*)
The decision is *altogether* wrong. (*completely*)

Allusion, Illusion

An *allusion* is a reference to something already known; an *illusion* is something imagined, not true. *Allude* is a verb.

Shirley has the *illusion* that she is beautiful when she is not.
The speaker made an *allusion* to the wisdom of Solomon.

Already, Yet

Already means *by now* or *by a certain time; yet* means *now* or *by a certain time.* *Already* is used with positive statements and *yet* is often used in negatives and questions. Both are used with the present perfect and past perfect tenses. Do not use *yet* with the past tense in the same clause.

The Harrisons have *already* come. (*by now*)
The Harrisons had *already* arrived when I came. (*by then*)
The Harrisons have *not* come *yet*. (*by now*—with present perfect tense)
The Harrisons had *not yet* arrived when I came. (*by then*—with past perfect tense)

As a conjunction, *yet* can mean *however.*   (see **Coordinating Conjunctions**)

Amount, Number

Use *amount* to refer to uncountable nouns. Use *number* to refer to countable plural nouns.   (see **Countable and Uncountable Nouns**)

The shopper bought a large *amount* of bread. (uncountable)
The shopper bought a *number* of items on her grocery list. (countable)

Another, Other, Others   (see **Determiners**) (For **one another**, see **each other** below.)

Use *another* (1) before singular countable nouns and (2) before *one*. Use *other* (1) before plural countable nouns; (2) following *the, all,* or *every*; and (3) before uncountable nouns.

Ted wants *another cup* of coffee. (countable, singular)
He wants *another one*. (countable, singular)
He wants *the other one*. (countable, singular)
Every other cup is broken. (countable, singular)
All other cups are broken. (countable, plural)
Ted prefers this coffee to *other kinds.* (countable, plural)
He really doesn't like *other coffee*. (uncountable)
Is there *some/any other* (a different kind of) *coffee* that will please Ted? (uncountable)

Use *another* (singular) or *the others* (plural) as a pronoun to replace a countable noun.

Here is one plate. Where is *another*? (countable, singular)
There are several *other plates*. Look for *the others*. (countable, plural)
Paul went on the first bus with some of the children, but Wilma waited to go with *the others*.
  (countable, plural)

Use *other* as a pronoun to replace an uncountable noun.

This bread seems stale. Is there any *other*?

Any, Some

Any and *some* can be adjectives or pronouns. Use *some* in positive statements; use *any* in negation and in questions. *Some* can also be used in questions when agreement is expected or in an invitation or request. *Any* can also be used in positive statements after *if* or to express doubt. Use compounds such as *anyone, anybody, someone,* and *somebody* in the same ways.

Ted doesn't want *any* coffee. (negative)
Ted, do you want *some* coffee? (positive answer expected)
Ted, do you want *any* coffee? (negative answer expected)
Would you like to have *some* coffee? (invitation to have coffee)
We *cannot* stop to drink *any* coffee now. (negative)
If you want to get *any* coffee, buy it now. (doubt)
I don't think there is *any* coffee in the house. (negative)
I doubt that there is *any* coffee in the house. (doubt)

Anybody and Anyone; Any Body, Any One

Use *anybody* and *anyone* as indefinite pronouns in questions and negation. (see **Pronouns, indefinite**) Use *any body* as a noun, *body* modified by *any*. Use *any one* as a pronoun, *one* modified by *any*.

Can *anyone/anybody* help? (it does not matter who)
Sharon's hair is limp; it does not have *any body*.
Bring me a pen from my desk. It doesn't matter which color; *any one* will do.

Any More, Anymore

Use *anymore* as an adverb in questions and negations to mean *no longer*. Use *any more* in questions and negatives to mean *none in addition*.

We never eat chocolate *anymore* because Carl is allergic to it. (no longer)
Harry does not want to eat *any more* chocolate. (none in addition—he has already eaten some)

As If, As Though, Like

As if and *as though* are conjunctions. Use *as if* and *as though* to introduce clauses. Use *like* as a preposition to introduce a prepositional phrase. (*Like* can also be a verb—see *like, please* in this section.)

Elizabeth feels *as though* / *as if* she is lost.

Coffee does not taste *like* tea.

Sweet potatoes taste *like* pumpkin.

At, In, On (Time)   (see **Prepositions, time**)

Use *at* with specific times of the day.

at 10:15, *at* night, *at* dinner (time), *at* noon, *at* midnight

Use *in* with more general times.

in 1903, *in* two weeks, *in* a { month, day, week, year }, *in* March, *in* a minute

Use *on* with days and dates.

on Saturday, *on* May 23, *on* the weekend (British: *at* weekends), *on* weekends

At, In, On (Place)   (see **Prepositions, space**)

Use *at* with a point in space.

at the airport, *at* school, *at* home

Use *on* with a surface.

on the street, *on* the table, *on* the floor, *on* the Mississippi River

Use *in* with three-dimensional space.

in the box, *in* the house, *in* a city, *in* New York City, *in* Canada

The choice of preposition may change according to what is in the writer's or speaker's mind.

at the store (location)
in the store (within a building)
sitting *on* the sofa (not enclosed)
sitting *in* an easy chair (back and arms around the body)

Bear, Bore, Born and Bear, Bore, Borne

Use *born* or *borne* as the past participle when *bear* means *carry* or *endure*. Use *borne* as the past participle when *bear* means *give birth to*. Use *born* to mean *be brought into existence*.

Marshall has *borne* his sorrows bravely. (*endured*)
Today machines *bear* the burdens that were once *borne* by men. (*carry*)
Mary has *borne* a son. (*given birth to*)
The new*born* baby was only a few hours old.
Strength is sometimes *born* out of difficulties. (*brought into existence*)

Because, Because of

Use *because* as a conjunction to introduce a dependent clause. Use *because of* as a preposition to introduce a prepositional phrase.

dependent
clause

Gene needs to wear a raincoat *because* it may rain.

prepositional
phrase

Gene needs to wear a raincoat *because of* the rain.

Before, Ago (see **Ago, Before**)

Beside, Besides

Beside is a preposition that means *next to; besides* can be an adverb or preposition that means *in addition* or a preposition that means *except*.

preposition
The kitten is sleeping   *beside*   her mother. (*next to*)

preposition
 Besides   milk we need eggs. (*in addition to*)

adverb
Besides, we need eggs. (*in addition*)

preposition
Everyone   *besides*   Tom will be there. (*except*)

adverb
I really want to stay home tonight; *besides* I have already seen that movie. (*in addition*)

Between . . . And . . ., From . . . To . . .

Always use *between* with *and* or use *from* with *to* when separating pairs of dates or times.

Between 1750 *and* 1800 rapid change took place.
From 1750 *to* 1800 rapid change took place.
The committee meeting lasted *from* 10:00 *to* 11:30.

Choice, Choices (Noun); Choose (Verb); and Device, Devices (Noun); Devise (Verb)

These words have a change in spelling (*c* to *s*) and sound (*s* to *z*) like that in *advice, advise. Choose* also has a vowel change.

Test Yourself

A. Cross out the errors and put the correct forms in the blanks to the left.

_____ 1. Mary and Charles live in 269 Oak Shadow Drive besides the Oak Shadow

_____   Elementary School.

_____ 2. Ever since ten years before, Charles and Mary have refused to live any-

_____   where except in the middle of the city because of they dislike traveling very

            far to get to work.

_____ 3. From 1983 and 1985 Charles and Mary had all ready finished most of the

_____   work of remodeling their house.

_____ 4. Some of their neighbors had not already finished fixing up their own

_____   houses; a large number of work needed to be done.

_____ 5. Charles and Mary gladly excepted all the advice and help they got and

_____   planned to repay their friends and neighbors by helping them after.

_____ 6. Mary and Charles were better at some things than at other; the first

_____   cabinet they built looked like a drunk man had made it.

_____ 7. When friends offered to help them, they cleared out a place at the floor in

_____   the dining room besides the windows in order to have room to store all
            their supplies.

_____   8.   They did not refuse some help that someone offered them.

_____

_____   9.   Mary and Charles did not finish remodeling their house all together, but at

_____   ten years they had most of the work finished.

_____ 10.   Because of their hard work, Charles and Mary do not plan to remodel

_____   another houses soon; they want to stay on 269 Oak Shadow Drive many
                 more years.

Do, Make

_Do_ and _make_ are verbs with similar meanings, but you cannot usually use one in place of the other. _Do_ is an operator, but _make_ is not.   (see **Operators**)

_Do_ the work.
    the dishes. (also _wash_ the dishes)
    the house or housework. (also _clean_ house or _clean the_ house)
    the laundry. (but _wash_ the clothes)
    research.

_do_ + _ing_ forms:

do the cleaning.
    the gardening.
    the ironing.
    the painting.
    the driving, etc.

_Do_ is often used with abstract ideas.

do business (buy or sell)
    one's best or worst, the best you can
    one's duty
    a favor
    good (charitable activities)
    well (make satisfactory progress)
    harm
    justice

An object after _do_ can change the meaning of the verb.

⎰ This medicine ⎱
⎱ A vacation ⎰ will _do you good._ (improve your sense of well-being)
⎱ A rest ⎰

Your picture does not _do you justice._ (show you as good or as beautiful as you are)
The book review does not _do the book justice._ (show it as good as it is)

In a question, *do* can mean to carry on a trade, occupation, or profession.

What does your roommate *do*? (What is her occupation?)
She *is* a teacher now, but she *was* a student until last year. (*Do* is not always used in the reply.)

Make often means to create or produce something that was not there before.

make a bargain (*agree*)
the bed (*straighten* sheets and blankets for a neat appearance)
a cake (also *bake* a cake)
believe (*imagine*)
an error, a mistake
a fire
(a) noise
a statement
war, peace
friends

Make + a noun can sometimes replace a verb related to the noun; using the single-word verb is better in writing because the phrase is wordy.   (see **Wordiness**)

make an agreement (with or about) or	agree (to or with)
an announcement (of)	announce
an answer (to)	answer
an attempt (to)	attempt (to)
a beginning (of)	begin (to)
a decision (to, about)	decide (to, about)
a discovery (of)	discover
and end (to)	end
an offer (of, for)	offer (to)
a profit (from)	profit (from)
a promise (to, about)	promise (to)
progress (in, with)	progress (in)
a search (for)	search (for)
a start (on, in + ing)	start (to)
a stop (for, to)	stop (for, to)
a turn	turn
a vow (to)	vow (to)

Some meanings are limited to one form only.

She *started* the engine. (not *made a start*)
Columbus *discovered* the New World. (not *made the discovery of*)

Make can be followed by an objective complement (*make* + noun or object pronoun + adjective or noun)   (see **Objective Complement**)

direct   objective
object complement
The people *made him   president*. (noun)

	direct object	objective complement

Getting out of school early *made* the *children*   *happy*.   (adjective)

Make can be a causative verb before another verb. (*make* + noun or pronoun object + bare infinitive)

	direct object	verb

The thunder   *made* everyone *run*   into the building.
The coach   *made* his team   *train* six hours a day.
Fear of the police *made* the thief *run*   away.

Each, Every, Everyone, All

Use *each* and *all* as pronouns or adjectives. Use *each* and *every* before *one* and before singular nouns. Use *all* before uncountable and plural countable nouns.

Singular Forms

Each ⎫
Every ⎭ child has a seat now.   (negative: no one)
                              (negative: no child)

Each one ⎫
Every one ⎬ has a seat now.   (negative: not one)
Everyone ⎭   (negative: not one)
                      (negative: no one)

Everyone and *everybody* are indefinite pronouns. *All* and *each* do not have similar one-word forms. Use *everyone* for people only. Do not use *everyone* before *of*, but use *every one*.

Everyone in the class went on the bus.

Every one ⎫
Each one ⎬ of the students went on the bus.

Although *every* and other words made with it must be followed by a singular verb *in writing*, *every* is close in meaning to *all;* you will often *hear* a plural verb with it. Use *single* as an intensifier with *every*.

Every plate was broken, *every single* one.

Use *each* when persons or things are thought of separately.

All the plates were broken, but *each one* had been broken at a different time.

Plural Forms

All (the) children have seats now. (negative: no children, none of the children)

NOTE: *All the* children is more definite than *all* children. Use *all the* children when the individual members of the group are known.

All children in the world need enough to eat.
All the children on this bus have their lunches with them.

Each Other, Every Other, One Another

Each other and *one another* are reciprocal pronouns: Each of two or more persons or things does something to the other one.

The lovers held *each other's* hands.
The cats snarled at *each other*.

Use *each other* for two persons or things and *one another* for more than two.

At the class reunion, many old friends greeted *one another*.

Every other can be the singular of **all others**, or it can mean *every second one* before countable nouns.

The car was not out of gas. We looked for *every other* possibility, but we could not find what the trouble was.
Write on *every other* line. (skip lines 2, 4, 6, 8, etc.)
Take this medicine *every other* day. (Monday, Wednesday, Friday, etc.; or Tuesday, Thursday, Saturday, Monday, etc.)

Every Day, Everyday

Every day is an adverb meaning the same as *each day*. Spelled as one word, *everyday* is an adjective meaning *usual* or *common*.

We have the newspaper delivered *every day*.
Carl works *every day* except Sunday.
These are my *everyday* clothes. (not special)
Not finding a place to park is an *everyday* problem. (common)

Except, Accept   (see **Accept, Except**)

Few, Only a Few, a Few

Few and *only a few* mean *not many* or *not enough*, emphasizing the lack of something; *a few* means a small number, but does not imply a lack or insufficiency. *Only a few* can replace *few*.

$$\left.\begin{array}{l}\textit{Few}\\ \textit{Only a few}\\ \textit{Not enough}\end{array}\right\}\text{ people came to the meeting, so we had to reschedule it for next week.}$$

A *few* people came to the meeting, so we were able to finish our business. (not many, but enough)

We found $\left.\begin{array}{l}\textit{few}\\ \textit{only a few}\end{array}\right\}$ apples on the trees, so we left them for the birds. (not enough to pick)

We found *a few* apples on the trees, so we picked what was there. (enough to pick)

NOTE: The difference between *few* and *a few* is also found between *little* and *a little*.

For, Since

Use *for* before a period of time with all tenses. Use *since* only before a specific point in time with reference to *now,* relating past to present.   (see **Prepositions, time**)

Hundred, Hundreds (also Tens, Dozens, Thousand(s), Million(s), and so on)

Do not change the adjective *hundred* to a plural form after a number. Use *hundreds, thousands, millions,* and so on only as indefinite pronouns (often followed by *of* + a noun or pronoun).

As Numbers
Two hundred men were there.
More than *two thousand* students voted for student president.
Over *six hundred* people were moved out of the flooded area.

As Indefinite Pronouns
Hundreds (*of* people) lined up to get tickets to the concert.
Thousands (*of* bees) swarmed after their queen.

Its, It's

Its is a personal possessive pronoun like *her* or *his; it's* is a contraction of *it is.* Use *its* to mean *of it.* Avoid using *it's* in formal writing.

Professor Hill's discovery is remarkable, but *its* practical value must be proved. (the value of *it.*)
The dog has buried *its* bone. (*of it*)
It's (*it is*) true that a storm is coming.
A decision has been made, and *it's* going to be a popular one.
The flight attendant said, *"It's* time to buckle your seat belts."

Lay, Laid, Laid and Lie, Lay, Lain

Use *lay, laid, laid* as a transitive verb (with a direct object) to mean *put* or *place.* Use *lie, lay, lain* as an intransitive verb (no direct object) to mean *recline.* Do not confuse *lie, lay, lain* with *lie, lied, lied,* an intransitive verb that means *say something that is not true.*

Present Tense
Criminals *lie* when they are caught.
Children *lie* in the grass to watch the clouds.

            direct object
Librarians *lay* the *guides* to the library on a table near the entrance.

Past Tense
The thief *lied* to the police. (from *lie*—told something not true)
The boy *lay* on his back in the grass. (from *lie*—recline)
The librarian *laid* the papers on the table. (from *lay*—put)

Present Continuous/Progressive
The criminal *is lying* about his burglaries.
The children *are lying* on their backs in the grass, watching the clouds.

                                     direct object
The librarian *is laying* some   *guides*   to the library on a table near the entrance.

Present Perfect
The thief *has lied* about his burglaries.
Father *has lain* down for a short nap.

                                  direct object
The librarian *has laid* some instruction   *booklets*   on the table.

Like, Please

One meaning of *like* is *find pleasant*; as a verb *please* can mean *make someone happy*. A person or personal pronoun must be the subject of *like*, but a person or personal pronoun must be the object of *please* in its active form.

subject
Robert likes chocolate cake.

      but

                                object
Chocolate cake always *pleases Robert*.

   subject
Most *children* like candy.

      but

                        object
This candy *pleases* the *children*.

Please (verb) is often used in the passive with a subject that refers to a person.

Robert is pleased with the cake.
  The *children are pleased with* the candy.

Formal announcements often use *it pleases* someone *to* . . .

It pleases us to announce the opening of a new store on Buckley Avenue.

Little, Only a Little, a Little

Little and *only a little* mean *not much* or *not enough,* emphasizing the lack of something; *a little* means *a small amount,* but does not imply lack or insufficiency. Use these words before uncountable (mass, noncount) nouns instead of *few, a few,* and *only a few.*

$\left\{\begin{array}{l}\textit{Only a little}\\ \textit{Little}\\ \textit{Not enough}\end{array}\right\}$ thought has been given to the problem, and no solution has been found.

After *a little* thought has been given to the problem, a solution will be found.

$\left\{ \begin{array}{l} \textit{Only a little} \\ \textit{Little} \\ \textit{Not enough} \end{array} \right\}$ milk is left for tomorrow.

A *little* milk is left; it will be enough for tomorrow.

Loose, Lose, Loss

Do not confuse the spelling of *loose* (*let go* or *untied*) and *lose* (*fail to find*). Use *lose* as a verb. Use *loss* as a noun meaning *the result of losing.* Use *loose* as an adjective (rarely as a verb).

The gate is open and the horses are *loose.* (*set free* or *strayed away*)
We may *lose* them if they are not found soon. (*fail to find*)
Losing them would be a great *loss.*
You must pay attention and not *lose* your place in the music. (*fail to find*)
Walter's bicycle lock is *loose* (*not held together securely*), but no one has stolen the bicycle yet.

Many, Much (see **Countable and Uncountable Nouns**)

Must, Have to, Ought to, Should—see **Modals,** p. 190

 **Test Yourself**

B. Cross out the errors and put the correct word or words in the blank to the left. Each sentence has two errors.

_____ 1. No one likes to do an error; everyone of us likes to do as well as possible.

_____

_____ 2. When students have to do a decision about their future, they will try to

_____ please their parents, so their parents will not loose confidence in them.

_____ 3. If students give little thought to the future, they will be able to decide what

_____ they want to do everyday for the next few years.

_____ 4. If all the students make a few errors, they will make their parents, friends,

_____ and teachers rejoiced.

_____ 5. Its impossible to please every one all the time.

_____

_____ 6. Young people have hundreds of chooses to do in a few years that may

_____   affect the rest of their lives.

_____ 7. Wise students choose to make few friends while they are studying because

_____   of friends are as necessary as studying is.

_____ 8. Everyday every one of us has almost fifteen hundreds minutes to use in

_____   some way.

_____ 9. Students must device ways to get much work done in little time in order to

_____   do a success of themselves.

_____ 10. When people help every other, they are more likely to be successful and

_____   have a few problems.

Numbers of, a Number of, the Number of

Use *numbers of* to mean *many* or *very many* (with a plural verb). Use *a number* to mean *some* or *many* (followed by *of* + a plural noun, it takes a plural verb). Use *the number* to mean quantity (followed by *of* + a plural noun, it takes a singular verb).

Numbers of birds *are* roosting in the trees by the school. (many birds)
A number of birds *are* roosting in the trees by the school. (a group, but it does not contain as many birds as in *numbers of*)
The number of birds that can live in this cage *is* four.
The number of birds that are roosting in the trees by the school *is* impossible to count.

Only (Adverb); Only a, the Only, and Only (Adjectives); Only (Conjunction); if Only = Wish

The basic meaning is *solely* or *nothing more*; the adjective meaning is *no one else*; the conjunction can be a very informal substitute for *but*.

The *only* clerk(s) who can answer your question is/are absent today. (*no one else*)
Only the staff may have reserved parking places. (*no one else*)
Martha is an *only* child. (*has no brothers or sisters*)
I would help, *only* I have to work tonight. (*but*)
Only a fool would think that! (*no one but*)
If only I could retake that test, I could make a better grade. (*I wish*)

Passed, Past

Use *passed* as the past tense and past participle of *pass,* but never use it as an adjective before a noun. Use *past* as an adjective, an adverb, a preposition, or a noun.

Time *passed* (by) slowly. (past tense)
Our troubles have *passed*. (past participle)
We saw the city hall as we drove *past*. (adverb)
We drove *past* the city hall. (preposition)
The days of summer are *past*. (predicate adjective)
The *past* can never come back. (noun)
The *past* few days have gone by quickly. (adjective)

People, Person(s)

Both *people* and *person(s)* stand for human beings. Use *people* only as a plural noun with a plural verb. Use *person* as singular and *persons* as plural.

$$\left.\begin{matrix} \text{Ten} \\ \text{Many} \\ \text{Fifty} \end{matrix}\right\} \left.\begin{matrix} \textit{people} \\ \textit{persons} \end{matrix}\right\} \text{are waiting}$$

One *person* is waiting.

Principal, Principle

Notice the difference in spelling. Use *principal* as an adjective or a noun to mean *chief, main,* or *the most important one.* Use *principle* as a noun to mean *rule, belief,* or *law of nature*.

Miss Blake is the *principal* of Roosevelt School (*head teacher*)
The *principal* actor in the play was very good. (*most important one*)
The mayor's *principal* interest was getting re-elected. (*chief*)
Make honesty your *principle*. (*rule*)
People who take their religion seriously have strong *principles*. (*moral beliefs*)
The *principles* of gravity never change. (*laws of nature*)

Principal sometimes means a sum of money that has been invested.

Many people try to spend their interest without using any of the *principal* of their investments.

Remember, Remind

Both are regular verbs. Use *remember* to mean *recall.* Use *remind* to mean *cause to recall*.

Oscar did not *remember* his dental appointment until the dentist's secretary called to *remind* him.
Remind me (*make me remember*) to pay the water bill tomorrow.

Result from, Result in

Use *result from* to mean *caused by*. Use *result in* to mean *cause*.

The fire *resulted from* (*was caused by*) faulty wiring.
The fire *resulted in* (*caused*) damage to the building.
Freezing temperatures *resulted in* (*caused*) ice on the lake.
Ice on the lake *resulted from* (*was caused by*) freezing temperatures.

Rise, Rose, Risen and Raise, Raised, Raised

Use *rise* as an intransitive verb (without a direct object) to mean *go higher*. Use *raise* as a transitive verb (with a direct object) to mean *make something higher*.

Smoke *rises*. (*goes higher*)
Eagles *rise* from the cliffs to hunt their prey. (*go up*)

direct
object

Every morning the students *raise* the *flag*. (*make it go up*)

direct
object

If you study hard, you may be able to *raise* your *grades*. (*make them go up*)

Shine, Shined, Shined and Shine, Shone, Shone

Use *shine* with a direct object to mean *make shiny or glossy*; use *shine, shone, shone* without a direct object to mean *give off light or brightness*.

direct
object

Peter *shined* (*made shiny*) his *shoes* until they *shone*. (*gave off light*)
The sun *shone* all day today. (*gave off light*)

Sit, Sat, Sat and Set, Set, Set

Use *sit* to mean *put oneself on a chair or on a flat place with one's back upright* or *to remain in one place*. (*Sit* is never used in English to mean *reside* or *live* in a place.) Use *set* to mean *place* or *put*; it must be followed by a direct object except with fowl or birds to mean *incubate eggs*.

The children are *sitting* quietly in their classroom.
Susan *sits* too much; she needs more exercise.

direct object
Louis *set* the *coffee pot* on the table. (*placed*)

direct object
Where has Tim *set* down his new *schedule*? (*put*)
The hen has been *setting* for a week (*incubating eggs*)

Some Time, Sometime, and Sometimes

Some time means *an indefinite amount of time; sometime* means *at a time not specifically stated;* and *sometimes* means *occasionally.*

Dr. Prentiss will be able to give you *some time* at 3:00 this afternoon. (amount of time is uncertain)

Dr. Prentiss will see you for fifteen minutes *sometime* this afternoon. (exact time of the appointment is uncertain.)

Dr. Prentiss has *sometimes* seen Marcia Blake. (*occasionally, not regularly*)

Stationary, Stationery

Stationary (adjective) means *not movable; stationery* (noun) means *writing paper.*

The new lights for the tennis courts are permanent and *stationary.* (*not movable*)
We need to order some new *stationery.* (*writing paper*)

Still, Already, Yet, and However

Still and *yet* can replace each other in meaning when they mean *however.*

Gerald is weak in mathematics; *still,* / *however,* he is strong in English.
Gerald is weak in mathematics, *yet* he is strong in English.

Note punctuation differences in the two sentences above. (see **Clauses, connectors**)

In any tense *still* can show that something continues or continued longer than expected and *already* can show that it begins or began sooner than expected. In this sense, when *yet* replaces *already* in negative statements, it corresponds to *still* in positive statements.

This ice cream is *still* frozen (*longer than expected*); I thought it would be melted *by now.* / *already.*

This ice cream is melted *already* (*sooner than expected*); I thought it would *still* (*up to now*) be frozen.
This ice cream has not melted *yet.* (*up to now*)

The baby is *still* crawling. (*longer than expected*)
The baby is *already* walking. (*sooner than expected*)
The baby is *not* walking *yet.* (*not as soon as expected*)

Still, Any More, Any Longer, No Longer

Still means *up to now; not . . . any more, not . . . any longer,* or *no longer* replace *still* in negative statements.

Are you *still* going to Paris in June?

No, I am *not* planning that trip $\begin{cases} any\ more. \\ any\ longer. \end{cases}$

I am *no longer* planning to go to Paris in June.

Struck, Stricken

Both *struck* and *stricken* are past participles of *strike*. Use *struck* in the sense of *a physical blow*, but use *stricken* to show *emotion* or *illness*.

The speeding car has *struck* a telephone pole.
The rebels have *struck* a blow for freedom.
The thoughtless daughter has been *stricken* with grief since her mother died.
Before a vaccine was developed, thousands of people were *stricken* by polio every year.

Such, Such a

Both *such* and *such a* come before an adjective that modifies the same noun. Use *such a* before singular countable nouns. Use *such* before uncountable and plural countable nouns. A phrase or clause beginning with *as* or a clause beginning with *that* can follow the nouns.   (see **Countable and Uncountable Nouns**)

	Adjective	Singular Noun	
Such a	(*cold*)	*day*	*as today* made Lucy shiver.
Such a	(*happy*)	*child*	made every one laugh.
		Uncountable Noun	
Such	(*unselfish*)	*friendship*	*as Mary's* is hard to find.
Such	(*good*)	*food*	*as this* is fit for a king.
		Countable Plural	
Such	(*difficult*)	*problems*	*as we are doing now* are too hard for me.

Andy makes *such* (long) telephone *calls*   *that* his phone is always busy.

That, Which, and Who, Whom, Whose

That, which, and *who, whom, whose* are relative pronouns. Some writers use *that* and *which* in the same way in essential adjective clauses. In the United States many writers prefer using *that* to introduce essential adjective clauses. Use *which* but never *that* to introduce adjective clauses that are nonessential. Use *who, whom,* or *whose* in both essential and nonessential clauses to refer to people. Some writers use *that* to refer to people but never *which*.   (see **Pronouns, relative**) *Which, who(m),* and *whose* can also begin questions.   (see **Questions**)

This, That, These, Those

Use *this* (singular) and *these* (plural) to refer to or modify someone or something nearer in space or time or just mentioned. Use *that* (singular) and *those* (plural) to refer to something farther away in space, time, or thought. (see **Pronouns, demonstrative**)

Do you prefer *this* cake or *that* pie? (space)
These pictures are much clearer than *those* we were looking at earlier. (time)

Their, There, They're

Their is the third person plural possessive pronoun; *there* is an adverb or an expletive; and *they're* is the contraction for *they are*.

Employees bring *their* families to the company picnic. (possessive)
There is a new motorcycle parked behind the gym. (expletive)
Dick's new motorcycle is parked over *there* behind the gym. (adverb)
They're too late for the concert now. (*they are*)

To, Too, Two

To is a preposition or the sign of the infinitive. *Too* is an adverb that means *also, very,* or *excessive*. *Two* is a number.

Sally is going *to* buy *two* tickets so we can go *to* the game Saturday. (infinitive, number, preposition)
She hopes the tickets aren't *too* expensive. (adverb—*very* or *excessively*)

Wear, Were, We're, Where

Wear means *to have clothing or something else on the body; were* is the past tense of *be* in all except the third person singular; *we're* is the contraction for *we are;* and *where* means *in* or *to what place?* or *in that place*.

Alan wonders what to *wear* today. (*have on clothing*)
The clowns *were* funny. (past tense of *be*)
We're early today. (*We are*)
Where are you going? (*to what place*)
Sally found her coat *where* she had left it. (*in that place*)

Weather, Whether

Weather means conditions related to the climate; *whether* means *if* (something happens) . . . *or not*. In formal writing, do not leave out *or not* after *whether*.

The *weather* today is better than predicted.
Whether it rains *or not*, the game will be played. **or** *Whether or not* it rains, ...

What . . . For? and Why?

Use *why?* in formal writing. *What . . .for?* is informal and can be used in conversation. NEVER SAY "*Why* are we doing this *for?*" or "*What for* are we doing this?" If you use *why*, do not use *for*. Never put *what* and *for* together at the beginning of a clause. *What for?* can be used to mean *why?* as a short question only if no clause completes the construction and the meaning is "*What is the purpose of?*" *How come* is sometimes used to mean *why* in very informal speech.

What are we helping him *for?* (informal)
What are we standing in line *for?* (informal)

Why are we helping him? (formal)
Why are we standing in line? (formal)

Your, You're

Your is the second person possessive pronoun; *you're* is the contraction for *you are*. Avoid *you're* in formal writing.

Where is *your* car? (car *belonging to* you)
Why have all of you forgotten *your* money? (money *belonging to* you)
You're on time, neither late nor early. (*you are*)

Test Yourself

C. Cross out the errors and put corrections in the blanks to the left. Each sentence has two errors.

_____ 1. Ruth and Frank need to remind to pay a deposit before they can get the

_____   electricity turned on in their new apartment; they had move out of their old
                one because their landlord rose the rent.

_____ 2. When Ruth and Frank moved, they asked number of there friends to help.

_____

_____ 3. They will miss their friends in their old apartment; still they plan to visit

_____   them some time to talk about passed good times.

_____ 4. Their move has resulted from their meeting the number of new people and

_____   making some new friends.

_____   5. The principle problem Ruth and Frank have had since they moved has been

_____   learning there new bus schedules.

_____   6. This schedules are very different from that at their old apartment.

_____

_____   7. Their pleased, however, because there buses now stop right in front of

_____   their apartment building.

_____   8. Some of Frank's friends wear upset because of a much more difficult

_____   problem: there car was struck by lightning.

_____   9. They had left their car in a parking lot were there were no tall stationary

_____   objects, buildings or trees, too attract the lightening away from the car.

_____ 10. Frank's friends, which have just had their car destroyed, will pay more

_____   attention to whether forecasts in the future.

Conjunctions

Conjunctions join ideas by joining grammatical structures. You must know the different kinds of conjunctions in order to punctuate sentences correctly and in order to express your ideas in the most effective way.

Coordinating conjunctions are *and, but, for, or, nor, yet,* and *so.* Coordinating conjunctions join grammatical structures of the same kind: words to words, phrases to phrases, and clauses to clauses.   (see **Coordinating Conjunctions**)

Word: Rice *and* potatoes are common foods.

Phrase: Today travelers go by plane *or* by bus.

Clause: Many trees lose their leaves in winter, *but* evergreen trees do not.

Correlative conjunctions are pairs of conjunctions that are used together.

both . . . and   not only . . . but also
either . . . or   neither . . . nor

Correlative conjunctions must be followed by the same grammatical structures.   (see **Parallel structure**)

                                   noun   adjective
Incorrect: *Either* the *meat* was tough to begin with *or overcooked.*

                                   noun   pronoun
Correct: *Either* the *meat* was tough to begin with   *or it*   was overcooked.
                                            adjective   adjective
                 The meat was *either tough* to begin with *or overcooked.*

Subordinating conjunctions introduce dependent clauses. (For examples of their use,   see **Clauses, connectors**)

Conjunctive adverbs show relationships between ideas but are not grammatically necessary in the clause.   (see **Interrupters**)

Test Yourself

The conjunctions are underlined in the following sentences. In the blank to the left put *cd* for a coordinating conjunction, *cr* for a correlative conjunction, *sb* for a subordinating conjunction, and *ca* for a conjunctive adverb.

_____ 1.   <u>Both</u> adults <u>and</u> children like to hear stories about monsters.

_____ 2.   Few adults, <u>however</u>, will admit that they believe in them.

_____ 3.   The Loch Ness Monster, <u>which</u> supposedly lives in a lake in Scotland, is one of the world's most famous monsters.

_____ 4.   Ancient stories <u>and</u> myths from many parts of the world tell about fearsome monsters as well as about the brave warriers who fought them.

_____ 5.   <u>Not</u> <u>only</u> dragons breathing fire <u>but</u> <u>also</u> human beings with frightening supernatural powers are found in folklore.

Contractions

Contractions are shortened forms of verbs that represent the sounds of speech. Contractions are written to show subject-verb combinations or negative-verb combinations. Avoid using them in formal writing.   (see **Style**)   All verb forms that can be contracted can be used as operators.

With Pronouns

I'm—I am
I've—I have
I'd—I had or would
I'll—I will or shall
You're, we're, they're, who're—You, we, they, who are
You've, we've, they're, who've—You, we, they, who have
You'd, we'd, they'd, who'd—You, we, they, who had or would
You'll, we'll, they'll, who'll—You, we, they, who will or shall
he's, she's, it's, who's—he, she, it, who is (sometimes he, she, it, who has)
he'd, she'd, it'd, who'd—he, she, it, who had or would
he'll, she'll, it'll, who'll—he, she, it, who will or shall
let's—let us

With Negatives

Ain't is considered colloquial or nonstandard. Do not use it in writing with any noun or pronoun. *Aren't I?* is sometimes used for *am I not?*

I, you, we, they, who don't—do not
                    haven't—have not

I, we, you, he, she, it, they, who didn't—did not
                              hadn't—had not

You, we, they, who aren't—are not
                    weren't—were not

He, she, it, who isn't—is not
                doesn't—does not
                hasn't—has not
                wasn't—was not

All nouns and pronouns can be used with the following forms (modal + *not*):

won't—will not
wouldn't—would not
can't—cannot
couldn't—could not
mustn't—must not
shouldn't—should not
mightn't—might not (rare)
needn't—need not (rare in U.S.)
oughtn't—ought not (rare)

In direct quotations, -*'s* may be used after a proper name to show *is* or *has*.

"John*'s* a good friend," he said. (John *is* a good friend.)
"Virginia*'s* had a hard year." (Virginia *has* had a hard year.)

Never use a positive contraction of a personal pronoun + *be, have, do,* or a modal as the last word of a clause. Negative contractions, however, are common at the end of a clause.

Virginia is my friend.	Yes, *she is.* (NEVER Yes, *she's.*)
	No, she *isn't.*
I'd go.	Yes, *I would.* (NEVER Yes, *I'd.*)
	I *wouldn't.*

Test Yourself

Rewrite the contraction that is underlined as it should be in formal writing. Put the correct form in the blank to the left.

_____ 1. We're sorry to hear that your letter of January 25 <u>didn't</u> reach us.

_____

_____ 2. If <u>we'd</u> known about your emergency needs, <u>we'd</u> have shipped a part to you by air.

_____

_____ 3. <u>Let's</u> know of your future needs, and <u>we'll</u> do our best to give you prompt service.

_____

_____ 4. <u>We're</u> sure you <u>won't</u> have any late deliveries in the future.

_____

_____ 5. If <u>there's</u> a question about <u>what's</u> already been shipped to you, please call us at once.

_____

Contrary to Fact Statements, see **Subjunctive**

Coordinating Conjunctions

Coordinating conjunctions join two or more words, phrases, or clauses in the *same* grammatical category.

and	for
but	so
or	yet
nor	and/or

NOTE: *For, so,* and *yet* are sometimes used in other ways in a sentence.

Meaning

Do not confuse the meanings of the coordinating conjunctions. (see **Clauses, Connecting Words**)

And shows addition:

Two *and* four make six.

But shows contrast:

Two and four make six, *but* two and three make five.
They bought eggs and bread, *but* they forgot to buy milk.

Or and *nor* show choice, separation, or negative addition.

Two and four *or* five and one make six.
They had enough money for eggs *or* bread, but not enough for both.
They did not buy eggs, *nor* did they buy bread.

Nor must follow *not* or *neither*. It is used in formal writing. Note that it is followed by an operator and the word order of a question.

So shows result:

They didn't have enough money to buy milk, *so* they bought only eggs and bread.

For shows cause:

They bought only eggs and bread, *for* they did not have enough money to buy milk.

Yet shows contrast and/or concession:

They bought eggs and bread, *yet* they forgot to buy milk.

For and *yet* are rarely used in speech in this construction, but they are often used in formal writing.

And/or means that what follows may be an addition to or a substitution for the previous statement. *And/or* is not used in a formal literary style, but it is often used in scientific writing:

Her letters are poorly typed. She needs a new typewriter *and/or* a new secretary.
The glassware is not clean. He needs a new dishwasher *and/or* better procedures.

Agreement

When *and* joins parts of the subject of a sentence, the verb is plural (see **Agreement of Subject and Verb**):

The *boys and* their *father are* going together.

When *or* or *nor* joins parts of the subject of a sentence, the verb agrees with the part of the subject closest to it:

Neither the boys *nor* their father *is* going.
Neither Father nor our uncle *nor the boys* are going.

Punctuation

When a coordinating conjunction joins two main clauses, put a comma before the coordinating conjunction. But when a coordinating conjunction joins two words, phrases, or subordinate clauses, do not put a comma before the conjunction unless there is another reason for it.   (see **Punctuation, comma**)

They bought bread and milk, but they forgot to buy eggs.
They had only enough money for eggs and bread or for eggs and milk.

Compound Constructions

Coordination means putting ideas into equal grammatical constructions that are called *compound.* Ideas in equal constructions should be of equal importance. If the ideas do not have the same importance, put the less important one in a less important (subordinate) construction.   (see **Subordinating**)

Use coordinating conjunctions and correlative conjunctions (*either . . . or, neither . . . nor, not only . . . but also*) to join constructions of equal importance.   (See **Parallel Structure** for special problems with correlative conjunctions.)

1   Join words:

compound subject
Paris, Rio de Janeiro, **and** *Tokyo* are three cities I would like to visit.

compound verb
Anne *played* in a band **and** passed a math course last summer.

compound subject   compound verb   compound verb
Anne **and** Peter *played*   together in a band *and took* one math course last summer. (Both parts of the subject act in both parts of the verb. Compare the compound sentences below.

compound direct object
John found the *books* **and** *coat* that he had left in the car.

compound predicate adjective
Basketball players are *tall* **and** *thin.*

compound infinitives
The children want to *go* **and** *play* now.

compound object of preposition
The children have an art class on *Monday, Wednesday,* **and** *Friday.*

2   Join phrases:

compound verb phrases   compound verb phrases
Anne *had been playng* in the band for several months **and** *had been taking* a math course too.

prepositional   prepositional
phrase   phrase

I have an art class *on Monday* **but** not *on Tuesday.*

gerund phase   gerund phase

Driving through heavy traffic **and** *finding a parking place* took the lawyer longer than she had planned.

compound adverb phrases

The bus is crowded *early in the morning* **and** *late in the afternoon.*

compound infinitive phrases

We decided *to go* now **and** *to see* as much as possible.

3 Join clauses:

Compound sentences are independent clauses joined by coordinating conjunctions.

independent clause   **so**

Anne *played* in the band last summer, **but** Peter *has* just joined it.

               and

independent clause

Correct: *John left his books in the car,* **and**

independent clause

        he left his coat in the library.

Compound sentences that have the same subject in both clauses are likely to be wordy. Reduce the number of words in the sentence above by changing to a compound object.

compound direct object

Improved: John left his *books* in the car **and** his *coat* in the library.

Dependent clauses can be joined by coordinating conjunctions.

dependent clause (noun)

Discovering (*that*) *the distance was too far* **and**

dependent clause (noun)

(*that*) *the time was too short,* we decided not to drive to Florida.

dependent clause (adverb)

When the experiment has been completed **and** (*when*)

dependent clause (adverb)

the results have been published, the supervisor should get a promotion.

To avoid wordiness reduce coordinate clauses whenever possible. (see **Wordiness**)

dependent clause

Correct: *If you have your test sheets* **and**

dependent clause

        if you have your pencil, you may begin to write now.

compound object

Improved: *If you have your test sheets* **and** *pencil,* you may begin to write now.

Test Yourself

In the blank to the left, put the coordinating conjunction that best shows the meaning of the sentence.

_____ 1. Locks _____ keys have been used for protection for thousands of years. (and, or)

_____ 2. Primitive people tried to protect themselves by rolling boulders in front of their caves, _____ modern people use locks instead of boulders. (so, for, but)

_____ 3. The Egyptian lock, invented around 2000 B.C., was a great improvement, _____ it could be opened by a key that could easily be carried away by one person. (so, for, but)

_____ 4. The Greeks improved on Egyptian locks by inventing the keyhole, _____ the lock could be opened from the outside. (so, for, but)

_____ 5. The Romans were not satisfied with the Egyptian keys based on a pattern of pins, _____ did they find the Greek curved key totally satisfactory. (and, but, or, nor)

_____ 6. The Romans changed the pins on the key to many different shapes to make each key difficult to copy, _____ they made the keys as well as the locks much smaller than they had been before. (and, but, or)

Countable and Uncountable Nouns

Countable and _uncountable_ refer to different kinds of nouns. _Countable_ nouns are sometimes called _count nouns._ Uncountable nouns are sometimes called _noncount_ nouns or _mass_ nouns. Nouns can be countable in one meaning and/or usage and uncountable in another meaning and/or usage.

Countable Nouns	_Uncountable Nouns_
have singular and plural forms	have only one form
take singular or plural verbs according to their use as singular or plural	take singular verbs
can have _a, an,_ or _one_ before them as modifier in the singular	cannot have _a, an,_ or _one_ before them as modifier
can have _many_ or _few_ before them as modifier in the plural	can have _much_ before them as a modifier
can have _some_ before them as modifier only in the plural	can have _some_ before them as a modifier
can have _a_ or _the number of_ before them only in the plural	can have _amount of_ before them
pronouns are _one_ (sing.); _many, few, some, number_ (pl.)	pronouns are _much, some, amount_

(see **Agreement of Subject and Verb; Articles; Determiners; Number; Pronouns, indefinite; and Quantity**)

Certain kinds of nouns are usually countable.

1   Names of persons, animals, plants, insects, and their parts:

Persons	*Animals*	*Plants*	*Insects*	*Parts*
a boy	a cat	a cactus	an ant	an ankle
a girl	a dog	a bush	a butterfly	a bone
a man	a horse	a flower	a caterpillar	a face
a student	a mouse	an oak	a fly	a head
a teacher	a tiger	a potato	a mite	a nose
a wife	a wolf	a rose	a tick	an ear
a woman	a zebra	a tree	a wasp	a wing

2   Objects with a definite shape:

a ball	a car	a house	a street	a typewriter
a building	a door	a mountain	a tent	an umbrella

3   Units of measurement (for length area, weight, volume, temperature, pressure, speed, and so on) and words of classification. Uncountable nouns can be measured or classified using words such as these:

a gram	a foot	a square foot,	a drop	a kind	a bit	a cup
an inch	a meter	meter	a degree	a type	an item	a spoonful
an ounce	a pound	a cubic inch,	a bunch	a piece	a part	a gallon,
		centimeter				liter

Classifications in society:

a family	a country	a language
a clan	a state	a word
a tribe	a city	a phrase

4   Some abstract words:

a help	an invention	a rest
a hindrance	a nuisance	a scheme
an idea	a plan	a taboo

Certain kinds of nouns are usually uncountable.

1   Names of substances and materials:

Food	*Materials and Metals*	*Natural Qualities*
bread	copper	lightness
cake	cotton	darkness
chocolate	dacron	heaviness
meat	grass	brightness
spaghetti	iron	dullness and other words in
spinach	rayon	*-ness*
butter	steel	luminescence
cheese	wood	adolescence

2   Names of liquids, gases, and substances made of many small particles:

Liquids	Gases	Grains and Other Solids Made of Many Small Particles		
coffee	air	barley	wheat	cement
milk	carbon dioxide	rice	cornmeal	sand
oil	oxygen	sugar	oatmeal	gravel
tea	smoke	popcorn	flour	salt

3   Names of languages: Arabic, English, Chinese, French, Japanese, Russian, Spanish, Swahili, Welsh.

4   Most *-ing* forms. Exceptions include *building, feeling, dealing, wedding,* and *helping* when it means a portion of food; a *saving* is an economy, but *savings* is an amount of money; *furnishings* is always plural.   (see **Gerunds**)

camping	hiking	parking	studying
clothing	learning	shopping	trying
dancing	lightning	smoking	waiting

5   Many abstract nouns, including words in *-ness, -ance, -ence,* and *-ity,* which are usually abstract and uncountable:

beauty	ignorance	peace	serenity	helpfulness	curiosity
equality	importance	plenty	selfishness	reticence	patriotism
happiness	obsolescence	sanity	verbosity	attendance	laziness

Many words that are countable in other languages are uncountable in English:

advice	courage	leisure	permission
anger	damage	luck	photography
applause	(harm)	luggage	and other
baggage	dirt	melancholy	disciplines in
behavior	education	money	*-graphy*
cash	equipment	moonlight	poetry
chaos	fun	mud	progress
chess and	furniture	music	publicity
names of	garbage	news (plural	rubbish
other games	harm	form but	safety
and sports	hospitality	takes singular	violence
china (dishes)	information	verb)	weather
conduct	laughter		

To measure or classify uncountable nouns, use *of.*   (see **Quantity**)

a *piece of* cake	an *amount of* leisure	a *bottle of* milk	a *breath of* air
a *slice of* bread	five *pounds of* sugar	a *yard of* cloth	an *acre of* land

A piece of, a bit of, and *an item of* can be used with many words. Other similar words can be used with only a few uncountable nouns.

a *slice of* bread, cake, meat	a *blade of* grass, wheat
a *bar of* chocolate, copper, candy, gold	a *grain of* rice, barley, wheat, sand
a *sheet of* paper, ice	a *lump of* coal, sugar

Many words have both countable and uncountable meanings. Substances, materials, activities, and abstract ideas often have countable meanings when one item or one specific example is meant.

Countable	*Uncountable*
an activity, activities (specific)	activity (abstract)
an agreement, agreements (specific)	agreement (abstract)
an art, arts (a method of doing something)	art (abstract)
a beauty, beauties (a person or thing that is beautiful)	beauty (abstract)
a bone, bones (piece or pieces)	bone (substance)
a brick, bricks	brick (substance)
a business, businesses (a particular activity or activities)	business (activity)
a cake, cakes	cake (substance)
a chocolate, chocolates (a piece, pieces of candy)	chocolate (substance)
a cloth, cloths (a piece or pieces)	cloth (substance)
a decision, decisions (action or actions)	decision (abstract)
a duty, duties (one requirement or requirements)	duty (abstract)
a fire, fires (one or more examples)	fire (substance)
a glass, glasses (for liquid); (eye) glasses	glass (substance)
a hair, hairs (one or more strands)	hair (substance and collectively for all the hairs on one person's head)
a history, histories (one or more accounts or events)	history (study of the past)
an honor, honors (act or acts of respect)	honor (abstract)
a hope, hopes (an expectation)	hope (abstract)
an iron, irons (a tool for pressing clothes, changing a tire, and so on)	iron (substance)
a kindness, kindnesses (a good deed or deeds)	kindness (abstract)
a language, languages (English, Chinese, and so on)	language (activity)
a light, lights (lamp or lamps or one source of light)	light (illumination)
a material, materials (a substance; especially of cloth)	material
a noise, noises (one or more sounds)	noise (usually unpleasant sound)
a pain, pains (one or more feelings)	pain (collective)
a paper, papers (sheet of paper, a composition, a newspaper)	paper (substance)
a pity (something unfortunate)	pity (emotion)
a pleasure, pleasures (thing or things that give happiness)	pleasure (emotion)
a silence, silences (a period or periods of time without sound)	silence (lack of sound)
a space, spaces (empty place or places)	space (the expanse of the universe)
a stone, stones (a piece or pieces)	stone (substance)

Countable	Uncountable
a success, successes (a person or event)	success (abstract)
a thought, thoughts (one instance)	thought (abstract)
a time, times (an occasion, occasions)	time (collective)
a trade, trades (a skill, an exchange)	trade (business)
a traffic, traffics (dealing, dealings)	traffic (business; the number of vehicles)
a war, wars (a particular instance)	war (activity)
a wine, wines (a kind of)	wine (substance)
a work, works (of art, of an author)	work (effort or employment activity)
a worry, worries (one or more instances)	worry (activity)

Some words have similar forms, one countable and the other uncountable.

Countable	Uncountable
clothes (plural only)	clothing
dance(s)	dancing
furnishings (plural only)	furniture
laugh(s)	laughter, laughing
machine(s)	machinery
moonbeam(s)	moonlight
payment(s)	pay
permit(s)	permission
sunbeam(s)	sunlight
use(s)	usefulness

When a prefix is added, the changed meaning may or may not have the same countability.

Countable	Uncountable
appreciation(s) (statement showing under-standing)	appreciation (rise in value; understanding; thanks)
	depreciation (loss in value)
apprehension(s) (fear; arrest)	apprehension (fear; understanding)
misapprehension(s) (failure to understand)	
malediction(s) (curse)	diction (choice of words or pronunciation)
benediction(s) (blessing)	
decision(s)	indecision
inequality, inequalities	equality
	inequality
justice(s) (person only)	justice (abstract idea)
injustice(s) (action)	injustice (abstract idea)
investment(s) (something invested)	investment (act of investment)
vestment(s) (ceremonial clothing)	

NOTE: The base word is usually the uncountable form, but not always. **Use your dictionary.**

Test Yourself

A. Change the following uncountable nouns into countable ideas by using units of measurement or idiomatic phrases.

1. rice	**5.** gold	**9.** iron	**13.** air
2. penicillin	**6.** milk	**10.** luggage	**14.** publicity
3. wheat	**7.** money	**11.** education	**15.** equipment
4. land	**8.** machinery	**12.** beauty	**16.** lightning

B. In the following sentences, choose the countable or uncountable form as the meaning requires.

_____ 1. Expensive _____ requires careful maintenance. (machines, machinery)

_____ 2. Jaguars and Porsches, for example, are expensive pieces of _____ .

(machine, machines, machinery)

_____ 3. Their _____ is not the most important reason for owning them. (use, usefulness)

_____ 4. Their expensive finishes and _____ make them status symbols. (equipment, furnishings)

_____ 5. In _____ they bring admiring looks from other drivers. (traffic, traffics)

_____ 6. Owning such machines is a matter of satisfaction and prestige rather than _____ . (transports, transportation)

_____ 7. _____ in the world are reflected in the kinds of transportation people use. (Inequality, Inequalities)

Dash, see **Punctuation, dash**

Determiners

Determiners modify nouns and gerunds (and sometimes pronouns), but the nature of the noun—countable, singular; uncountable; or countable, plural—tells which determiner is possible.   (see **Countable and Uncountable Nouns**)

Determiners always come before the nouns they modify. Other modifiers can come between a determiner and the noun it modifies.   (see **Adjectives, word order**)

Use only one determiner before any one noun unless one of the determiners is in a prepositional phrase.

my
some books—*some* of *those* books
their

"Predeterminers" (*all, both,* and *half*) are explained at the end of this section.   See **Confusing Choices** for special problems with some pairs of determiners: **a lot**, *lots, lots of;* **all**, *all of, whole;* **another**, *other;* **any**, *some;* **any body**, *any one, anybody, anyone;* **any more**, *anymore;* **each**, *every, everyone, all;* **each other**, *every other;* **few**, *a few;* **little**, *a little;* **numbers**, *a number, the number;* **one**, *another, other, others.*

140

Table of Determiners

	Noun-Singular Countable (takes singular verb)	Noun-Uncountable (takes singular verb)	Noun-Plural Countable (takes plural verb)
Article	the, a, an, no	the, zero (no) article, no	the, zero (no) article, no
Possessive Forms	my, our, your, his, her, its, their	my, our, your, his, her, its, their	my, our, your, his, her, its, their
Relative Forms	whose, which(ever), what(ever)	whose, which(ever), what(ever)	whose, which(ever), what(ever)
Demonstratives	this, that	this, that	these, those
Indefinite Forms	one, any, some, every, each, either, neither, (the) other, another	some, any, much, enough, more, most, (the) other, such, little, less, least, the amount (of)	some, any, both, many, enough, more, most, other(s), such, few, fewer, fewest, the number (of)
Cardinal Numbers	one		numbers of two, three, etc.
Ordinal Numbers	(the) first, second, third, etc., (the) last	(the) first, second, third, (the) last	(the) first, second, third, (the) last

Use *other* as the adjective form before plural noun, but use *others* as a pronoun to replace a plural noun.

Determiner		Kind of Noun
The	*book* is here.	(singular, countable)
Our	*books* are here.	(plural, countable)
Some	*day* they will come.	(singular, countable)
Some	*milk* is on the table.	(uncountable)
	Milk is on the table.	(uncountable)
Some	*books* are on the table.	(plural, countable)
Whatever	*milk* was left on the table has turned sour.	(uncountable)
This	*book* is on the table.	(singular, countable)
This	*milk* has turned sour.	(uncountable)
	Books are on that table, not magazines.	(plural, countable)
These	*books* are on the table.	(plural, countable)
Every	*book* on the table is for sale.	(singular, countable)
Enough	*milk* is on the table for all of us.	(uncountable)
Enough	*books* are on the table for all of us.	(plural, countable)

You can put an *of the* phrase after the indefinite pronoun forms.

Any (of the) books will do.   (singular, countable)
Some (of the) milk is on the table.   (uncountable)
Some (of the) books are on the table.   (plural, countable)
Enough (of the) milk is on the table.   (uncountable)
Enough (of the) books are on the table.   (plural, countable)

NOTE: *Each* can be followed by *one,* but *no + one* becomes *none* or *not one.* (Use *no one* only for a person.)

Each (one) of the books is on the table.   (singular, countable)
None (not one) of the books is on the table.   (singular, countable)

Predeterminers

Predeterminers that modify nouns come before determiners. They can be used without an *of* phrase to modify a noun.

All, Both, Half
All the boys are here.
Half a loaf is better than none.
Both the children are asleep.
Half these apples are rotten.
Half this milk is spoiled.
All his children are here.
All John's children are here.
All whose names are called must come forward.

In a related construction, *all, both,* or *half* can be followed by an *of* phrase.

Half of these apples are rotten.
Half of this milk is spoiled.
All of his children are here.
All of John's children are here.

NOTE: After *of* use *those whose* instead of *whose* by itself

All of those whose names are called must come forward.

With an *of* phrase, these words can be followed by a pronoun as well as a noun.

All of the boys (all of them) are here.
Half of the loaf (half of it) is better than none.
Both of the children (both of them) are asleep.

Word Order of Predeterminers
All and *both* can come after the noun or pronoun they modify.

The *people all* have problems.
They all have problems.
The *children both* are here.
They both are here.

Words showing multiplication can be predeterminers only. Do not use an *of* phrase directly after them or put them after the word that they modify.

Correct: Double that salary will be too much

Incorrect: Double *of* that salary will be too much.

Correct: Four times the number of people were killed by hurri-
                  canes this year as compared to last year.

Incorrect: Four times *of* the number of people were killed by
                  hurricanes this year as compared to last year.

Correct: Twice the number that we expected registered today.

Incorrect: Twice *of* the number that we expected registered today.

But you can put an *of* phrase after *number.* Always use a plural noun or pronoun after *number of.*

Correct: *Twice* the number of student*s* that we expected registered today.

NOTE: *Doubled, tripled,* and so on can follow the noun they modify.

That salary *doubled* will not be enough.

Fractions
Fractions can be predeterminers and can also be used with an *of* phrase. Put a hyphen between the number parts of a fraction.

One-fourth (of) the class was absent.
One-third (of) my income goes for rent.

One in a fraction can be replaced by *a* and sometimes by *the.* Do not put a hyphen after an article.

We will come in *a* half hour, but we still have *a* half mile to go. **or** half *an* hour, half *a* mile
You don't know *the* half of it.

Test Yourself

Correct the errors in the following sentences. Cross out the word that is incorrect. If it needs to be changed, write the correct form over it.

1. The distance from the earth to the moon is about thirty times of the earth's diameter.

2. Astronomers call the distance from the earth to the sun, approximately 93,000,000

    miles, a one astronomical unit.

3. A distances as great as that from the earth to the sun is hard to understand.

4. This distances of space even in our own solar system are very great.

5. The amount of distance from our sun to Pluto is forty astronomical units.

6. No one of the planets in our solar system is farther from the earth than Pluto.

Direct Objects

A direct object follows an active verb. Somebody or something (subject) acts in some way (verb) on somebody or something (direct object).   (see **Voice**)

Subject	Verb	Direct Object
Mary	threw	the ball.
Mary	bought	some ice cream.
Mary	loves	John.

The direct object is something or somebody different from the subject except for the rare direct object that is a reflexive pronoun.   (see **Pronouns, reflexive**)

Subject	Verb	Direct Object	
John	hit	a ball (it)	over the fence.
John	hit	himself (reflexive pronoun)	on the elbow.

The direct object can be a noun, a noun phrase, an object pronoun, a noun clause, an *-ing* form, or an infinitive.

Subject	Verb	Direct Object
Mary	threw	the ball. (noun)
Mary	bought	some ice cream. (noun phrase)
Mary	bought	it. (pronoun)
Mary	bought	whatever we wanted. (noun clause)
Mary	likes	eating ice cream. (*-ing* form)
Mary	likes	to eat ice cream. (infinitive)

An indirect object can show *to* or *for* whom the action is done.   (see **Indirect Object**)

Direct Speech

Writers in English have two ways of showing what other people say or write: *direct* speech and *reported* speech. Reported speech is sometimes called indirect speech. (see **Reported Speech**)

Direct speech is a written record of someone's exact words. A phrase that identifies the speaker or writer can come either before or after the quotation. This phrase is sometimes called a *dialogue guide*. Direct speech is sometimes called *direct quotation, direct discourse,* or *quoted speech.*

	quotation	dialogue guide
Direct Speech:	"We want to go," the students said.	

or

	dialogue guide	quotation
	The students said, "We want to go."	
Reported Speech:	The students said that they wanted to go.	

Punctuating Direct Speech

1   Put quotation marks (sometimes called inverted commas) around the speaker's exact words. Double quotation marks are usually used in the United States.   (see **Punctuation, quotation marks**)

"We want to go," the students said.
"Tomorrow is a holiday," the bank clerk told us.

2   Put a capital letter at the beginning of the speaker's exact words. The speaker's exact words (direct quotation) may begin at the beginning of the sentence,

"**W**e want to go," the students said.
"**T**omorrow is a holiday," the bank clerk told us.

or the speaker's exact words (direct quotation) may begin in the middle of the sentence,

The students said, "**W**e want to go."
The bank clerk told us, "**T**omorrow is a holiday."

3   Use a comma, a question mark, or an exclamation point to separate the speaker's exact words from the rest of the sentence. Do not use a period to separate the direct quotation from the phrase telling who speaks unless there are several sentences together in a longer passage (see below, rule 5).

"We want to go**,**" the students said.
"May we go**?**" the students asked.
"Help**!**" the students shouted.

NOTE: The phrase telling who speaks does *not* begin with a capital letter if it is not at the beginning of the sentence, even if it follows a question mark or an exclamation point.

4   Always put periods and commas inside (to the left of) the second part of the pair of quotation marks.

"We want to go**,**" the students said.
The students said, "We want to go**.**"

5   When the exact words of more than one speaker are written together, a special format is used. Indent at the beginning of the line to show a change of speaker.

First Speaker: "Peter, will you return these books to the library for me when you go there to work on your research paper this afternoon?" Sue asked. "I cannot take them back today, and they are due now."

Second Speaker: "Will tonight be soon enough?" Peter answered. "I have to report
                            for the first meeting of the track team this afternoon, but I plan to go
                            to the library tonight, and I can take them for you then."

First Speaker: "That will be fine; thanks a lot," Sue said.

Third Speaker: "If you do Sue a favor," Jan said, "then you can ask her to help you
                            study for your chemistry test next week, Peter. Maybe she can help me,
                            too."

First Speaker: "Of course, I could never refuse to help my friends," Sue agreed.

6   Always use a verb in the phrase that tells who is speaking in formal written
English. Do not use a name followed by a colon without a verb unless you are writing
or copying a play. People who write plays follow a special format.

7   When the dialogue guide (phrase telling who is speaking) interrupts the
speaker's exact words, do not put a capital letter at the beginning of the continuation
unless a new sentence begins there.

"We want to go as soon as we can because we are afraid the game will be over before we get
    there," the students said.
"We want to go as soon as we can," the students said,

          continuation of the speaker's exact words in the same sentence
"because we are afraid the game will be over before we get there."

"Connie, come here," Aunt Marian said.

                          continuation
"Connie," Aunt Marian said, "come here."

8   You can invert the order of words in the dialogue guide when they come
within the direct quotation or at the end of it. Normal word order is always correct,
however.

                                                          subject   verb
Normal Word Order: "We are the ones who are coming," *Charlotte said.*

                                              verb   subject
Inverted Word Order: "We are the ones," *said Charlotte,* "who are coming." (within)
                            "We are the ones who are coming," *said Charlotte.* (at the end)

Normal Word Order: "No one else knows as much as Ellen," *Margaret said.*

Inverted Word Order: "No one else," *said Margaret,* "knows as much as Ellen." (within)
                            "No one else knows as much as Margaret," *said Ellen.* (at the
                                end)

9   Use ellipses (three spaced periods) to show that you have left out part of a
direct quotation.   (see **Punctuation, ellipsis**)

"My purpose," wrote Wordsworth about the language of his poetry, "was to imitate and . . .
    adopt the very language of men."

NOTE: When you use a quotation from a written source, do not indent the beginning
of the quotation if it comes in the middle of a paragraph of your own writing.

10 Use brackets around your own explanation within a quotation. (see
Punctuation, brackets)

"My purpose [in choosing a poetic style] was to imitate and . . . adopt the very language of
men," Wordsworth wrote.

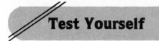

Test Yourself

Write conversations for the following situations. Write at least three parts: one person
speaks, a second person answers, and the first person speaks again.

1. Your friend Jane bought a television set yesterday, but now it has no picture. She talks
   about her problem with a clerk at the store where she bought the set.
2. Joe needs to make a telephone call at a pay phone. He has a one-dollar bill but no
   change. He asks Sally if she can make change for a dollar.

Do

Do is both a main verb and an auxiliary (helping) verb. For uses of *do* as a main verb
compared with *make,*   see **Confusing choices, *Do*** and ***Make*.**   For uses of *do* as
an auxiliary (helping) verb,   see **Auxiliary Verbs** and **Operators.**   For contracted
forms of *do,*   see **Contractions.**   *Do* has irregular forms: *does, did* (past), and *done*
(past participle).

 **Expletives**

An expletive is a meaningless word or filler, usually at the beginning of a sentence. (Sometimes *expletive* means an oath or a violent or profane word used to express strong feeling.) *There* and *it* can be expletives in the sense of fillers. Putting the true subject of the clause at the beginning often makes a better written sentence.

Always use a singular verb after *it*.

Correct: It is useless to go now.

Improved: To go now is useless.
            Going now is useless.

Correct: It has been a short vacation.

Improved: Our vacation has been short.

Use *it* to begin a sentence about the weather or time.

Correct: It is raining/hot/cold, ten o'clock, spring, and so on.

148

Use a singular verb after *there* if the noun following the verb is singular; use a plural verb if the noun following the verb is plural. Put the true subject at the beginning of the clause if possible.

Correct:	singular There *is* no *one* here to help.
Improved:	No *one is* here to help.
Correct:	plural There *are* many *students* standing in line.
Improved:	Many *students are* standing in line.

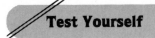

Test Yourself

Rewrite the following sentences to remove the unnecessary expletives.

1. There is nothing more frightening than an earthquake.
2. It is the feeling of helplessness that upsets people in an earthquake.
3. It is true that certain belts across the earth's surface are known to be earthquake zones.
4. There are landslides, tidal waves, and cracks in the earth that are possibly results of earthquakes.
5. There are shock waves that go in all directions from the center of an earthquake.
6. It is frightening to think of the earth shaking, rolling, or moving under one's feet.
7. There is no place more dangerous than inside a building during an earthquake because the building can collapse.
8. Although scientists know many things about earthquakes, no one knows for sure what it is that triggers them.

F

Finite Verbs

A finite verb is a verb form or forms that can be used as the main verb in a clause. (see **Clause**) A finite verb may be just one word or it may be several words together in a finite verb phrase.

A finite verb can show tense, voice, mood, and aspect. In order to show all these different meanings, a finite verb phrase can include modals and auxiliaries as well as the head verb (the head verb carries the dictionary meaning). (see **Mood; Passive Verbs,** and **Tense**) In the present tense and in all verb phrases formed with *is/are* or *has/have,* verb forms also show number. (see **Agreement of Subject and Verb**)

Indicative Mood (Statement)

Present Tense, Active Voice:	John *throws* the ball.
Past Tense, Active Voice:	John *threw* the ball.
Present Tense, Progressive/Continuous Aspect, Active Voice:	John *is throwing* the ball.
Present Tense, Perfect Aspect, Active Voice:	John *has thrown* the ball.
Present Tense, Passive Voice:	The ball *is thrown* (by John).
Imperative Mood, (Command):	*Throw* the ball.

150

Agreement

A finite verb must agree with its subject in person and number.   (see **Agreement of Subject and Verb**)

Aspect

Aspect is sometimes used to distinguish the perfect and continuous/progressive verb forms. Many grammars, however, treat the perfect and progressive forms as tenses rather than as separate aspects.

The children *learn* easily. (present)
The children *have learned* easily. (present perfect)
The children *are learning* easily. (present continuous/progressive)

Tense

Show tense in a finite verb phrase only in the head word (main verb), the modal, the auxiliary, or *be*. (*Be* is listed separately from the auxiliaries *have* and *do* in the table.)   (see **Tense**)

John *goes*. John *went*. John *will go*.
John *can go*. John *could go*.
John *is* going. John *was* going.
John *has* to go. John *had* to go.
John *wants* to go. John *wanted* to go.

Do not repeat the tense in an infinitive that follows the finite verb.

Incorrect: Leslie *liked* to *walked* to the office.

Correct: Leslie *liked* to *walk* to the office.

Incorrect: My sister *did* not find time to *studied* last night.

Correct: My sister *did* not find time to *study* last night.

Do not repeat the tense in the head verb after *do, does,* or *did*. (This form of the head verb is called the simple or bare infinitive form.)

Incorrect: Leslie *did* not *walked* to the office.

Correct: Leslie *did* not *walk* to the office.

Incorrect: My sister *did* not *found* time to study last night.

Correct: My sister *did* not *find* time to study last night.

Few verbs can be used in all the possible forms of a finite verb. Only active verbs have direct objects, for example. Some verbs are never used as commands.

Word Order

Put the words in a verb phrase in the required order. Form verb phrases in the order given below for a statement, starting at the left. Most phrases will be made of two or three words. (See **Conditional Sentences, Direct Speech, Operators,** and **Questions** for changes in word order in special circumstances.)

		Modal$^{T(not)}$	+ Auxiliary$^{T(not)}$	+ be$^{T(not)}$	-ing Form	Head Verb: Base or Past Participle	Object and/or Inf/Ger
They	1.	could				go.	
	2.	will				go.	
	3.	will		be	going.		
	4.			are	going.		
	5.			were	going to	walk.	
	6.	will				have	to go.
	7.	might	have	been		found.	
	8.	might	have	been	hiking.		
	9.			are	being	taught	to obey.
	10.	may	have	been	asking		her to come.
	11.			are	being	examined.	
	12.		did			find	the report.

1   *T:* Only these three forms marked *T* can show tense in a finite verb phrase. **Show tense in only *one* of these forms.** Working from left to right on the chart above, you can

show tense by changing *will, shall,* or *may* to *would, should,* or *might* if one of these words is in the verb phrase

or

use *will* or *shall* to show future tense

or

show tense by changing *have* or *do* to *had* or *did*

or

show tense by changing *be* to *is, are, was, were,* or *been.*

2   *Not:* Working from left to right on the table, you can put *not* after the modal if there is one (*may not*)

or

put *not* after any form of *have* or *do* if there is no modal (*have not* or *do not*)

or

put *not* after a form of *be* if it is the first word in the verb phrase or if it is the only verb.

3 *Have, did,* and *be* can be head verbs. You can use them as the head verb and as the auxiliary in the same sentence.

He *has* (aux.) *had* (head verb) to work hard.
She *did* (aux.) not *do* (head verb) her work.
They *are* (aux.) *being* (head verb) difficult.

4 Use the head verb only once. In a finite verb phrase, you can use the base (simple, bare infinitive) form **or** the *-ing* form **or** the past participle of the head verb.

5 Do not put more than one *-ing* form in any one finite verb phrase except after *going to be.*

6 With *going* as a semiauxiliary in the future and intentional meaning, add *to*.

7 After certain base forms, you can add an infinitive or gerund.   (see **Infinitive/-*ing* choice**)

Test Yourself

Find the errors in the verb forms in the following sentences and put the correct forms in the blanks to the left.

_____ 1. Early people did not had very good methods for preserving food.

_____ 2. They were able to dried berries, grains, nuts, and roots.

_____ 3. After the discovery of fire, they probably could smoked and dried meat.

_____ 4. People in ancient Rome imported ice and snow to used in preserving food.

_____ 5. People had to learned about how bacteria and other microorganisms cause food to spoil before they could develop satisfactory methods of preservation.

_____ 6. A Frenchman named Nicolas Appert invent the process of canning in the early nineteenth century.

_____ 7. Appert preserved food in glass bottles; later other people learned how they could used tin-plated cans.

_____ 8. Clarence Birdseye worked to developed the quick-freezing process in the 1920s.

_____ 9. More recent developments in methods for drying food have gave us convenient products such as powdered milk and instant coffee.

_____ 10.   Irradiation has been show to slow decay and kill bacteria and insects in perishable foods.

_____ 11.   In the future people are going have a greater variety of foods available than ever before because of better methods of preservation.

_____ 12.   Living far from the places where food grown will not keep people from having balanced diets in the future.

Fragments

A fragment is a group of words that is punctuated like a sentence, but it is not. A capital letter begins the group of words, and a period ends it. But between the capital letter and the period, some part that is necessary has been left out or put in a wrong form, resulting in a fragment. A sentence fragment is a serious error in composition.

1   A dependent clause that is **not attached to an independent clause** is a fragment.   (see **Clauses**)

A subordinating word such as *that,* the WH-words, and the subordinating conjunctions (*after, because, if,* and so on) make a clause dependent. However, WH-words can introduce **questions** of only one clause.   (see **Clauses** and **WH-Words**)

Incorrect: **1.** *When* Charles came to visit us. (*fragment*)

Incorrect: **2.** *If* Margaret has missed the first bus today. (*fragment*)

Incorrect: **3.** *That* Harold told us about. (*fragment*)

Incorrect: **4.** *Who* was looking for a new apartment. (*fragment*)

The first two sentences above can be corrected by leaving out the subordinators (in these sentences the subordinators are subordinating conjunctions). NOTE: Sentence 4 would be correct as a question, but it is not correct as a statement.

                     independent clause
Correct: **1.** Charles came to visit us.

                       independent clause
Correct: **2.** Margaret has missed the first bus today.

Leaving out the subordinators does not always correct sentences, however. Sentences 3 and 4 above can be corrected by changing *that* and *who* (relative pronouns) to personal pronouns.

Correct: **3.** Harold told us about *it*.

Correct: **4.** *She* was looking for a new apartment.

In the examples above, *it* and *she* refer to an unknown antecedent in a longer passage. Since sentence fragments are usually part of a longer composition, **they can often be**

attached to the sentence that comes before them or to the sentence that comes after them, keeping the subordinating word. You put in the subordinator because it shows the meaning you wanted when you first wrote the sentence. That meaning is important. Keep subordinating words in your sentence if possible when correcting them.

　　　　　　　　　　dependent clause　　　　　　　　independent clause
　　1. When Charles came to visit us, he brought us some flowers.

　　　　　　　　　　　dependent clause　　　　　　　　　　independent clause
Correct:　**2.** If Margaret has missed the first bus today, she will have to take a later one.

　　　　　　　independent clause　　　dependent clause
　　3. This is the book that Charles told us about.

　　　　　　independent clause　　　　　　dependent clause
　　4. My sister Helen is the one who is looking for a new apartment.

　　2 A statement that begins with a capital letter and ends with a period is a fragment if it **does not have a subject and a finite (main) verb.** Verbals (*-ing* and *to* + verb) cannot be the main verb in a clause.

Fragments
Margaret missing the first bus today.
Margaret to miss the first bus today.

An *-ing* or an infinitive can be changed to a finite verb.

Correct:　Margaret $\left\{ \begin{array}{l} \text{will miss} \\ \text{missed} \\ \text{has missed} \\ \text{is going to miss} \end{array} \right\}$ the first bus today.

Verbal phrases can also be **attached to an independent clause or a sentence before or after them.**

Correct:　Margaret, missing the first bus today, was late to work.

Correct:　Margaret was sorry to miss the first bus today.

Incorrect:　Margaret's alarm clock did not wake her up this morning, and she left her apartment later than usual. *Missing* the first bus today.

Correct:　Margaret's alarm clock did not wake her up this morning, and she left her apartment later than usual, missing the first bus today.

Do not punctuate prepositional phrases as sentences, even when they have verbals in them. Always connect them to an independent clause.

Incorrect:　Margaret *as a result of missing the first bus.* She was late to work.

Correct:　As a result of missing the first bus, Margaret was late to work.

Incorrect:　Margaret was late to work. Even after running to the bus stop.

Correct:　Margaret was late to work even after running to the bus stop.

NOTE: Sentence fragments are very common in spoken English. They are acceptable in a written record of actual speech, but avoid them in formal writing unless you are recording the exact words that someone has actually said.

 Test Yourself

Find the fragments in the following paragraph. Put *C* in the blank to the left if the numbered item is correct, but put *F* if the words are only a fragment. Then rewrite the entire paragraph to correct errors. Some sentences may be combined in your final version. Add transition words and phrases if necessary.

_____ 1. (1) Comfort is an idea of very modern times in Europe. (2) Although the

_____ 2. technical knowledge for being comfortable has been around for

_____ 3. thousands of years. (3) People in earlier times knowing a great deal about

_____ 4. comfort. (4) Nearly four thousand years ago, the inhabitants of

_____ 5. ancient Crete had sanitary plumbing. (5) Which can be seen today in

_____ 6. the ruins at Knossos. (6) The ancient Romans who had central hot-air heating to use during cold weather and incredibly luxurious baths.

_____ 7. (7) People in Europe during the Middle Ages lost the knowledge of how

_____ 8. to be comfortable. (8) No longer thinking that comfort or what we

_____ 9. think of as common cleanliness was necessary. (9) Dignity and prestige

_____ 10. were more important to the upper classes. (10) Who could have had

_____ 11. comfort. (11) Hard, straight chairs were preferred to padded chairs that caused the person sitting in them to relax and thus lose dignity

_____ 12. and respect. (12) Even more important, the chair being reserved

_____ 13. for those in power. (13) In the Middle Ages only the great had

_____ 14. chairs. (14) Even today, "the chair" showing the person in charge of a

_____ 15. meeting, the president or chairperson. (15) The one who directs the

_____ 16. proceedings. (16) Large buildings with great halls and huge rooms that were necessary to impress the lower classes were impossible to heat comfortably.

_____ 17. (17) Modern houses that are smaller than the great palaces of earlier times being much easier to heat to a comfortable temperature during

_____ 18. cold weather. (18) While Europeans were cold, uncomfortable, and dirty, people in other parts of the world that knew a great deal about cleanliness and comfort that was later rediscovered in Europe.

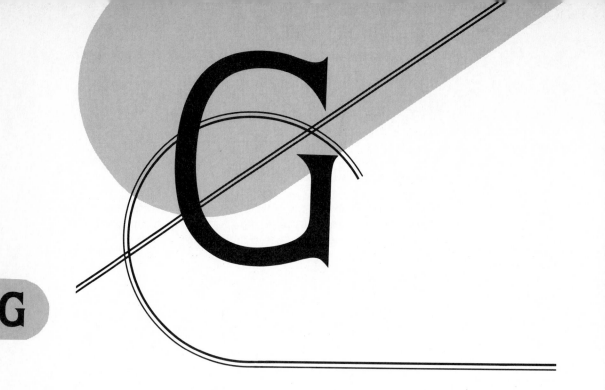

 Gender

Most nouns in English have the same form for male and female. The only pronouns that show sex distinction are *he* and *she* and the other forms related to them. *It* shows that sex is unknown, absent, or unimportant. English has a few words with two related forms, one for male and the other for female. (See **Word Formation**) Some words can be used for only one sex.

Some Words with Masculine and Feminine Forms

Masculine	*Feminine*
man	woman
widower	widow
host	hostess
god	goddess
steward	stewardess
waiter	waitress
lion	lioness
drum major	drum majorette

158

Some Words That Can Be Used for One Sex Only

People

Male	Female
father	mother
husband	wife
boy	girl
son	daughter
uncle	aunt
brother	sister
nephew	niece
gentleman	lady

Animals, Birds, and Fowl

Male	Female	Common Word
bull, steer*	cow	cattle (plural)
stallion, gelding*	mare	horse
boar	sow	pig, hog
ram	ewe	sheep
buck	doe	deer
cock, rooster, capon*	hen	chicken
gander	goose	goose
drake	duck	duck
dog	bitch	dog

* Used for a male that has been castrated.

Some people object to words for occupations and professions that are marked to indicate sex differences. *Flight attendant* is preferred to *steward* and *stewardess,* for example.   (See **Women, terms referring to**)

Adjectives do not change to show gender. Possessive pronouns, however, must show the sex of the person they stand for (antecedent), never the sex of the noun they modify.

masculine   masculine feminine
  Ralph brought   *his*   *mother* some roses. (*his* refers to *Ralph,* not to *mother*)

feminine   feminine masculine
Lucy   found   *her*   *brother* in the library. (*her* refers to *Lucy,* not to *brother*)

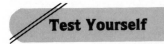

Test Yourself

Write the correct form in the blank to the left.

_____ 1. English words for family relationships are different from those of some
other languages; a young girl or woman may speak of _____ cousin whether
the cousin is male or female.

_____ 2. A boy can speak of _____ sister,

———— 3. and a man can speak of ——— mother.

———— 4. An aunt is always a girl or woman; an aunt may like to visit ——— niece or

nephew.

———— 5. A niece enjoys seeing ——— uncle or aunt; a niece is the daughter of a

brother or sister. Grandparents are two generations removed from their

grandchildren;

———— 6. often a grandmother is fonder of ——— grandson

———— 7. or ——— granddaughter

———— 8. than of ——— own children.

 Gerunds

Gerunds are *-ing* forms of the verb that are used as nouns. Gerunds name actions. Use them in a sentence the same ways nouns are used.   (see **Nouns**)

Subject:	*Learning* the new bus schedule is easy. *Making* new friends can be difficult.
Predicate *Nominative:*	My student job this year is *working* in the library. Paul's favorite sport is *running*.
Direct Object:	Paul likes *running*. Jim enjoys *playing* golf.
Object of a *Preposition:*	Paul likes most sports *except fishing*. Some people are afraid *of speaking* in public.
Objective *Complement:*	The police officer considered the offense *speeding*. The teacher called the children's play *learning*.

Although gerunds are used in clauses as nouns, they keep the qualities of verbs. Gerunds can be followed by direct objects, indirect objects, adverb modifiers, and predicate adjectives if their meaning allows these constructions.

Gerund		direct
Followed by	gerund	object
Direct Object:	*Learning* the new bus *schedule* is easy.
	Making	new *friends* can be difficult.

NOTE: When an article or an adjective modifies the gerund, the gerund is followed by a prepositional phrase instead of by a direct object.

Modifiers			prepositional
Before a	adjective	gerund	phrase
Gerund:	*Constant learning of new bus schedules* is annoying.		

Gerund		indirect	direct
Followed by		object	object
Indirect Object:	*Giving Jim* new golf *clubs* would please him.		
	Buying Paula new		*shoes* is expensive.

Gerund	adverb
Followed by	modifier
Adverb Modifier:	*Learning quickly* is easier for Pat than for Steve.
	Eating fast is bad for the digestion.

Gerund	
Followed by	predicate
Predicate	adjective
Adjective:	*Feeling happy* makes Ray sing.
	Being kind can be difficult.

Use a possessive pronoun before a gerund. Using an object form of the pronoun changes the meaning and emphasis of the sentence. Use an object pronoun if the -*ing* form is a participle that modifies the pronoun. (Both forms are grammatically correct; the emphasis is different.)

Object Pronoun	
Followed by	
Participle:	We heard *the dog barking*.
	We heard *it barking*. (emphasis on *it*—*barking* modifies *it*)
	We saw *John sleeping*.
	We saw *him sleeping*. (emphasis on *him*—*sleeping* modifies *him*)

Possessive Pronoun	
Followed by	
Gerund:	We heard the *dog's barking*.
	We heard *its barking*. (emphasis on *barking*—*its* modifies *barking*)
	We were annoyed by *John's sleeping*.
	We were annoyed by *his sleeping*. (emphasis on *sleeping*—*his* modifies *sleeping*)

Many compound nouns are made from a gerund and another noun. They usually show the *purpose* to which the head noun is put.

a drinking fountain—a fountain for drinking

shopping carts—carts for shopping

an ironing board—a board for ironing

a landing field—a field for landing

a parking lot—a lot for parking

a reading room—a room for reading

a swimming pool—a pool for swimming

a dining room—a room for dining

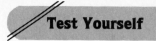

Test Yourself

1. Underline the gerunds in the following sentences.

    Making fire was a difficult task for primitive people. Most primitive

    people made fire by rubbing dry sticks together very fast until the

    friction sent off sparks. The sparks ignited dry material called tinder.

    Later striking flint and steel together to make sparks replaced the

    rubbing sticks. Because making fire was so difficult, guarding fire and

    keeping it going were important household tasks. Often borrowing

    coals from a neighbor was easier and faster than starting a new fire.

    According to writers of earlier times who wrote about making fire

    with flint and steel, the process could often take half an hour. Caring

    for fire was important. Changing to matches after they were invented

    in Sweden in 1844 made life easier for many people.

2. Make the following phrases into compound nouns that show purpose.

    a dog for hunting   a bag for sleeping
    licenses for building   shoes for running
    a car for racing   fixtures for lighting
    a board for cutting (food)   courses for training

3. Replace the underlined words in the following passage with a compound noun of
    purpose.

    The Scout troop drove to a (1) place for camping that was two hun-

    dred miles away from town. When they arrived, they had to unpack

    their (2) gear for camping before the sun went down. They put up

    their (3) tents for sleeping, unpacked their (4) bags to sleeping, and

    arranged their (5) utensils for cooking. They had brought (6) pots for cooking and (7) <u>pans</u> <u>for</u> <u>frying</u>. Before the sun went down, they also

had time to pitch their (8) <u>tent</u> <u>for</u> <u>dining</u>. All of the Scouts had

(9) <u>boots</u> <u>for</u> <u>hiking</u> and some had also brought (10) <u>gear</u> <u>for</u> <u>fishing</u>.

They knew they would have a good time.

H

Have

Have is both a main verb and an auxiliary (helping) verb. It is also used in many idiomatic phrases.

As a main verb, *have* has many different meanings. Many of its meanings are related to possessing, getting, accepting, and causing someone to do something, but there are many others also. Look up *have* in a dictionary if you see it used in a way that you do not understand. British and North American usages differ.

For uses of *have* as an auxiliary (helping) verb, see **Auxiliary Verbs; Operators** and **Tense.**

For word order of *have* in verb phrases, see **Finite Verbs.**

For special uses of *have* (*have to, had better*), see **Modals.**

For the use of *had* to replace *if* in contrary-to-fact clauses that have inverted word order, see **Conditional Sentences.**

For contracted forms of *have*, see **Contractions.**

Homonyms, see **Spelling**

Hyphens, see **Punctuation, hyphen**

164

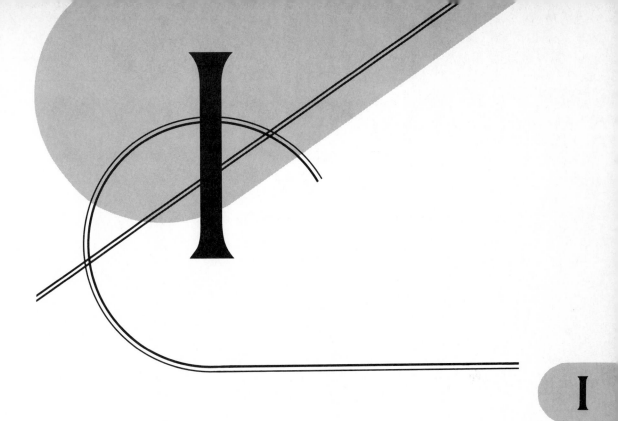

Indirect Object

An indirect object is always in a clause in which the main verb is a transitive active verb. The indirect object is almost always the person *to* whom or *for* whom something is done.

active verb	indirect object	direct object
Mary threw	*John*	the ball.

In the sentence above the indirect object comes before the direct object. It can also come after the direct object, following *to* or *for*. Most verbs can have the indirect object in either place.

	active verb	direct object	indirect object
Mary	threw	the ball	*to John.*

		indirect object	direct object
Mary	brought	*Fred*	a sandwich.

		direct object	indirect object
Mary	brought	a sandwich	*for Fred.*

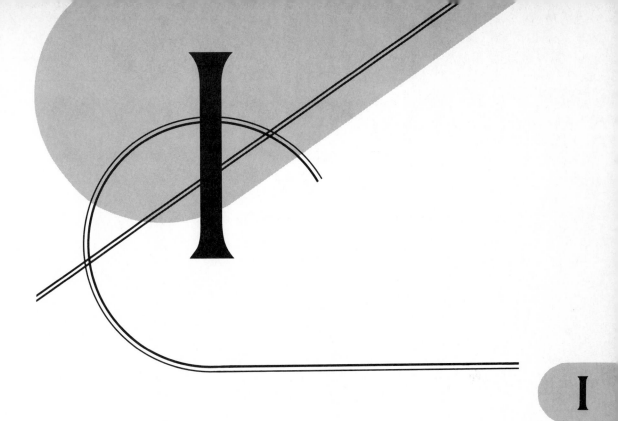

165

An object pronoun can be an indirect object.

	indirect object	direct object	
Mary threw	*him*	the ball.	(more common word order)

	direct object	indirect object	
Mary threw the ball to		*him.*	(possible word order)

A nonpersonal indirect object is possible with verbs such as *give, owe, pay,* and *send.*

	indirect object	direct object	
Frank paid the	*bank*	the amount that he owed.	

Word Order of Indirect Objects

1   With most verbs, if the *direct object* is a *noun,* the indirect object can be put either before it or after it.

subject	active verb	indirect object	noun direct object	indirect object
Paul	gave	*Jane*	the book.	
Paul	gave	*her*	the book.	
Paul	gave		the book	*to her.*

2   If the *direct object* is a *pronoun,* the indirect object usually comes after the direct object.

	direct object pronoun	indirect object
Paul gave	it	*to her.*
Wilma bought	them	*for John.*

3   If either the direct object or the indirect object is long or has many modifiers, it usually comes last. Put an indirect object that is modified by a clause or a long phrase after the direct object.

	direct object	indirect object
Paul gave	the book to	*the girl who was waiting for it.*
Terry cooked	dinner for	*the Boy Scout troop.*

Put a direct object that is a noun clause or that has an adjective clause in it after the indirect object.

	indirect object	direct object
Paul gave	*the girl*	the book that he had just bought.
Terry cooked	*the Boy Scouts*	a dinner that they would never forget.
Wilma asked	*them*	what the answer was.

	indirect object	direct object
The teacher explained to	*the class*	whatever they had difficulty understanding.

Avoid putting both a long direct object and a long indirect object in the same sentence. If you do, you are likely to confuse the reader.

4 Certain verbs must have *to* or *for* with the indirect object. The *to* or *for* phrase usually comes after the direct object. (For exceptions, see rule 3 above.) Some of the most common of these verbs are the following:

admit:	She *admitted* her mistakes *to* her mother.
communicate:	The dean *communicated* the decision *to* the student.
announce:	The judges *announced* the winner *to* the crowd.
dedicate:	The football team *dedicated* the game *to* their injured teammate.
describe:	The tourist *described* the beautiful view *to* (*for*) us.
entrust:	They *entrusted* their money *to* their best friend.
explain:	The professor *explained* the problem *to* (*for*) him.
indicate:	The guide *indicated* the way *to* me.
introduce:	Albert will *introduce* you *to* his friends.
mention:	Charlotte forgot to *mention* her accident *to* her husband.
outline:	The director *outlined* the work *to* (*for*) us.
prescribe:	The doctor *prescribed* medicine *for* the patient.
propose:	The chairman *proposed* a new plan *to* the committee.
prove:	The lecturer *proved* his theory *to* the audience.
recommend:	My friends have *recommended* this restaurant *to* me.
repeated:	I will *repeat* the problem *to* (*for*) you one more time.
report:	The new members of the team *reported* the problem *to* the coach.
return:	My brother *returned* the book *to* me.
suggest:	The doctor *suggested* a vacation *to (for)* him.

5 If a WH-word is the indirect object in a clause, the sentence will be a question. In that case, follow the word order for questions.   (see **Questions**)

	indirect object	direct object	
Informal:	*Who(m)*	did Terry cook dinner for?	

Formal:	For *whom* did Terry cook dinner?

6 With some verbs, the indirect object as well as the direct object can become the subject of a passive sentence.   (see **Passive Verbs**)

		indirect object	direct object
Active:	Paul gave	*Jane*	the book.
	Wilma asked	*them*	a question.

	subject
Passive:	*Jane* was given the book (by Paul). (indirect object becomes subject)

or

The book was given to Jane (by Paul). (direct object becomes subject)
They were asked what the question was. (indirect object becomes subject)

or

A *question* was asked. (direct object becomes subject)

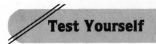

Test Yourself

A. In the following sentences, change the underlined words to pronouns. Which object, direct or indirect, is changed to a pronoun? Should the word order be changed?

1.   In sports and games, players and athletes score and win in many different ways; in

      many games and sports, players throw <u>other</u> <u>players</u> balls or other objects.

2.   People throw Frisbees to <u>their</u> <u>friends</u>.

3.   Some people even train <u>their</u> <u>dogs</u> to catch Frisbees.

4.   In a popular track event, athletes throw <u>javelins</u> as far as they can, and the judges

      measure <u>the</u> <u>distance</u> <u>of</u> <u>the</u> <u>throw</u>.

5.   In badminton, players hit <u>a</u> <u>birdie</u> over the net to the players on the opposite team.

      They hit <u>the</u> <u>other</u> <u>players</u> a birdie.

6.   In soccer, players pass <u>their</u> <u>teammates</u> the ball; they kick <u>the</u> <u>ball</u> toward the goal

      of the opposing team.

7.   In baseball and cricket, movements of the players give the teams points. In most

      other games, movements of the ball give <u>the</u> <u>teams</u> winning points.

8.   Judges give points to <u>the</u> <u>performers</u> for the movements of their bodies in sports

      such as gymnastics, diving, and skating.

9.   Winning runners must beat <u>their</u> <u>opponents</u> to the finish line.

10. "Handicaps" sometimes give <u>less</u> <u>skillful</u> <u>players</u> a chance to win.

B. In the following sentences underline words that are incorrect or in the wrong place and rewrite the sentences correctly.

1.   The boys playing in the street threw their brother Jim, who was walking with his arms

      full of groceries, a ball.

2. The boys threw him it.

3. Their brother quickly put down the groceries, caught the ball with one hand, and threw them it back.

4. Then he gave them a scare by chasing them down the street and finally threw the ball that he had caught with one hand to them.

5. The boys explained him that they were only joking.

6. Jim suggested them a better place to play ball.

7. Jim gave to them directions to the park.

Indirect Speech and **Indirect Questions**, see **Reported Speech**

Infinitives

The infinitive is the form of the verb that follows *to.* In every verb except *be,* the same form is used in the present tense for all persons except the third person singular. (see **Be**)

I, you, we, they *run;* but he run*s.*
I, you, we, they *have;* but he *has.*

> **1**   Use the infinitive phrase (*to* + infinitive)

as a noun:

Subject of the Clause:	*To know* Donna well is difficult.
Predicate Nominative:	To know Donna well is *to love* her.
Direct Object:	Ed hates *to study.*

After *prepositions,* however, use *-ing* forms except after *but, except,* and *about* in certain meanings.

		object of preposition	
Incorrect:	*After*	*to study*	Ed turned out the light.
Incorrect:	*Before*	*to get*	a driver's license, you must pass a test.

		object of preposition	
Correct:	*After*	*studying,*	Ed turned out the light.
Correct:	*Before*	*getting*	a driver's license, you must pass a test.

Correct: If you want to drive, you have no choice *but* / *except*   *to get*   a driver's license.

(object of preposition)

Correct: My sister is *about*   *to get*   her driver's license.

(object of preposition)

2   Use the infinitive phrase to modify a noun or pronoun:

(noun   modifier)

Correct: *Permission to drive* depends on getting a driver's license.

(noun   modifier)   *(pronoun modifier)*

Correct: Ed's *ability to study* is greater when he has a quiet place in *which   to do*   it.

3   Use the infinitive phrase to *complete it is + adjective*   (see **Adjectives, constructions that follow the verb,** and *It*):

(adjective   infinitive)

Correct: Sometimes it is *difficult   to get* a driver's license.

(adjective   infinitive)

Correct: It is not   *easy   to learn* another language well.

In formal writing, leave out *it is* and move the infinitive phrase to the beginning of the clause. An *-ing* form can also be the subject of the clause.

(subject)

Improved: *To get*   a driver's license is sometimes difficult.
            Getting a driver's license is sometimes difficult.

Improved: *To learn* another language well is not easy.
            Learning another language well is not easy.

4   Use the infinitive phrase after certain verbs of command or request   (see **Subjunctive**):

The conductor *told* the chorus *to sit* down.
The cashier *asked* John *to show* his driver's license as identification.
The captain *commanded* the company *to be* at ease.
The clerk *required* Pamela *to show* her insurance receipt before issuing her license.

5   Use the infinitive phrase to *complete many verb constructions*:

Some verbs must be followed by an infinitive phrase (with *to*), some verbs can be followed by an *-ing* form, and some verbs can be followed by a *bare infinitive* (without the *to*). Some verbs can be followed by either an infinitive phrase or by an *-ing* form.   (see **Infinitive/-ing choice**)

Verb followed by an infinitive phrase:

Mr. Jefferson *needs to leave* now.
Ben *offered to finish* the experiment today.

Verb followed by an infinitive phrase or by an *-ing* form:

Mrs. Parker *likes to go* shopping on Saturdays.
Mrs. Parker *likes going* shopping on Saturdays.

6 Use the *bare infinitive* (simple verb form)
a after modals:

Ed $\begin{Bmatrix} must \\ can \\ will \end{Bmatrix}$ *study* in California next year.

The weather $\begin{Bmatrix} will \\ could \\ might \end{Bmatrix}$ *be* worse tomorrow.

b Use the *bare infinitive* after *do, does,* or *did* if the main verb in the clause cannot be an operator   (see **Operators**):

Question: Why *did* Ed *study* in Texas last year?

Negative Statement: Ed *did not study* in New York last year.

Question: Why *does* everyone *love* Donna?

Negative Statement: Marcia *does not love* Donna.

c Use a *bare infinitive* after certain verbs such as *make* and *let*   (see **Infinitive/-ing Choice**):

John's brother *let* him *borrow* his car.
The bank *made* both of us *sign* the check.

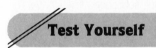

Test Yourself

A. Look at the underlined words. In some places, *to* is used as an infinitive and is followed by the simple verb form. In other places, *to* is a preposition and is followed by a noun, a pronoun, or a verbal noun (gerund). In the blank to the left, put *I* if *to* is an infinitive, but put *P* if *to* is a preposition.

_____ 1. A "fixed star" is one that never seems <u>to</u> <u>move</u>.

_____ 2. Unlike the sun, which appears <u>to</u> <u>rise</u> and <u>set</u> in the sky every day,

_____ 3. fixed stars do not appear <u>to</u> <u>change</u> their positions in relation

_____ 4. <u>to</u> <u>one</u> <u>another</u>.

_____ 5. Compared <u>to</u> <u>the</u> <u>distance</u> between the earth and the sun, the distance from

_____ 6. the earth <u>to</u> <u>the</u> <u>nearest</u> <u>star</u> is enormous.

_____ 7. The distance from earth to <u>Proxima</u> <u>Centauri</u>, the nearest star, is a little

more than four light-years.

_____ 8. We are not accustomed to <u>thinking</u> about such great distances.

_____ 9. We can understand why the fixed stars do not appear to <u>have</u> any motion

in the heavens when we realize how far away they really are.

_____ 10. Only when astronomers study these stars over a long period of time and

make very accurate measurements to <u>plot</u> their positions can their move-

ments be shown.

_____ 11. In addition to <u>plotting</u> the movements of stars, astronomers also keep

accurate records of their changes in brightness.

_____ 12. For thousands of years astronomers have tried to <u>record</u> accurately the

positions of heavenly bodies.

B. Put _measure, to measure,_ or _measuring_ in the blank in the sentence. Then copy the correct form in the blank to the left.

_____ 1. It is important to be able _____ great distances accurately.

_____ 2. Astronomers try _____ accurately.

_____ 3. Scientific advances let astronomers _____ more accurately today than they

were able to do in the past.

_____ 4. Clear atmospheric conditions are essential _____ accurately.

_____ 5. Smog and other forms of air pollution make accurate _____ more difficult.

_____ 6. Without proper atmospheric conditions, astronomers cannot _____ accu-

rately.

———— 7.   Astronomers have to learn how ——— great distances.

———— 8.   Ancient astronomers did not ——— as accurately as modern astronomers do.

In the sentences above, are there any places that <u>measurement</u> or <u>measurements</u> could be used?

Infinitive/-*ing* Choice

An infinitive or an -*ing* form may be added to certain verbs to complete their meanings. Deciding whether to use the infinitive or the -*ing* form is difficult. You may also need to put in a person or a pronoun referring to a person. You may use all the constructions with a few verbs, but not with most verbs. With some verbs a different construction changes the meaning. In general, the *to* form shows purpose. The -*ing* form is more general, more descriptive, and less active.   (See **Gerunds, Infinitives, and Participles**)

1   *Infinitive (to + verb) Constructions*

   a   An infinitive form can follow the main verb. The subject of the main verb is also the subject of the infinitive.

subject +	verb	+ infinitive
Susan	likes	to go.
Mary	wanted	to go.

   b   An infinitive form can follow a noun or pronoun that is not the subject of the main verb. (If the stated subject of an infinitive is a pronoun, that pronoun must be an object pronoun.)

subject +	verb	pronoun + noun or	+ infinitive
Susan	wants	*us*	to go.
Mary	wanted	*John*	to go.

   c   An infinitive form can follow a noun or pronoun that is not the subject of the main verb, as in **b**, but the only infinitive form that can be used with these verbs is *to be*.   (See **Objective Complement** for a similar construction without *to be*.)

Susan considered the book *to be* useless.
Mary declared Paul *to be* the winner.

A few verbs follow the patterns shown in **a, b,** or **c** except that you must leave out the *to*. These verbs are noted in the lists as *bare* or *unmarked* infinitives.

They made us *go*.
They let us *go*.

NOTE: The patterns given in the table—**a b c**—do not apply to all meanings.

TABLE 1   Some Verbs That Can Be Followed by Infinitives

† advise (b)	enable (b)	learn (a)	report (b)
agree (a)	encourage (b)	let (b bare)	request (b)
† allow (b)	expect (a,b)	† like (a,b)	† require (b)
appoint (b)		† listen to (b bare)	resolve (a)
ask (a,b)	fail (a)	love (a,b)	return
† attempt (a)	† fear (a)		[go back] (a)
	† feel (c)	make (b bare)	return
† be (a)	† find (c)	manage (a)	[take back] (b)
† bear (a)	† forbid (b)	mean	
beg (a,b)	force (b)	[intend] (a,b)	say (a)
† begin (a)	† forget (a)		† see (b bare)
believe (c)		need (a,b)	seem (a)
bother (a)	go	neglect (a)	send (b)
	[purpose] (a)	notify (b)	† start (a)
call on (b)	guess (c)		stop (a)
care (a)		offer (a)	suppose (c)
† cause (b)	happen (a)	order (b)	
challenge (b)	† hate (a,b)		teach (b)
choose (a,b)	hear (b bare)	† permit (b)	tell (b)
claim (a)	help (a,b,b bare)	persuade (b)	tempt (b)
come (a)	hesitate (a)	plan (a)	tend (a)
command (b)	hire (b)	pledge (a)	think (c)
compel (b)	hope (a)	† prefer (a,b)	train (b)
consent (a)		prepare (a,b)	trust (b)
† consider (c)	imagine (c)	pretend (a)	try (a)
† continue (a)	induce (b)	promise (a)	
	inform (b)	prove	† understand (c)
dare (a,b)	instruct (b)	(a with *to be,* c)	urge (b)
decide (a)	intend (a,b)		used to (a bare)
declare (c)	† investigate (b)	† quit (a)	
demand (a)	invite (b)		wait (a)
† deserve (a)		refuse (a)	want (a,b)
desire (a)	judge (c)	regret (a)	warn (b)
determine (a,c)		† remember (b)	wish (a,b)
discover (c)	know (c)	remind (b)	
drive (b)	lead (b)		

† These verbs can also be followed by an *-ing* form (see Table 3). See note following Table 3 about *remember/forget* and verbs of the senses.

NOTE: Modals are not included in this table.   (see **Modals**)

Test Yourself

A. Fill in the blanks in the following sentences with the correct infinitive form of the verb at the end of the sentence. Then copy the correct form and put *a*, *b*, or *bare* in the blank to the left to show the infinitive construction used in the sentence.

_____   1.   Many people do not want _____ in areas where floods are common. (live)

_____   2.   Flooding makes people _____ their houses and livestock. (leave)

_____ 3. In some areas of the world such as near the Mississippi River in the United

States and near the North Sea in The Netherlands, people trust dikes or

levees that are walls of earth _____ floods away. (keep)

_____ 4. Sometimes farmers and other property owners refuse _____

_____ 5. because they hope _____ their property by staying and taking care of it.

(leave, save)

_____ 6. People who choose _____ after the authorities have

_____ 7. told them _____ may lose their lives as well as their property. (stay, leave)

_____ 8. The police and military units that often help in natural disasters do not

force the residents _____ but let the people who live there

_____ 9. _____ if they insist. (leave, stay)

_____ 10. After a flood has subsided, residents return _____ their lives and clean up

the debris the flood has left behind. (resume)

More Constructions That Must Be Followed by the Infinitive

1 _Purpose:_ Many verbs can be followed by _in order to_. Sometimes _in order to_
is shortened and becomes _to_. In expressing purpose, both _to_ and _in order to_ are
followed by an infinitive verb form.

The tourists rented a boat _to go_ on the lake.
The tourists rented a boat _in order to go_ on the lake.
The men escaped _to_ avoid punishment.
The men escaped _in order to_ avoid punishment.

Test Yourself

B. In the following sentences, cross out "in order" and leave "to" as the infinitive of
purpose.

1. Engineers build dams in order to control flooding below the dam.
2. They also build dikes and levees in order to keep the water in the river banks when
    floods come.

3. Engineers in The Netherlands have been building dikes for hundreds of years in order to keep out the waters of the North Sea.

2 **Complement:** *be* + adjective + infinitive. After an adjective following the main verb *be* (and sometimes after other linking verbs) an infinitive phrase can be used. (see **Adjectives**)

	verb	adjective	infinitive
The results of this experiment	are	difficult	to get.
This book	is	easy	to understand.
Our friends	were	pleased	to see us.
My friends	were	disappointed	to miss you.

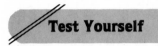
Test Yourself

C. Complete the following sentences with the correct form of *be* and the verb and adjective given.

1. Lowlands near the deltas of great rivers _____ from flooding. (difficult, protect)

2. Accurate weather forecasts _____ people about dangers from flooding. (necessary, warn)

3. Accurate weather forecasts _____ . (easy, make—negative)

4. Knowing more about the earth's weather patterns from studying satellite pictures _____ prevent loss of life and property from floods. (likely, help)

3 **After WH-words:** If a WH-word follows the main verb, an infinitive phrase can follow the WH-word and include the meaning of *can* or *should*. (see **Reported Speech**) The two classes of these verbs are shown by *a* and *b*.

a The subject of the main verb is also the subject of the infinitive.

subject +	verb	+ WH-word +	infinitive	
They	asked	*which*	book *to buy.*	(they can/should buy)
We	are deciding	*when*	*to go.*	(we can/should go)

b The subject of the main verb is not the subject of the infinitive, but another noun or pronoun before the WH-word is the subject of the infinitive. If the subject of the infinitive is a pronoun, use an object pronoun.

subject +	verb	noun or + pronoun +	WH-word +	infinitive	
They	told	*us*	which	book *to buy.*	(we can/should buy)
We	are advising	*them*	how	*to go.*	(they can/should do)

TABLE 2   Some Verbs That Can Be Followed by WH-Words + Infinitives

advise (b)	forget (a)	know (a)	† show (b)
ask (a)	guess (a)	learn (a)	teach (b)
consider (a)	hear (a)	† observe (a)	tell (b)
decide (a)		plan (a)	think (a)
discover (a)	imagine (a)	remember (a)	understand (a)
	inform (b)		
† explain (a)	† inquire (a)		† wonder (a)
† explain to (b)	investigate (a)	say (a)	
		see (a)	

† These verbs are not in Table 1. All other verbs in this list also appear in Table 1.

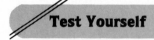

Test Yourself

D. Change the clause that begins with a WH-word into a WH-word + infinitive.

1. Governments ask engineers where they should build dams for flood control.

2. Governments advise residents of floodplains what they ought to do in case of flooding.

3. Residents of floodplains need to plan how they can protect life and property in case of flooding.

4. When ordinary people understand what they can do to help themselves, they cooperate with authorities who are trying to help them.

2   *-ing Forms*

Many verbs can be followed by *-ing* forms.

  a The *-ing* form can follow directly after the main verb.

subject +   verb   + -ing form
John   delayed   *going.*

  b The *-ing* form can follow a noun or pronoun different from the subject of the main verb. If the word before the *-ing* form is a pronoun, use a possessive form. (see **Gerunds**)

subject +   verb   + pronoun + -ing form
John   delayed   their   going
Martha   appreciated   his   *helping* her.

Use the possessive form of nouns in formal writing.

Martha appreciated *John's* helping her.

Use the object pronoun after verbs of the senses.

Martha watched *him* washing the car.
Martha noticed *him* cleaning the lab.

TABLE 3   Some Common Verbs That Can Be Followed by -ing Forms

admit (a)	detest (a,b)	keep (a)	purpose (a)
† advise (a,b)	dislike (a,b)	keep from (a)	put off (a,b)
† allow (a)	dread (a,b)	keep (him) from (a)	
appreciate (a,b)	endure (a,b)		† quit (a)
† attempt (a)	enjoy (a,b)	† like (a,b)	
avoid (a)	escape	† listen to (b)	recall (a,b)
	[avoid] (a)	love (a,b)	regret (a)
† be (a)	excuse (b)		† remember (a,b)
† bear		make (a)	† require (a)
[endure] (b)	favor (a,b)	mean	resent (a,b)
begin (a)	† fear (a,b)	[signify] (a,b)	resist (a,b)
believe (a,b)	† feel (b)	mind	resume (a,b)
	† find (b)	[object to] (a)	risk (a,b)
† cause (a,b)	finish (a,b)	miss (a)	
complete (a)	† forbid (a,b)		save (a,b)
consider (a)	† forget (a,b)	need (a)	† see (b)
† continue (a)		neglect (a)	stand (a,b)
control (a,b)	get [start] (a)		† start (a,b)
	go—activity (a)	object to (a,b)	stop (a,b)
decrease (a,b)	give up (a)	omit (a,b)	suggest (a,b)
defend (b)			
defer (a,b)	† hate (a,b)	† permit (a)	† try (a)
delay (a,b)		postpone (a,b)	
deny (a)	† imagine (a,b)	† prefer (a)	† understand (b)
describe (a,b)	† increase (a)		
† deserve (a)	† investigate (b)		
despise (a)			

† These verbs can also be followed by an infinitive (see Table 1). See notes below about *remember/forget* and verbs of the senses.

Test Yourself

E. Fill in the blanks in the following sentences with the correct form of the verb at the end of the sentence. Then copy the correct form in the blank to the left.

_____ 1.   Some engineers favor _____ large dams and levees to control

_____ 2.   _____ . (build, flood)

_____ 3.   Other scientists believe _____ trees and _____ soil

_____ 4. _____ erosion and runoff at the source is better. (plant, control)

_____ 5. Ecologists resist _____ large areas for highways and parking lots because

water in these areas cannot soak into the ground. (pave)

_____ 6. When engineers and ecologists disagree, governments may delay their

_____ to get the opinions of the people who will be affected. (plan)

_____ 7. Engineers and ecologists consider _____ dangers from floods an important

goal. (avoid)

Problems in Choosing Between the Infinitive and the -ing Form

1 The *-ing* form can be used after prepositions. (Because certain words can introduce either a prepositional phrase or a clause, be careful not to use an *-ing* form as the only verb form in a clause.)

	subject verb -ing form
Correct:	He fears going.

	subject verb preposition -ing form
Correct:	He is afraid of going.

	subject verb infinitive
Correct:	He is afraid to go.

	infinitive
Incorrect:	Before *to go* she will see you.

	preposition -ing form
Correct:	Before *going* she will see you.

(*Before* is a preposition.)

	subordinating conjunction subject verb
Correct:	Before she *goes,* she will see you.

(*Before* is a subordinating conjunction.)

2 *For* can introduce an infinitive with a stated subject.

They are waiting *for us to go.*
(*Us* is the subject of *to go.*)

NOTE: A pronoun that is the subject of an infinitive must be the object form: *us,* not *we.*

3 Sometimes *to* is a preposition. When it is, it can have an *-ing* form following it instead of an infinitive. To tell which form to use, ask this question: Can I put *that thing* or *that one* after *to*? or can I use *do that* after *to*? Does the *used to* mean *accustomed to*? or does it show habitual action in the past?

The student became used to *that one.* (If *that one* completes the idea correctly, use -*ing* form.)

He became used to *working* hard.

The student became used to *getting* up early.

He used to *that one.* (*That one* does not follow; try *do that.*)

Correct: He used to *do that.*

Correct: He used *to work* hard. (If *do that* works, use the infinitive to show repeated action in the past.) He used *to get up* late.

4   Certain phrases with *to* as a preposition may be followed by an -*ing* form.

accustom(ed) to going	look forward to going
adapt(ed) to going	pay (paid) attention to going
adjust(ed) to going	put a stop to going
agreeable to going	preferable to going
alternative to going	resistant to going
change(d) from . . .	solution to losing
to . . .	submit(ted) to training
(in) contrast(ed) to going	
introduce(d) to driving	
limit(ed) to going	

5   In a comparison, put the -*ing* form both before and after the adjective if possible.   (see **Parallel Structure**)

Going up a ladder is **easier** than   *coming* down.
Succeeding is   **preferable** to *failing.*

Test Yourself

F. In the following sentences choose the correct form from those in parentheses. Put it in the blank in the sentence and then copy it in the blank to the left.

_____   1. Soil that washes into riverbeds increases the chances that rivers will

_____ their banks. (overflow, to overflow, overflowing)

_____   2. Engineers used to _____ the harmful effects of dam and

_____   3. see _____ them only as a benefit. (ignore, ignoring; build, to build, building)

_____   4. People who live in floodplains become used to _____ with danger. (live, living)

_____   5. One alternative _____ with danger is _____ away

_____   6.   from an area that is likely to be flooded. (live, to live, to living, living; move, to moving, moving)

_____   7.   Before _____ to leave an area that is liable to flood, people usually have had several bad experiences with floods. (decide, to decide, deciding)

_____   8.   People resist _____ from dangerous areas because other places to live are not available or are far from friends and families. (move, moving, to moving)

_____   9.   For some people _____ in the same place is easier than moving away from it. (stay, to stay, staying)

_____   10.   In some parts of the world, people have learned how _____ yearly floods. (predict, to predict, predicting)

_____   11.   Farmers do not try _____ some of these floods but let

_____   12.   them _____ new, rich soil to the area. (control, to control, controlling; bring, to bring, bringing)

G. Correct the errors in the following sentences. Cross out and change words that are wrong. Put the correct forms in the blanks to the left.

_____   1.   Flooding causes people moving from their homes.

_____   2.   Engineers who design flood-control projects avoid to damage the environment as much as possible.

_____   3.   Engineers investigate many places build dams before to decide on

_____   4.   the best place.

_____   5.   People who own land where dams are to be built object to give up

_____   6.   their land in order to having it turned into a lake.

_____   7.   When people know what to expect, move is easier.

_____ 8. The agencies that plan how develop the water resources of a nation must also consider human problems.

_____ 9. Flood control is a very complicated process when the difficulty of move people is added to all the other problems.

_____ 10. Sometimes engineers, ecologists, and social workers must all understand how working together.

6   You can use either the infinitive or -*ing* form after *forget* and *remember,* but the meaning is different. The -*ing* form shows *memory* of action before the time of the action of the main verb.

Frank remembers *going.* (Frank has a memory that he went.)
Frank forgot *having borrowed* the book. (Frank had no memory that he had already borrowed the book.)

The infinitive shows *action* or *lack of action* after the main verb.

Frank remembered *to go.* (Frank remembered and then he went.)
Frank forgot *to go.* (Frank did not go.)

Some evidence suggests that certain other verbs are completed by infinitives or gerunds according to the same principles that control *forget* and *remember.* These verbs are followed by an infinitive when the action of the infinitive is not complete at the time of the main verb, but they are followed by an -*ing* form when the action is complete or going on at the time of the main verb.

Karen *stopped to eat* because she was hungry. (She had not yet eaten when she stopped.)
Karen *stopped eating* ice cream because she wanted to lose weight. (She was already eating ice cream at certain times before she stopped.)

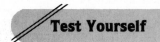

Test Yourself

H. In the following sentences, use the correct verb form after *forget* or *remember.* Then write the correct form in the blank to the left.

_____ 1. Ben did not remember _____ to the dentist yesterday. (go)

_____ 2. Ben now remembers _____ the appointment two weeks ago. (make)

_____ 3. He remembers _____ that he would have time to go to the dentist on the fifteenth of the month. (think)

_____ 4. He remembered _____ the appointment down on his calendar. (write)

_____ 5. But he forgot _____ the appointment in the pocket diary he carries with him. (write)

_____ 6.   On the day of the appointment, Ben was so busy he forgot

_____ 7.   _____ in his diary and he forgot _____ . (look, go)

_____ 8.   He doesn't remember _____ in his diary at all yesterday. (look)

7   You can use either an infinitive or an *-ing* form with verbs of the senses. The subject of the infinitive or *-ing* form is usually expressed. *To* is always left out. The bare infinitive emphasizes the completion of a single act; the *-ing* form shows a process and/or emphasizes the duration of the action.

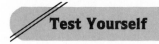

subject	verb	object/subject	infinitive	-ing
Brenda	saw / will hear / is watching	him	go	/ going

We watched the flag bearers *dip* the flags as they passed the reviewing stand. (one action)
We watched the flags *flying* at the top of the stadium. (continuing action)

Verbs of the senses that can follow this pattern:

feel	listen to	observe	see	notice
hear	look at	overhear	smell	watch

Test Yourself

I. In the following sentences, underline the verbs of the senses and the verb forms that follow them. Be prepared to explain the choice of the bare infinitive or the *-ing* form.

1.   The lion stalking her prey watched the herd of antelope grazing peacefully.

2.   The lion noticed a newborn gazelle struggle to its feet.

3.   The lion saw the baby's mother waiting for it.

4.   Hearing its mother calling, the baby struggled to keep up with her.

Interjections

An interjection is a word that shows strong comment or emotion. An interjection is not a grammatical part of its clause, and it is always followed by an exclamation mark or a comma.   (see **Punctuation, exclamation mark**)

Oh! There you are.   **or**   Oh, there you are.
Well! Where were you?   **or**   Well, where were you?
Help! The baby fell in the lake!

Do not confuse *oh* with *O*. Use *oh* as an exclamation. Use *O* in formal direct address, in prayer, and in literary usage (often in poetry and personification). Always capitalize *O* and never put a punctuation mark directly after it. (Direct address of things that are not living is called *apostrophe.*)

O God, grant our prayers.
O mighty ocean waves!
O powerful western fallen star!

Test Yourself

Cross out words that are incorrect and write the correct form above them. Some sentences may be correct.

1. O, why did you buy that kind of bread?

2. Oh my darling, will you marry me?

3. Oh, there you are.

4. Where, o where, did I leave my hat?

5. Oh, God, bless this solemn occasion.

Interrupters

Interrupters are transitional words or phrases. They are often called *conjunctive adverbs.* (see **Clauses, connecting words**) Learn these facts about them:

1. They show the relationship between ideas within a sentence or between sentences.
2. They cannot replace coordinating conjunctions between independent clauses unless you use a semicolon between the clauses.
3. They are often set off by commas within their own clause (single words of four letters or fewer are not usually set off by commas).
4. They are movable within their own clause.

To Add Information and Reasons	*To Compare*	*To Show Cause and Effect*	*To Contrast*
also	by comparison	accordingly	however
besides	likewise	as a consequence	instead
equally	similarly	as a result	in spite of that
further	in the same way	consequently	anyhow
furthermore	*To Show Logical Order*	then	nevertheless
in addition	first, second, . . .	therefore	on the contrary
moreover	finally	thus	on the other hand
too	last		otherwise
			still

To Explain, Give Reasons	To Summarize	To Show Chronological Order	To Show Concession
actually	in all	subsequently	admittedly
admittedly	in a word	later	after all
certainly	in brief	next	all the same
for example	briefly	after that	at any rate
in fact	in short	afterwards	however
indeed	in summary	then	in any case
really		now	in spite of that
of course		nowadays	nevertheless
that is		concurrently	still
		simultaneously	
		soon	
		first	
		formerly	
		earlier	
		previously	
		before that	

NOTE: *Actually, indeed,* and *in fact* often introduce something you believe is true. But if what comes earlier is not true, these words show contrast.

BE CAREFUL: The most common writing errors with interrupters are comma splices and run-on sentences. Interrupters alone cannot join independent clauses. You must put a semicolon or a comma and a coordinating conjunction between the clauses in addition to the interrupter.   (see **Clauses** and **Comma Splices**)

Differences Between Coordinating Conjunctions and Interrupters

Punctuation and Word Order:

Coordinating Conjunctions

1. Put a comma before a coordinating conjunction that joins clauses.

2. Do not separate a coordinating conjunction **from the rest of its own clause** with a comma.

3. Put a coordinating conjunction first in its clause when using it to join clauses.

Interrupters

1. Put a semicolon between two or more independent clauses if a coordinating conjunction is not used.

2. Separate an interrupter from the rest of its own clause with a comma or commas if it is a long word or a phrase.

3. Move an interrupter within its own clause for emphasis and rhythm.

Result:

Examples of Coordinating Conjunctions and Interrupters

Jeff left his apartment very dirty when he moved out of it, *so* he lost his deposit.

Jeff left his apartment very dirty when he moved out of it; *consequently,* he lost his deposit.

Time: Jeff moved out of his apartment last week(,) *and* later he moved in with Warren.

Jeff moved out of his apartment last week(;) *subsequently,* he moved in with Warren.

Explanation: Marian thought she had lost her keys(;) *actually,* she had left them in the door.

Contrast: Marian thought she had lost her keys(,) *but* she found them later.

Marian thought she had lost her keys(;) *however,* she found them later.

Marian thought she had lost her keys(;) she found them later(,) *however.*

Further Explanation: All the club members agree to the proposal(,) *and* they are very happy about it.

All the club members agree to the proposal(;)

in fact(,)
indeed(,) } they are very happy about it.
actually(,)

Contrast: We thought we had enough money for the trip Saturday(,) *but* everyone must pay more.

We thought we had enough money for the trip Saturday(;)

in fact(,)
actually(,) everyone must pay more.

Test Yourself

Punctuate the following sentences correctly.

1. Fruits are the seeds of plants together with the parts of the plant that enclose the seeds in addition in common use the word *fruit* is usually used for the fleshy, pulpy tissue that surrounds the seeds.

2. *Vegetables* however grow on plants that die at the end of one growing season.

3. Vegetables may also be other parts of the plant for example they may be roots, stems, or leaves.

4. Most people think of tomatoes as vegetables however they are botanically fruits.

5. Furthermore the fact that tomato plants live only one year also makes people think of them as vegetables.

6. Fruits can also be classified according to where they grow that is some grow in tropical climates, others grow in subtropical climates, and still others grow in temperate climates.

Intransitive Verbs, see **Sentence Patterns**

Inverted Word Order

Inverted word order means moving a word, phrase, or clause out of its usual position in a sentence. (See **Conditional Sentences; Direct Speech; Operators,** and **Questions**)

Irregular Verbs, see **Verbs, irregular forms**

It, Impersonal Use

Use *it* as the subject of the sentence in impersonal constructions that show temperature, weather, and time.

It is hot.
It is raining.
It is getting late.
It is too early to go now.
It is time to go now.

It sometimes replaces a subject that comes later in the sentence.

It is true that Gerald is my brother.
(That Gerald is my brother is true.)
It is impossible to decide now.
(To decide now is impossible.)
It is a good idea to find out now.
(To find out now is a good idea.)

Using *it is* . . . is often wordy. Avoid this construction in formal writing if you can. Put the true subject in the subject position at the beginning of the sentence. Do not use *it* to refer to the whole idea of a clause.

Incorrect: Because Kathy oversleeps, she has to drive too fast on her way to work; *it* is so dangerous I am afraid to ride with her.

Improve the sentence above by putting *her driving* in place of *it.*

Improved: Because Kathy oversleeps, she has to drive too fast on her way to work; *her driving* is so dangerous I am afraid to ride with her.

Incorrect: When children watch too much violence on TV, *it* may affect their behavior.

In the sentence above, *it* has no antecedent (word that it stands for). Improve the sentence above by rewriting it completely.

Improved: Watching too much violence on TV may affect children's behavior.

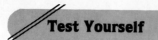

Rewrite the following sentences, avoiding the impersonal use of *it* wherever you can improve the style and make the sentence less wordy by doing so.

1. It is a good thing that you wrote us about your problems with your last shipment of software.

2. It is true that our offices will be closed for the Columbus Day weekend.

3. However, it is not true that you will be unable to reach a service representative until after the holiday.

4. If you call our Chicago office today, it will be possible to arrange a service call Friday morning.

5. When customers tell us about their problems, it is easier for us to correct them.

Markers

Markers are endings and other changes in words that show a change in their meaning and use in the sentence. Regular markers in English are spelled *-s*, *-'s*, and *-s'* on nouns and *-s*, *-ed*, and *-ing* on verbs. The unmarked form of a word is often called the *base word*.

Noun: *Boy* (unmarked) can be changed to boy*s*. (plural)
                                                        boy*'s*. (singular possessive)
                                                        boys*'*. (plural possessive)

Verb: *Walk* (unmarked) can be changed to
              walk*s* (third person singular, present tense)
              walk*ed* (past and past participle)
              walk*ing* (present participle and gerund)

Markers can be irregular. (see **Nouns** and **Verbs, irregular**) Always look in a dictionary if you have any doubt about the correct form. If no irregular form is shown after the base form in the dictionary, you can assume that changes in the word are regular. (See **Spelling** for rules for adding endings.)

189

Clause Markers

A word that introduces a dependent clause is sometimes called a clause marker. Other terms are often used to identify special kinds of clause markers. *Relative pronouns* introduce dependent clauses that function as nouns or adjectives. *WH-words* introduce direct and indirect questions. *Subordinating conjunctions* introduce dependent clauses that function as adverbs.   (see **Clauses, dependent** and **WH-Words**)

Everyone knows someone *who* talks too much. (relative pronoun)
Catch the hat *that* is blowing down the street. (relative pronoun)
The hat fell in the mud *after* the wind blew it away. (subordinating conjunction)

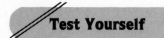

Test Yourself

A. Underline the noun and the verb markers in the following sentences.

1. Peaches are a kind of fruit that originated in Asia.

2. Travelers carried fruit to ancient Persia.

3. Alexander the Great's armies introduced peaches from Persia to Europe.

4. Spanish ships transported the first peaches to the Americas.

B. Underline the clause markers in the following sentences.

1. The British Navy discovered that sailors who drank lime juice did not get scurvy, which

    was a disease common among sailors who were away at sea for many months.

2. Since British sailors drank lime juice, they were called "limeys."

3. Much later scientists discovered that sailors who did not get the vitamins in fresh fruits

    and vegetables developed scurvy because their diet was deficient in vitamin C.

Mass Nouns, see **Countable** and **Uncountable Nouns**

Modals

Can, could, may, might, shall, should, ought to, will, would, and *must* differ in form and meaning from other verbs. (The modal forms of *need* and *dare* are used so rarely in the United States that they will not be considered here.) Related verb phrases are *be able to, have to, had better, used to,* and *be used to.*

Forms and Constructions of Modals

Learn the following facts about modals:

1. Modals never change—no *-s* in the third person singular present.
2. Modals have no *-ing* form.
3. Modals can show the future (except *can* in the sense of ability) and some show the past by using adverbs.
4. Modals act as operators. (see **Operators**)
5. Modals can never be followed directly by another modal.
6. Modals must be followed by bare infinitives (simple forms) of other verbs in verb phrases.
7. Modals never follow directly after *to*.

Most modals can be contracted with *not*, and some can be contracted with the pronoun. (see **Contractions**)

Back-shift in reported speech is irregular and differs in some cases for different meanings of the same modal. (see **Reported Speech,** p. 330, for an explanation of *back-shifting*)

Meanings of Modals

Modals show many meanings that are shown by the subjunctive or another mood in many other languages. They generally do not show a happening or event but show thoughts about actions: Permission, for example, means that you are allowed to do something but not necessarily that you do it.

Permission:	*May* we cook? (Do you object? or Is there a regulation against cooking?)
Advisability:	*Should* we cook? (Is cooking a good idea?)
Necessity:	*Must we cook?* (Are we required to cook?)

The questioners are not necessarily cooking at the time they ask the questions above. We do not know for sure whether or not they will cook in the future, although the implication here of *may* is that they want to cook, and if the answer is "yes," they probably will cook. The implication of *must* is that the questioners do not want to cook, and if the answer is "no," they probably will not.
Adverbs often show the time setting of modals.

Could (in the meaning of *ability*)
The chef could cook tomorrow. (future)
The chef could cook every day. (present habitual)
The chef could cook yesterday. (past)

The tense of other verbs in the sentence can also show the time setting.

The chef could cook while the waiters *are* setting the tables.
The chef could cook well when he *came* here last year.

Without an adverb, modals can mean "now and in the future."

We should respect our parents. (present and future)

Although the *can/could, may/might, will/would,* and *shall/should* pairs sometimes have a present/past relation, *could, might, would,* and *should* have special meanings that do not always correspond to those of the "present" part of the pair.

Never use a modal directly after *to*.

Can and Could

Use *can* and *could* for ability, possibility, and permission.

1   *Ability* (*is able to, is capable of,* and sometimes *knows how to*) *Be able to* can replace *can* if more precise tense distinctions are needed, and must be used for *capability* in the future.

can in the present and future negative and positive (is able to)

Students taking calculus *can* do these problems easily, but students taking algebra *cannot.*
   (Note spelling of *cannot.*)
The new attendant *can* start working tomorrow.

Use *be able to* instead of *can* in the future for learned ability.

The new counselor *will be able to* swim better when he takes more lessons.
The new employee *will be able* to use the computer after she finishes the training course.
Students who have taken calculus *will be able* to do these problems easily on the test tomorrow,
   but others will not.

Back-shift into reported speech in the past. (see p. 330)

The professor thought that the students *could* do these problems easily.

Past:	At one time the students *could (were able to)* do these problems by themselves.
Past Negative:	At one time the students *could* not *(were not able to)* do these problems by themselves.

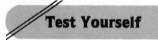

Test Yourself

A. Correct the errors in the following sentences.

1.   Paul can swim better when he finishes his swimming course.

2.   Last summer he thought he can swim well, but once he almost drowned.

3.   Then he decided he would take swimming lessons at his college if he can.

4.   He can go to the first class tomorrow if he could buy a new swimsuit by then.

2   *Possibility* with *can* and *could* (something may happen if conditions are suitable)

No one is perfect; everyone *can* make mistakes. (Mistakes are possible.)
Even good cooks *can* prepare bad food at times. (It is possible sometimes to prepare bad food.

Could in place of *can* in the present and future meanings of possibility shows doubt, not a change in tense.   (see **Conditional Sentences**)

Even good cooks *could* prepare bad food at times. (possible but not very likely)
The dean *can* see you at 2:30. (a definite possibility for an appointment)
The dean *could* see you at 2:30. (Perhaps an appointment might be arranged.)
Our team *can* win the volleyball match. (Winning is a definite possibility.)
Our team *could* win the volleyball match. (Winning is unlikely but possible if certain conditions are met.)

In all the sentences above with *could*, a conditional *if*-clause is implied.

Even good cooks *could* turn out bad food if . . .
The dean *could* see you at 2:30 if . . .
Our team *could* win the volleyball match if . . .

Negatives with possibility show that something is *impossible*.

Normal growth *cannot* occur without adequate nutrition. (Normal growth is impossible.)
The results of this experiment *cannot* be correct. (The results are impossible.)
It *cannot* snow in Miami in August. (Snow in Miami in August is impossible.)

Past possibility: *could have* + past participle + adverb(s) and/or a finite verb in the past:

adverb
The dean *could have seen* you *yesterday*.

past verb
The dean *could have seen* you but you *broke* your appointment.

Direct Speech:	Long ago people said, "Ships sailing too far west *can* fall off the edge of the earth."
Back-Shift After Reported Speech:	At one time people said that ships sailing too far west *could* fall off the edge of the earth.

Past condition contrary to fact: *could* + *have* + past participle:

When the flood came, the water *could have risen* higher than it did (something could have happened but it did not); the damage *could have been* worse.
Everyone complained about the heat yesterday, but it *could have been* hotter. (Even hotter weather was possible.)

Negative:	The judge *could not have* sent him to jail just for getting a parking ticket. It *could not have snowed* in Zanzibar.

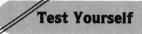
Test Yourself

B. Correct the errors in the following sentences.

1.　Since our team is undefeated so far this year, we believe we could win the basketball championship in our region.

2.　If we had done as well last year as this year, we would be able to win last year too.

3.　Unless we completed the experiments carefully, we can misinterpret the results.

4.　The rain yesterday cannot have flooded the basement because it did not rain very hard at all.

C. Put *can, could,* or a form of *be able to* in the blanks.

1.　We _____ not go on a picnic yesterday because of the rain.

2.　We have been told we _____ use the state park for our club's next picnic.

3.　Some students _____ learn the new vocabulary in time for the next test tomorrow. (future negative)

4.　The tutor told them that they _____ get extra help tomorrow.

5.　Now that the student from Thailand has moved into an apartment, he _____ cook the kind of food he likes.

6.　I know I don't have an appointment, but _____ the doctor possibly see me this afternoon?

3　*Permission* with *can* and *could* (*be allowed to, be permitted to, have permission to*) Although many authorities have preferred *may* to *can* to show permission, even in much formal writing both are used in the present and future to show permission. See below under *may* for differences in its usage in the past.

Anyone with a library card from the main library *can* borrow books from the branch libraries. You *can* hand in your composition tomorrow instead of today if you need to revise it.

Past *could* (usually with an adverb or with a clause that has a verb in the past tense) shows that permission was given at some time in the past but is no longer given under the conditions described.

At one time anyone *could* travel without a passport. (but not now)
Once anyone *could* buy land here, but now no one can.

Permission can also be shown by *have permission to, is permitted to,* and *was allowed to. Have permission to* means that permission is necessary and has been granted. *Are permitted to* and *is allowed to* mean that special permission is not necessary.

At one time anyone *was allowed to (could)* swim in the Warner's lake, but now the only people who *are allowed to (can)* are those who *have permission*.

Other Uses of Can and Could

In polite questions, *could* is considered more polite than *can*.

Can you see me now?
Could you see me now? (more doubt and thus more possibility of an easy refusal)

Polite commands with *can* put the speaker on the same level as the person to whom the command is given.

You *can* finish typing this letter while I make a phone call. (politely, "Finish typing this letter.")

How can or *How could* show disapproval in the form of questions. They mean *you shouldn't (have)*!

How can you come so late!
How could you have forgotten our anniversary!

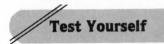

Test Yourself

D. Fill in the blanks in the following sentences with a form of *can* or *could*. Then rewrite the sentences using a form of *be able*, changing other words and word order as necessary.

1. I know I missed my appointment this morning, but _____ the doctor possibly see me this afternoon? (hesitant, very polite)

2. If my bus had not broken down, I _____ kept my appointment this morning. (I did not keep my appointment this morning.)

3. If another bus had come along sooner after the first one broke down, I _____ kept my appointment this morning. (I did not keep my appointment.)

4. If another bus had not come along, I _____ kept my appointment this morning. (I kept my appointment.)

5. If my bus had not come on time, I _____ kept my appointment this morning. (I kept my appointment.)

6. If I _____ (negative) see the doctor this afternoon, I

7. _____ come back until Thursday. (negative)

May and Might

Use *may* and *might* for permission and possibility.

1 *Permission* with *may:* Although *may* and *can* are usually interchangeable, some authorities prefer *may* in formal writing. *Might* is sometimes used to show the past, but it is often replaced by *could.* Adverbs and other verbs make the time reference clear.

present
You *may* wait here *now* until the doctor can see you.

past, reported speech
The nurse *told* them that they *could* (*might*) wait in the waiting room.

future
You *may* come back at ten o'clock *tomorrow.*
You *may* remind me again *next week.*

Past permission is not shown with *might.* (see *could,* permission, above)

2 *Possibility* with *may* and *might*:

My car *may* need new tires.
The answer to this problem *may* not be correct.
Causes of the poor tests results *may* be understood later.

Might shows more doubt than *may* does (see *could,* above).

My car *might* need new tires.
The answer to this problem *might* not be correct.
Causes of the poor test results *might* be understood later.
We *might* go to Florida this winter, or we *might* go to Texas instead.

NOTE: *May* and *might* in the meaning of possibility are not generally used in questions. *Can* and *could* are usually used.

Past possibility (not yet certain): *may + have +* past participle:

They *may have found* a solution to the problem.
Warren and Sally *may have had* an accident.

May becomes *might* or *could* in the past:

He thought that his car *might* need new tires.
He found that his car *could* need new tires.

Test Yourself

Use *may* or *might* in the following sentences.

1. _____ we sit here?

2. You _____ ; there is plenty of room.

3. We _____ have to leave before the program is over, but we hope not.

4. We _____ not _____ hear very well from these seats. (may, might; can, be able to)

5. You _____ hear better than you expect; a lot of work was done to improve the acoustics in this auditorium. (possibility)

6. We thought these _____ be poor seats, but they were the only ones we could get.

7. We _____ have done better if we had bought tickets earlier, but since we do not have season tickets for this series, we always have to take what is left.

Will and Would (for will as a sign of the future tense see p. 370)
Use *will* and *would* for agreement, polite commands, and prediction.
1   *Agreement* with *will* (with a personal subject only, in all tenses):

I *will* (agree to) help you.
We *will* sign the contract immediately.
I *will* be there at 10:15 tomorrow. (a definite appointment)

2   *Polite commands, offers, and invitations* (*Would* shows more doubt)
(see **Commands**):

Will you please open the door for me.
Would you please open the door for me. (even more polite)
Will (*would*) you want another cup of coffee?
Will you come to dinner at my house tomorrow?

(See **Conditional Clauses** for *would* following *if* or *unless* [They *would* if they *could,* but they *cannot.*].)

As past habitual, *would* shows an action repeated in the past. You can often use *would* instead of *used to.*

When we were children, we *would* often *make* our mother angry by pretending to quarrel. We *would disagree,* we *would complain* about each other, and sometimes we *would* even *wrestle* and *pretend* to hit each other. We *would do* all these things just to get our mother's attention.

3   *Prediction* with *will,* also a statement of natural law, especially in scientific and technical writing, shows a result that is likely or certain.

Water *will* freeze at 0° Celsius (32°F). (It always freezes. . . .)
When these chemicals are mixed, the reaction *will* be as follows. (The reaction is always. . . .)
Boys *will* be boys. (Boys and men always behave a certain way.)

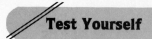

Test Yourself

A. Look at exercise D that follows *can* and *could* on p. 195. Can you use *will* or *would* in any of the sentences in those exercises? How does using *will* or *would* change the meaning?

B. Put *will* or *would* in the blanks in the following sentences.

1. _____ you accept a prize of $10,000?

2. I _____ if there are no conditions attached to it.

3. When I was a child, I _____ often dream of winning a great deal of money.

4. My plans for spending it _____ be worked out in great detail.

5. If I could return to my childhood, I _____ have no difficulty deciding how to spend $10,000.

6. But now I see many more possibilities in life than I did as a child, and I know I must be prepared for unexpected problems that _____ come in the future.

Shall and Should

Questions in the first person: *shall* is used in questions before *I* or *we* in the sense of "would you like me to?"

Shall (should) I close the door now?
Shall (should) we go to Florida next spring?
Shall (should) I fix lunch now?

Should (above) shows more doubt or uncertainty on the part of the speaker. It can also introduce a question of advisability. (see exercise below)

Test Yourself

Put *shall* or *should* in the blanks in the following sentences.

1. _____ I start to pack our lunches for the picnic now? (no hesitation)

2. I don't know; perhaps we _____ wait to see what the weather will be.

3. We _____ have good weather this time of the year.

4. Why _____ we worry?

Should and Ought To

Use *should* and *ought to* to show ***advisability*** and ***obligation.***

General Truths: Children *should* be respectful to older people.

Children *ought to respect* older people.

Drivers *should* be careful when it rains.

Drivers *ought to* be careful when it rains.

Ought to is rarely used in the negative.

Children *should not* be disrespectful to older people.
Drivers *should not* be careless when it rains.

Show definite time with adverbs of time or tenses of other verbs:

Tomorrow you *should* pay the gas bill.
Tomorrow you *ought to* pay the gas bill.
Jonathan *should* be making better grades than he *is*.
Jonathan *ought to* be making better grades than he *is*.

Special Uses of Should

After verbs of command and request, *should* + main verb can be used instead of the subjunctive. (see **Subjunctive**)

The commander ordered that the flag (*should*) fly at half mast.
Government regulations require that the price (*should*) be cut.

NOTE: A more common sentence pattern uses the infinitive for commands and requests.

The commander ordered the flag *to be flown* at half mast.

With should *or*
Subjunctive: The police directed that *we* (*should*) *take* the detour. (subject pronoun)
With Infinitive: The police directed *us to take* the detour. (object pronoun)

Should can replace *if* in conditional sentences.

If she comes early, tell me.
Should she *come* early, tell me.

If Herb finds shoes that fit him, he will buy them.
Should Herb *find* shoes that fit him, he will buy them.

(see **Conditional Sentences** for *should* following *if* and *unless*)

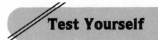

Test Yourself

Put *shall, should,* or *ought to* in the following sentences.

1.   National flags _____ be treated with respect because they stand for the nation.

2. When the head of state dies, all government agencies are told that their flags _____ fly

   at half mast.

3. People _____ respect the flags of their own and of other countries.

4. Flags are symbols of a country that _____ be respected.

5. _____ flags not be respected, the country is insulted.

6. Many rules for the use of flags differ from country to country; however,

   everyone _____ know what burning a flag means.

Must and Have to
Use *must* and *have to* to show necessity and prohibition.

Necessity:
Have to can replace *must* in the positive; *had to* replaces *must* in the past.
Have to can follow another auxiliary or a modal.

You *must* (*have to*) pass a test before you enter the computer course.
If you don't make a high enough test score, you *might have to* repeat your course.
You *must* (*have to*) pay for all your groceries at the cash register.
Alan and Martha *must* (*have to*) get a marriage license before the wedding. (*will have to* is
   possible)

Past Necessity is shown by *had to.*

All applicants *had to* take eye tests before renewing their driver's licenses.
Some students *had to* buy five books this term.

Lack of Necessity (does not need to) is shown by *do not have to.*

Present: We *do not have to* (do not need to) buy many books this term. (British: *need
               not*)
             Some students *do not have to* work because their families give them enough
               money to go to school.
Past: Doris *did not have to* pay as much as she expected to repair her car.
             The class *did not have to* hand in homework last week.

Logical Necessity—*Must be* can indicate a deduction or an inference from the facts
given.

Present
He has many accidents; he *must be* a careless driver.
She came in with her umbrella dripping; it *must be* raining outside.
My answer to problem two is wrong; I *must be* using the wrong formula to solve it.

NOTE: *Must* in a question such as *Must you go?* implies *I don't want you to go.*

Past (must + have + past participle):
You *must have studied* hard to get such good grades.
He *must have had* many accidents to lose his driver's license.

Future:
If the main verb is *be*, use *must + be*. If the main verb is not *be*, use *must + be + ing* form of the
  main verb or *must + be + going to + main verb.

be *As the Main Verb:*
Everyone in the play practiced late today; the dress rehearsal *must be* tomorrow.

Other Verbs as Main Verbs:
Andy is looking everywhere for his new tennis racket; he *must be planning* to play tennis this
  afternoon.
Clara cleaned house today; she *must be having or must be going to have* company.
The sky is clear and the temperature is dropping fast; it *must be going to freeze* tonight.

Prohibition—must + negative: or *must* + a verb such as *avoid* or *stop* +
ing form

Pedestrians *must not* cross the expressway except on the bridge.
Drivers *must not* throw trash in the parking lot. (*must stop throwing*)

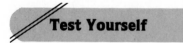

Test Yourself

Put *should, ought to, must, have to,* or *had to* in the blanks in the following sentences.

1. _____ you go now? I wish you would stay longer so we could finish this contract

   today.

2. I do not _____ leave immediately; I can stay a bit longer.

3. We _____ be able to have a longer talk tomorrow after I have been able to put all the

   statistical tables together.

4. There is a strict deadline for us to submit our proposal; we _____ get the first draft

   finished tomorrow.

5. We are late with the statistical tables because we _____ wait to get the latest figures

   from the census office yesterday afternoon.

6. But don't worry; although we may _____ ask for a short delay, we will get the

   contract without any difficulty.

7. We _____ not ask for a second delay, however.

8. We _____ not appear inefficient.

9. Does the manager have all the licenses and permits we _____ have for the construction work?

10. If the manager has been doing his job properly, he _____ have already got the licenses and permits.

11. We _____ work carefully.

12. This _____ be the most important contract we have ever bid for.

13. The management _____ be planning to expand if we get this contract.

14. Because the future of our company depends on this contract, we _____ do our best work in the next few days.

Related Phrases

Be able to—see above under *can* (can follow a modal)

Have to—see above under *must* (can follow a modal)

Had better—shows advisability and means nearly the same as *should* and *ought to,* but with the idea that the advice is suitable or advantageous. A bad result may follow if the advice is not taken. Even though the form is past, it is used only with a present meaning. *Had better* is always followed by the bare infinitive.

You *had better move* your houseplants indoors before a freeze, or they will die.
Becky *had better get* new tires for her car before she has an accident.

Used to + infinitive shows habitual action in the indefinite past. Do not use a time phrase beginning with *since* with *used to*. Often the same idea can be shown by *would* in the past. (See above for *would* and see **Tense, present** for habitual present.) *Used to* cannot follow a modal. Use a bare infinitive (simple verb form) after it.

Travelers *used to cross* the Atlantic by ship and then take a train, but these days they fly all the way.
When I was a small child, I often *used to argue* with my brother, but now we agree most of the time.
People *used to believe* that the earth was flat, but now we know that it is a sphere.
When we were children, we often *used to make* our mother angry by pretending to quarrel. We *used to disagree*, we *used to complain* about each other, and sometimes we *used to wrestle* and *pretend* to hit each other. We *used to do* all these things just to get our mother's attention.

Be (or *get*) *used to* + *-ing* form or a noun or pronoun means *be accustomed to*. The tense is shown on *be* or *get*.

Our cat *is used to sleeping* in a basket.
People who *are used to* (*get used to*) *drinking coffee* when they get up in the morning do not like to go without it.
When I lived in northern Canada I *was used to* cold weather, but now that I live in southern Florida, I *am used to* the heat.

Test Yourself

A. Put *had better, used to,* or a form of *be used to* or *get used to* in the blanks in the following sentences.

1. Our small company _____ preparing bids for such a large project as the one we are working on now. (negative)

2. We _____ employ only fifteen people fulltime.

3. We realize that now we _____ plan for a great expansion.

4. When large construction projects were advertised for bids, we _____ think we were too small to apply.

5. Now we believe we will be able to _____ being large and successful.

6. Everyone should have the opportunity to _____ success.

7. Our company _____ make plans now for expansion.

B. Now put *should, must,* or *would* where possible in the sentences above.

Which blanks are unfilled? How can you rewrite these sentences using different forms?

Meanings of Modals and Related Phrases
(All can be used with *not*; see also **Contractions**)

Ability/Capability	Tense	Opportunity Realized:	Tense
can (cannot)—	present and future	can (cannot)—	present
		be able to—	present, past and future
could—	present and past		
		Not Realized:	
		could not have	past

Advisability

shall I? should I?—	questions, future
should—	present, past, and future
had better (had better not)—	present

Deduction/Inference

must—	present, past, and future

Intention/Insistence

shall—	(future meaning)
will—	(future meaning)
be going to (is not going to)—	present, past, and future

NOTE: Past intention is usually shown with *wanted to* or *desired to.*

Necessity/Obligation
    (in order of emphasis)

must—	present and future
have to (not have to)—	present, past, and future
ought to (ought not)—	present, past, and future
should—	present, past, and future
need (to) (need not or does not need)—	present, past, and future
to be (see **Be**)—	present, past, and future

Offer

will—	future
would like (would not like)—	present and future

Permission

may—	present and future
can (cannot)—	present and future
could—	past
let + personal object—	present and future

Possibility/ Impossibility

can (cannot)—	present and future
could—	present and future
may—	present and future
might—	present and future
could have (could not have)—	past
may have (may not have)—	past
might have (might not have)—	past

Prediction/ Natural Law

will—	present and future

Prohibition

must not—	present and future
must never—	present and future

NOTE: Also shown by *do not, no + ing* form, *it is forbidden to,* and *it is unlawful to.*

Repeated Action in the Past

would—	past tense
used to—	past tense
past tense	

Repeated Action in the Present
    present tense

Becoming Accustomed to Something

get used to—	all tenses
be used to—	all tenses

NOTE: *Not* and *never* can follow all modals of one word. Their correct order in phrases is shown. Spell *cannot* as one word.

Modifiers

Modifiers affect the meanings of other words in some way. Nouns can be modified by adjectives, articles, determiners, participles, and infinitives. Verbs can be modified by adverbs; adverbs can also modify adjectives and other adverbs. Phrases and clauses can modify both nouns and verbs, but their word order in the clause may be different from the word order of a one-word modifier. Noun forms can modify other nouns, both in their common forms and in their possessive forms. Certain forms of pronouns can modify nouns.

The word that is modified is often called the *head word*. Words that come before the head word are called *premodifiers*. Words that come after it are called *postmodifiers*.

Some Examples of Modifiers of Nouns

Kind of Modifier	Premodifier	Headword-Noun	Postmodifier
Article **or** Determiner	The **or** this	horse . . .	
Predeterminer	All the	horses . . .	
Possessive Noun (Proper)	Ruth's	horse . . .	
Possessive Pronoun	Her	horse . . .	

In the following examples, you must use a determiner in the singular, and you may use one in the plural, depending on the meaning of the sentence. *The* as shown in the table is one of many possible determiners.   (see **Determiners**)

Kind of Modifier	Premodifier	Headword-Noun	Postmodifier
Possessive Noun (Common)	(The) girl's	horse	
Single-Word Adjective	(The) big	horse	
Adjective of Comparison	(The) slower	horse	*or* slower than mine
	(The) fast	horse	*or* as fast as mine
A-word Adjective	(The)	horse	alone
Intensive Pronoun	(The)	horse	itself
Prepositional Phrase	(The)	horse	in the pasture
Adjective Clause	(The)	horse	that she bought
Noun	(The) show	horse	
Noun, Appositive	(The)	horse,	the mare,
Infinitive	(The)	horse	to buy
Present Participle	(The) working	horse	
	(The)	horse	running away
Past Participle	(The) trained	horse	
	(The)	horse	found yesterday

Although predicate adjectives and predicate nouns modify nouns and pronouns that are the subject of the clause, they are usually called complements, not modifiers. (see **Predicate Complements**)

See **Adjectives, order of** for a chart of the word order when several premodifiers modify the same noun.

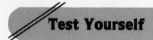

Test Yourself

Modifiers of Nouns

Put the letter of the correct modifier in the blank to the left.

A. single-word adjective	F. past participle
B. possessive noun	G. prepositional phrase
C. possessive pronoun	H. noun used as adjective
D. intensive pronoun	I. appositive noun
E. present participle	J. adjective clause

1. _____ Polar bears are large (1) *white* bears

2. _____ (2) *that live in arctic climates.*

3. _____ With their strong muscles and claws, they are very (3) *dangerous*

4. _____ animals. With their (4) *fur* coats they can live, sleep, hunt,

5. _____ and play in extremely (5) *cold* weather without

6. _____ shelter. (6) *Living* on ice floes in winter, they

7. _____ are able to hunt seals, the (7) *mainstay*

8. _____ (8) *of their diet.* Because of

9. _____ (9) *their* white coats, the bears

10. _____ (10) *themselves* are difficult to see against

11. _____ the ice and snow of the (11) *frozen* arctic.

12. _____ Polar bears are good swimmers. The (12) *bears'*

13. _____ small heads, long necks and (13) *slender*

14. _____ bodies (14) *compared* to those of

15. _____ (15) *other* bears help them move quickly on land and in water.

Are there any modifiers of nouns in the sentences above that are not italicized? How are they used?

Some Examples of Modifiers of Verbs (All modifiers of verbs can be called adverbs.)

Kind of Adverb	Verb	Adverb
Single Word	(He) ran	quickly.
Prepositional Phrase	(He) ran	down the street.
Clause	(He) ran	when he saw us.

See **Adverbs** for other examples of words that adverbs can modify and for the word order of adverbs in a clause.

Mood

Four terms have traditionally been used to describe the different ways verbs can express an idea:

the indicative—makes a statement.
the imperative—gives a command. (see **Commands**)
the interrogative—asks a question. (see **Questions, direct**)
the subjunctive—shows a condition contrary to fact, such as an unreal statement after *if*, a command, a request, or necessity. (see **Conditional Sentences** and **Subjunctive**)

Some grammars use *mode* instead of *mood* to show the differences in the way the verb idea is expressed. Many languages make changes in the verb form to show the ideas such as obligation, permission, and necessity that English can show by using modal and auxiliary verbs before the main verb. (see **Modals** and **Auxiliary verbs**)

Be Used in Different Moods

indicative (a statement)

Frances *is* a good student.

imperative (a command)

Be a good student.

interrogative (a question)

Is Frances a good student?

subjunctive (a statement after *if* that is not real)

If Frances *were* not a good student, she would leave school. (She *is* a good student.)

Were is usually used in written nonreal statements after *if* for all persons.

Negation

Negation shows disagreement, denial, absence of somebody or something, or an opposite idea or quality.

Formation of a Negative Clause (see **Operators**)

1 Put *not* directly after all operators (all forms of *have* and *do* acting as auxiliaries and after *am, is, are, was, were, shall, should, will, would, can, could, may, might, must,* and *ought*). (see **Contractions**)

Deborah *will do* the work.	She *will not* do it.
	She *won't* do it.
	She'll not do it.
Russell *is walking* to work today.	He *is not* walking to work today.
	He *isn't* walking to work today.
	He's not walking to work today.

Word Order: Put *not* after the first modal or auxiliary in a verb phrase. (see **Finite Verb, table of word order**)

208

NOTE: In speech, using *not* as a separate word instead of in a contraction emphasizes the negative idea. In formal writing, avoid using contractions.

   2   Make the negative of all other verbs with the required form of *do* and *not* or the contracted forms *don't, doesn't,* or *didn't.*

They *do not (don't)* see you very often these days.
She *does not (doesn't)* walk to work every day.
They *did not (didn't)* find the lost dog.

Tag questions are always positive following negative statements and negative following positive statements.   (see **Tag Questions**)

   In negative questions, keep *-n't* with the verb operator when you move the operator to the beginning of the clause.   (see **Operators**)

Do*n't* they see you often these days?
Does*n't* he walk to work every day?
Did*n't* they find the lost dog?

The strong form of *not* follows the subject in formal writing.

Do they *not* see you often these days?
Does he *not* walk to work every day?
Did they *not* find the lost dog?

WH-questions also keep *-n't* with the operator (the verb that follows the *WH*-word) or put *not* after the subject.

Why is*n't* he on time?
Why is he *not* on time?

   3   For strong emphasis, put *not* or another negative adverb at the beginning of the clause and invert the subject and verb.

                         verb   subject
Not since the 1930s *have there been* the *droughts* that we are seeing now.
Not in our lifetimes *will we see* another   *leader* like our late president.
Rarely   *has* the   *world seen* such courage!

Test Yourself

In some of the following sentences, *not* or *no* is in the wrong place or is the wrong form (*no*). Cross it out if it is wrong and move it to its correct place in the sentence. Change the word if necessary.

1.   Clouds do always not mean rain; they mean that there is moisture in the upper air or

     atmosphere.

2.   Fog no is different from clouds; it is a kind of cloud that is not in the air but is on the ground.

3.   The shapes of clouds are always not the same, but change constantly.

4.   Why not are clouds the same all over the world?

5.   They are different because winds are no the same in the tropics as in other parts of the world.

6.   Outside tropical areas, winds in the upper atmosphere do no always blow at exactly the same speed or in exactly the same direction as winds at the earth's surface.

Answers to Negative and Positive Questions

Negation in English is related to the positive statement. English-speaking people agree or disagree with the underlying positive statement, not with a negative question, even if the only statement they hear or see is negative.

Affirmative Statement:	Chris likes to eat bananas.
Affirmative Question:	Does Chris like to eat bananas?
Affirmative Answer:	Yes, he does. (agreement)
Negative Answer:	*No,* he does*n't.* (disagreement)
Negative Question:	Chris doesn't like to eat bananas, does he?
Affirmative Answer:	Yes, he does. (agreement—he likes to eat bananas)
Negative Answer:	*No,* he does*n't.* (disagreement—he does not like to eat bananas)

Notice that *yes* is always followed by a positive verb, and that *no* is always followed by a negative form. Use the same answer for both the affirmative and negative question. The following answers are likely to be misunderstood.

Incorrect:	No, he does. (disagreement with the question because he likes to eat bananas)
Incorrect:	Yes, he doesn't. (agreement with the question because he does not like to eat bananas)

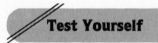

Test Yourself

Write a short, correct answer that gives the meaning shown in parentheses.

1. You haven't bought your book yet, have you? (No book has been bought.)

2. The professor didn't tell us which book to buy to use tomorrow, did she? (She failed to tell us.)

3. The manager of the bookstore hasn't called to tell us the new books have come in, has he? (He called yesterday.)

4. The students have already finished reading today's assignment, haven't they? (No assignment was given for today.)

5. Will the students who registered late be able to buy books? (They will be able to buy them tomorrow.)

Other Negative Words and Double Negatives

Since formal English rarely puts more than one negative word into one clause, you must remember which words in English have this negative effect.

not (in the verb, and modifying words other than the verb)
nor   (see **Coordinating Conjunctions**)
neither, nor   (see **Coordinating Conjunctions**)
unless   (see **Conditional Sentences**)

no	nobody	rarely	hardly
never	nothing	seldom	scarcely
none	nowhere	barely	

Correct
No one is ever here.
There is *no* way to do that.
They do *not* have much money.
They have *hardly any* money.

Incorrect
No one is *never* here.
There's *not no* way to do that.
They *don't* have *no* money.
They *don't* have *hardly any* money.

Words beginning with negative prefixes, such as *nonaligned* and *nonexistent,* although they have a negative meaning, may be used with other negatives in the same clause.   (See **Word Formation, prefixes,** for more examples with a negative meaning.)

Our country is *not non*aligned because it has treaties with other countries.
One can*not* say human kindness is *non*existent.

Without and certain verbs of negative meaning such as *fail* or *lack* can occur in the same clause with the negative words listed above.

He is *not* without his faults. (He has some faults.)
They do *not* lack water. (They have enough water.)
The first experiment did *not* work, and the second one failed, too.

Use *either* in negative statements and answers after *not* to indicate an additional negative item or idea.

Do Mary and Margaret both want bananas?
Mary does*n't* want any, and Margaret does*n't* either.
The first experiment did *not* give the expected results, and the second one did *not either*.

Use *neither* in a similar construction, omitting *not* in the second clause and invert the subject and verb.   (see p. 236)

The first experiment did *not* give the expected results, and *neither* did the second one.

NOTE: *Either* and *neither* are more often used as correlative conjunctions.   (See **Parallel Structure** for other adverbs used to emphasize negative ideas.)

To make the negative command, put *don't* or *do not* before the main verb.

Pick up the book.	Do *not* pick up the book.
	Do*n't* pick up the book.
Let him pick up the book.	Do *not* let him pick up the book.
	Do*n't* let him pick up the book.
Someone open the door.	Do *not* (let) anyone open the door.
	Do*n't* (let) anyone open the door.

NOTE: *Some* and words beginning with *some* usually change to *any* in the negative sentence. *Not* follows *let's* or *let us*.

Let's open the door.	Let's *not* open the door.

Public signs often state negative commands as *no* before an *-ing* form.

No smoking   *No* running   *No* standing   *No* loitering

Stop has the sense of negation.

Stop smoking (do *not* smoke)   Stop pollution (do *not* pollute or allow others to pollute)

NOTE: Do not use **no** as an adverb; always use **not** to modify a verb. Use **no** to modify a gerund: **No** swimming/smoking/parking

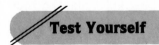

Test Yourself

Correct the errors in the following sentences.

1. The Andes Mountains form the world's longest mountain range, but no the highest.

2. Not nowhere in the Andes is there a mountain as high as Mount Everest in the Himalaya Mountains in Nepal.

3. But several peaks in the Andes are no much lower than those in the Himalayas.

4. Volcanoes and earthquakes are no uncommon in the Andes.

5. The mountains in the southern Andes are not nowhere so high as those in the central

 area.

6. Although not no higher than Mount Everest, which is 29,000 feet high, Mount Aconca-

 gua in Argentina at almost 23,000 feet is the highest peak in the Western Hemisphere.

Transferred Negatives

After some verbs such as *think, believe,* or *expect,* the *not* can move from the *that* clause in which it logically belongs to the main clause.

Main Clause:	I do *not* think that you have tried very hard to finish this work.
	means
that Clause:	I think that you have *not* tried very hard to finish this work.
Main Clause:	She does *not* believe that you care about her as much as you say you do.
	means
that Clause:	She believes that you do *not* care about her as much as you say you do.

The *that* may be omitted in a noun clause used as a direct object if it is not the subject of its own clause.   (see **Clauses, dependent**)

Negatives and Style

Contractions are used in speech and informal writing, but the strong form of *not* is often very formal and disturbs the rhythm of the sentence. Writers, therefore, often express the negative idea in other ways when they do not want to write in a very formal style.

Why is*n't* he on time? (informal)
Why is he *not* on time? (formal) = Why is he *late?* (less formal, less emphatic)
They do*n't* have much money. (informal)
They do *not* have much money. (formal) = They have *hardly any* money. (less formal)
The stars are*n't* visible. (informal)
The stars are *not* visible. (formal) = The stars are *in*visible. (formal or less formal)

 **Test Yourself**

Give a one-word substitution for the underlined negative phrases.

1. Why is Pat <u>not in class</u> today?

2. She is <u>not at home</u>.

3. Physical exercise is good for people, but it is <u>not</u> <u>required</u>.

4. Stopping at red lights is <u>not</u> <u>optional</u> for drivers or pedestrians.

Non-count nouns, see **Countable and Uncountable Nouns**

Nouns

Nouns are words that name things such as persons, animals, places, ideas, and institutions. A noun can be the subject of a clause. Nouns are sometimes called *substantives,* a term that means any word or group of words that can be used as the subject of a clause. A noun, a pronoun, a noun phrase, a gerund, a gerund phrase, or an infinitive phrase can be substantives.

Kinds of Nouns

Countable and Uncountable (see **Countable and Uncountable Nouns**)

Proper Nouns and Common Nouns

Proper nouns are names of particular people, places, or things. They are capitalized. All other nouns are *common* nouns.

Ruth Anderson and *George Allen* attend *Lakeview College.*
Monday, June 15, is *Peter Thompson's* birthday.

Proper nouns take articles or determiners only if two or more people, places, or things have the same name.

My brother is named Bill Johnson and my cousin is also named Bill Johnson. *The Bill Johnson* who lives across the street from me is my brother.

Common nouns can be classified into abstract nouns and concrete nouns. *Abstract* nouns name ideas, emotions, qualities, and processes: justice, beauty, happiness, length, weight, classification. *Concrete* nouns name persons or things that can be known directly through the senses; ball, boy, bread, chair, heat, noise, fire, smoke, ice, water, and so on.

Collective Nouns

Collective nouns are special nouns that stand for a group of people, animals, birds, or insects. Collective nouns take singular or plural verbs depending on whether the group acts as a unit (singular) or as separate individuals (plural). (see **Agreement of subject and verb**)

Some collective nouns for people are

army	choir	congregation	team
audience	chorus	group	troop
band	clan	orchestra	unit
brigade	class	patrol	youth

Some collective nouns for animals, birds, and insects are

a herd of cattle, sheep, goats   a hive of bees
a flock of birds, chickens   a swarm of ants, bees, flies

Spelling of Nouns

Most nouns are *regular* in spelling the pural. Add -*s* to the end of the singular form.

boy, boys   book, books   pencil, pencils

Add -*es* to make plurals of nouns that end in -*s* or in a similar sound (*ch, sh-, tch, x, z,* and *dg*).

bun*ch,* bunch*es*   pat*ch,* patch*es*   fo*x,* fox*es*   e*dg*e, e*dg*es

(See **Spelling** for irregularities in nouns ending in -*ch, dg, -s, -sh, -tch, x,* and *z,* in -*o,* and in -*y.*)

Some nouns are *irregular* in the plural and/or the related verb.

1   A final -*f* or -*fe* becomes -*ves* in some nouns (some of the -*f* nouns are related to a verb in -*ve*).

Noun in -f	*Plural Noun*	*Verb*
cal*f*	cal*ves*	cal*ve*
belie*f*	belie*fs* (regular plural)	belie*ve*
el*f*	el*ves*	—
hal*f*	hal*ves*	hal*ve*
hoo*f*	hoo*ves* (also hoo*fs*)	—
kni*fe*	kni*ves*	kni*fe*
lea*f*	lea*ves*	—
li*fe*	li*ves*	li*ve*
loa*f*	loa*ves*	—
proo*f*	proo*fs*	pro*ve*
relie*f*	relie*fs* (rare in plural)	relie*ve*
sel*f*	sel*ves*	—
shel*f*	shel*ves*	shel*ve*
thie*f*	thie*ves*	thie*ve* (*thieving* common; other forms rare)
wi*fe*	wi*ves*	—
wol*f*	wol*ves*	wol*f*

NOTE: *Roof* is regular: roof, roof*s*

2 Most nouns in *-th* have regular plurals, but have related verbs.

Nouns in *-th*	Plural	Verbs in *-the*
breath	breaths	breathe
cloth	cloths	clothe
	(*clothes* is a different noun that means *clothing*)	
tooth	teeth (irregular)	teethe
wreath	wreaths	wreathe

3 Some old English plural forms are still used.

man, men
woman, women
fireman, firemen
workman, workmen, and other compounds with *-man*
mouse, mice
louse, lice
goose, geese

child, children
ox, oxen
brother, brethren (religious use only—brothers in other uses)
foot, feet
tooth, teeth

4 Some nouns can keep the singular form in a collective plural meaning.

Animals, Birds, and Fish

Mr. Parker hunts
{
deer.
pheasant.
elephant.
duck.
}

He catches
{
trout.
perch.
bluefish.
}

Trees and Plants (Grains)

The Allens planted
{
pine
oak
wheat
corn   on their farm this year.
rye
sorghum
barley
}

People

Everyone—*man, woman,* and *child*—is affected by air pollution.
Student and *teacher* alike signed the petition.

Test Yourself

A. Put the correct form of the word in parentheses in the blank in the sentence, and then copy it in the blank to the left.

_____ 1. Cats are so clever at getting out of difficulties that people say cats have nine _____ . (life)

_____ 2. Cats have padded _____ so they can move quietly when they hunt. (foot)

_____ 3. The _____ of cats are called kittens. (baby)

_____ 4. Like the young of many other mammals, kittens lose their baby _____ . (tooth)

_____ 5. Cats like to hunt rats and _____ . (mouse)

_____ 6. People have kept cats for thousands of years to destroy the vermin that eat _____ and other grains. (wheat)

_____ 7. People have many different _____ about cats. (belief)

_____ 8. In some places people think cats bring good _____ . (luck)

_____ 9. "Honest as a cat when the cream is out of reach" means that _____ do not steal when they do not have the chance to do so. (thief)

_____ 10. The _____ that ancient Egyptians worshiped cats are the mummies and statues of cats that have been found there and pictures of them in ancient paintings. (proof)

5 Some Latin and Greek plurals are used. Writers in science often use the Greek or Latin forms even though most writers use English plurals if one exists.

Words Keeping Foreign Plurals (Always use the foreign plural if there is no entry under English plural.)

Singular	_Foreign Plural_ _Scientific Use_	_English Plural_ _General Use_

Words ending in _-a_ in the singular and _-ae_ in the plural:

amoeba	amoebae	amoebas
alumna	alumnae	
antenna	antennae	antennas
formula	formulae	formulas
larva	larvae	
nebula	nebulae	nebulas

Singular	Foreign Plural Scientific Use	English Plural General Use

Words ending in *-ex* or *-ix* in the singular and *-ices* in the plural:

ap*ex*	ap*ices*	ap*exes*
append*ix*	append*ices*	append*ixes*
cerv*ix*	cerv*ices*	cerv*ixes*
ind*ex*	ind*ices*	ind*exes*

Words ending in *-is* in the singular and *-es* in the plural:

analy*sis*	analy*ses*
ax*is*	ax*es*
bas*is*	bas*es*
cris*is*	cris*es*
diagnos*is*	diagnos*es*
hypothes*is*	hypothes*es*
neuros*is*	neuros*es*
oas*is*	oas*es*
parenthes*is*	parenthes*es*
synops*is*	synops*es*
thes*is*	thes*es*

Words ending in *-on* in the singular and *-a* in the plural:

criter*ion*	criter*ia*
phenomen*on*	phenomen*a*

Words ending in *-um* in the singular and *-a* in the plural:

agend*um*— also agend*a*	agend*a*	
bacteri*um*	bacteri*a*	
dat*um*	dat*a*	
curricul*um*	curricul*a*	curricul*ums*
errat*um*	errat*a*	(error, errors)

medi*um*	medi*a*	(*mediums* has a
		    different mean-
		    ing)

memorand*um*	memorand*a*	memorand*ums*
		    (often memo,
		    memos)

strat*um*	strat*a*	
symposi*um*	symposi*a*	symposi*ums*

Words ending in *-us* in the singular and *-i* in the plural:

bacill*us*	bacill*i*	
cact*us*	cact*i*	cactus*es*
fung*us*	fung*i*	fungus*es*
nucle*us*	nucle*i*	
radi*us*	radi*i*	
stimul*us*	stimul*i*	
syllab*us*	syllab*i*	syllabus*es*
termin*us*	termin*i*	(terminal, terminals)

Singular	Foreign Plural Scientific Use	English Plural General Use

Words ending in *-im* in the plural (from Hebrew):

cherub	cherub*im*	cherub*s*
seraph	seraph*im*	seraph*s*

Test Yourself

B. Put the correct plural form of the word in parentheses in the blank in the sentence, and then copy it in the blank to the left.

_____ 1. Scientists use many words of foreign origin in developing their _____ .

(hypothesis)

_____ 2. Scientists depend upon objective _____ (criterion)

_____ 3. when they make _____ (analysis) of problems.

_____ 4. In order to draw accurate conclusions, they collect large amounts

of _____ (datum) related to the problem they are studying.

_____ 5. Scientists often give the results of their studies at _____ (symposium).

_____ 6. When the results of new investigations are published, other researchers can

find them by looking in the _____ (index) to the scholarly publications.

_____ 7. _____ (synopsis) of scholarly papers are short summaries that are usually

called *abstracts*.

Some nouns with regular plural spelling do not have a singular form. (These nouns take plural verbs when they do not follow a preposition.)

Nouns that can follow *a pair of*:

binoculars	scissors
glasses (eyeglasses)	shorts
pants	slacks
pliers	socks
pajamas	stockings
scales (countable in other	tights
meanings)	tongs
	trousers
	tweezers
	twins

Some nouns are rarely or never used in the singular or preceded by a number in certain meanings:

archives
arms (weapons)
belongings
clothes
congratulations
credentials
earnings
looks (appearance)
manners (courteous behavior)
misgivings
odds
particulars (details)
premises (land and buildings on it)

proceeds
quarters (place to live)
regards
remains
resources (assets)
riches
shortcomings
suds
surroundings
thanks
valuables
whereabouts

Some nouns end in *-s* but have a singular meaning (they take singular verbs):

checkers (draughts)
chess
economics
mathematics
means
measles

metropolis
molasses
mumps
news
physics
tennis

diseases in -itis:
    appendicitis
    bronchitis
    tonsillitis
(-itis means *an inflammation*)

People, police, and *clergy* have singular forms but always take plural verbs. Series and statistics have the same form in singular and plural. (See **Agreement of Subject and verb** for more about irregular forms.)

Test Yourself

C. Replace the underlined words in the exercise below with a word from the following list:

archives   credentials   materials   means   misgivings
particulars   premises   proceeds   quarters   news

Joan decided to go to the state <u>building where records are kept</u> to see what she could find out about her family's history. Even though she had no <u>evidence of her qualifications</u> as a researcher, she was able to get an identification card on the <u>spot</u>. She gave the librarian the <u>details</u> of her family history in order to find the location of the books relevant to her family. She had to pay a small fee to use the <u>collection</u>; the <u>money from fees</u> can help pay the staff. Joan had some <u>fear</u> about looking into her family history because she knew that every family has had some bad people in it. Most people dislike finding out that one of their ancestors was a criminal. Sometimes, however, researchers find that their ancestors were people of <u>wealth</u> and high position. Such good <u>information</u> encourages them to keep looking to find out even more about their families.

Uses of Nouns

See each of the headings below in its own section for more examples of nouns used in different ways in a clause.

1   Subject

subject
Father just came.

2   Predicate nominative

predicate
nominative
Mr. Jefferson is my *father*.

3   Direct object

direct
object
The children love their *father*.

4   Indirect object

indirect
object
The children gave their *father* a hug.

5   Object of a preposition

object of
preposition
We are waiting for our *father*.

6   Objective complement

objective
complement
Sally never called her stepfather *father*.

7   Appositive

appositive
Mr. Jefferson, the *father* of one of our students, is here now.

8   Possessive   (see **Punctuation, apostrophe**)

Father's car is out of gas.

9   Modifier of another noun   (see **Adjectives, order of**)

A *father* figure is important to a child's psychological development.

Test Yourself

D. Identify the way the word *sister* is used in the following sentences:

1. My roommate next term will be John's sister.

2. My sister is studying in Canada.

3. I wrote my sister a letter last week.

4. Chris, my sister, always wants to know what I have been doing.

5. John jokingly calls me his sister, but I'm not.

6. John often waits for his sister after class.

Endings of Nouns

Certain endings are common on nouns. Do not confuse words that have the same root but that have endings that show they are different parts of speech.

noun
The newspaper article contained informa*tion* about Latin America.

adjective
An informa*tive* article about Latin America was in the newspaper today.

(see **Word Information, suffixes, nouns,** for a more complete list of noun endings)

Number, Singular and Plural

English grammar usually shows the difference between one and more than one. *One* is called *singular; more than one* is called *plural.* Nouns that can be either singular or plural are called *countable.* Certain nouns that English-speaking people think of as abstract or as masses usually have a form that looks singular. These nouns are called *uncountable* or *mass nouns.* To be sure about the way English uses a word, look it up in a reference book such as the *Oxford Advanced Learner's Dictionary* or the *Longman Dictionary of Contemporary English.* (see **Countable and Uncountable Nouns** and **Agreement of Subject and Verb**)

Numbers, Use in Formal Writing

Numbers should usually be spelled out in the text of formal writing if you can spell them in one or two words: *seventeen, forty-one, two hundred, nine thousand,* and so on.

Put a hyphen between the parts of compound numbers from twenty-one through ninety-nine and between the parts of fractions. (see **Punctuation, hyphen**)

Never begin a sentence with figures. If the number is long, rewrite the sentence so that the number is not the first word.

Incorrect: 9,725 people visited the exhibit last month.

Correct: Last month 9,725 people visited the exhibit.
Forty-two people visited the exhibit yesterday.

If you have both long numbers and short numbers in the same sentence or list, use figures for all of them.

Correct: Last month 9,725 people visited the exhibit, and yesterday 42 people visited it.

(see p. 120 for usage of *a number of, the number of,* and *numbers of*)

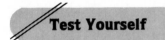

Test Yourself

Correct the errors in the use of numbers in the following sentences:

1. 19,340 feet above sea level is the height of Mount Kilimanjaro, the highest mountain in Africa.

2. North of Mount Kilimanjaro at 19,340 feet is Mount Kenya, which is seventeen thousand and forty feet high.

3. The 5 highest mountain peaks in the world are in or near Nepal.

4. 12,795 feet above sea level, La Paz, Bolivia, is the highest city in the world.

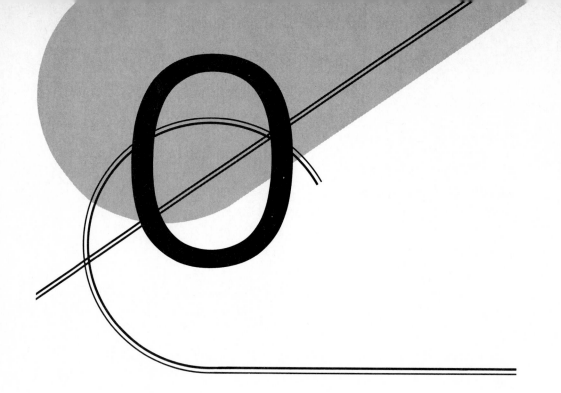

O

Object Complement

An object or objective complement modifies or gives additional information about a direct object. An object complement always follows a direct object. Only a few transitive verbs can take object complements.

	Subject	Verb	Direct Object	Objective Complement
Active:	The club	elected	Helen	treasurer. (noun)
Passive:	Helen	was elected		treasurer. (noun)
Active:	We	found	the baby	crying. (adjective)
Passive:	The baby	was found		crying. (adjective)
Active Only:	Charles	made	his mother	happy. (adjective)
Active:	The training	made	the team	a winner. (noun)

Some of the verbs that can be followed by both a direct object and an objective complement are listed in the following chart.

224

Verbs That Can Be Followed by a Direct Object + a Noun or an Adjective	*Verbs That Can Be Followed by a Direct Object + a Noun Only*	*Verbs That Can Be Followed by a Direct Object + an Adjective*
believe	appoint	color (it) red, . . .
call	elect	cut (it) short
consider	name	force (it) open
declare		hold (it) open
find		kick (it) loose
imagine		knock (it) open
keep		paint (it) blue
leave		pull (it) tight
make		push (it) shut
pronounce		set (it) right
report		wash (it) clean
think		work (it) loose

These verbs can also be followed directly by the adjective if the noun object is followed by a long modifier: We forced *open the door that was blocking the way.* Compare word order after separable two-word verbs.   (see **Two-Word Verbs**)

NOTE: Two other constructions similar in meaning to the object complement are possible with some verbs: *as* or *to be* sometimes follow the direct object. A few verbs can be followed by a direct object + object complement, by a direct object + *as,* and by a direct object + *to be.* Some verbs can be followed by two of these structures, and some verbs can be followed by only one.   (See **Infinitive/-*ing* Choice** for verbs that can be followed by a direct object + *to be.*

Some verbs that can be followed by a direct object + *as* are listed below.

<pre>
                direct
                object
The club elected John treasurer. (<i>Treasurer</i> is the object complement.)
                    to be treasurer.
                    as treasurer.
</pre>

<pre>
                direct
                object
The judge declared the defendant guilty. (<i>Guilty</i> is the object complement.)
                         to be guilty.
</pre>

<pre>
                direct
                object
Mrs. Johnson accepted the money <i>as</i> a gift.
</pre>

Some verbs can be followed by a direct object + *as:*

accept + dir. obj. + as	interpret + dir. obj. + as
acknowledge + dir. obj. + as	know + dir. obj. + as
classify + dir. obj. + as	recognize + dir. obj. + as
characterize + dir. obj. + as	regard + dir. obj. + as

consider + dir. obj. + as   report + dir. obj. + as
define + dir. obj. + as   take + dir. obj. + as
describe + dir. obj. + as   treat + dir. obj. + as
intend + dir. obj. + as   use + dir. obj. + as

The coach {
accepted
interpreted
considered
recognized
regarded
reported
took
treated
} direct object my remarks as   an insult. (noun)
rude. (adjective)

Test Yourself

Underline the object complements.

1. When we painted our house, we painted the window frames blue.

2. Hold the doors open, please.

3. The fire inspector declared the building unsafe.

4. Paul always called his sister *Sis*.

Objects, Kinds of

Direct objects and indirect objects follow transitive verbs in the active voice. Prepositions are followed by objects. Direct objects can take objective complements after a few verbs.   (see **Direct Objects; Indirect Objects; Prepositions,** and **Objective Complements**)

Pronouns used as objects must be the object form (objective case).

Gerunds and infinitives can take objects in the same way the main verb in the clause does.

Gerunds and infinitives can replace single-word objects.   (see **Gerunds** and **Infinitives**)

Noun clauses can replace single-word objects.   (see **Clauses, noun**)

Operators

An operator (sometimes called a *special* verb, an *x*-word, or a green word) is a verb form that can come first in a question: it is an auxiliary or a modal. An operator does special things in a clause.   (see **Auxiliaries, *Be*, Modals, Negation,** and **Questions**)

Auxiliaries (can also be the main verb)
be: *am, is, are, was, were*
have, has, had (an operator when it is an auxiliary but rarely an operator as main verb in the United States)
do, does, did (replaces or is used with all verbs that are not operators when an operator is needed)

Modals (can be the main verb or can be followed by the bare infinitive of another verb)
can, could
may, might
shall, should
will, would
must
need (an operator mainly in British usage)
dare (mainly British usage)
ought (rarely an operator; usually replaced by *should* in questions)

All operators and only operators contract with not.

When verb phrases that are semiauxiliaries or semimodals have an operator as part of the phrase, use the word already in the phrase as the operator.

In *be going to, be (is)* acts as operator:

Is he going to find his book?

In *had better, had* acts as operator:

*Had*n't she better come now?

In a positive question, *had better* is replaced by *should:*

Should she come now?
She *had* better buy a new car.
Should she buy a new car?

Constructions Requiring an Operator: Questions

Yes/No Questions

1   With an operator already in the statement:

Statement: Flora *will* come with us tomorrow.

Question: *Will* Flora come with us tomorrow?

Statement: Patrick *is* looking for a new job.

Question: *Is* Patrick looking for a new job?

Statement: The student assistants *were* pleased with their new schedule.

Question: *Were* the student assistants pleased with their new schedule?

Statement: We *must* go now.

Question: *Must* we go now?

2 Without an operator already in the statement:

Present Tense

If the verb already in the statement is

> third person singular—use *does* + infinitive
> all other persons—use *do* + infinitive

Past Tense

All forms—use *did* + infinitive

Never put the past form of the main verb after *did*.

Statement: Flora *came* with us yesterday.

Question: *Did* Flora *come* with us yesterday?

Statement: Patrick *changes* jobs often.

Question: *Does* Patrick *change* jobs often?

Statement: The student assistants *liked* their new schedule.

Question: *Did* the student assistants *like* their new schedule?

  dependent clause
Statement: They *think* (that) they should go now.

  dependent clause
Question: *Do* they *think* (that) they should go now?

NOTE: The verb in the independent clause changes to make the question. The verb in the dependent clause does not change.

Short answers to *yes/no* questions must use the operator that is in the question.

Question: *Will* Flora come with us tomorrow?

Short Answer: Yes, she *will.*   **or**   No, she *won't* (*will* not).

Question: *Is* Patrick looking for a new job?

Short Answer: Yes, he *is.*   **or**   No, he *isn't.*

Question: *Were* the student assistants pleased with their new schedules?

Short Answer: Yes, they *were.*   **or**   No, they *weren't.*

Question: *Must* we go now?

Short Answer: Yes, we *must.*   **or**   No, we *don't have to.*

Question: *Did* Flora come with us yesterday?

Short Answer: Yes, she *did.*   **or**   No, she *didn't.*

Question: *Does* Patrick change jobs often?

Short Answer: Yes, he *does.*   **or**   No, he *doesn't.*

Question:	*Do* the student assistants like their new schedule?
Short Answer:	Yes, they *do.* **or** No, they *do*n't.
Question:	*Do* they think (that) they should go now?
Short Answer:	Yes, they *do.* **or** No, they *do*n't.

WH-Questions

1   If the WH-word is the subject of the statement, or if it modifies the subject, do not change the verb form to make the question.

	subject	verb	
Statement:	Charles	*wants*	to see me.
WH-Question:	*Who*	*wants*	to see me? (*Who* refers to *Charles.*)
	Who(m) did Charles	*want*	to see? (*Who(m)* refers to *me.*)
Statement:	Your dog	*barked*	last night.
WH-Question:	*Which* dog	*barked*	last night? (*Which* modifies the subject.)
	When did your *dog*	*bark?*	(*When* is an adverb.)
Statement:	Pat's books	*fell*	off the table.
WH-Question:	*Whose* books	*fell*	off the table? (*Whose* modifies the subject.)
	How many books	*fell*	off the table? (*How many* modifies the subject.)
	Where did the books	*fall?*	(*Where* is an adverb.)

2   If the WH-word is not used as the subject or a modifier of the subject, use an operator in the question.

a   With an operator already in the statement:

| *Statement:* | He *will* leave tomorrow. (*Will* is an operator.) |

| | | subject | |
| *WH-Question:* | *When will* | he | leave tomorrow? |

| | | subject | |
| *WH-Question:* | *Why will* | he | leave? |

b   Without an operator already in the statement:

| *Statement:* | He *leaves* tomorrow. |

| | | subject | |
| *WH-Question:* | *How does* | he | leave? |

| | | subject | |
| *WH-Question:* | *Why* does | he | leave so soon? |

Tag Questions

Use an operator in a tag question, a shortened question form at the end of a statement. If the statement is positive, the tag question is negative. If the statement is negative, the tag question is positive. (Tag questions are rarely used in formal writing. Contractions are usually used in tag questions in speech.)

   1 With an operator already in the statement (a negative statement always has an operator):

Flora *is* coming with us, *isn't* she? (*is* she *not?*)
Flora *isn't* coming with us, *is* she?

The student assistants *were* pleased with their new schedules, *weren't* they? (*were* they *not?*)
The student assistants *weren't* pleased with their new schedules, *were* they?

We *must* go now, *must*n't we? (*must* we *not?*)
We *don't have* to go now, *do* we?

   2 Without an operator already in the statement:

Flora *came* with us yesterday, *did*n't she? (*did* she *not?*)
Flora *did*n't *come* with us yesterday, *did* she?

Patrick *changes* jobs often, *does*n't he? (*does* he *not?*)
Patrick *does*n't *change* jobs often, *does* he?

The student assistants *like* their new schedules, *do*n't they? (*do* they *not?*)
The student assistants *do*n't *like* their new schedules, *do* they?

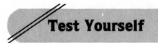

Test Yourself

The King and the Spider

A. Turn the statements below into questions.

(1) Robert the Bruce was a king of Scotland in the fourteenth century. (2) Robert had been defeated six times by his enemies. (3) He was hiding from them in a cave. (4) He watched a spider trying to attach its thread to the wall of the cave where he was hiding. (5) He noticed that it kept trying again and again even though it kept failing. (6) It failed six times. (7) The king decided that if the spider could succeed on its seventh try, he too ought to go out to battle and try again. (8) The spider attached its thread on the seventh try. (9) Robert was encouraged. (10) He went out and defeated his enemies.

B. Finish the questions based on the passage above.

   1. Why . . . ?

   2. How . . . ?

   3. How many times . . . ?

   4. Where . . . ?

   5. When . . . ?

   6. How often . . . ?

7. What . . . ?

8. Who . . . ?

9. Which . . . ?

10. From whom . . . ?

How many of the sentences you have just written have operators in them?

C. Turn the questions you have just written into statements. How many of the statements have operators in them?

D. Write tag questions for the sentences in "The King and the Spider."

Constructions Requiring an Operator: Negatives

1 With an operator already in the positive statement, put *not* after the operator (see **Adverbs, order of,** and **Negation**):

Flora *will not* come with us tomorrow.
Patrick *is not* looking for a new job.
The student assistants *were not* pleased with their new schedule.
We *must not* go now.

2 Without an operator in the positive statement, use *do, does,* or *did*. Never put the past form of the main verb after *did*.

Flora *did* not *come* with us yesterday.
Patrick *does* not *change* jobs often.
The student assistants *do* not *like* their new schedule.
They *do* not *think* (that) they should go now.

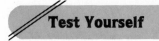

Test Yourself

E. Make the following sentences negative. Do not change the tenses.

(1) John wanted to buy a house in Toronto. (2) He liked living there. (3) He enjoyed cold weather because he was used to it. (4) The rest of his family would have liked to live in Florida. (5) They wanted to compromise by finding a place halfway between Miami and Toronto.

F. (1) Write tag questions for the sentences above. (2) Write tag questions for the negative forms of the sentences above.

Constructions Requiring an Operator: A Repeating Verb

After *so* in a shortened clause (the subject and verb must be inverted after *so*):
    1 With an operator already in the first clause:

Flora *will* come tomorrow, and *so will* Patrick.
Patrick *is* looking for a new job, and *so am I.* (Use the form of *be* that agrees with the subject of the clause the operator is in).
The student assistants *were* pleased with their new schedule, and *so was* Dr. Jackson.
We *must* go now, and *so must* everyone else.

2   Without an operator already in the first clause:

Flora *came* yesterday, and *so did* Patrick.
Patrick *changes* jobs often, and *so does* Paul.
The student assistants *liked* their new schedule, and *so did* Dr. Jackson.
They *think* (that) they should go now, and *so does* Roger.

After *as* or *than* in a comparison an operator must be used, or the verb may be left out if the meaning is clear without it.   (see **Adjectives, comparison**)

Flora *is* as quick as Patrick *(is).* *(quicker than)*
Flora *came* as soon as Patrick *(did).* *(sooner than)*
The lab assistants *were* as pleased as Dr. Jackson *was.* *(more pleased than)*
The lab assistants *liked* their new schedule as much as Dr. Jackson *did.*

If the number or tense changes after *so* in a shortened clause or after *as* or *than* in a comparison, repeat the verb in its correct form.

Flora *is* as unhappy today as Patrick *was* yesterday. (change in tense)
Ted and Patrick *are* as happy today as Flora *was* yesterday. (change in tense and number)
Flora *was* happy yesterday, and *so were* Ted and Patrick. (change in number)
Flora is happi*er* today *than* Ted *was* yesterday. (change in tense)

3   After *neither* or *nor* with inverted order in the second clause:

Flora *did not finish* yesterday, and *neither did* Patrick.
The student assistants *did* not *like* their new schedule, *nor did* Dr. Jackson.

Test Yourself

G. Fill in the blank in the sentence with an operator and then copy it in the blank to the left. You may also have to add a *not*.

_____ 1.   There was a thunderstorm west of town this morning, and there _____ one

in the center of town now.

_____ 2.   It rained hard west of town this morning, and it _____ raining at the lake

then too.

_____ 3.   The painter had to stay home because he could not work in the rain, and his

boss _____ too.

_____ 4. The storm was so bad one bus was stalled for over an hour, and

so _____ many cars.

_____ 5. Traffic was blocked a long time this morning, but it _____ any more.

_____ 6. Stalled cars were blocking traffic, and so _____ the bus.

_____ 7. Winds cause problems during storms by blowing down trees and branches,

and so _____ heavy rain when the streets flood.

Constructions Requiring an Operator: Parallel Structures

4 In parallel structure after *not only* with inverted order in the first clause: (see **Parallel Structure**)

Not only was the young girl beautiful, but she *was* also a talented musician.
Not only did the authorities decide to build more schools, but they also *raised* teachers' salaries.

Test Yourself

H. Put the correct verb in the blank in the sentence, and then copy it in the blank to the left.

_____ 1. Not only _____ *The New York Times* omit information about the earthquake

in Nepal, but *The Times of India* omitted it also.

_____ 2. Not only _____ information about the disaster lacking in Europe, but there

was also no news of it even in Singapore.

Parallel Structure

Parallel structure means repeating the same grammar patterns to show that the ideas in them have the same importance. Putting sentences and longer passages into parallel structure requires thinking ahead. Because the writer or speaker must plan parallel structures before writing or speaking, parallel structure is rarely used in informal speech, but it is used in formal writing or in speeches that are carefully written out before they are given. Coordinating conjunctions usually join parallel structures. (see **Coordinating Conjunctions**)

Parallel Structure with Single Words or with Phrases

With *-ing* forms:

Parallel: Evelyn likes hik*ing*, swimm*ing*, and bicycl*ing*.

With infinitive phrases:

Parallel: Evelyn likes *to hike, to swim,* and *to ride* a bicycle.

Do not mix the forms.

Not Parallel: Evelyn likes *to hike, to swim,* and *riding* a bicycle.

NOTE: Although the verb *like* can be followed either by the *-ing* form or by an infinitive phrase, use the same form in one sentence to keep the structure parallel. Use *to* before all verbs or only before the first one.

Not Parallel: Evelyn likes *to hike, to swim,* and *ride* a bicycle.

Parallel: Evelyn likes *to hike, swim,* and *ride* a bicycle.

Do not mix prepositional phrases and *-ing* forms.

Not Parallel: Anthony liked to spend his time *studying* in the library, *working* in the biology laboratory, and *at* soccer games.

Parallel: Anthony liked to spend his time *in the library, in the biology laboratory,* and *at soccer games.*

Parallel Structure with Clauses

Not Parallel: Anthony was happy *when he was studying math, working on his biology experiments,* or *to watch soccer games.*

Parallel: Anthony was happy *when he was studying math, when he was working on his biology experiments,* or *when he was watching soccer games.*

A parallel structure that begins with clauses must keep on with clauses. Do not change to another pattern or change the voice of the verb from active to passive or from passive to active.

Parallel: *Whoever requests* my allegiance, *whoever demands* my loyalty, *whoever requires* my trust—that leader must be *both wise* and *trustworthy.*

Parallel independent clauses make a special kind of compound sentence that is called a *balanced sentence.* The structures in its parts are the same.

Not Balanced: The hare was *fast* but erratic; the *slow* tortoise was persistent.

| independent clause | independent clause |
Balanced: The hare was *fast but* erratic; the tortoise was *slow but* persistent.

The first sentence above is grammatically correct, but it is not *balanced* because the adjective *fast* follows the verb in the first clause and *but* emphasizes the idea of contrast. The adjective *slow* comes before the noun in the second clause, however, and *but* is left out. Both sentences are compound sentences, but only the second one is balanced.

Not Balanced: A wise leader does not ask for loyalty but gets it; when a foolish leader demands loyalty, he fails to get it.

Balanced: A wise leader does not ask for loyalty but gets it; a foolish leader demands loyalty but fails to get it.

Lists after a colon:

Not Parallel: Use your dictionary for the following purposes: to find word *meanings, pronunciation, spelling,* and *looking up* irregular forms. (*Looking up* cannot be the object of *find.*)

                                                                  noun

Parallel: Use your dictionary for the following purposes: to find word *meanings,*

                       noun   noun   noun

    pronunciation, spelling, and irregular verb *forms.*

Parallel: Some punctuation marks are rarely used: *slashes,* the *periods* of ellipsis, and *brackets.*

Parallel: Use the library for the purposes for which it was intended: *reading, studying,* and *looking* up information, not for *talking* and *sleeping.*

Use correlative conjunctions in pairs.

both . . . and . . .
either . . . or . . .
neither . . . nor . . .
not . . . but . . .
not only . . . but also . . .

Use inverted order—verb before subject—after *not only.*

                                    noun   noun

Parallel: {*Both* / *Neither* / *Not only*} the parents {*and* / *nor* / *but also*} the children enjoyed the program.

    Either   the parents   *or*   the children will attend, but not both.

                                              noun   noun

    The program was attended *not* by the parents *but* (only) by the children.

Put the same structure directly after each correlative conjunction.

                                                       prepositional
                                      infinitive   phrase

Not Parallel: The coach has decided *neither   to go* to Miami *nor to Chicago.*

                                          prepositional   prepositional
                                          phrase   phrase

Parallel: The coach has decided to go *neither   to Miami   nor to Chicago.*

                         noun   noun

Parallel: *Neither* the *results* of the first experiment *nor* the *results* of the second one were the results we expected.

                              noun   noun

Parallel: *Not only* did the *parents* enjoy the program, *but* the *children* enjoyed it also.

Do not change the verb from active to passive or from passive to active in the second clause of a balanced sentence.

	active	passive

Not Parallel: Both the parents *enjoyed* the program, and also it *was enjoyed* by the children.

	passive

Not Parallel: Not only *was* the program *enjoyed* by the parents, but the children

active
enjoyed it too.

	passive	passive

Parallel: Not only *was* the program *enjoyed* by the parents, but it *was enjoyed* by the children too.

	active	active

Parallel: Not only *did* the parents *enjoy* the program, but the children *enjoyed* it too.

Test Yourself

Put the following sentences in parallel structure wherever possible. Some useful vocabulary: core, cork, heavy, hollow, inflated, light, oblong, solid, string, thread, twine, yarn

1. Some sports such as running, wrestling, and to go fishing are popular in many parts of the world.
2. People like to watch sports they understand, such as bicycle races and they also like auto racing.
3. A sport that is very popular in many parts of the world is horse racing; soccer is another sport that millions of people like.
4. Games of strategy and skill have been played for thousands of years; archaeologists have found board games in the ancient pyramids of Egypt.
5. Many games are played with a ball, which may be stuffed with rubber, cork, yarn, or animal hair, or even filled with string or twine.
6. The outer covering of a ball may be leather or made of rubber or plastic.
7. In sports such as basketball, volleyball, and football, players use an inflated ball made of leather; but a golf ball has rubber thread wound tightly around a small core filled with liquid.
8. A ball for a game may be hard or soft, solid or have air inside it.
9. Most games are played with a round ball, but oblong balls are used in American football and rugby.
10. Bowling balls, made of hard rubber or plastic, may weigh as much as sixteen pounds; only one-tenth of an ounce is the weight of a celluloid table tennis ball.

Parentheses, see **Punctuation, parentheses**

Participles

Participles are forms of the verb that are used in verb phrases to form tenses.

He *was walking*
has walked many miles.

Or they can be adjectives.

The man *walking* down the street seems *tired.*

Present participles and *past participles* are special forms of the verb.

Make present participles by adding *-ing* to the present form of the verb according to regular spelling rules. Make past participles of regular verbs by adding *-ed* to the present form according to regular spelling rules. (see **Spelling**) Learn the past participles of irregular verbs. (see **Verbs, Irregular**) In some books the simple past form is called the *-ed* form and the past participle is called the *-en* form.

Uses of Participles   (see **Tense**)

In **verb phrases,** use a form of *be* + a present participle to form the progressive tenses.

The man {
is *walking.* (present progressive)
was *walking.* (past progressive)
will be *walking.* (future progressive)
}

Use a form of *have* + a past participle to form the perfect tenses.

The man {
has *walked.* (present perfect)
had *walked.* (past perfect)
will have *walked.* (future perfect)
}

Use past participles to form the passive voice of transitive verbs.

The man {
is *seen* often. (present passive)
has been *seen* often. (present perfect passive)
was *seen* often. (past passive)
had been *seen* often. (past perfect passive)
}

As **adjectives,** present participles show that the time of the action of the participle is the same as the time of the action of the main verb.

The man *walking* down the street *seems* happy. (*Walking* and *seems* are happening at the same time.)

Perfect participles show that the time of the action of the participle was *before* the time of the action of the main verb.

The man, *having walked* for several miles, *seems* tired.
Having walked for several miles, the man *seemed* tired. (*Having walked* happened before *seemed tired.*)

Having been walking for several miles, the man *seemed* tired. (The perfect progressive form is rare but possible.)

Past participles also show that the action of the participle has already happened, but the emphasis is on the present state or condition rather than on the action in the participle.

The dish *broken* into a dozen pieces cannot be mended. (*Having* broken and *having been* broken are rare but possible.)

The money *found* on the street was soon claimed.

Participial phrases can include a subject, complement(*s*), and adverbs.

the players

Subject: We left   *them*   sleeping. (Use an object pronoun for the subject of a participle.)

NOTE: The main verb in the sentence above is *left,* which can be followed by an *-ing* form. Some verbs can be followed by only an *-ing* form, other verbs can be followed by only an infinitive form, and still others by either form, sometimes with a change in meaning.   (see **Infinitive/-*ing* Choice**)

If the main verb in the clause can be followed by either a present participle or a gerund, choose the form that gives the emphasis you want.   (see **Gerund**)

Participle: Use an object pronoun. The emphasis is on the object.

emphasis
on
object   present
pronoun   participle

We watched   *him*   *running.*

Gerund: Use a possessive pronoun. The emphasis is on the gerund.

                    emphasis
possessive   on
pronoun   gerund

We watched   *his*   *running.*

Object: Participles made from transitive verbs can take direct and indirect objects.

direct
object

Finding the *course* too difficult, Jim decided to drop it.

indirect   direct
object   object

Lending Doris the *book,* Joe told her she could keep it for a week.

Predicate Complement: Participles made from linking verbs can take predicate nominatives and predicate adjectives. (*Being* is often left out.)

predicate
adjective

(Being)   *sad*   about losing the game, the team dressed quietly.

predicate
nominative

(Being) the   *home*   of childhood, the house held many memories.

Adverb Modifiers: Participles can be modified by single words, phrases, and clauses.

single-word adverb
quickly,

prepositional phrase

Returning the papers   *with a smile,*   Robert thanked Anne for the chance

adverb clause
as soon as he could,

to look at them.

Absolute phrases are formed with participles.   (see **Absolutes**)

The rain *having* already *begun,* we decided to spend the afternoon at home.
Jobs *being* difficult to find, Pat decided she would have to move.

NOTE: Participles and participial phrases are often reduced forms of dependent clauses.   (see **Subordinating and Reducing** and **Wordiness**)

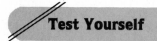

Test Yourself

A. Fill in the blank with the correct form of the verb in parentheses.

Reptiles, (1) _____ (have) no temperature controls (2) _____ (build) into their bodies, are (3) _____ (limit) to (4) _____ (live) in areas (5) _____ (provide) shelter from the cold. In many parts of the world, lizards are the reptiles most often (6) _____ (see), (7) _____ (lie) in the sun (8) _____ (warm) themselves and (9) _____ (hunt) insects. Closely (10) _____ (relate) to lizards, snakes lack legs; they move by (11) _____ (curve) their backbones and (12) _____ (press) their scales against a firm surface. Snakes, generally (13) _____ (stay) on the ground, cannot be (14) _____ (observe) as easily as lizards. Snakes that have been (15) _____ (import) as exotic pets and then (16) _____ (free) are (17) _____ (cause) difficulties in some places because they are (18) _____ (survive) in the wild where the climate is warm enough.

B. Explain the use of each participle in the passage above.

C. Put the correct participle in the blank in the sentence and copy it in the blank to the left.

_____ 1. Where is the doctor _____ (acquaint) with the original diagnosis?

_____ 2. The medicine _____ (give) to the patient last night seems to have had some

effect.

_____ 3. Changes in the medication _____ (make) yesterday may help.

_____ 4. _____ (break) arms heal quickly in children but more slowly in adults.

_____ 5. The patient _____ (bite) by the snake was

_____ 6. _____ (discharge) this morning.

_____ 7. Bones _____ (set) quickly heal faster.

For additional exercises on the use of verb forms in reduced clauses, see pp. 82–83 and pp. 418–423.

Common Errors with Participles

Do not write *dangling participles,* participles that do not modify a noun in the same clause. Participles at the beginning of the clause usually modify the subject.

Dangling: *Having* already *chosen* a new bicycle, the old one was put up for sale. (What does *having chosen* modify? Who chose? It cannot modify *the old one* since bicycles cannot choose.)

Correct: *Having* already *chosen* a new *bicycle, Max* put *his* old one up for sale. (*Having chosen* now modifies *Max.*)

Dangling: *Finding* no coffee in the cupboard, tea was used instead. (*Finding* cannot modify *tea.* Who found no coffee? There is no word in the sentence for *finding* to modify.)

Correct: *Finding* no coffee in the cupboard, the *cook* made tea instead.

Do not write *fragments* by using the *-ing* form **by itself** as the main verb in the sentence. Use a form of *be* in the progressive tenses.   (see **Fragments**)

participle
alone

Fragment: The cherry trees *blossoming* in the spring.

Correct: The cherry trees *are blossoming* this spring.
The cherry trees *were blossoming* last month.
The cherry trees *have been blossoming.*
Cherry trees *blossom* in the spring.

Fragment: The wind *blowing* the branches nearly to the ground.

Correct: The wind *is blowing* the branches nearly to the ground.
                The wind *was blowing* the branches nearly to the ground.

Do not confuse the past and past participle forms of irregular verbs when those forms are not the same.   (see **Verbs, Irregular,** groups 1 and 4)

Incorrect: The painters *done* the work.

Correct: The painters *did* the work.
                The painters *have done* the work.

Incorrect: The chorus *sung* the song.

Correct: The chorus *sang* the song.
                The chorus *has sung* the song.

Do not use infinitives after verbs that require *-ing* forms or use *-ing* forms after verbs that require infinitives.   (see **Infinitive/-*ing* choice**)

Incorrect: We *enjoy to go* to the movies.

Correct: We *enjoy going* to the movies.

Incorrect: We *want going* to the movies.

Correct: We *want to go* to the movies.

 **Test Yourself**

D. In the following sentences you will find several kinds of errors with participles: dangling participles *(dp)*, fragments *(fr)*, incorrect forms of irregular verbs *(vf)*, and infinitives where participles are needed *(inf)*. Underline the incorrect part of the sentence and put the symbol that shows the error in the blank to the left. Make changes in the sentence needed to correct it. Put *c* if the sentence is correct.

_____ 1. Fossils have showed that dinosaurs once lived in many parts of the earth.

_____ 2. Some dinosaurs being as much as twenty feet tall.

_____ 3. Although dinosaurs were not lizards, their name comes from Greek words meaning *terrible* and *lizard*.

_____ 4. Some dinosaurs ate plants, but others ate animals, even other dinosaurs.

_____ 5. The dinosaurs that ate plants (herbivores) tried to avoid to be eaten by those that ate other animals (carnivores).

_____ 6. The largest meat-eating animal that ever lived was the fierce *Tyrannosaurus*, which, it is believed, attacking other dinosaurs.

_____ 7. Having been found almost complete in some places, scientists can reconstruct skeletons from fossil bones.

_____ 8. Weighing up to fifty tons, evidence shows dinosaurs were the largest land animals that have ever lived.

_____ 9. Dinosaur eggs have been founded in Mongolia.

_____ 10. Some scientists believing that dinosaurs died out because of their small brains.

Word Order of Participles

Use participial phrases that are nonessential modifiers before or after the words that they modify. Use participal phrases that are essential modifiers only after the words that they modify.

A **nonessential modifier** *does not identify* the word it modifies or tell *which one.* Use commas to separate nonessential modifiers from the rest of the clause.

nonessential modifier
Finding the course too difficult, Pat dropped it.
Pat, *finding the course too difficult,* dropped it.

An **essential modifier** *identifies* and tells *which one.* Do not separate essential modifiers from the rest of the clause with commas.

essential modifier
The money *found on the street* was soon claimed by the man who had lost it.

Participles Used as Adjectives

Most participles cannot come between an article or determiner and the word they modify, but a few can.

In standard English you would not say *the sung song,* but you can say *the lost child.* Participles such as *lost, open, closed, broken, finished, recorded,* and *spoken* can be used as adjectives before nouns.

All the words in this list show mental states or opinions. They can be used in the four patterns on pp. 244–245.

-ing Forms	*Past Participles*
alarming	alarmed
amazing	amazed
amusing	amused
annoying	annoyed
astonishing	astonished
bewildering	bewildered
boring	bored
confusing	confused
contrasting	contrasted

-ing Forms	*Past Participles*
damaging	damaged
	defeated
	delighted
disappointing	disappointed
distinguishing	distinguished (different meanings)
disturbing	disturbed
embarrassing	embarrassed
encouraging	
entertaining	
exciting	excited
fascinating	fascinated
frightening	frightened
	honored
interesting	interested
intimidating	intimidated
irritating	irritated
lasting	
	limited
	lost
	organized
pleasing	pleased
promising	
puzzling	puzzled
rewarding	
satisfying	satisfied
shocking	shocked
startling	startled
surprising	surprised
tiring	tired
wearing (in the sense of *tiring*)	worn
worrying	worried

NOTE: Words in *-ing* that show purpose can be used before nouns but cannot be modified by *very:* clothes that are used *for hiking,* or fields that are used *for playing,* for example. Such words include *running, riding, swimming,* and *flying.* (see **Gerunds**)

1 A participle can be used before a noun:

The *disturbing* news shocked everyone.
The *disturbed* crowd began to shout.

2 A participle can be used after *be:*

The news was *disturbing.*
The people were *disturbed.*

3 A participle can be used as an objective complement:

The police found the boys *disturbing* the peace.
The doctor declared the criminal *disturbed.*

4   Some participles can be used with *very:*

The news was *very disturbing.*
The people were *very disturbed.*

Notice the difference in meaning in the present and past participle forms after *be*. The *-ing* form can be completed by a personal object and is active.

The news was *disturbing me.* (disturbing news)
The day was *boring me.* (a boring day)
My coach was *encouraging me.* (an encouraging coach)

With the past participle, the meaning is passive. Something is happening to the subject.

The man ⎰ was disturbed (by something)—a disturbed man.
⎱ was bored (by something)—a bored man.
  was encouraged (by something)—an encouraged man.

Use an adjective form before a noun if it exists:

A *delightful* day, **but** I was *delighted.* (do not use *a delighting day*)

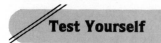

Test Yourself

E. Put the correct participle in the blank in the sentence, and then copy it in the blank to the left. (combined forms)

_____   1.   Learning a new language can be _____ (embarrass).

_____   2.   _____ friends try not to laugh when Anna makes funny mistakes. (amuse)

_____   3.   _____ by conversations with her friends, Anna is learning fast. (help)

_____   4.   Anna finds her English classes helpful and _____ (interest)

_____   5.   Anna is an _____ listener to radio and TV programs even

_____   6.   when she cannot understand everything that is _____ . (interest, say)

_____   7.   _____ her to try speaking English as much as possible, Anna's teachers

praise her progress. (encourage)

_____   8.   _____ by her teachers' praise, Anna is always looking for people who will

have a conversation with her. (encourage)

_____   9.   Studying a new language can be _____ (reward)

_____ 10.   but it is also _____ . (tire)

F. Many verbs have related adjective forms. Which of the following verbs have adjective forms with different meanings from those of the present participle? Look the words up in your dictionary and write correct sentences with the present participle and the adjective form or forms. If your dictionary gives the past participle form as a separate entry and labels it *adjective,* that means that you can use the form before the adjective, as in the chart on pp. 243–244.

1. advise	**4.** explode	**7.** learn
2. defend	**5.** favor	**8.** love
3. dread	**6.** imagine	**9.** rest

Parts of Speech

Parts of speech are the classes into which words are put according to their grammatical uses. The same word is sometimes used as different parts of speech without any change in form. Endings (suffixes) added to the base form or root of the word often show changes in the part of speech, however.   (see **Word Formation, suffixes**)

The following sections related to parts of speech are in the text in alphabetical order: **Adjectives, Adverbs, Articles, Conjunctions, Determiners, Interjections, Nouns, Prepositions, Pronouns, Two-Word Verbs,** and **Verbs**.

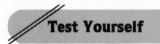

Test Yourself

A. Mark the words used as nouns, adjectives, verbs, adverbs, and prepositions in the following sentences. Write *n, adj, v, adv,* or *prep* above the words to be identified.

1. Printed communication on paper has been important for hundreds of years. Most education today is still based on the use of books and handwritten materials in the classroom.

2. The exact origin of the alphabet is unknown. Scholars believe it was probably invented in Asia long ago. Paper of vegetable fibers was also invented in Asia. Chinese people first developed movable type. Later it was reinvented separately in Europe in the first half of the fifteenth century.

3. Two kinds of alphabets exist today: those that are based on sounds (English and other European languages) and those that are based on ideas (Chinese).

B. The words in each of the following groups have the same root or base, but different endings may change the word to another part of speech. Mark each word as to its part of speech before you begin to fill in the blanks. Use your dictionary to look up words you are not sure about. Words may be used more than once in the same section.

a. right, righteous, righteousness, rightful, rightfully

	Word	*Part of Speech*	

1. _____ _____   People always want to get the (1) _____ answers

   to problems and feel that they have done

2. _____ _____   the (2) _____ thing. Idealistic people want to

3. _____ _____   (3) _____ the wrongs that they see in the

4. _____ _____   world. (4) _____ people are willing to

5. _____ _____   assume their (5) _____ responsibilities.

6. _____ _____   Some religious leaders teach people how to be in a

7. _____ _____   state of (6) _____ , but other religious people

8. _____ _____   believe that only God is (7) _____ , and that such a term

   cannot (8) _____ be applied to human beings.

b. organ, organic, organically, organism, organization, organize

1. _____ _____   An _____ is a specially functioning part of a

2. _____ _____   living body; the whole body is called an _____ .

3. _____ _____   _____ substances come from a living

4. _____ _____   _____ . Some people prefer to eat foods that

5. _____ _____   are grown _____ without artificial

6. _____ _____   chemical pesticides or fertilizers. The _____

7. _____ _____ of such farming is expensive. _____ foods

8. _____ _____ often cost more. Interested people may ____ farms where

they can grow their own food.

c. memory, memorabilia, memorable, memorably, memorize

1. _____ _____ Developing a good ____ is especially important to musicians.

In contests, they often

2. _____ _____ have to ____ new and unfamiliar

3. _____ _____ material quickly. A ____ occasion is one that is easy to re-

member, such as a contest in which a prize was won. Fine

musicians who travel to other parts of the world often go to

visit museums to see

4. _____ _____ ____ of great musicians of the past. They like to remember

occasions

5. _____ _____ when they performed _____ . A person who

6. _____ _____ has difficulty committing simple things to ____ will have diffi-

culty becoming a musician.

Passive Verbs

A passive verb is a form of transitive verb: The subject receives the action instead of acting. Many active verbs can be changed into passive verbs, but not all can. Most passive verbs can be changed into active verbs. Although passive verbs used carelessly make writing dull and wordy, passive verbs have specific uses.

Formation of the Passive

Make the passive from a form of *be* + the past participle of the main verb.

Passive Voice of *Paint*

Tense		Singular	/ Plural	Past Participle of Main Verb
Present	The house(s)	*is*	*are*	painted.
Present Perfect		*has been*	*have been*	painted.
Past		*was*	*were*	painted.
Past Perfect		*had been*	*had been*	painted.
Future		*will be*	*will be*	painted.
Future Perfect		*will have been*	*will have been*	painted.
Present Progressive		*is being*	*are being*	painted.
Past Progressive		*was being*	*were being*	painted.

All passive verbs have some form of *be* in them.

By + an agent after a passive verb gives the same information that the active subject gives in the active voice. You can leave this information out in the passive voice.

	Passive
	past participle
Present:	The experiment *is completed* (by the technician).
	Active
	The technician *completes* the experiment.
Present	*Passive*
Progressive:	The experiment *is being completed* (by the technician).
	Active
	The technician *is completing* the experiment.
	Passive
Past:	The experiment *was completed* (by the technician).
	Active
	The technician *completed* the experiment.
	Passive
Past Progressive:	The experiment *was being completed* (by the technician).
	Active
	The technician *was completing* the experiment.

Passive infinitives are possible with some verbs.

After a storm the roof needs to *be inspected* for damage. (direct object)
To be struck by lightning is a frightening experience. (subject)
This engine was the first one *to be made* entirely of plastic. (adjective)

Passive gerunds are possible with some verbs.

Being chosen captain of the team is a great honor. (subject)
The thief was afraid of *being discovered*. (object of a preposition)
Last month he achieved his goal, *being elected* president of the club. (appositive of *goal*)

Passive participles are possible with some verbs. In the present tense, *being* is often left out, and *having been* or *had been* is sometimes left out of perfect participial phrases that are passive.

(*Being*) *chosen* car of the year, the Ford is a good buy.
(*Having been*) *chosen* car of the year last year, the Ford is not eligible again.
(*Being*) *made* entirely of plastic, the engine was carefully tested.

With some verbs, the indirect object can become the subject of the passive.

	indirect object	direct object	
Active:	Don sent	Mary	a letter.

Passive: A letter was sent (by Don) (to Mary).

Passive: Mary was sent a letter.

Active to Passive and Passive to Active

As shown in the examples below, active sentences must have a subject, verb, and direct object. But the passive must have only a subject and verb. Additional information is optional in the passive.

subject	active verb	optional indirect object	direct object	optional indirect object
Active: Shirley	paid	(him) (the waiter)	the bill	(to him). (to the waiter).

subject	passive verb	optional indirect object	optional agent
Passive: The bill	was paid	(to the waiter)	(by Shirley).

Active: Shirley paid (the waiter)/(him) the bill (to him).

Passive: The bill was paid (by Shirley) (indirect object or agent—rarely both).

Passive: The waiter was paid (by Shirley).

See **Indirect Object** for more on position of the indirect object, for verbs which must have *to* or *for* before the indirect object, and for constructions in which the active direct object becomes the passive subject.

Not all active clauses can be changed to passive ones, nor can all passive clauses be changed to active ones. Some active constructions do not occur in the passive at all:

1   *have* when it means *possess, eat,* or *drink*

Active: My parents *have* a new car.

Active: The child *has* already *had* breakfast.

2   constructions in which a pronoun referring to the subject is part of the direct object

Active: They helped *each other*. (reciprocal pronoun)

Active: The player hit *himself* on the head with his bat. (reflexive pronoun)

   3   clauses in which a possessive pronoun modifies the direct object:

Active: Tom drove *his car* to the concert. (*His refers to subject.*)

   4   clauses in which the direct object is made from the same root as the verb:

Active: Sarah *dreamed* an unusual *dream* last night.

Some verbs do not naturally occur in the passive in the meanings in these sentences (they may occur in the passive in other meanings).

Active: My brother *got* a new job.
Active: Susan *wanted* many friends.
Active: John *resembles* his brother.
Active: The stadium *seats* (*holds*) 50,000 people.
Active: Chris *lacks* enough money to pay her bills.
Active: Peter *likes* ice cream.
Active: Charles *hates* spinach.

Some constructions cannot change directly from passive to active with certain verbs.

Passive: John *was said* to be in Chicago.
Incorrect: His friends *said* John to be in Chicago.
Active: John's friends *said* that he was in Chicago.

With certain verbs, the direct object can become the subject of the same verb, as in a passive form, but with an intransitive meaning:

	transitive active verb	direct object		intransitive verb		passive verb	
John	*broke*	the	cup.	The cup	*broke*	The cup	*was broken*.
The pilot	*flew*	the plane high.		The plane	*flew* high.	The plane	*was flown* high.

Some other examples of transitive/intransitive crossovers are

bend	feed	help	rest	spin
blow	fill	hurt	roll	split
burn	fit	increase	shake	steady
burst	freeze	land	shine	stretch
close	grow	melt	shrink	tear
decrease	hang	move	shut	thaw
empty	heal	open	spill	vibrate

Advantages of the Active Voice

   1   An active clause can give **more information in fewer words.** (see **Wordiness**)

2   An active verb makes your writing **livelier and more vivid.**

3   In an active clause the subject is in a strong position, but in the passive construction you may leave out some information in the active subject or put it in a weak position after *by.* The active form **emphasizes the subject.**

4   The **indirect object is stronger** in the active sentence.

Uses of the Passive Voice

1   A passive construction emphasizes the **result** in an impersonal style. This emphasis is sometimes good in scientific and technical writing. Today, however, many editors of scientific and technical journals prefer a style that avoids the passive.

Water *was produced* by mixing two parts of hydrogen and one part of oxygen.
The effects of confinement in a small space *were* repeatedly *observed* in the experimental
    animals.

2   A passive verb emphasizes a **victim** or the **result of a disaster**.

Active: The *motorcycle* injured the child.

Passive: The *child* was injured.

When the injury of the child is more important than the motorcycle, the passive sentence is better. Usually in accidents and disasters the result is more important than the cause.

Active: The *tornado* blew the roof off Mr. Halwell's house.

Passive: Mr. Halwell's *roof* was blown off (by the tornado).

3   Use a passive verb **when the agent or actor is unimportant or obvious**.

The *school auditorium* was built in 1912. (Who did the construction is unimportant.)
The *thief* was arrested. (Unless several law enforcement agencies are working on the same case,
    you can assume that the agent is the local police.)

4   Use a passive verb if you want to **hide the name of the person who is responsible** for an unpleasant decision or result. Bureaucrats and administrators write in the passive so that no specific person can be blamed for unpopular decisions and rulings.

The proposal to raise taxes was approved. (no agent)
An increase in tuition fees was proposed. (no agent)

Who is responsible? These sentences do not tell us.

Test Yourself

Rewrite the following paragraph, turning active verbs into passive ones. You may want to change other words and add some transitional words. In most sentences you can leave out the agent when you turn the active verb into a passive one.

All over the world (1) *people drink tea*. (2) *People prepare it* differently in different places. In China (3) *people make tea* by pouring boiling water over tea leaves, but in Japan (4) *people pound the leaves* into a powder. Then (5) *they mix the powder* with boiling water. (6) *People often associate the English* with tea drinking, but their discovery of tea actually came much later. In England at first (7) *people considered tea* a medicine, and (8) *both the English and the French added milk to it* for medicinal value. (9) *A tea salesman in the United States developed iced tea*. (10) *He invented it* during a heat wave at the Saint Louis World's Fair in 1904. (11) *Someone in the United States also invented the tea bag*. In Russia (12) *people make a strong essence of tea* in a small teapot; then (13) *they pour it into a glass and thin it* with hot water from a samovar. (14) *People in Tibet make very strong tea*, probably the strongest anywhere. (15) *People in Tibet boil tea* for several hours to get the full flavor of the leaves.

Period, see **Punctuation, period**

Person

As a grammatical term, *person* means the way the writers express their ideas: as their own (first person), directly to the reader (second person), or as ideas of others (third person). Pronoun forms that show these differences are called personal pronouns. (see **Pronouns, personal** and **Point of View**)

Besides the forms of *be*, the only *verb* form that changes to show person is the third person singular in the present tense: I, you, we, they *walk*, but he, she, or it *walks*. Put an *-s* on the end of all third person singular verbs in the present tense except modals, *have*, and *be*. Verbs ending in *-o* such as *go* and *do* add *-es*: *goes* and *does*. (See ***Be*** for its irregular forms in the present and past tenses; see **Agreement of Subject and Verb;** and see **Spelling** for rules about adding *-s* to verbs.)

Phrases

A phrase is two or more words that work together as a unit and/or as the same part of speech. The main word in a phrase is sometimes called the *head* word. A clause has a subject-finite verb combination, but a phrase does not have both a subject and a finite verb. A noun phrase can be the subject of a clause, however, and a verb phrase can be the main verb of a clause. Verb phrases can be finite or nonfinite; that is, they can be the main verb of a clause (finite); or they can be infinitives, participles, or gerunds (nonfinite). (See **Finite Verbs, Prepositions,** and **Infinitives**.)

A noun phrase is a noun and its modifiers.

Noun Phrase: *The large white house* was sold yesterday.

A (finite) verb phrase includes all the finite verbs in one clause.

Verb Phrase: The house *has been sold*.

A nonfinite verb phrase includes an infinitive, a gerund, or a particple and its object and modifiers, if any.

Infinitive
Phrase: The house *to be sold* is across the street.

Gerund Phrase: *Selling the house* may be difficult.

Participal
Phrase: *Having sold the house,* he was happy.
                     Found guilty of breaking into the house, the thief went to jail.

A prepositional phrase includes a preposition and the noun or noun phrase that is its object.

Prepositional
Phrase: The house *on the next corner* has been sold.

An adverbial phrase can be a prepositional phrase used as an adverb.

Prepositional
Phrase: The house has been sold *since last week.*

or an adverb and another adverb that modifies it.

Adverb Phrase: They sold the house *very quickly.* (*Quickly* modifies *sold* and *very* modifies *quickly.*)

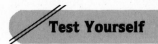

Test Yourself

Underline the kind of phrase shown by the instructions in parentheses.

1. Selling goods to consumers in small quantities is called retailing. (verb)

2. Retailers are the last link between producers and users. (prepositional)

3. Retailers break large wholesale lots into smaller units. (noun)

4. Large retail establishments such as department stores and oil companies very often provide credit to their customers. (adverb)

5. Mail-order businesses offering services to customers without the time to shop in person have prospered. (participial)

6. Some large department store chains do business internationally. (noun)

7. Small specialty shops often try to attract customers by offering special services or hard-to-find items. (infinitive)

8. Many successful businesspeople have begun their careers in retail sales. (verb)

9. Understanding the needs of customers helps retailers succeed. (gerund)

Point of View

Choosing a point of view, a writer speaks directly (*I*), or to the reader (*you*), or about someone or something else (*he, she, it,* or *they*). Most academic and journalistic writing is done in the third person, and most academic writing is done in the present tense. Since the third person singular, present tense verb has an *-s* ending, you must be especially careful to use the correct forms: he agree*s*, she think*s*, Professor Armstrong state*s*, and so forth. (see **Agreement of Subject and Verb**) You must be *consistent*; you must not change, but keep writing in the same point of view all through your paper unless you have a good reason to change. You must make your changes very clear to the reader. The following paragraph contains several unnecessary changes.

> Visiting Paris for the first time is an exciting experience. I[1] could hardly wait to see the Eiffel Tower. As our[2] bus came from the airport into the center of the city, you[3] could not see it, but they[4] all kept trying. You[5] must see the Eiffel Tower to see Paris.

[1] I—first person, singular
[2] our—first person, plural
[3] you—second person
[4] they—third person, plural
[5] you—second person

The following paragraphs keep a consistent point of view.

> First-time visitors[1] to Paris always want to see the Eiffel Tower as soon as possible. Coming into the city on the bus, they[2] look for it but cannot see it although they[3] keep trying. The Eiffel Tower, most tourists[4] think, is the most important sight to see in Paris.

[1] visitors—third person, plural
[2] they—third person, plural
[3] they—third person, plural
[4] tourists—third person, plural

> The first time I[1] landed at the Paris airport, I[2] could hardly wait to get into the city to see the Eiffel Tower. As my[3] bus was going into the city, I[4] kept looking out the window hoping to catch sight of it. I[5] thought that the Eiffel Tower was the most important thing to see in all of Paris.

[1] I—first person, singular
[2] I—first person, singular
[3] my—first person, singular
[4] I—first person, singular
[5] I—first person, singular

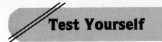

Test Yourself

In the following passage, make the point of view consistent.

Niagara Falls, New York, and Niagara Falls, Canada, are interesting places that you ought to visit if you ever get the chance because one of the world's great waterfalls is between them. Tourists visit the Falls from either the Canadian or the U. S. side. They can cross a bridge and go to the other side after they get there. You can go into the caverns under the falls on the Canadian side. *The Maid of the Mist*, a small boat, takes visitors to the base of the falls. You can also go up to the top of observation towers for a view of the entire area.

Possessives

Two constructions can show *possession* or *source*. A construction that follows *of* is easy to make. The construction with *-'s* or *-s'* is sometimes confusing. (Some grammars call possessive forms *genitives*.)

Nouns

Apostrophe + s or Apostrophe Alone

Nouns can be changed to the possessive by adding *-'s* or, if the word already ends in *-s*, by adding an apostrophe by itself.   (See **Punctuation, apostrophe** for more about the apostrophe with possessive forms.)

's and ' Forms

the dog*'s* bark (singular)   Curtis*'* friend (plural)
a day*'s* work (singular)   the Johnsons*'* house (plural)

of *Phrase after Nouns Not Related to People*
the tires *of the truck*   the roof *of the barn*
the surface *of the road*   the leaves *of the tree*

NOTE: With nouns not related to people, the word that follows *of* can usually be used as an adjective without *'s: truck tires, road surface, barn roof.*

Choice between 's and of *Possessive Forms*

1   Nouns connected with people and human activity usually take the *'s* form:

proper names: Abraham Lincoln's speech
personal nouns: the girl's book
collective nouns: the team's success
nouns relating to human activity: the body's ability
geographical names: Canada's history
institutions: the University's budget, the museum's members

2 Many phrases of time and money take the 's form:

a month's pay   two weeks' vacation   fifty dollars' worth of groceries
a year's work   season's greetings   our money's worth

3 Certain idioms take the 's form:

a hair's breadth   within arm's reach

4 Higher animals can take the 's form:

the dog's life   the kitten's cry
the horse's mane   the cat's meow

The noun following an 's possessive can be left out if the context makes the meaning clear.

Martha's course is harder than Grace's. (Grace's course)
Paul's dog is well trained, but Kevin's is not. (Kevin's dog)
They bought their furniture at Scott's. (Scott's furniture store)

Double possessives using both *of* and the 's form are common with proper nouns when the reference is definite and personal.

a novel of Conrad's   a friend of my father's
a symphony of Beethoven's   a painting of Picasso's

Double possessives are also possible with pronouns (see below).

a friend of mine   a book of hers   an acquaintance of ours

Pronouns

Two forms of pronouns are possessive: one form goes before the noun the way the 's noun form does, and the other form follows *of.* (see **Pronouns, possessive**)

my friend   a friend of mine
our friends   friends of ours
their friends   friends of theirs

Test Yourself

Correct the errors in the following sentences.

1. Bicycle's riders want to be sure to get their money's worth when they try out a new

    bicycle that they are thinking of buying.

2. They want to check the bicycle's seat to be sure it is comfortable.

3. They do not want to spend a month's pay for a bicycle that will not stand up to theirs

    needs.

4. An expensive racing bicycle may not be necessary for everyday's use.

Predicate

Predicate means the verb phrase and all the complements and modifiers related to it. A predicate can be just a single word, or it can include several words in a verb phrase, objects or predicate nominatives and their modifiers, and adverbs in the form of single words, phrases, and clauses.   (see **Adverbs** and **Complements**)

Subject	Predicate
The boy	laughed.
The boy	laughed and ran away.
The boy	laughed at the cat.
The boy	caught the ball.
The boy	tried to catch the ball.
The boy	tried to reach the ball that was rolling across the playground.
The boy	tried to reach the ball that was rolling across the playground, but slipped and fell.

Predicate Complements

Predicate complements (also called subjective complements) of two kinds follow linking verbs (also called copulas). Linking verbs are *intransitive*.   (see **Sentence Patterns**)

> *Predicate nominatives* are nouns or noun substitutes that restate the subject.
> *Predicate adjectives* modify the subject. Do not add an *-s* to an adjective.
> Common linking verbs are *be, become, appear, feel, look, remain, rest, seem, smell,* and *taste*.

Subject	Linking Verb	Predicate Complement
The house	is	a *mansion*. (noun restates *house*)
The house	appears	*large*. (adjective describes *house*)
The house	seems / is / appears / feels	*empty*. (adjective describes *house*)
The apple	looks / seems / smells / tastes	*rotten*. (adjective describes *apple*)

The answer   is still ⎫
                remains ⎭   *what I told you yesterday.* (noun clause restates *answer*)

Your prize   will be   *whatever you choose.* (noun clause restates *prize*)

Other verbs can be linking in special meanings, usually when they mean *become.*

The food *grew* cold.   My uncle *fell* sick.   The house *stands* empty.

The weather *turned* bad.   Our dream *came* true.   The milk *went* sour.

                             Get ready.

Use adjective forms after linking verbs: The weather turned *bad,* not *badly.*   (see
Adjective/Adverb Choice)

NOTE: Adverbs of place can complete the meaning of *be.*   (see **Be, meanings**)

The bread is *on the table.*   *Here* is your paper. (inverted)

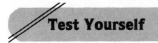

Test Yourself

A. Underline the predicate complements in the following sentences. Identify them in the blank to the left as *noun* or *adjective*

_____ 1. Optical illusions are strange.

_____ 2. Things that we think we see are sometimes different from reality.

_____ 3. When wheels turn fast, the spokes appear solid.

_____ 4. Colors appear brighter next to darker colors.

_____ 5. Straight lines look curved next to certain angles.

_____ 6. Colors and lines that fool the eyes are optical illusions.

B. Underline the predicate complements in the following sentences and then correct any errors you find.

1. Some people think that women are more beautifuls in candlelight.

2. Colors appear differents under colored lights.

3. Some people who are color-blind can see only white, gray, and black; being color-blind

    is inconveniently.

4. Color blindness does not become more bad as people grow older, but is a problem

    from birth.

5. Telling the difference between red and green traffic lights is difficulty for people who are color-blind.

6. Both the kind of light and the physical structures of the eyes are a factors in how we see what is around us.

Prefixes, see **Word Formation, prefixes**

Prepositions

Prepositions show relationships in time and space and relationships between ideas (logical relationships). Prepositional phrases can modify as adjectives *or* adverbs. A preposition in a prepositional phrase is followed by a noun, a pronoun, or another word that can replace a noun, such as an *-ing* form (gerund). Always use the object form of a personal pronoun after a preposition.

	preposition	noun
A child put the book	*on*	the *table*.
The dog went	*with*	its *owner*.

		pronoun
The dog went	*with*	*her*.

noun
With practice the elderly man learned to ski.

-ing form/
gerund
With training the dog learned to obey.

Prepositions of Space and Movement

Most of the following prepositions can be used for both space and movement, depending on the meaning of the rest of the sentence.

above	beside	inside	over
across	between	inside of	past
against	beyond	in the	round
along	by	middle of	through
alongside	by (the edge/	into	throughout
among	side of)	near	to
around	down	next to	towards
at	far (away) from	off	under
away from	from	on	underneath
before	as (far) as	opposite	up
behind	in	out	
below	in back of	out of	
beneath	in front of	outside	

Do not put *of* after another preposition unless the dictionary shows it. Do not, for example, write *off of* or *behind of.* When the *of* can be used or left out, leave it out.

Do not put a preposition before an adverb:

		adverb
Incorrect:	They went *to*	downtown
	They looked *in* everywhere	
Correct:	They went downtown.	
	They looked everywhere.	

Many prepositions can be used as adverbs, but not all of them can. Some of the adverb forms must have another word added: *Away* and *far* are adverbs, but *away from* and *far from* are prepositions.

The messenger is waiting *outside* the door. (prepositional phrase used adverbially)
The messenger is waiting *outside.* (adverb)

The prepositional phrase gives more information than the single-word adverb.

Some adverbs are very similar to but not exactly the same as related prepositions.

The taxi was waiting *near the hotel.* (prepositional phrase)
The taxi was waiting *nearby.* (adverb)

Learn the set phrases with prepositions of space.

Harriet lives	*in* Denver. (a city)
	in Colorado. (a state or province)
	on Green Avenue. (street without a number)
	at 261 Green Avenue. (street with a number)
	in Room 261 or Apartment 210-A. (specific room or apartment)
Harriet's friend lives	*in* Canada. (country)
	at or *away from* home.
	on a farm.
	in a dormitory, apartment, house, student hostel.
	in poverty, wealth, a city, a suburb, a town, a village.
	in the South, West. (region or section), an area (of_)
The plane landed	*in* Chicago.
	at O'Hare Airport.
	at the Chicago airport.
Harriet lives	*at* 261 Green Avenue, Denver, Colorado.
The plane landed	*at* O'Hare Airport, Chicago.
We visited my cousin	*in* Denver.
He is	*in* college.
	at the university.
We are going	*across* the Rocky Mountains.
	across the Mississippi River.
	across the desert.

Their house is (located)	*on* the beach.
	on the ocean.
	at the shore.
	in the mountains.
	on the river, bay, lake.
	in the desert.
	on the plains.

NOTE: When you do not put a preposition between different items of information about place, use a comma.   (see **Punctuation, comma**)

Use *between* to show a location that has two points of reference, but use *among* to show a location that has more than two points of reference.

Our house is *between* the house of the Andersons and the house of the Simpsons.
My car is parked *among* hundreds in the parking lot, *between* Joe's car and Cliff's car.

Use *to* to show directions in some phrases.

| perpendicular *to* | *to* the north, south, east, west |
| horizontal *to* | next *to* |

but

north, south, east, west *of* the library

NOTE: Compound compass directions made of two words are written as one word and always begin with *north* or *south*. Precise directions for navigation are usually given in degrees.

| northeast | southeast | east by northeast |
| northwest | southwest | west southwest |

Do not capitalize points of the compass when they mean direction.   (see **Capitalization**)

Prepositions that show space and movement often introduce essential information that tells *which one*. These phrases are adjective phrases and follow the noun or pronoun they modify. Do not put commas before or after them.

The buses *in the city* run every ten minutes.
The houses *on the bay* were damaged by the hurricane.

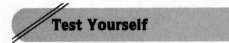

Test Yourself

A. Fill in the blanks in the following paragraph with a preposition from the list below.

across	by	on
around	in	through
at	from	to

When Joe and Chris inherited some money, they decided to take a trip (1) _____ the world. They started (2) _____ San Francisco and flew (3) _____ Honolulu, where they stayed (4) _____ a hotel (5) _____ Waikiki Beach. Then they flew (6) _____ Manila (7) _____ the Philippines. (8) _____ Manila they went on (9) _____ Hong Kong and then Bangkok. (10) _____ Bangkok they visited several famous temples and looked (11) _____ silk (12) _____ the shops. Arriving (13) _____ India, they spent a few days (14) _____ the mountains and then visited the Taj Mahal. Because Chris had always wanted to travel (15) _____ the Trans-Siberian railroad, they flew (16) _____ the U.S.S.R. (17) _____ Nakodhka near Vladivostok they started their long journey (18) _____ Siberia. When they got (19) _____ Moscow, they had traveled more than five thousand miles (20) _____ the train. (21) _____ Moscow they flew (22) _____ London, landing (23) _____ Heathrow Airport. Renting a car, they drove (24) _____ England (25) _____ one end (26) _____ the other. Finally they turned their car in (27) _____ the airport, caught another plane, and returned (28) _____ their home (29) _____ a ranch (30) _____ Texas.

B. Write out the following information about yourself, using correct prepositions. Write your answers in complete sentences.

1. Where do you live? (house, apartment, dormitory, rented room)
2. What is your address? (street, number, city, state or province, country)
3. What was your last address before your present address? (street, number, city, state or province, country)

Prepositions of Time

after	on
as (late) as	prior to
at	since (+ point in time)
before	to
by	till
during	until
for (+ period of time)	up to
in	

Most prepositions of time cannot be used as single-word adverbs in the way that prepositions of space and movement can. *After, before, since,* and *until* can introduce dependent adverb clauses, however.   (see **Clauses, adverb**) Do not use *after* as a single-word adverb.   (see **Confusing Choices, after**)

Since can be used as a single-word adverb to mean *since then.*

The dogs chased the cat, and the cat has not been seen *since.*

During, for, and *since* have special uses. *During* and *for* can be followed by a period of time. *During* means *while the event or period is in progress. For* marks the *length* of time or an *appointed* time.

This tree has been here *for* two hundred years. (length of time)
The train will stop *for ten* minutes; then it will leave. (length of time)
Is your appointment *for* 3:00? (an appointed time)
During the 1960s many nations of Africa became independent. (length of time)
We sat on the grass *during* the concert in the park. (length of time of the concert)

Since marks the *beginning* of a period of time. It can be used with a point in time and means *from that time until now.* As a preposition, *since* is usually used with the present perfect or the present perfect progressive tense in the main clause.

The patient *has been waiting since* 2:30.
Since 1960 many nations of Africa *have become* independent.
We *have been sitting* on the grass *since* 5:00 waiting for the concert to start.
Since finding a new roommate, Martha *has been* happier.

NOTE: As a conjunction, *since* is used with a perfect or present tense in the *main clause* when it refers to time. (There are no tense restrictions when it means *because.*)

I *have been* very busy *since* I saw you last week.
It *is* at least ten years *since* the family moved to Portland.

Learn the set phrases of time.

One student always comes	as *early/late/soon* as possible.
	at ten o'clock. (specific time)
	on time.
	late for class.
	in time for class, *in time to* go to class.
	up to fifteen minutes late.
	after ten o'clock.
	before ten o'clock.
	by (no later than) ten o'clock.
The doctor waited/did not wait came/did not come	*until (till)* ten o'clock.
	on (upon) the hour. (minute, day)
The patient returned/did not return	*a year to the day* after his first appointment. (exactly)
The doctor came here	*in* 1980. (year)
	in May. (month)

on May 18. (date)
on Wednesday. (day of the week)
in the morning, afternoon, evening, daytime, the
    night.
at noon, midnight, night.

period of time

Great social changes have taken
place

in/during the past ten years, the past decade, and
    the past century.
for ten years, a century

specific time
since 1960, then, that time.

Test Yourself

C. Fill in the blanks in the following paragraph with words from the list below.

after	before	during	later	since
at	by	in	on	up to

Terry has spent her holidays in Washington, D. C., this year. She will be flying back to

Houston (1) _____ January 3. To get to the airport (2) _____ time to catch her plane, she

will have to leave her friends' apartment (3) _____ (no later than) 4:30 a.m. because

her plane leaves (4) _____ 6:30 (5) _____ the morning. She will arrive in Houston

(6) _____ 7:32 a.m. because of the difference (7) _____ time zones between Washington

and Houston. She will stay with friends in Houston (8) _____ three days (9) _____ she

goes back to her classes. She has been studying in Houston (10) _____ early July;

(11) _____ that she studied Spanish in Madrid (12) _____ six months. (13) _____ another

six months she plans to return home to look for a job with an international company.

(14) _____ the time Terry has spent in Houston, she has made many new friends.

(15) _____ now she has had a good time there, and she expects to enjoy the rest of her

studies. (16) _____ she leaves, she plans to return to visit her friends as often as possible.

Prepositions That Show Logical Relationships

The following examples deal with some common problems with prepositions, but they do not cover all meanings of each preposition. Use a dictionary written for students of English to study and learn additional meanings.

1   Use *of* to show the relationship between a part or parts and the whole. (When *one* comes before *of, one* is the subject of the clause and takes a singular verb even though the noun or pronoun after *of* **must be plural.**   (see **Agreement of Subject and Verb**)

One *of* our friend*s* has a car.
One *of* the best method*s* is the one that you used yesterday.
but
Much *of* the water is polluted. (uncountable)

Plural nouns must be replaced by plural pronouns.

One *of them* has a car.
One *of them* is the one that you used yesterday.
Many *of them* have cars.
Ten *of them* are missing.
Some *of them* are here.

An uncountable noun can follow *of* and can usually be replaced by *it*.

Some of the *rice (it)* has been burned.
Much of the *advice (it)* that I get is useless.
All of the *news (it)* is good today.
None of the *information (it)* was helpful.
Chris is a doctor *of* dentistry.
Bart is a professor *of* biology.

2   Learn the uses of *of, out of,* and *from* to show origin and material.

Willis is a citizen *of* Australia.
Sara is a student *from* Mexico. (Her home is in Mexico.)
George is a student *of* Mexico. (He studies about Mexico.)
They are residents *of* the United States.
Amanda is a doctor *from* Massachusetts. (Her home is in Massachusetts.)
Amanda is a doctor *of* medicine. (kind of doctor)
The desk is made *of*/*from*/*out of* wood.
This cloth comes *from* India; it is made *of*/*from*/*out of* silk.
This jam is made *of*/*from*/*out of* strawberries.
Butter is made *of*/*from*/*out of* cream.

Of can also show material or content.

We bought a basket *of* tomatoes. (Tomatoes were in the basket.)
We bought a basket *of* straw. (The basket was made out of straw.)

3   Use *for* to show *purpose.*

Thelma is going *for* an interview tomorrow.
Larry needs a new case *for* his camera.

    4 Use *on* and *about* to show a *subject*.

I just bought a book *on/about* botany.
Walter has read many articles *on/about* opera.

    5 Use *except* and *but* to show *omission*.

No one *but/except* Catherine saw the new schedule.
Everyone is ready *except/but* Arthur.

Test Yourself

D. In the sentences below, use a preposition that will show the meaning given in parentheses.

_____ 1. Michael just bought a basket _____ flowers. (to put flowers in)

_____ 2. The basket is made _____ dried vines. (material)

_____ 3. Now he has flowers in the garden that he can cut, but later he will have to

                 buy a bunch _____ flowers to put in the house. (content)

_____ 4. Marcia just bought a book _____ flower arranging. (subject)

_____ 5. The new basket can also be used _____ flower arrangements. (purpose)

_____ 6. After the flowers die, the basket can be used _____ fruit. (purpose)

_____ 7. Everyone _____ Jo likes daisies; she doesn't want them in the house because

                 they make her sneeze. (omission)

_____ 8. Jo hopes Michael doesn't bring her a basket _____ daisies. (content)

    6 Use *by* and *with* to show an agent and *without* to show the lack of an agent.
(Use *with* only for inanimate agents.)

They traveled *by* foot, car, plane, train, etc.
The small boy tied his shoes *by* himself.
                            without any help.
                            with no help from anyone.

(See **Passive Verbs** for special uses of *by* and *to* with transitive verbs.)

7 Use *on account of, because of, owing to,* and *due to* to show *cause.*

Owing to
Due to
On account of
Because of
} his age, the teenager could not get the job he wanted.

Do not confuse *because of* with *because. Because* introduces a dependent clause; it must be followed by a subject and verb.

subject verb
Because he was too young, he could not get the job he wanted.

preposition
Because of his age, he could not get the job he wanted.

8 Use *besides, together with, as well as, with,* and *in addition to* to *add* ideas and information. Do not confuse *beside* and *besides.* (See p. 111.)

Three teams *besides/in addition to/together with/as well as* ours played in the tournament.

(*Besides* is usually the best choice to avoid wordiness.)

The teams *with* their supporters filled the gym.

9 Use *without* to show lack or omission.

Without their supporters, the teams played in an empty gym.

10 Use *in spite of* or *despite* to show concession.

Despite
In spite of } the bad weather, our trip to the mountains was a success.
Many people are cheerful *in spite of* their problems.

11 Use *like* to show similarities when it is a preposition. Use *as* as a preposition only when it means *in the role of.* Otherwise, use *as* as a conjunction. (see **Adjectives, comparison**)

Like father, *like* son.
He looks *like* his father, walks *like* his father, and eats *like* his father.

preposition   preposition
Now I am speaking not   *as*   your doctor but   *as*   your friend.

conjunction   conjunction
She is not   *as*   friendly   *as*   her brother is.

Test Yourself

E. Correct errors in the following sentences.

1. On account several kinds of difficulties, many people have problems paying their bills

   on time.

2. Ruth didn't get her water bill in time to avoid a late penalty because of the mail was delivered to the wrong box.

3. Ruth's bills were already more than she could afford with no any penalty.

4. One of the best methed of paying bills is by check, but not if you have no money in your checking account.

5. Paying by check is convenient; beside, it gives a written record of the payment.

6. In spite their problems, most people pay their bills on time.

7. One of the problem with bills is that they come at different times of the month.

8. Because of bills are sent out at different times during the month, not everyone gets bills and money to pay them at the same time.

9. You may not get your bills at the same time like your friends get theirs.

10. You may not be able to pay your bills with no some help from your friends.

Grammatical Problems with Prepositional Phrases

1   When you use a prepositional phrase as an adjective, put it directly after the word that it modifies.

<pre>
                  adjective
            prepositional phrase
</pre>
The *principal of my high school* (*of my high school* modifies *principal*) is the

<pre>
              adjective
        prepositional phrase
</pre>
man with the cane. (*with the cane* modifies *man*)

2   When you use a prepositional phrase as an adverb, put it at the beginning or at the end of the clause it is in, never between the verb and the direct object.

<pre>
                    adverb
              prepositional phrase
</pre>
The Thompsons planted trees *along their driveway.*

<pre>
              adverb
        prepositional phrase
</pre>
Along their driveway the Thompsons planted trees.

Put a comma after a long prepositional phrase or phrases (four words or more) at the beginning of a clause.   (see **Punctuation, comma**)

Along the curving driveway, the Thompsons planted trees.
Along the driveway leading to the house, the Thompsons planted trees.

3   Prepositions can introduce noun clauses, especially in formal writing.   (see **Clauses, noun**)

	preposition	noun clause
The club is giving free tickets   *to*   *whoever asks for them.*

| | | noun clause |

The president will give the job   *to*   *whomever he chooses.*

4   Prepositions often come at the end of a clause in speech and in informal writing, but writers avoid putting them at the end of a clause in formal writing.

Informal Speech: We *don't* know *who* the package was delivered *to.*

Formal Writing: We *do not* know *to whom* the package was delivered **or** who received the package.

Prepositions and adverbs that are part of two-word verbs often come at the end of a clause.   (see **Two-Word Verbs**)

The firemen put out the fire.
They put it out. (*It* cannot follow *out.*)
Will was annoyed with Allen.

Emphasis on One: Allen was the one (that) Will was annoyed *with.*

Formal: Allen was the one *with whom* Will was annoyed.

5   Only three prepositions can be followed by an infinitive phrase: *but, except,* and *about.* Other prepositions can be followed by *-ing* forms if the meaning allows them.

We had no choice *but to go.*
We had no choice *except to go.*
They were *about to leave* when their friends came.

They had no hope *of leaving* early.
Charles is helpless *about doing* his own cooking.
The artist has been waiting for an answer ever *since applying* for a grant.

6   Do not confuse *to* as a preposition with *to* in the infinitive phrase.   (see **Infinitive** and **Infinitive/-ing Choice** (pp. 179–180))

The preposition *to* must be followed by an *ing* form. (Certain verbs must be followed by *to* + *ing* form; other verbs must be followed directly by the *ing* form without *to.*)

They keep *going.* (no *to*)
We object *to* their *going.*
Pay attention *to* your *driving.*

The infinitive *to* must be followed by the simple verb form.

They want *to go*.
Paul needs *to pay* his bills at once.

Test Yourself

F. Correct the errors in the following sentences.

1. The Watsons planned to buy at the end of the month their son a new bicycle.

2. Of several different makes they looked at bicycles.

3. For test rides they took several bicycles out.

4. Their son really did not like the first bicycle because it did not for him have enough gears.

5. They finally found a bicycle their son liked, but on it they didn't see the price tag.

6. They wanted to paying cash for the new bicycle.

7. They had to applying for credit, however.

Prepositions with Adjectives and Verbs

Use only certain prepositions with certain verbs and adjectives. Learn the correct prepositions when you add new verbs and adjectives to your vocabulary. Many verbs have very different meanings when combined with prepositions and adverb particles.   (see **Adjectives** and **Two-Word Verbs**)

Participial Prepositions

A number of *-ing* forms can be followed by nouns or pronouns in a construction similar to that of a prepositional phrase.

barring	excepting	regarding
concerning	pending	respecting
considering		

Barring a delay, the package should arrive Monday.
Concerning your parking violation, you will have to pay the fine by the date below.
Excepting only those with a doctor's excuse, all students must register for physical education.

You will often see these phrases in business letters.

Figurative Use of Prepositions

Prepositions of space are often used in a figurative sense to show logical relationships.

What are the reasons *behind* your proposal?
The doctor's reputation is *above* reproach.
The costs have gone *above/beyond* the estimate.

Test Yourself

G. Put words from the list below into the blanks in the letter.

concerning   behind   pending
barring   beyond

Dear Mr. Johnson,

(1) _____ the difficulties you wrote us about, please accept our apologies. (2) _____ an unexpected delay, you should receive the parts you ordered no later than Friday. The reasons (3) _____ the delay are (4) _____ our control and we do not expect them to cause difficulties in the future. (5) _____ confirmation from you, we shall hold further shipments in our warehouse.

Principal Parts of Verbs

The principal parts of verbs must be used only in certain ways.

Use the **simple form** (the same as the bare infinitive)

1   as the main verb in the clause (add a final *-s* in the third person, singular, present tense—*be, do, go,* and *have* are irregular):

They *see* a great deal of work to do these days. (statement, independent clause)
See the balloon! (command)
Friends always speak to us when they *see* us. (statement, dependent clause)

2   directly after modals and forms of *do:*

They *will see* their friends at the lake.
They *can see* the answer by looking in the back of the book.
They *must see* the truth of that statement.
They *had better see* the director today.
Did you *see* the director yesterday? No, I *did* not *see* him.

3   after *to* in an infinitive phrase:

They used *to see* us often.
They have *to see* the director today.
They wanted *to see* the director.

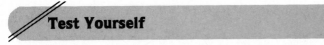

Test Yourself

A. Correct the errors in the following sentences.

1.   Marie's new car does not gets as many miles on a tank of gasoline as she had expected.

2.   She could returned it for service and find out what is wrong with it.

3.   Did she asked about the mileage before she bought it?

4.   She tried to asked the salesman, but he ignored her question.

Use the **past** as the main verb, past tense:

They *saw* us yesterday.

Negative forms change in the present tense and the past tense. Use *did + not +* bare infinitive.   (see **Negation** and **Operators**)

They *did* not *see* us yesterday.

NOTE: All regular and some irregular English verbs have the same form for the past and past participle, but some irregular verbs have different forms for the past and past participle.   (see **Verbs, Irregular**)

Test Yourself

B. Correct the errors in the following sentences. Look up irregular verb forms on pp. 389–393.

1.   Marie seen a new car that she wanted to buy.

2.   She liked it very much after she driven it.

3.   She come again yesterday to look at it.

4.   She told the salesman she would have to wait to buy it until she payed for her old car.

5.   If the price rised, she would never be able to afford a new car.

Use the **past participle**

1   after *has, have,* or *had* to form perfect tenses:

They *have seen* us many times.
They had seen us already before we saw them.
She *has* not *seen* us yet.

2   as an adjective after or separated from the noun; a few past participles can come before the noun (see **Participles**).

The man *seen* in the bank was not the thief.
Stars *seen* at night are not the only stars in the sky.
The Southern Cross, *seen* by early explorers from Europe, was a constellation Europeans had never observed before.

3   in passive forms after the verb *to be*   (see **Passive Verbs**):

They *are* often *seen* at the concerts.
She *is seen* there every day.
He *has been seen* here many times.
The dog *was never seen* again.
She likes to *be seen* in public places.

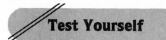

Test Yourself

C. Correct the errors in the following sentences.

1. Marie has not decide what to do about her car.

2. Her car was take to the garage for repairs yesterday.

3. She wants to get it fix as soon as possible.

4. As soon as the repairs are did, she will decide what to do next.

5. She has often took her car to the garage for repairs.

Use the **present participle** (*-ing* form)

1   in the progressive tenses after some form of *be:*

The girl with the sprained ankle will *be seeing* the doctor again tomorrow.
She *is seeing* the doctor often these days.

NOTE: The verb *see* and other verbs of the senses are not usually used in the progressive tenses. Here, however, *see* means *visit;* therefore, the progressive tenses are possible in the two sentences above.

2   as an adjective after or separated from the noun; a few present participles can come before the noun. See pp. 243–244

Seeing the accident, the man stopped to help the victims.

3   as a noun   (see **Gerunds**)

Seeing is believing.

Test Yourself

D. Correct the errors in the following sentences.

1. Marie's aunt, who has never driven a car, is taken driving lessons now.
2. Even driven with an instructor in the seat next to her, she is afraid she will have an accident.
3. Seen a police officer always frightens her.
4. She is afraid of get a ticket whether she has done anything wrong or not.
5. Marie has been written down all her aunt's adventures in the car to give to her when she finally gets her license.

Pronouns

Most pronouns stand for a noun or a noun phrase. *I, me,* and related pronouns stand for the speaker or writer. The word or words that a pronoun stands for are its *reference* or *antecedent*.

Learn how to use different kinds of pronouns correctly. You will find them in this order: Personal, Reflexive, Intensive, Reciprocal, Demonstrative, Indefinite (including Quantity and Numbers), Interrogative, Relative. "Pronoun Reference" follows.   (see **Confusing Choices**,   *amount,* number; *another,* other, others; *any,* some; *any body* and *any one; anybody* and *anyone; each,* every, everyone, all; *each other,* every other, one another; *few,* only a few; *its,* it is; *little,* only a little, a little; *many,* much; *who,* that, which; *your,* you're)

Personal and Related Pronouns

Person	Personal		Possessive		Reflexive/
	Subject	Object	Determiner/	Noun	Intensive
Singular:	*Form*	*Form*	*Adjective*	*Replacement*	
First	I	me	my	mine	myself
Second	you	you	your	yours	yourself
Third					
Masculine	he	him	his	his	himself
Feminine	she	her	her	hers	herself
Neuter (Common)	it	it	its	—	itself
Plural:					
First	we	us	our	ours	ourselves
Second	you	you	your	yours	yourselves
Third	they	them	their	theirs	themselves

A pronoun must agree in *number* (singular or plural) and *gender* (masculine, feminine, neuter, or common) with the word it stands for (its antecedent).

Use a *subject* or *object* or *possessive* form according to the use of the pronoun in its own clause.   (see **Case** and **Gender**)

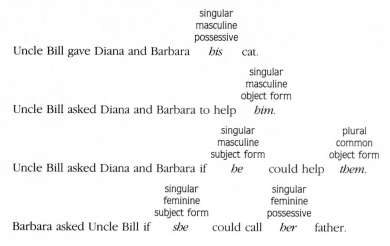

singular
masculine
possessive

Uncle Bill gave Diana and Barbara   *his*   cat.

singular
masculine
object form

Uncle Bill asked Diana and Barbara to help   *him.*

singular   plural
masculine   common
subject form   object form

Uncle Bill asked Diana and Barbara if   *he*   could help   *them.*

singular   singular
feminine   feminine
subject form   possessive

Barbara asked Uncle Bill if   *she*   could call   *her*   father.

Gender of Personal Pronouns

In the third person singular, choose the pronoun that agrees with the sex of the person referred to. Animals closely related to people can be referred to by *he, him,* and *his* or *she, her,* and *hers.* Gender distinction in lower animals and other forms of life may sometimes be appropriate.

The dog is looking for *his/her/its* bone.
The hen cackled after *she/it* laid *her/its* egg.

Use *it, its* to refer to inanimate objects except ships, which are always referred to as *she.* Sometimes other machinery closely associated with people is referred to as though it were human, usually a woman. Countries are sometimes referred to as *she* or *her,* from the idea of "motherland."

Traditionally the *he, him, his,* pronouns have been used for mixed groups or groups in which the sex is unknown. Since many people now object to this use, you can avoid the problem by using plural forms.   (see **Gender** and **Women, terms referring to**)

Traditional: *Everybody* brought *his* own lunch.

Awkward: *Everybody* brought *his* or *her* own lunch.

Acceptable: *All* the students brought *their* own lunches.

NOTE: If *I, me, my,* or *mine* or *we, us, our,* or *ours* is part of a pair or a series, put it last.

The storm destroyed *his* car and *mine,* too.

Barry helped George with *his* work, and he will help us with *ours* tomorrow.

Test Yourself

Put the correct pronoun forms in the blanks.

A. Arthur went to the airport yesterday morning to meet (1) _____ mother, but

(2) _____ didn't arrive because (3) _____ had missed (4) _____ connection in New York.

(5) _____ mother had asked the airline to call (6) _____ son so (7) _____ would know

what had happened to (8) _____ , but the message never reached (9) _____ . The mixup

upset (10) _____ both.

B. When I asked Sylvia to help both (1) _____ brother and (2) _____ with

(3) _____ computer science problems, she told (4) _____ that she could help

(5) _____ Thursday afternoon. (first person)

Problems with Personal Pronouns (Reference)

Do not use impersonal *they* without an antecedent or *you* in a way that is not clear.

Unclear: When a clown at the circus wants to make *you* laugh, he falls down.

Improved: When a clown at the circus wants to make the audience laugh, he falls down.

Unclear: As soon as *they* open the doors to the theater, *you* can go in.

Improved: As soon as the ushers open the doors to the theater, we/the audience can go in.

or

As soon as the doors are opened, we can go in.

Do not use a pronoun to refer to one of several possible antecedents.

Unclear: The little *boy* asked the *man* selling balloons if *he* could help.

Clear: The little boy asked the man selling balloons for help.

Clear: The little boy offered to help the man selling balloons.

Impersonal Uses

Use *it* in certain constructions of weather and time.   (see **It**)

It is rainy and cold today.
It is still early in the evening.

Avoid using *it, you,* or *they* in an indefinite meaning if you can write a clearer sentence. Many constructions that are common in speech should be avoided in writing.

Weak: *It* says almost nothing in our world literature textbook about writers from South America.

Improved: Our world literature textbook says almost nothing about writers from South America.

Weak: When *you* change a tire, first jack up the car and then *you* take off the hub-cap.

Improved: To change a tire, first jack up the car and then remove the hubcap.

Weak: When I came to register, *they* told me to come back in a week.

Improved: When I came to register, the clerk told me to come back in a week.
                                  or

Improved: When I came to register, I was told to come back in a week.   (see **Passive Verbs**)

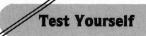

Test Yourself

C. Rewrite the following sentences to make the pronoun references clearer.

1. When the little boy and his father saw the clown at the circus, he laughed at him.

2. They always try to make you laugh.

3. If you get there early, you can go into the circus tent as soon as they open the gates and you can get a good seat.

4. Whenever they say a circus is coming to town, we like to go to it.

5. Sometimes it is hard to get tickets to the circus.

Problems with Possessive Forms

Use the possessive forms, not the article, before parts of the body and personal possessions. Use the article in prepositional phrases and in passive constructions only.

Active:	Cary blinked *her* eyes constantly. (not *the* eyes)
Active:	Ted washed *his* face and put on *his* glasses. (not *the* face and *the* glasses)
Active:	The ball hit *John's* head.
	The ball hit *his* head.
Prepositional Phrase:	The ball hit John on *the* head.
	his
Passive:	John was hit on *the* head by the ball.

(See also **Possessives,** p. 257 for double possessive forms.)

Choosing the Right Pronoun

Follow the distinction English makes between the personal (people and some-times higher animals) and nonpersonal (lower animals, inanimate things, events, ideas, and so on). Use forms of *he, she, they,* and *who* to refer to the personal; use forms of *it, they,* and *that* or *which* to refer to the nonpersonal.

Use of *Own*

Use the intensifier *own* only with possessive forms. You can use it two ways: after a personal possessive as a pronoun *(our own)* or between a possessive and a noun *(our own house)*.

The face that I saw in the mirror was *mine.*
The face that I saw in the mirror was *my own.*
The face that I saw in the mirror was *my own face.*

Old Forms of Personal Pronouns

Old forms for the second person singular pronouns are *thou, thee,* and *thine,* and an old form for the plural is *ye.* You will see these forms in poetry and older literature, but do not use them. Old pronoun forms are often used with old verb forms in *-st,* such as *thou didst, hast,* and so on. Another confusing use of *ye* is to replace *the: Ye* Meeting House. In this phrase *ye* is an article, not a pronoun.

Possessive Pronouns That Replace a Noun

He put his hand on *mine.* (my hand)
That is Julie's bicycle, but this is *mine.* (my bicycle)
This book is *yours.* (belongs to you)
Her family lives in Oregon, but *his* lives in California. (his family)

Reflexive Pronouns

Use a reflexive pronoun only as the object of a verb form or preposition to refer to the subject of the sentence. The phrase *by* + pronoun + *self* means *alone* or *without any help.* An even more emphatic form is *all by* + pronoun + *self.*

The child is able to dress *himself.*
Albert hit *himself* on the elbow with a bat.
The hunter accidentally shot *himself* in the foot.
The boy is old enough to go on the bus *all by himself.*

NOTE: In prepositional phrases that show space, use the object pronoun instead of the reflexive form.

They put their books on the tables *in front of them.*
Walter looked up at the light *above him.*
The little girl hid her dirty hands *behind her.*

Intensive Pronouns

The intensive form is the same as the reflexive form. Put an intensive form directly after the word it modifies or at the end of the clause.

The president *herself* spoke to us. **or** The president spoke to us *herself.*
The drivers *themselves* were to blame for the accident. **or** The drivers were to blame for the accident *themselves.*
The dean *himself* visited the class. **or** The dean visited the class *himself.*
Margaret and I did the work *ourselves.* (at the end of a clause after a compound subject)

If you use a first-person pronoun with a second-person pronoun or with a third-person noun or pronoun, use the first person form pronoun later in the clause to refer to both the other pronouns. If you use a second-person pronoun with a third-person noun or pronoun, use a second-person form later in the sentence to refer to both the other pronouns.

third	first		first	
person	person		person	

Don and I found *ourselves* wandering through the building looking for the right classroom.

second	third			second	
person	person			person	

You and Paul lost control of *yourselves* at the party last night.

	third	first				first
	person	person				person

Betty, Helen, and I have already told you that these places are *ours.*

Reciprocal Pronouns

Each other and *one another* must be objects of verb forms or objects of prepositions. They mean that each part of the subject did the action and also received the action. *Each other* is used for two people or things and *one another* for more than two, but some speakers do not make this distinction.

Martha and Harold gave *each other* gifts on their wedding anniversary.
The students greeted *each other* after their long summer vacation.
Members of the class were asked to prepare questions for *one another.*

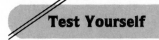

Test Yourself

D. Choose the best form and put it in the blank to the left.

_____ 1. Athletes in different sports can get different kinds of injuries while participating in (it, him, them).

_____ 2. A soccer player is liable to be injured on (his, her, the) knee or thigh.

_____ 3. Contact sports such as football and basketball can cause injuries to (his, her, the) head.

_____ 4. Runners may collapse because of strain on (their, the) heart, especially if they are out of condition.

_____ 5. Carol sprained (her, his, the) ankle when she slipped and fell during a basketball game.

_____ 6. Julia has played on her school teams for three years now without any injuries to (herselves, herself, themselves).

_____ 7. Most players never hurt (himself, themself, themselves).

_____ 8. In some sports players wear special equipment to protect certain parts of (their, the) body from injuries.

_____ 9. Even with good equipment players need to pay attention to (each other, each others, one another, one anothers) to avoid injuries.

_____ 10. Sports medicine is a new specialty to help people like Joe, who broke (his, the) leg waterskiing.

_____ 11. Sports medicine specialists treat injuries to different parts of (his, our, their, the) body.

_____ 12. After Joe got out of the hospital, he said, "Between you and (I, me), I am really thankful for the way the doctors were able to put me back together."

_____ 13. Joe warned (his, her) sister Debbie to be more careful while waterskiing than he had been.

_____ 14. Joe thought the water level in the lake was too low for safety; if rain didn't bring (her, his, the, it's) level up,

_____ 15. (her, hers, she) shouldn't try to ski.

_____ 16.   Debbie told (her, his) brother not to worry

_____ 17.   about (her, hers, she).

_____ 18.   She told him that she could take care of (herself, himself, themselves).

_____ 19.   She said that if she got into trouble the fault would be (her, hers, hers) own.

_____ 20.   After all, she (herself, himself, themselves) had taught him how to water-ski.

Underline other personal pronouns in the sentences above. Are they subject, object, or other forms? Why?

Demonstrative Pronouns

Use demonstratives alone as pronouns or before nouns as determiners.   (see **Determiners**) Demonstratives can show distance or contrast not connected with distance.   (see **Adjectives, endings**)

	Singular	*Plural*
Nearer the Speaker **or** *On the One Hand:*	this	these
Farther from the Speaker **or** *On the Other Hand:*	that	those

Distance: One car is parked at the curb; another is in the parking lot.
This car is parked at the curb; *that* is in the parking lot over there.
This is mine here; *that* is yours over there.

Contrast but Not Distance: Which of these two cakes would you like, *this* one or *that* one?
Two courses of action are possible: on the one hand *this* course seems correct, but on the other hand *that* one seems safer.

Those can be an indefinite pronoun meaning *people* or *ones; those who* can be replaced by *whoever* + singular verb.

Those who eat too much gain weight. or *Whoever eats* too much gains weight.
Those who are friendly have many friends. or *Whoever is . . . has. . . .*
The supplies for drafting cost more than *those* for art.

That can also be used as an indefinite pronoun to replace a singular or uncountable noun. Use it in comparisons to avoid repeating nouns.   (see **Adjectives, comparison and contrast**)

The *lumber industry* of Finland is more important than *that* of Spain. (replaces a singular noun modified by an *of* phrase)

The *bread* baked this morning tastes fresher than *that* baked yesterday. (replaces an uncountable noun)

Test Yourself

E. Put *this, that, these,* or *those* in the blanks in the sentences, and then copy the correct word in the blank to the left.

_____ 1. The weather that we are having now is unusually pleasant for _____ time of

year.

_____ 2. _____ who like outdoor sports appreciate being able to work out outside.

_____ 3. We cannot expect _____ fine days to last much longer.

_____ 4. Remembering _____ stormy days we had last year, we can look for a change

in the weather soon.

_____ 5. The weather _____ month is much warmer than

_____ 6. _____ of a year ago.

_____ 7. The storms here are less severe than _____ farther north.

_____ 8. _____ who are afraid of tornadoes should avoid living in areas where they

often develop.

Indefinite, Quantity, and Number Pronouns

Use singular verbs with the first eight pronouns if they replace uncountable nouns, but use plural verbs if they replace countable nouns. Compound pronouns—see below—are always singular.   (See **Countable and Uncountable Nouns, Agreement of Subject and Verb, Confusing Choices, p. 109** for differences in usage between *any* and *some,* and **Quantity and Measure.**)

Singular Countable	Singular Uncountable	Plural
	all	all
	any	any
	enough	enough
	half	half

Singular Countable	Singular Uncountable	Plural
	more	more
	most	most
	none	none
	some	some
another	other	others
(or)		
determiner + other		
each		
either		
neither		
one		
		ones
		several
	less	few
	much	many
one, the first, the second, and all ordinal numbers		two, the second, three, the third, and all cardinal and ordinal plural numbers
	a lot (informal)	lots (informal)
	a $\begin{array}{c}\text{good}\\\text{great}\end{array}$ deal (informal)	a $\begin{array}{c}\text{good}\\\text{great}\end{array}$ deal (informal)

Many single-word indefinite pronouns and words of quantity and number can be determiners before nouns.   (see **Determiners**)

See **Confusing Choices,** pp. 108–109, for usage of *another, other, others.*

Test Yourself

F. Put *another, other,* or *others* in the blanks, and then copy the correct answer in the blanks to the left. As adjectives, these words never end in *s.* Use *others* only if it is a pronoun that stands for a plural noun.

_____ 1. When Sam spilled coffee on his suit, he didn't have _____ suit to wear to the

party.

_____ 2. His _____ suits were at the cleaner's.

_____ 3. He didn't have any _____ at home.

_____ 4. At first he couldn't decide whether to stay home or to wear some

_____ clothes.

_____ 5.   While he was deciding what to do, _____ idea came to him.

_____ 6.   He decided to tell the _____ at the party that he was really a cowboy who

wore jeans when he dressed up.

G. Put _any_ or _some_ in the blanks.

_____ 1.   When Sam got to the party last night, he could not find _____ of his friends.

_____ 2.   _____ of them had told him they would be there.

_____ 3.   No one had seen _____ sign of the people he knew.

_____ 4.   _____ of the food was good,

_____ 5.   but _____ of it was new to him and he didn't like it at all.

_____ 6.   He hadn't really expected to find _____ food he liked,

_____ 7.   but he had expected to find _____ of his friends.

Compound Indefinite Pronouns

Personal:			none		another
	anyone	everyone	no one	someone	other ones
	anybody	everybody	nobody	somebody	others
	any one	every one			another
Nonpersonal:	anything	everything	nothing	something	other ones
		every one	none		others
Pronouns That Can _Also Be Adverbs:_	anywhere	everywhere	nowhere	somewhere	

Number

Use a singular pronoun to refer to _each, either, neither, no one, nobody, everybody, everyone, everything, anyone, anybody, someone,_ and _somebody,_ in formal writing. (Plural pronouns are often used to refer to compound pronouns in speech.)

Formal: _Anyone_ who has lost _his_ friend in this crowd will never find _him_ again today.

Informal: _Everybody_ can find _their_ own seats in the theater.

Formal: _Nobody_ brought _his_ book.

Informal: _Nobody_ brought _their_ books.

(see **Negation** for use of _no-_ compounds)

To avoid using *he, him,* or *his* to refer to an unknown person who may be female, put the sentence in the plural or leave out the pronoun.   (see **Women, terms referring to**)

Correct: Someone has left *his* umbrella. (*Their* is often used in speech)

Correct: Someone has left *an* umbrella.

Correct: Everyone wants *his* breakfast now.

Correct: Everyone *wants* breakfast now.

Spelling
When *every one* or *any one* means each person or thing, spell it as two words. Spell *no one, other ones, each one, either one,* and *neither one* as two words. These phrases are usually followed by *of* or *of* is implied.

Possessive Forms
Make all the compound pronoun forms possessive by adding *-'s.*

Possessives: *Somebody's* car was just towed away.
                  Everybody's business is *nobody's* business.

Modifying Compound Pronouns
Adjectives follow compound pronouns.

adjective
Someone intelligent is needed.
Nothing   sensible   has been done yet.

ELSE: Use *else* after compound pronouns to emphasize the idea of *other* or *more* or *different.*

Someone *else* can try now.
No one *else* can help us.

Else can be a possessive following a compound pronoun that refers to a person.

Someone *else's* friend came too.
Anyone *else's* ideas are welcome.

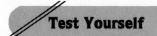 **Test Yourself**

H. Choose the correct forms in the letters below and put them in the blanks.

Dear Customer Relations:

I am very unhappy with the fact that (1) _____ (none, no one) in your organization has

answered my complaints about the television set I bought from you last month.

(2) _____ (Not none, Nobody, Not one) of your employees has given me a satisfactory answer. I would think that (3) _____ (some body, some one, someone) could help me, but I have been unable to find help (4) _____ (somewhere, anywhere, nowhere). A business such as yours, that constantly advertises its customer services, should do better. Can (5) _____ (any one, anyone, everyone) help me?

Sincerely,

Marian Brown

Dear Ms Brown:

We regret that you have had an unfortunate experience with the television set you bought from us. You need to give us more information, however, before (6) _____ (any thing, anything, everything) can be done to help you. (7) _____ (Nobody, Nothing, None) of us can help you without more facts. From which store did you buy your television set? Did you buy a set off the floor with (8) _____ (something, everything, every thing) in working order, or did you buy a set in its shipping carton? Did (9) _____ (anyone, none, another) demonstrate the set for you? What do you want us to do? Do you want your set repaired, or do you want (10) _____ (another one, other, others)? Or would you prefer credit on your account to be applied on (11) _____ (something else, other, another)? Your credit account will be good (12) _____ (everywhere, nowhere, somewhere) we have a store. Remember, your satisfaction is more important to us than (13) _____ (others, something else, anything else). We want you to be pleased with (14) _____ (everything, all things, everyone). By not responding immediately to your complaint, someone has neglected (15) _____ (a, his, their) responsibility. We regret your inconvenience. After we receive further information from you, (16) _____ (everything possible, possibly something, possibly everything) will be done to resolve your problem to (17) _____ (everyone, everyone else's, everyone's) satisfaction. Please let us know if there is (18) _____ (anything, anything else) we can do to serve you.

Yours truly,

B. B. White, Customer Service

Question (Interrogative) Pronouns

Who, whom, whose, which, and *what* can begin questions. Use *who, whom, whose,* and *which* to refer to persons. Use *which* and *what* to refer to things or events. Although *who* is often used in conversation as both a subject and an object form, use *who* for the subject of a clause and *whom* for the object of a preposition or verb in formal writing.   (see **WH-Words,** and **Questions**)

subject   subject
 Who remembers *what* they did?

    object
To *whom* was the request originally made?

possessive
 Whose   voice will the people follow?

Relative Pronouns

Relative pronouns (sometimes called clause markers) introduce dependent clauses (sometimes called subordinate clauses). They may introduce dependent clauses used as adjectives or nouns.   (see **Clauses**)

In Adjective Clauses
    Relative pronouns used in adjective clauses are *that, who, whom, whose, which, when* and *where.*
    That may introduce a relative clause used as an adjective. If *that* could be used but is left out, the clause is called *unmarked.* If two *that* clauses are used in the same sentence, at least one will usually be unmarked. Both may be unmarked.

The best pie *that* I have eaten lately is the one *that* you made last night. (marked)
The best pie I have eaten lately is the one you made last night. (unmarked)

That, which, and *whom* are the only relative pronouns you can leave out. Do not put commas around clauses beginning with *that* since *that* should be used only in essential clauses.   (see **Punctuation, comma**)
    Who, whom, and *whose* can be used in both essential and nonessential clauses. (These words can also begin a question in an independent clause—see **Questions.**)

In informal writing, *whom* is not always used when an object is needed, but in formal writing *whom* must be used.   (see **Style**)   Decide between *who* and *whom* by asking whether you could use *he* or *him* or *they* or *them*.

Dale is my friend *who* was in my history class last year.
> *he* was in my history class—*who* is correct.

Beth is the girl *who/whom* you saw in the park yesterday.
> you saw *she/her*—you saw *her* is correct.
> *whom you saw in the park yesterday* is correct.

Often *that* can replace *whom* in less formal writing, or the clause can be unmarked.

Some earlier poets *who* influenced Shakespeare can be identified. (subject)
These are the earlier poets *from whom* Shakespeare drew many of his ideas. (object, formal)
These are the earlier poets *that* Shakespeare drew his ideas *from.* (less formal)
These are the earlier poets Shakespeare drew his ideas *from.* (less formal with unmarked clause)
The earlier poets *whose* ideas Shakespeare used can be identified. (possessive, formal)

Use *whose* for persons and use *it* or *its* with animals and things. Use *whose* with animals and things if necessary to avoid awkward constructions. Never use *which* for people.

The man *whose* hat blew off chased *it* down the street.
The car *whose* brakes failed finally stopped at the corner.

Use *which* in nonessential clauses. Separate nonessential clauses from the rest of the sentence by commas.

Our TV set, *which* has been broken for three weeks, should be ready this afternoon.

NOTE: Some writers use *which* instead of *that* in essential clauses, but most writers in the United States prefer *that* in essential clauses.

Do not use *which* to refer to a whole clause, sentence, or paragraph. You should always be able to show a noun or pronoun that the *which* stands for. In the sentence above, *which* stands for *set.*   (see **Pronouns, reference**)

Incorrect: A good watchdog barks loudly when strangers come on your property, *which* gives you a feeling of security.

In the sentence above, *which* refers to all the ideas in the sentence that go before it, including a verb, *barks,* and the entire clause following *barks.* Improve the sentence by leaving out *which* and changing the following verb to an *-ing* form or by changing the subject.

Correct: A good watchdog barks loudly when strangers come on your property, giving you a feeling of security.

or

Knowing your watchdog barks loudly when strangers come on your property gives you a feeling of security.

Use *which* or *whom* after prepositions in formal writing. In less formal writing, the preposition followed by *which* or *whom* may be replaced by *that* or the clause may be unmarked.

Mr. Johnson is the man *to whom* I sent my application. (*that* I sent my application *to*)
Ajax Manufacturing is the company *to which* I sent my application. (*that* I sent my application *to*)

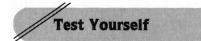

Test Yourself

I. Put *that, which, who, whom,* or *whose* in the following sentences and put the correct word in the blank to the left. Choose the best word for formal style.

_____ 1.   Ms. June King, _____ is the personnel manager of Stilerite, accepted Susan's job application.

_____ 2.   Mrs. Axelheim is the one to _____ Susan sent her application, but she was out of town when the application arrived.

_____ 3.   The designer's job at Stilerite, _____ is the job Susan has always wanted, is now vacant.

_____ 4.   The best job _____ Susan has ever had is the one she has now in New York, but she wants to move back to her hometown.

_____ 5.   The division manager, _____ promotion to corporate headquarters has already been announced, recommended Susan for the job.

_____ 6.   Ms. King has already told Susan about the kind of person _____ is likely to get the designer's job.

In Noun Clauses

Relative pronouns used in noun clauses are *that, what, whatever, whoever, whomever,* and *whichever.*   (see **Reported Speech** for **WH**-Clauses in indirect questions)

Use *that* or *what* after *say* and similar verbs in indirect speech. Use *what* if the dependent clause has no direct object after a transitive verb. In all other cases use *that* or no relative pronoun.

Mary $\begin{cases} \text{said} \\ \text{told us} \\ \text{explained} \end{cases}$ $\begin{array}{l} \textit{that} \text{ she had lost her schedule.} \\ \textit{what} \text{ she had done.} \end{array}$

Whatever may be used to introduce a clause used as a subject or object.

noun clause as subject
Whatever you discover will be interesting.

noun clause as direct object
He will do   *whatever he likes.*

BE CAREFUL: Choose *who/whom/whose* and *whoever/whomever* after looking at how the word is used *in its own clause.* The way a dependent clause is used in the whole sentence—subject or object—does not affect the choice of *who* or *whom.*

The whole noun clause is the object of *scolded:*

The teacher scolded *whoever came* late. (*Whoever* is the subject of *came.*)

The whole noun clause is the object of *scolded:*

The teacher scolded *whomever* he *disliked.* (*Whomever* is the object of *disliked.*)

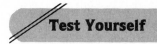
Test Yourself

J. Put *who, whom, whoever,* or *whomever* in the following sentences.

_____ 1. To _____ it may concern: Margaret Simpson has completed all requirements to enter the nursing program.

_____ 2. Margaret will ask_____ is willing to help her to recommend her for a scholarship.

_____ 3. Are you the person for _____ this letter was intended?

_____ 4. No, the director of admissions is the one to _____ it should have been addressed.

_____ 5. Tell _____ addressed the letter that a mistake was made.

_____ 6. This letter was sent out several weeks ago; we cannot find out_____ is responsible for the error because we have all new employees in this department now.

Special Problems with Relative Pronouns

1 Never use a relative pronoun and a personal pronoun in the same clause to stand for the same antecedent.

	relative	personal
antecedent	pronoun	pronoun
Incorrect:	The book *that* he borrowed	*it*	is very difficult to understand.

In the sentence above, *that* refers to *book* and *it* refers to *book;* leave out *it*.

relative
antecedent pronoun

Correct: The *book that*   he borrowed is very difficult to understand.

Even if the dependent clause is unmarked (*that* is left out), do not use a personal pronoun to refer to the antecedent of the omitted *that*.

personal

antecedent   pronoun

Incorrect: The *book* (*that* omitted) he borrowed   *it*   is very difficult to understand.

Correct: The *book* he borrowed is very difficult to understand.

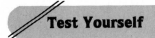

Test Yourself

K. Cross out pronouns that are wrong.

1. The package that I took it to be mailed this morning cost more than I expected.
2. The price of postage for the letters that I mailed them overseas is very expensive.
3. The package that it was delivered late can be returned tomorrow.
4. The postmark on the tax return that you mail it in must be stamped before midnight, December 31.
5. The reports that they are due tomorrow are on Mr. Smith's desk.
6. Albert owns the dog that the letter carrier is afraid of it.

    2   Do not use *that* immediately after a subordinating conjunction at the beginning of an adverb clause.

Incorrect: Because *that* Janet is my friend, she helps me.

Correct: Because *Janet* is my friend, she helps me.

Incorrect: Since *that* we have moved here, we have been happy.

Correct: Since we have moved here, we have been happy.

Test Yourself

L. Cross out *that* wherever it is used incorrectly.

1. Joan takes the daily newspaper that is published in her city because that she wants to know about the bargains that are advertised.
2. We have not read a newspaper, however, since that we have been here on vacation; we have read only the books that we brought with us.
3. After that we have had a good rest, we may feel strong enough to go back to the reading that is waiting for us at home.
4. Which article is it that you want us to read before that we leave?

3 Look at the antecedent of *who, that,* or *which* when used as subject to decide whether the verb following should be singular or plural. (see **Agreement of Subject and Verb**)

The *man who is* coming is my father. (The antecedent of *who* is *man,* singular; so the verb following *who* must be singular.)

The *men who are* coming are from my hometown. (The antecedent of *who* is *men,* plural; so the verb following *who* must be plural.)

The *book that is* on the table was returned today. (The antecedent of *that* is book, singular; so the verb following *that* must be singular.)

The *books that are* on the table were returned today. (The antecedent of *that* is *books,* plural; so the verb following *books* must be plural.)

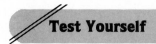

Test Yourself

M. Choose the correct form and put it in the blank to the left.

_____ 1. The librarians are the ones who (knows, know) where all the reference books are.

_____ 2. A set of encyclopedias can be found on shelves that (is, are) opposite the main entrance to the reference room.

_____ 3. Reference books in different subjects are in the south section, the section that (is, are) near the windows.

_____ 4. Many students who (takes, take) books off the shelves forget to leave them for the librarians to put back.

_____ 5. When students try to put books back themselves, they often put them in the wrong place, a place that (make, makes) locating the books difficult for others.

Pronoun Reference

Avoid unclear pronoun reference in writing. Check your writing to be sure you use pronouns correctly.

1 A pronoun must have the same number (singular or plural) and gender (masculine, feminine, or neuter-common) as the **word it stands for.** (see p. 276)

2 A pronoun must be the correct one to stand for a person or for something that is not a person. (see p. 279)

3 Do not use *it, you,* or *they* in a way that is not clear. (see p. 277)

4 Do not use both a relative pronoun and a personal pronoun in the same clause to stand for the same word. (see pp. 291–292)

5 Put a relative pronoun close to the word it stands for.

A pronoun should follow its antecedent closely. Relative pronouns that introduce adjective clauses usually follow immediately after their antecedents.

		relative	
	antecedent	pronoun	
Incorrect: The books can be sold now *that* are on the table.

	relative	
	antecedent pronoun	
Correct: The books *that* are on the table can be sold now.

		relative	
	antecedent	pronoun	
Incorrect: The man is coming *who* is my best friend.

	relative	
	antecedent pronoun	
Correct: The man *who* is my best friend is coming.

		relative	
	antecedent	pronoun	
Incorrect: The car is in the garage *that* was in a wreck.

	relative	
	antecedent pronoun	
Correct: The car *that* was in a wreck is in the garage.

6 Do not confuse the reader by using a pronoun that can stand for more than one antecedent (ambiguous reference). (see p. 277)

7 Do not put too much material between the antecedent and a personal pronoun. If a different sentence comes between the antecedent and the pronoun, repeat the antecedent or use a synonym for it.

Incorrect: Anna's mother is coming to visit her. Next week will be a good time for a visit because of the Independence Day holidays. *She* is excited because *she* has been away from home for two years now, and *she* has not seen *her* in all that time.

The pronouns in the passage above are unclear for two reasons: *She* and *her* are ambiguous and could refer to either *Harriet* or *her mother,* and they are also too far from their antecedents, the words they stand for.

Improved: Anna is excited because she has not seen her mother since leaving home three years ago. Next week will be a good time. . . .

8 Do not use *this, that, which,* or *it* to refer to an implied idea (especially to an idea in the verb only) or to one of several ideas. Make sure you have one specific noun or pronoun as the antecedent for every pronoun that requires one.

Unclear: The cook made a mistake and put too much salt in the soup, *which* made it impossible to eat.

Improved:	The cook's mistake, putting too much salt in the soup, made the soup impossible to eat.
Improved:	Too much salt in the soup made eating it impossible.
Unclear:	The little girl cried when the cat died. *This* upset everyone. (The little girl's crying or the cat dying?)
Improved:	The little girl's crying when the cat died upset everyone.
Improved:	The cat's death upset everyone so much that the little girl cried.
Improved:	The little girl cried when the cat died. Her grief upset everyone.

Test Yourself

Combined Exercise on Pronoun Reference

Find the unclear or ambiguous pronoun reference and put the pronoun that is unclear in the blank to the left. Then rewrite the sentences to remove the problems.

_____ 1. For thousands of years wealthy people have collected wild animals and

_____ 2. kept them in captivity so they could look at them. (2) The first collection of animals was in Paris that was made for scientific

_____ 3. study. (3) Zoological gardens, or *zoos,* as they are usually called, are developed to show wild animals to people who could never see them in their natural places; this helps everyone understand wild animals

_____ 4. and their habits. (4) Some people feel sorry for wild animals who

_____ 5. are kept in zoos. (5) The favorite animal of many children is the elephant, which they like to feed it and see it using its trunk to eat.

_____ 6. (6) Giraffes are usually easy to find because of its head sticking

_____ 7. up above everything else. (7) They are trying to take animals out of cages and put them in places to live that are as much like their natural

_____ 8. homes as possible. (8) This is better not only for the animals, but also for the visitors, who can learn more about how the animals really

_____ 9. live if the zoo tries to put them in realistic settings. (9) You can

_____ 10. watch the polar bears outside playing in their cool water. (10) It tries to make a visit to see animals as enjoyable as possible.

Punctuation

Apostrophe (')

1 Use an apostrophe to show possession, source, ownership, or a relation similar to ownership, usually for people.   (see **Possessive**).

a If a noun does not end an *s* or *z* sound, add an apostrophe and an -*s*. These words are usually singular, but not always.

The jackets of the child*en*   The childr*en's* jackets
The jacket of the chil*d*   The chil*d's* jacket
The jacket of Mrs. Mar*ch*   Mrs. Mar*ch's* jacket

b If a noun already ends in an *s* or *z* sound, put the apostrophe after the *s*.

The jackets of the girl*s*   The girls' jackets
The jacket of Charle*s*   Charles' jacket
The jackets of the student*s*   The students' jackets
The jacket of Mr. Pitt*s*   Mr. Pitts' jacket

NOTE: You will see -*'s* after nouns ending in -*s*, but current usage does not require the second *s*.

c Never put an apostrophe on a personal pronoun even when it ends in -*s*.

my books, mine   our books, our*s*
your books, your*s*   their books, their*s*
her books, her*s*   its (the dog's) bone, *its*
his books, hi*s*   NOTE: *It's* always means *it is*.

d Use an apostrophe and -*s* to make possessive forms of impersonal pronouns.

anyone*'s* books   nobody*'s* books
everyone*'s* books   everybody*'s* books

e The -*'s* follows the last element of a hyphenated word. (The -*s* for plural follows the first element.)

    singular   plural
My sister-in-law*'s* house   My sisters-in-law*'s* houses
The commander-in-chief*'s* order

f Avoid uses of the possessive form that are unclear. *Jane's photograph* may mean

a photograph that Jane owns, or
a photograph that is a picture of Jane, or
a photograph that Jane has taken.

2 Use the apostrophe and -*s* in certain conventional expressions not related to people, usually of time. In this construction, -*s* replaces a prepositional phrase beginning with *of*.

a day's, month's, year's *work*
an hour's, a day's, two-weeks' *wait* or
   delay

an hour's, a day's, week's, month's, year's
   wages
a month's, two months', a year's *salary*

And in other conventional expressions:

at death's door (near death)
a hair's breadth (exremely narrow)
to your heart's content (as much as you
   want)

to the journey's end (to the end)
in the mind's eye (in imagination)
fifty dollars' worth of groceries

3   Use an apostrophe and *-s* to form plurals of dates and of words, letters, or symbols being discussed as words, letters, or symbols. (Some styles leave out the apostrophe.) (also see p. 319)

He always forgets to cross his *t*'s and dot his *i*'s when he writes fast.
Most people in the world cross their 7s, but people in the United States do not.
The *1960*'s were years of rapid change.

4   Use an apostrophe to show that a letter or letters have been left out of a word. (see **Contractions**)

it's   it is or it has
it isn't   it is not
I'd   I had or I would
didn't   did not, and so on

Other common forms:

o'clock   of the clock
ma'am   madam

Forms used in songs and poetry:

e'en   even
e'er   ever
ne'er never
o'er over

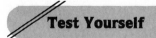 **Test Yourself**

A. Turn the following phrases into possessive or noun modifiers.

1. a book that belongs to Elizabeth.

2. a leg of the table

3. the wages of a day

4. the ideas of Charles

5. the shoes of Chris

6. a class of Professor Martin

7. a requirement of the college

8. the house of Mr. and Mrs. Roberts

9. a tire on the bicycle

10. shoes of Pat

B. Put apostrophes wherever they are needed in the following sentences. Some sentences are correct.

1. Its difficult to sleep when a dog barks all night.

2. Whose dog is it?

3. The dog belongs to Mr. and Mrs. Jones; its name is Sparky.

4. Its barking because it thinks its lost its master.

5. The Joneses are moving away, but they plan to come back today to pick up the dog and some other things of theirs they left behind.

6. Theyll be here by ten oclock this morning.

7. They plan to stop at Mrs. Jones sister-in-laws house down the street before they leave.

8. Shes the one whos been feeding the dog for them.

9. She wouldnt hurt anyones feelings by saying so, but shell be glad to say good-bye to that dog.

Asterisk (*)

1 Asterisks were used in the past to indicate footnotes if there were very few footnotes. (Numbers set slightly higher than the line of type are usually used to indicate footnotes now.)

2 Asterisks are used in linguistics to show incorrect examples.

* They no know how to do it.   * They do not know how doing it.

Absence of an asterisk in linguistics shows that an example is correct.

They do not know how to do it.

3 Three asterisks *** show an ellipsis, especially in older writing. Three periods show an omission ellipsis of parts of sentences or sentences. Three asterisks usually show that a whole paragraph or an even longer passage has been left out. (See "Ellipsis" in this section, p. 310.)

Brackets ([])

Always use brackets in pairs. They show that you have put an explanation of your own into a direct quotation.

Poets sometimes use contractions that are not common in speech: "'twas [it was] the night before Christmas. . . ."

Colon (:)

Never put a colon at the beginning of a line. Use a colon to separate a statement from a further explanation or detail.

1 A colon may introduce a list or explanation that is not grammatically necessary to the sentence.

list

An elderly man bought several items at the bookstore: a notebook, two pens, and some typing paper.

explanation

Some writers have difficulty understanding punctuation rules: they think the examples are not clear.

Never use a colon immediately after a preposition or a verb.

Incorrect: He went to the store for: milk, bread, cheese, and tea.

Incorrect: The cities in the United States that I would like to visit are: Miami, San Francisco, and New York.

Sentences must be grammatically complete before the colon.

Correct: He went to the store for several items: milk, bread, cheese, and tea.

Correct: The cities in the United States that I would like to visit are three: Miami, San Francisco, and New York.

Correct: The cities in the United States that I would like to visit are Miami, San Francisco, and New York.

2   Use a colon to introduce a long quotation separated from the rest of the text.

William Wordsworth wrote about nature:

> "My heart leaps up when I behold
> A rainbow in the sky:
> So was it when my life began;
> So is it now I am a man:
> So be it when I shall grow old,
>   Or let me die!"

3   In a book or article title, a colon separates the title from the subtitle.

Writing Research Papers: A Complete Guide
Women at Work: Case Studies of Working Mothers

4   A colon separates hours and minutes:

2:15 p.m.

A colon also separates minutes and seconds, if necessary:

2:15:03 (two hours, fifteen minutes, and three seconds)

5   A colon shows a ratio:

4 : 1 (four to one)

Test Yourself

Put colons wherever necessary. Some sentences may be correct.

1. Libraries offer many services lending books, offering reference services, and providing comfortable places to read and study.
2. Three kinds of libraries are public libraries, school libraries, and research libraries.
3. Specialized libraries supported by business, government, religious, and professional groups have special collections in law, medicine, science, and religion.
4. College and university libraries provide books in many disciplines art, music, literature, science, social science, and health fields, for example.
5. Readers can sometimes find libraries in unexpected places hospitals, resorts, and airports in some places have libraries.
6. The public library in Madison opens at 830 A.M. and closes at 930 P.M.

Comma (,)

Never put a comma at the beginning of a line. Never use a comma without a reason for doing so.

1   Put a comma **AFTER** each item except the last in a series of three or more words, phrases, or short clauses.

Words: Debbie, Sue, and Janet have all made the team.

Phrases: The mayor of the city, the sheriff of the country, and the governor of the state are all elected officials.
She put down the phone, picked up her purse, and left.

Clauses: The dog growled, then he barked, and finally he began to chase the cat.

2   Put a comma **AFTER** a person's last name if the last name is written before the first name.

On the application for a new job, Jane had to write her last name first: Ashford, Jane. She also had to give her father's name: Ashford, William.

3   Put a comma **AFTER** every item in an address or date if there is more than one item (month and date together count as one item).

One Item: On May 15 she will be ten years old.
Only in New York can you see the Statue of Liberty.

More Than   He was born on March 23, 1965, the youngest of four brothers.
One Item: She lives in New Haven, Connecticut, before she moved to Denver, Colorado, with her family.
They have lived at 291 Redfern Avenue, Dayton, Texas, since September, 1976, in a house that is a hundred years old.

In addresses, use *at* when the street number is given, but use *on* when the street is given without the number. *In* can replace a comma between street and city in a sentence but not in a mailing address.

They lived *on* Redfern Avenue *in* Dayton, Texas.
They lived *at* 291 Redfern Avenue.

Do not put a comma between state and zip code numbers in writing a mailing address.

Miss Susan Jackson
291 Redfern Avenue
Dayton, Texas 76109

4   Put commas **AFTER** certain words, phrases, and clauses at the beginning of a sentence.
a   after a word that does not flow into the rest of the sentence. (To express stronger emotion, use an exclamation mark.)

Oh, I wish I could go with you.
Yes, you have the right number.

Well, that was the end of that.
Stronger: Well! That was the end of that!

No, that is not the right answer.
Stronger: No! That is not the right answer.

b   after a long participial, infinitive, or prepositional phrase at the beginning of the sentence and after an absolute phrase.   (see **Absolutes**)

Participial: Seeing his father coming down the street, the child shouted and ran to the door.

Both present and past participles can be used.

Phrase with Present Participle:	Tying the manager's hands and feet, the robber warned him not to make any noise.
Phrase with Past Participle:	Tied hand and foot, the manager struggled to reach the burglar alarm.
Infinitive Phrase:	To find the street you are looking for, turn left at the first stop sign.
Prepositional Phrase:	Before making a final decision on a career, you should think about what you dislike as well as what you like.

NOTE: The comma is often left out after a short phrase (usually four words or fewer) at the beginning of a sentence.

   c Put a comma **AFTER** an introductory dependent clause introduced by a word such as *if, when, after, since, although,* or *because.*   (see **Clauses, dependent**)

When he heard that she had already left, he rushed out of the house.
After she had locked the door and shut the curtains, she turned out the light and went to bed.

A NOTE ON WORD ORDER: When infinitive phrases, prepositional phrases, or dependent adverbial clauses come at the *end* of a sentence, do not separate them from the rest of the sentence by a comma.

Phrase at Beginning:	To find the street you are looking for, turn left at the first stop sign.
Phrase at End:	Turn left at the first stop sign to find the street you are looking for.
Phrase at Beginning:	Before making a final decision on a career, you should think about what you dislike as well as what you like.
Phrase at End:	You should think about what you dislike as well as what you like before making a final decision on a career.
Clause at Beginning:	When he heard that she had already left, he rushed out of the house.
Clause at End:	He rushed out of the house when he heard that she had already left.
Clause at Beginning:	After she had locked the door and shut the curtains, she turned out the light and went to bed.
Clause at End:	She turned out the light and went to bed after she had locked the door and shut the curtains.

   5 Put a comma **BEFORE** a tag question or other contrasting phrase or an absolute phrase at the end of a sentence.   (see **Absolutes**)

The secretary is late today, isn't she?
They will not leave early, will they?
He wore his new suit, not his old one.

The secretary is late today, having missed the bus.
They will not leave early, still having work to do.
He wore his new suit, having left his old one at the cleaners.

6   Put a comma **BEFORE** a coordinating conjunction that connects two independent clauses (*and, but, for, or, nor, yet,* or *so*).   (see **Coordinating Conjunctions** and chart, pp. 317–318)

He walked down the street to the bus stop, and he waited for a bus for nearly twenty minutes.
Nelson is always complaining about not having any friends, but he is not a friendly person himself.

Do not put a comma before or after a coordinating conjunction that joins two verbs in the same clause.

He *went* down the street to the bus stop *and waited* for a bus for nearly twenty minutes.
Nelson *is* always *complaining* about not having any friends *and is* not a friendly person himself.

Test Yourself

Comma exercises, Rules 1–6

Put commas wherever needed.

1.   When Abraham Lincoln was twenty-one years old his family moved settling in Illinois.

2.   Living at home another year he helped his father build a cabin plant a crop and split rails for fences.

3.   In the early part of 1831 Lincoln traveled to New Orleans Louisiana at the mouth of the Mississippi River the farthest he had ever gone from home.

4.   Lincoln saw slaves being bought and sold while he was in New Orleans.

5.   When Lincoln returned to Illinois he moved to New Salem lived in the back of a store and tried to support himself with odd jobs borrowing books to read after work.

6.   Nine months later Lincoln enlisted in the local military unit to fight the Indians in the

Black Hawk War; although he did no fighting the men in his company elected him captain.

7. Abraham Lincoln was one of the most famous presidents of the United States wasn't he?

8. He is remembered today as a lawyer and president not a soldier.

7   Put a comma **BETWEEN** coordinate adjectives which can be separated by *and*.   (See **Adjectives, order of,** for more rules and examples.)

They were well-trained and intelligent horses.
They were intelligent, well-trained horses.

or

They were well-trained, intelligent horses.

Her rich and famous brother was coming to visit her.
Her rich, famous brother was coming to visit her.

or

Her famous, rich brother was coming to visit her.

Do not use commas instead of *and* to separate coordinate adjectives that follow the verb as predicate adjectives.

Her brother was rich and famous.

Test Yourself

Comma Exercises, Rules 1–7.

Put commas wherever they are needed.

1. Abraham Lincoln had several nicknames among them "Honest Abe"; this nickname showed his honest upright character.

2. He was so honest and upright that for several years he worked long and hard to pay off debts his business partner left.

3. Lincoln's energetic hard work made people respect him when he decided to run for political office.

Put commas **AROUND** certain words and phrases.

8 Use a comma or *pairs* of commas to set off certain words, phrases, and clauses from the rest of the sentence. When these words, phrases, and clauses come at the beginning or end of the clause, put only one comma.

a Words and phrases such as *however, nevertheless, furthermore, in addition, of course, consequently, on the other hand, namely, that is, as a result, subsequently,* and *after that.* (see **Interrupters**)

In the Middle of the Clause:	Most authorities, however, disagree with these conclusions.
At the Beginning of the Clause:	However, most authorities disagree with these conclusions.
At the End of the Clause:	Most authorities disagree with these conclusions, however.
In the Middle of the Clause:	The results, therefore, seem to be conclusive.
In the Middle of the Clause:	A final judgment, of course, must wait for more evidence.

Do not put an interrupter between two independent clauses and leave out the semicolon. (see **Fragments**)

Wrong:	The results of this experiment were very interesting, however, most authorities disagree with the conclusions.
Right:	The results of this experiment were very interesting; however, most authorities disagree with the conclusions.

b Use a comma or a pair of commas to separate the name or title of a person spoken to from the rest of the sentence.

A Pair of Commas in the Middle of the Clause:	Please, John, come early tomorrow.
One Comma at the End of the Clause:	Thank you for the help, Mrs. Johnson.
One Comma at the Beginning of the Clause:	Mark, bring those notebooks here now.

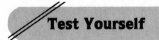 **Test Yourself**

Comma Exercise, Rule 9

Put commas wherever needed.

(1) Abraham Lincoln's name was linked with that of a girl named Ann Rutledge; some historians doubt however that he ever planned to marry her. (2) Ann died in 1835; at that time Lincoln grieved for her very much. (3) Nevertheless Lincoln proposed to a girl in Kentucky only eighteen months later. (4) The girl in Kentucky refused his proposal however; after that he married Mary Todd in 1842 when he was thirty-three years old.

9   Use a comma or a pair of commas to set off words, phrases, and clauses that give additional information or rename a person or thing already identified.

Modifiers such as adjectives, participial phrases (*-ing* forms), and dependent clauses may be either *essential* or *nonessential*. (Some grammars use the terms *restrictive/nonrestrictive* or *limiting/nonlimiting* for this difference.)

Essential modifiers are necessary to identify the word they modify. They tell "which one." Nonessential modifiers give additional information about something that is already identified. A proper name is almost always complete identification, so additional information about somebody or something called by a proper name is almost always nonessential.

Do not set off essential modifiers from the rest of the sentence by a comma or a pair of commas. Set off nonessential modifiers from the rest of the sentence by a comma or a pair of commas.   (see **Punctuations, commas**)

Essential: My neighbor who likes to swim hates rainy days. (*who likes to swim* tells which neighbor.)

Nonessential: Dr. Brown, who likes to swim, hates rainy days.

Essential: Students who need a receipt may apply here. (Some students need a receipt.)

Putting commas in the sentence above changes the meaning from *some students* to *all students*.

Nonessential: Students, who need a receipt, may apply here. (All students need a receipt.)

Essential: Drivers in the city who obey traffic laws have fewer accidents. (Some drivers in the city obey traffic laws; only these drivers have fewer accidents.)

Nonessential: Drivers in the city, who obey traffic laws, have fewer accidents. (All drivers in the city obey traffic laws and have fewer accidents than drivers outside the city.)

In spoken English the difference between essential and nonessential modifiers is shown by a change in intonation and by slight pauses before and after nonessential modifiers. Show these pauses in your writing by using a comma or commas to show nonessential modifiers.

Essential: My brother James is a student here. (I have more than one brother. One is named James. That one is a student here.)

Nonessential: My brother, James, is a student here. (I have only one brother; his name is James. He is a student here.)

Essential modifiers tell which one.

Essential: The word *receive* is often misspelled.

Essential: The planet Pluto is the planet in the solar system that is the farthest from earth.

Do not set off the *-self* pronouns with commas.

I *myself* will go.
The drivers *themselves* could not avoid the accident.

CLAUSES: (see **Pronouns, relative**) An **essential** clause can begin with *that*, it can begin with its own subject if *that* is left out, it can begin with a WH-word, or it can begin with a preposition followed by a WH-word. If you can use either *that* or *which*, use *that* in essential clauses in formal writing (British usage allows *which*).

	Essential Clause	
that	The man *that* I told you about	is here.
that *left out; subject* begins the clause	The man *I* told you about	is here.
WH-*word*	The man *whom* I told you about This is the place *where* we searched.	is here.
preposition + WH-*word*	The man *of whom* I spoke	is here.

A **nonessential** clause begins with a WH-word or with a preposition followed by a WH-word.

	Nonessential Clause
WH-*word*	Joyce Harris, *who*(*m*) I saw yesterday, asked about you. (Use *whom* in formal writing.)
WH-*word*	Joyce Harris, *who* came back from vacation yesterday, asked about you.
WH-*word*	Joyce Harris, *whose* mother is in the hospital, left early today.
preposition + WH-*word*	Joyce Harris, to *whom* I sent an invitation to our party, asked about you.
WH-*word*	Chicago, *which* is known as "the windy city," gets the wind off Lake Michigan and from the plains.

Although proper names are usually followed by nonessential modifiers, proper names that stand for more than one person, place, or thing can be identified by essential modifiers. Put *the* before the proper noun to indicate one specific item out of more than one.

Essential: The Miami *that is in Ohio* is a smaller city than the Miami *that is in Florida*.

Essential: That is the Joe Green *who is the football player,* not the Joe Green *who is the singer.*

Test Yourself

Comma Exercise, Rule 9

Put commas wherever needed. Some sentences may be correct.

1. Abraham Lincoln's mother Nancy died when he was nine years old.

2. The following year Lincoln's father Thomas went to Kentucky and married Sarah a widow he had known before she married the first time.

3. Sarah Lincoln's stepmother encouraged and helped the young Abe.

4. Lincoln himself said that the formal education he received was limited to "the three R's" which stands for "reading 'riting and 'rithmetic."

5. Lincoln borrowed books from anyone who would lend them to him.

6. He borrowed Weem's *Life of Washington* which he later said made a big impression on him.

7. Lincoln and his family who lived on a farm on the Indiana frontier moved farther west when he was twenty-one.

8. They moved to Illinois a state that was considered the far west in those days.

9. Lincoln got his first steady job in New Salem a town that was near the state capital of Springfield.

10. Lincoln's lack of formal education which had not been available in Indiana was a handicap to him.

11. Lincoln borrowed books when he was a young man in Illinois just as he had borrowed them earlier from friends and neighbors who lived in Indiana.

12. He studied law by reading law books borrowed from a lawyer who was his friend.

10 Put a comma or commas in a direct quotation to set off the speaker's exact words from the rest of the sentence. (see **Direct Speech** for complete rules, examples, and exercises)

"The patient needs to have her lunch now," the nurse said.
The nurse said, "The patient needs to have her lunch now."

Test Yourself

Combined Comma Exercises

Put commas wherever necessary and be prepared to give the rule that applies.

1. The story of Abraham Lincoln's life is the story of a man who rose to be President of the United States from humble origins that were not uncommon however in his own time.

2. Although his family seems very poor by today's standards his kind of life was not considered unusually hard on the frontier.

3. Writing about his early life Lincoln himself said "God bless my mother; all that I am or ever hope to be I owe to her."

4. Nevertheless deaths of family members lack of schools and life in primitive log cabins seem like severe hardships to most people today.

5. Lincoln not only had a hard life as a child but he also had a difficult life as President of the United States a country that was divided and at war during his presidency.

6. From almost the time that Lincoln was inaugurated on March 4 1861 to his death on April 14 1865 the northern and southern states of the United States were at war.

7. Lincoln's body was returned to Springfield Illinois for burial; his tomb there which is visited by thousands of people every year is an impressive monument.

Dash (—)

Avoid using a dash in most formal writing. In informal writing a dash can replace a colon, and a pair of dashes can replace a pair of commas or parentheses.

Colon: The Scouts checked their camping equipment carefully: backpacks, tents, clothing, and food.

Dash: The Scouts checked their camping equipment carefully—backpacks, tents, clothing, and food.

Pair of Commas: The Scouts checked their camping equipment, especially the backpacks and tent, before leaving for the mountains.

Parentheses: The Scouts checked their camping equipment (especially the backpacks and tent) before leaving for the mountains.

Dashes: The Scouts checked their camping equipment—especially the backpacks and tent—before leaving for the mountains.

Use a dash or a pair of dashes to set off a long interrupter that already has commas in it.

The Scouts checked their camping equipment carefully—backpacks, tent, camping equipment, clothing, and food—before leaving for the mountains.

All of John's family—his father, mother, brother, and sister—will visit him next summer.

NOTE: In typing use two hyphens to make a dash.

Test Yourself

A. Put dashes wherever they are possible in the following sentences.

1. Lawyers also called attorneys, counsel, or counselors give legal advice and represent their clients in court.
2. The word *engineer* can refer to several different kinds of people someone who works in a branch of engineering, someone who manages things cleverly, or someone who drives an engine.
3. People who teach others teachers, professors, instructors must enjoy working with people.

B. Can you use parentheses instead of dashes in any of the sentences above?

C. Can you use a colon instead of a dash in any of the sentences above?

Ellipsis (. . .)

An ellipsis is three dots indicating that part of a direct quotation has been left out. If the words left out are at the end of a sentence, a fourth dot is added for the period.

"So was it when my life began . . . so be it when I shall grow old . . ."

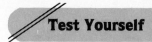 **Test Yourself**

Shorten the following quotation from Abraham Lincoln. Begin with the first *you*. Use ellipsis to show that this word is not the first word in the sentence. Use quotation marks to show that this passage is a direct quotation.

It is true that you may fool all the people some of the time; you can

even fool some of the people all the time; but you can't fool all of the

people all the time.

Exclamation Point (!)

Never put an exclamation point at the beginning of a line. Put an exclamation point after a statement or a word of strong feeling.

Well! When can you come?	They are looking for you!
Watch out!	Run!
Help!	Call the ambulance!

 **Test Yourself**

To show strong feeling, use exclamation points instead of commas or periods.

1. Help, the building is on fire.
2. The man is drowning. Come help us.
3. "No," he shouted. "I positively will not take you with me."

Hyphen (-)

Never put a hyphen at the beginning of a line. Put a hyphen slightly above the line if you are writing by hand on lined paper. Never put a hyphen below the line.

1 Use a hyphen to separate parts of words as conventional spelling indicates.

vice-president	but	vice admiral
mother-in-law	but	stepmother
pre-engineering	but	premature

Look up the word in a dictionary if you are not sure whether or not it needs a hyphen.

2 Use a hyphen between all spelled-out numbers of two words from twenty-one through ninety-nine and in compound numbers that contain them.

thirty-three (33)
one hundred thirty-three (133)

3 Use a hyphen between the parts of fractions when they are written as words but not if an article replaces *one*.

three-fourths (¾)   one-fourth (¼)
seven-eighths (⅞)   **but** a/the half

4 Use a hyphen to separate syllables of a word between the end of one line and the beginning of another. *Always* put the hyphen with the *first* part of the word. (see **Syllable Division**)

He is holding his hands together, making a big fist, rhythmically rub-
    bing one thumb against the other.

5 Use a hyphen to join compound adjectives; that is, if two words together modify a noun that follows them, they are joined by a hyphen.

We bought hamburgers at a *fast-food* restaurant.
Mrs. Patterson paid a *special-delivery* fee for an important letter.
A hospital must have a *germ-free* environment.

6 A woman who wants to keep her maiden name after she marries may use a hyphen to join her name to her husband's name.

Martha Arnold may become Martha Arnold-Smith after she marries John Smith.

7 Use a hyphen in scientific and business style to replace *to* in short phrases of time and place.

The second quarter (May-June) was weak in economic activity. (the hyphen here means *up to and including*)
The Manila-Hong Kong flight was late.

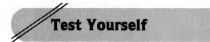

Test Yourself

Put hyphens wherever they are needed in the following sentences.

1. On Tuesday last week the vice president of the First National Bank presented an opti mistic report.
2. She announced that new building starts have risen by one third in the past year and that in the twenty six shopping days remaining in the current reporting period, retail sales are expected to be at least ten percent better than they were during the same period last year.
3. In the second quarter (April June) three new fast food franchises opened.
4. Additional airline activity such as local flights connecting with the new Atlanta Paris nonstop flight may boost the economy further in the January March period in the new year.

Parentheses ( )

Never put any other punctuation mark before the opening parenthesis mark. In a very long parenthetical explanation, end punctuation (period, question point, or exclamation mark) is possible before the close of the parenthesis. A comma, a colon, a semicolon, or end punctuation is possible after the close of a parenthesis. Use parentheses to enclose incidental information, details, and explanations.   (see **Comma**, rule 10, and **Dash**)

Changes in the money supply from 1980–1985 can be clearly seen (Figure D and Table 8). Many new laws were passed during this period (1875–1880); some of these new laws were not enforced, however.

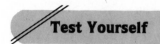
Test Yourself

Put parentheses wherever possible in the following sentences.

1. Abbreviations are used more often in certain styles of writing scientific, technical, and business than in others humanities.
2. The term *eighteenth century* does not mean the 1800's 1800–1899 but it means the 1700's 1700–1799.
3. Prefixes on words can be confusing: *disinterested impartial* does not mean the same as *uninterested* not *interested*.

Period (full stop) (.)

1   Put a period, question mark, or exclamation point at the end of every sentence. (These three marks are called *end punctuation*.)

It is raining.
This is a rainy day!
Is it raining?

2   A period follows many abbreviations.   (see **Abbreviations**)

etc., a.m./p.m., Mrs., Mr., Dr., Ms. **but** not Miss

But not all abbreviations are followed by a period:

UNESCO (*U*nited *N*ations *E*ducational, *C*ultural, and *S*cientific *O*rganization), WHO (*W*orld *H*ealth *O*rganization), and other acronyms (abbreviations formed from the first letters of words).

If a period for an abbreviation ends a sentence, do not put a second period as end punctuation.

3 Use a period as a decimal point in money expressed in a decimal system and in mathematics.

$4.95 (four dollars and ninety-five cents)
9,743.75 (nine thousand, seven hundred forty-three and seventy-five hundredths)

4 Use a period after numbers and letters used in outlines and lists but not after an item in a list or outline that is not a complete sentence.

Three steps must be completed before a decision is made.
1. Determination of need
2. Estimate of costs
3. Time required for completion of project

Test Yourself

Put periods wherever they are needed.

1. Mr and Mrs Philip Adams and their daughter, Miss Patsy Adams, are leaving for Singapore tomorrow
2. Since they are citizens of the U S, they did not need passports to go to Canada last year
3. On this trip in Southeast Asia they will need passports to show their citizenship and WHO cards to show their inoculations

Question Mark (?)

Never put a question mark at the beginning of a line.
  1 Put a question mark at the end of a direct question.

Will you be leaving soon? (replacing a period)
"How many days are left?" he asked. (replacing a comma)

2 Never put a question mark after an indirect question. (see **Reported Speech**)

They asked whether the storm would be severe.
She wants to know when you will come back.

3 Use a question mark to show uncertainty about facts.

The dates of Socrates are 470?-399 B.C. (The date of birth is uncertain.)

4 A question mark is sometimes left out after a polite request or command put in the form of a question.

Would you please carry these books for me. (Meaning: Please carry these books for me.)

Would you hold the door open, please. (Meaning: Please hold the door open.)

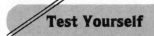
Test Yourself

Put periods and question marks wherever necessary. In sentence 3, use a question mark to show that the date is not certain.

1. Did Mr Sharp lecture on the history of mathematics at 8:00 P M
2. Yes, he asked if we knew how ancient many mathematical concepts are
3. Geometry goes back to the ancient Egyptians, who in 1650 B C used a value for *pi* that was nearly accurate
4. An exact value for *pi* is impossible in decimals, but it is close to 314159

Quotation Marks (" " and ' ')

Double marks are usual in American usage; single marks (sometimes called inverted commas) are usual in British usage.

1 Use quotation marks to set off the exact words of a speaker or to show material quoted from writing.   (see **Direct Speech**)

"Come over here," the doctor said; "I want to look at you." (speaker's exact words)
Lincoln's Gettysburg address begins, "Fourscore and seven years ago." (quoted from a book)

Do not put quotation marks around indirect or reported speech.   (see **Reported Speech**)

The doctor said that he wanted to look at me.

2 Show titles of works that are not published separately by putting quotation marks around them.   (See also **Titles**: titles of works published separately are underlined in handwriting and typing.)

A short story: "The Last Leaf"
A poem: "The Raven"
A magazine or newspaper article: "The State Visit of the President"
A chapter in a book: "The Vertebrates"

These are titles of works by other people. **Never put quotation marks around the title of a paper that you are writing.**

3 If quotation marks are needed inside a passage that is already enclosed in quotation marks, use single marks instead of double marks. (British usage reverses this order.)

"Now," he said, "I have finished reading 'The Raven'."

4 Quotation marks are always used in pairs. The first *opens* and the second *closes* the quotation. Always put periods and commas inside the close of quotation marks.

"Now," the mechanic said, "I have finished the work."

5   Other punctuation marks may be inside or outside the quotation marks, depending on the meaning and structure of the sentence.

What is the theme of "The River"?
He asked, "Have you finished reading 'The Raven'?"
Only three characters appear in the story "A Worn Path": Phoenix, a man, and a nurse.

Test Yourself

Put quotation marks wherever they are needed.

1.   The desire to take medicine is perhaps the greatest feature that distinguishes man

from animals, said a famous doctor, Sir William Osler.

2.   Take your medicine, Mrs. Penney said to her little boy; it will make you feel better.

3.   A famous proverb says, A merry heart does good like a medicine.

4.   People have often commented that sometimes the medicine is worse than the disease.

Slash (also called diagonal or virgule) (/)

Use a slash between two words to show that both or either one of them can give the correct meaning.

Mary and/or Bob must sign the checks in their joint account.
Infinitive/gerund choice is difficult to learn. Some verbs can be followed by only a gerund, other verbs can be followed by only an infinitive, and some can be followed by either gerunds or infinitives.

Semicolon (;)

Never put a semicolon at the beginning of a line.

1   Two independent clauses may be joined by a semicolon.   (see **Comma Splices**)

The athletes who were training for the championships were running six miles every day; they were also eating a special diet.

2   Two independent clauses may be joined by a comma and coordinating conjunction. The comma may be replaced by a semicolon, however, if there are other commas in the sentence.

Comma and Coordinating Conjunction

The athletes who were training for the championships were running six miles a day, but I was not.

Semicolon and Coordinating Conjunction

The athletes who were training for the championships were running six miles a day, lifting weights, swimming every afternoon, and eating a special diet; but I was not.

Punctuation Chart for Joining and/or Separating Clauses with Transition and Connecting Words

Coordinating Conjunction: comma + coordinating conjunction

Independent Clause	Comma	Coordinating Conjunction	Independent Clause
It was raining	,	so	traffic moved slowly.
It was raining	,	and	traffic moved slowly.
Traffic moved slowly	,	for	it was raining.

Interrupter (conjunctive adverb): semicolon + movable interrupter in second clause

Independent Clause	Semicolon	Independent Clause
		interrupter
It was raining	;	as a result, traffic was moving slowly.
It was raining	;	therefore, traffic was moving slowly.
		interrupter
It was raining	;	traffic, therefore, was moving slowly.
		interrupter
It was raining	;	traffic was therefore moving slowly.

NOTE: Commas around interrupters may be left out when the interrupter comes between two parts of a verb phrase.

Subordinating Conjunction: Turn one clause into a dependent construction. Put a comma between the clauses *only* when the dependent clause comes first.

Dependent Clause	Comma	Independent Clause
subordinating conjunction		
Because ⎫		
Since ⎬ it was raining	,	traffic moved slowly.
When ⎭		

Independent Clause	No Comma	Dependent Clause
		subordinating conjunction
		because ⎫
The traffic moved slowly		since ⎬ it was raining.
		when ⎭

Separate Sentences: (grammatically correct but may appear childish and/or give up the meaning of the transition word)

Independent Clause	Period + Capital Letter	Independent Clause
It was raining.		The traffic moved slowly. Therefore, the traffic moved slowly. As a result, the traffic moved slowly.

NOTE: A subordinating conjunction always makes the clause it introduces into a dependent clause. *Since it was raining.* is incorrect. It is a fragment.   (see **Fragments**)

Test Yourself

Replace commas with semicolons wherever semicolons are needed in the following sentences.

1. Sports injuries have been the subject of much research recently, many people who once would have been permanently crippled can now be treated successfully.
2. A runner who wants to avoid injuries must train regularly, wear correct shoes, and do stretching exercises before and after running, and a serious runner must also pay attention to diet.

Underlining (Italics)

Words that are printed in italics are indicated by underlining in handwriting or typing.

1   Underline titles of complete publications: books, periodicals, movies, television programs, record albums, and plays, but not the Bible or other sacred writings or their parts. (NOTE: In scientific writing, book and periodical titles are not always underlined.)

	Handwriting/Typing	*Print*
Books:	A Tale of Two Cities	*A Tale of Two Cities*
Newspapers:	The New York Times	*The New York Times*
Magazines:	The Reader's Digest	*The Reader's Digest*
Sacred Writings:	the Koran, the Bible, the Gita, Genesis, the Gospels	

Do not underline the title of a paper that you are writing, either on that paper or on the title page for that paper.

2   Underline foreign words and phrases.

She did not know he was a Frenchman until he said, "Bonjour, mademoiselle."
The abbreviation for the Latin word confer, cf., is often used in scholarly writing. It directs the the reader to compare one idea with another.

3   Underline words or numbers used as words or numbers.

He crossed his t's and dotted his i's carefully.
I never know whether to use it's or its.
Write your 1's, 7's, and 9's so that people will not confuse them.

4   Underline for emphasis, but *very* sparingly.

Do not bring that dog in here!

5   Underline the names of ships, trains, and aircraft.

The Queen Elizabeth II is sailing today.
The Goodyear blimp Liberty is over the stadium.

Test Yourself

Combined Exercise on Underlining and Quotation Marks

Underline and add quotation marks wherever necessary.

1. When Abraham Lincoln was a young boy, his family had a Bible; he borrowed other

    books such as Pilgrim's Progress and Robinson Crusoe.

2. Three books about Lincoln are Citizen of New Salem, The Great Proclamation, and

    Lincoln as They Saw Him.

3. Sections called Lincoln, Abraham in encyclopedias contain good summaries of Lincoln's

    life.

4. When people are very precise, sometimes others say about them, They dot all their i's

    and cross all their t's.

5. The sinking of the Titanic while it was crossing the North Atlantic was a famous

    disaster at sea.

Puns, see **Spelling**

Quantity and Measure

Choose a word of quantity according to the kind of noun it refers to. Different words are used with countable and uncountable nouns.   (see **Articles, Countable and Uncountable Nouns, Pronouns,** and **Determiners**)

Traditional English (yard, pound, quart) and metric (meter, gram, and liter) measuring systems are used in different parts of the English-speaking world. Consult a dictionary for equivalents (most dictionaries have a table of measures at the back).

Measurements, containers, and portions as well as certain idiomatic words are used to make uncountable nouns countable or as collective nouns to group items for convenience. They follow a set pattern: a/an/the + measure + uncountable noun.

		liter/quart	*of*	wine, milk, beer, etc.
		meter/yard	*of*	cloth, string, rope
		kilometer/mile	*of*	highway, road
Measure:	*a/an/the*	kilogram/pound	*of*	rice, meat, butter
		milligram	*of*	aspirin (metric always for medicines)
		cubic centimeter	*of*	penicillin
		hectare/acre	*of*	land
		ream	*of*	paper

320

Container:	a/an/the	bottle	of	soda, beer, milk, sauce
		can (Br. tin)	of	soda, soft drink, vegetables
		box	of	cereal, grapes, apples
		bag/sack	of	rice, groceries, potatoes
		pitcher (Br. jug)	of	water, milk, juice
Portion:	a/an/the	piece, portion, slice	of	bread, cheese, cake, meat
Idiomatic Words:	a/an/the	bunch	of	grapes
		ear	of	corn
		loaf	of	bread
		hand	of	bananas
		head	of	lettuce, cabbage, cauliflower
		stalk	of	celery

NOTE: Always put a countable noun directly after a number: *two dozen eggs, two boxes of eggs, three hundred sacks of rice, a box of a dozen pencils, one package of gum.* Numbers do not have *s* in the plural.   (see p. 117)

Test Yourself

Correct the errors in the following sentences.

1. Bill went to the bookstore to buy a ream of paper and a dozen of pencils.

2. He also needs one of laboratory workbooks.

3. He bought aspirin tablets, a one hundred box.

4. Then he went to the grocery story to buy threes cabbages.

5. He bought six pounds cabbage.

Question mark, see **Punctuation, question mark**

Questions, Direct and Indirect

Direct questions give the speaker's exact words. In dialogue they are enclosed in quotation marks.

Indirect questions report what was said but do not give the speaker's exact words.   (see **Reported Speech**)

If you have difficulty with the question forms in English, think of the statement before changing it into a question. Look at the verb. Is it an operator verb? If it is not an operator verb, you must use a form of *do.*   (see **Operators**)

Yes-No questions expect an answer of agreement or disagreement, often in a short form without the main verb repeated. Put the operator before the subject in a Yes-No question.

To form a Yes-No question, look for a form of *BE,* for a form of *HAVE* as an auxiliary, or for a MODAL in the sentence. If the question has one of these forms, move it to the beginning of the sentence. If the question does not already have one of these words, put *do, does,* or *did* at the beginning of the sentence and change the verb to the *simple* (bare or unmarked infinitive) form.

Statement: John *is* studying. John *studies* every day.
     He *will* study tomorrow.

Question: *Is* John studying? *Does* John study every day?
     Will he study tomorrow?

The short answer is made with the same verb that is moved to make the question (the operator):

	Agreement	Disagreement (Negative)
Answer (Short):	Yes, he *is (does).* **or**	No, he *isn't/is (doesn't/doesn't).*
	Yes, he *will.* **or**	No, he *won't/will* not.
Answer (Long):	Yes, he *is* (he's) studying. **or**	No, he *is* not (isn't) studying.
	Yes, he *studies.* **or**	No, he *does not (doesn't)* study.
	Yes, he *will* (he'll) study tomorrow. **or**	No, he *will* not (won't) study tomorrow.

Test Yourself

Solomon

Solomon was a wise king who lived long ago. When people had difficult problems they went to him to settle them. One day two women came to Solomon. They both claimed the same baby. The first woman said it was hers, and the second one did, also. When they could not agree, Solomon told them that he had a simple solution to their problem: he would cut the baby in half and give each of them one part of it. The first woman agreed, but the other one began to cry and told the king to give the baby to the other woman, not to kill it. Then King Solomon decided that the woman who wanted to save the baby's life was its real mother. He gave the baby to her.

A. Write Yes-No questions based on the story about Solomon that begin with the following words:

1. Did two women . . . ?
2. Was Solomon . . . ?
3. Did the first woman . . . ?

4. Were both women . . . ?
5. Did Solomon . . . ?
6. Was one woman . . . ?
7. Did the real mother . . . ?

B. Now turn the questions you have just written into statements. How are the verb forms different in the statements?

WH-questions are questions that begin with *WH* or *H*: *who, whose, whom, what, which, when, where, how,* and *why.* If *who, what,* or *which* is the **subject** or modifies the subject of the sentence, it is followed by the normal word order of a statement.

	subject	verb

Statement: *Those students* lost their books.

Question: *Who* lost their books?

Answer: Those students.

Statement: *Finding the book I need* is difficult.

Question: *What* is difficult?

Answer: Finding the book I need.

Statement: *That dog* bothered him yesterday.

Question: *Which dog* bothered him yesterday?

Answer: That dog.

Statement: *Registration* *is* frustrating.

Question: *What* is frustrating?

Answer: Registration.

Statement: *My oldest sister* is here.

Question: *Which sister* is here?

Answer: The oldest one.

Question: *How many sisters* are here?

Answer: Only one, the oldest one.

Whom (*who* in informal English), *what,* and *which as* **objects** form questions by putting the WH-words first and *do, does, did,* or another operator second.

subject   verb   object
Statement: He   wanted his brother.

object   verb subject   verb
Question: *Who (whom) did*   he   *want?*

Answer: His brother.

subject   verb   object
Statement: The teacher *ate* an *apple* this morning.

object verb   subject   verb
What did the teacher *eat* this morning?

Answer: An apple.

object
Statement: The farmer mowed the *grass.*

object
Question: *What* did the farmer mow? (The information wanted is the direct object.)

Answer: *The grass.* The farmer mowed the *grass.*

When the action of the verb is the information the questioner wants, the *main verb* is not used in the question but is replaced by *do:*

Question asking for *action* in the answer:

verb
Question: *What* did the farmer *do?* (The information wanted is the action of the verb.)

verb   verb
Answer: He mowed. He mowed the grass.

Notice that the long answer for both of the last two questions is the same: *He mowed the grass.*

Statement: Sally can fix her own bicycle.

Question: *What can* Sally *do?* (Asks for action of the verb.)

Answer: (Sally can) fix her own bicycle.

A modal *(can)* cannot be replaced by *do, does,* or *did.* The *do* here replaces the main verb, *fix,* because the question is asking for an action.

Which? (The answer will be one of two or one of a limited group.)

Statement: He did *Part II* first on this examination.

Question: *Which part* did he do first?

Answer: Part II. He did Part II.

When? (The answer will be a time or an occasion.)

Statement: He is leaving *tomorrow.*

Question: *When* is he leaving?

Answer: Tomorrow.

Where? (The answer will be a place or a situation.)

Statement: They went to *New York* yesterday.

Question: *Where* did they go yesterday?

Answer: To New York. They went to New York.

How? (The answer will show manner, means, or degree.)

                verb verb

Statement: We *are* going by bus. (The verb has a form of *be*.)

                verb   verb

Question: *How are* you going?

Answer: By bus. We are going by bus.

                verb

Statement: We *went* by bus. (The verb is a form of *go*.)

                verb   verb

Question: *How did* you *go*?

Answer: By bus.

Statement: The word *receive* is spelled R-E-C-E-I-V-E.

Question: *How is receive* spelled?

Answer: R-E-C-E-I-V-E. It is spelled R-E-C-E-I-V-E.

Statement: This family is *very* happy.

Question: *How* happy do you think this family is?

Answer: Very happy. This family is very happy.

How much? (The answer will be connected with an uncountable [mass] noun.)

Statement: I need *a lot* of money.

Question: *How much* money do you need?

Answer: A lot, a great deal.

How many? (The answer will be connected with a countable noun.)

Statement: I am taking *four* courses, which is too many.

Question: *How many* courses are you taking?

Answer: Four, which is too many.

How often? (The answer will indicate frequency.)

Statement: The best student goes to the lab *every day*.

Question: *How often* does she go to the lab?

Answer: Every day.

How come? is an informal spoken form that means *why is it that* . . . ? Avoid using it in writing.

Why? (The answer will be a reason.)

Statement:	The messenger is leaving early *to avoid the heavy traffic.*
Question:	*Why* is the messenger leaving early?
Answer:	To avoid the heavy traffic.
Statement:	He had difficulty registering *because the records from his former school were lost.*
Question:	*Why* did he have difficulty registering?
Answer:	Because the records from his former school were lost.

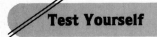 **Test Yourself**

Exercises on WH-Questions

A. In the blank to the left of the question, put the WH-word that can be used to get the information needed. In sentences 11–15, do not use *what.* Which WH-word can you use if you want to find out

_____   1.   the time,

_____   2.   directions to get to the bus stop,

_____   3.   the location of the bus stop,

_____   4.   the way your friend who has been in bed with a bad cold is feeling now,

_____   5.   the place your friend is going for a vacation,

_____   6.   the date of your sister's wedding,

_____   7.   the things you have to do to get a telephone,

_____   8.   the answer to Problem 3,

_____   9.   the weather forecast for tomorrow,

_____   10.   the method to follow in the second experiment,

_____   11.   the way to spell a word in French,

_____   12.   the amount of rice needed to feed four hungry people (two words)

_____ 13.   the number of people on a soccer team (two words)

_____ 14.   the frequency of your friend's visits to the library, (two words), and

_____ 15.   the reason for your friend's regular visits to the library?

B. Write complete questions needed to get the information in *A*.

C. Write questions based on the story of Solomon on p. 322. Write a question that begins with each of the following words:

1.   Where . . . ?
2.   Why . . . ?
3.   How . . . ?
4.   How many . . . ?
5.   Which . . . ?
6.   Who . . . ?
7.   To whom . . . ?
8.   Whose . . . ?
9.   What kind of . . . ?
10. What . . . ?

Reported (indirect) questions are not followed by a question mark.

Yes-no questions are introduced in reported speech by *whether* or *if*. *If* is considered informal.

Direct:	The driver asked, "Do you want to go?"
Reported:	The driver asked whether she wanted to go (or not).
	The driver asked if she wanted to go.

Indirect questions after a WH-word follow the subject-verb word order of a statement. Notice the pronoun and tense changes.   (see **Reported Speech**)

Direct:	The child asked her sister, "*When will you* go?"
Reported:	The child asked *when she would* go.
Direct:	Amy asked her brother, "*Where are you* going?"
Reported:	Amy asked *where he was* going.
Direct:	Mr. Jones asked the boys, "*How can you* finish on time?"
Reported:	Mr. Jones asked the boys *how they could* finish on time.
Direct:	Mrs. Jones asked the girls, "*What are you* doing?"
Reported:	Mrs. Jones asked the girls *what they were* doing.
Direct:	We asked them, "*Why don't you* come now?"
Reported:	We asked them *why they didn't* come now.

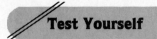

Test Yourself

Exercises on Indirect Questions

A. Look at the story "Solomon" on p. 322. Write indirect questions based on the information in it.

1. Solomon asked the women why . . .
2. Solomon asked the women if . . .
3. Solomon asked the first woman if . . .
4. Solomon asked the second woman why . . .

B. Write indirect questions that complete the sentences started. Sarah and George plan to help their father and mother start a new restaurant.

1. George asked Sarah if she knew when . . .
2. George also asked if she knew where . . .
3. Sarah asked George if he knew how many hours a day . . .
4. George wanted to know how soon . . .
5. George and Sarah asked their parents if . . .
6. They also asked what kind of . . .
7. They had several questions about how . . .
8. Their parents asked them who they thought would . . .
9. The whole family wondered how . . .
10. They also wondered if . . .

C. Rewrite your answers to *B* as direct questions. Begin each question "George asked . . ." or with another dialogue guide.

Quotations, see **Direct Speech**

Quotation marks, see **Punctuation, quotation marks**

 Reported Speech

Reported or indirect speech tells what a person says or writes without using the exact words. In reported speech, the phrase telling who speaks or writes must come first.

Direct Speech: "We want to go," the students said.

                    or

                The students said, "We want to go."

Reported Speech: The students said that they wanted to go.

Reported speech does not use quotation marks and capital letters to show the beginning of the words that a person actually speaks or writes. Reported speech uses words such as *say, said, say that,* or *said that* to introduce the indirect quotation. Sometimes the word *that* is left out, but if the meaning is not clear without it, use it.

The students said (that) they wanted to go.

Verbs in Reported Speech

Tell must be followed by a word referring to a person.

The students told $\begin{Bmatrix} us \\ John \\ the\ teacher \end{Bmatrix}$ (that) they wanted to go.

or

The students told   *us*   to go.

Other verbs that give the ideas of reported speech have an infinitive phrase (to + simple verb) after the main verb and are not followed by *that*.

The students
$\begin{matrix} demanded \\ begged \\ asked \\ wanted \end{matrix}$ to go.

Some verbs require other forms.

The students
insisted on going.
asked for permission to go.
requested permission to go.
wondered if they could go.

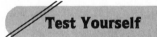

Test Yourself

Exercise on Verbs in Reported Speech

Correct the errors in the following sentences.

1. The safety inspector told to wear safety gloves.

2. The workers asked gloves.

3. The foreman insisted our wearing safety goggles.

4. When Betty cut her arm, she asked go to the nurse.

5. She requested permission go to the nurse for first aid.

Back-shifting of Tense in Reported Speech

Tense in reported speech can be different from tense in direct speech if the main verb is in the past tense.

   1 *After a main verb in the present tense* in reported speech, the reporting verb stays the same.

The students say that they *want* to go. ("We *want* to go.")
The students say that they *will* go. ("We *will* go.")
The students say that they *went.* ("We *went.*")

2 *After a main verb in the past tense,* the reporting verb changes if it is not already past or past perfect; do not use a present-tense verb after a main verb in the past tense.

The students said that they *wanted* to go. ("We *want* to go.")
The students said that they *would* go. ("We *will* go.")
The students said that they *had gone.* ("We *went.*")

A verb in the *present becomes past* if it follows a main verb that is past.
A verb in the *future becomes past* if it follows a main verb that is past.
A verb in the *past becomes past perfect* if it follows a main verb that is past.

Exceptions
1 The verb *to be* rarely becomes the past perfect but usually stays past.

He said, "I *was* sorry about that." becomes
He said that he *was* sorry about that.

2 The historical present tense shows ideas that are reported in the past but may still be considered to be true.

He believed that might *makes* right.
They taught that God *is* love.
Didn't you know that I *am* living in California now?

3 The present tense may be used when reporting opinions, statements, and comments from writers and characters in literature, even though they actually happened in the past.

The lecturer explained how Shakespeare shows us the danger of ambition.

Adverbs in Reported Speech

Adverbs in reported speech must often be changed when the tense of the verb is changed.

Direct: The director said, "Come back *tomorrow.*"

Reported: The director told us to come back *the following day.*

Direct: Harry said, "I found my book *yesterday.*"

Reported: Harry said that he had found his book *the day before.*

Direct: They said, "We were married *last year.*"

Reported: They said that they were married *a year earlier.*

Pronouns in Reported Speech

Pronouns in reported speech must be changed if they are first person (I/me, we/us, and so on) or second person (you, your, yours). They must be changed to third person (he/him, she/her, they/them, and so on).

Direct: The students say, "*We* want to go."

Reported: The students say that *they* want to go.

Direct: Mary said, "*I* want to go."

Reported: Mary said that *she* wanted to go.

Direct: John asked Peter, "Do *you* want to go?"

Reported: John asked Peter if *he* wanted to go.

Indirect Commands

Reported (indirect) commands are usually made with *tell* + a word referring to a person + an infinitive phrase.

Direct: The dean said, "Register on March 15."

Reported: The dean told *the students to register* on March 15.

Direct: My uncle always said, "Prepare for the future."

Reported: My uncle always told *us to prepare* for the future.

Indirect Questions

Indirect Questions keep the word order of a statement. Do not use a question mark (see **Questions**) after an indirect question.

                 Yes-No Question
Direct: The ticket agent asked, "Do you have your ticket?"

Indirect: The ticket agent asked if we had our tickets.

                 WH-Question
Direct: The ticket agent asked, "Where are your tickets?"

Indirect: The ticket agent asked where our tickets were.

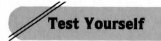

Test Yourself

Exercise on Reported Speech

When Peter applied for the job with the city as a draftsman, the personnel manager interviewed him. Put the conversation between Mrs. Mason, the personnel manager, and Peter into indirect speech.

1. "Our city," Mrs. Mason said, "tries to keep its pay scales similar to those of industry. We also have good health insurance."
2. "Where did you get your training?" the personnel manager also asked.
3. "I have an associate in science degree from Ephraim Technical College," Peter replied. "I finished my course last May."
4. Mrs. Mason asked, "Do you have any experience?"
5. "I have been working full time all summer for Heatling Construction Company, and I also worked afternoons and Saturdays while I was taking my college courses," Peter answered.
6. "Can you start work tomorrow?" the personnel manager asked.
7. "I am ready to start any time," Peter said. "Tomorrow will be fine."
8. "Be here tomorrow morning at eight o'clock then. We'll see how you do for two weeks," Mrs. Mason said.

See also **Exercise, Tense, Past,** p. 365.

Roots, see **Word Formation**

# Run-on Sentences

A run-on sentence is a serious error in sentence construction. It is sometimes called a *fused* sentence. *Never* write two or more independent clauses without any punctuation at all between them.   (see **Comma Splices**)

independent clause   no punctuation

Incorrect: Jane is going to Miami on her vacation

independent clause

Mary is going to New York.

independent clause no punctuation

Incorrect: Jane has already been to New York   therefore,

independent clause

she is going to Miami on her vacation.

Connect independent clauses in one of four ways:

  1 Put a semicolon between two independent clauses. Use an interrupter as a transition word.   (see **Interrupters**)

independent clause

Correct: Jane is going to Miami on her vacation;

independent clause

Mary, however, is going to New York.

independent clause

Correct: Jane has already been to New York; therefore,

independent clause

she is going to Miami on her vacation.

2 Put a comma and a coordinating conjunction between independent clauses. The coordinating conjunctions are *and, or, nor, but, yet, so,* and *for.* (see **Coordinating Conjunctions**)

Correct:

independent clause

Jane is going to Miami on her vacation,   , + coordinating conjunction

and
but

independent clause

Mary is going to New York.

Do not be confused by words like *therefore* and *however*. Putting them between the two clauses and putting commas before and after them does not correct the sentence. You then have a comma splice. These words, called interrupters or conjunctive adverbs, cannot join independent clauses unless you also put a semicolon between the clauses. (see **Interrupters**)

In a series of independent clauses, put a coordinating conjunction between the last two clauses.

Correct:

independent clause   independent clause

Jane is going to Miami on her vacation, Mary is going to New York,

, + coordinating conjunction   independent clause

and   Brenda is going to Chicago.

3 Put a period and a capital letter between independent clauses, making them separate sentences.

Correct: Jane is going to Miami on her vacation.
              Mary, however, is going to New York.

Correct: Jane has already been to New York. Therefore, she is going to Miami on her vacation.

4 Make one of the independent clauses into a dependent clause or into another subordinate construction. (see **Subordinating and Reducing**)

Correct:

dependent clause

Because Jane has already been to New York,

independent clause

she is going to Miami on her vacation.

participial phrase   independent clause

Correct: Having already been to New York, Jane is going to Miami on her vacation.

Keep at least one independent clause, or you will have a sentence fragment. (see **Fragments**)

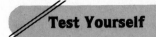

Test Yourself

Exercise on Run-on Sentences

Rewrite each of the following sentences in four ways: (1) put a semicolon where it is needed, (2) put a comma and a coordinating conjunction between two independent clauses, (3) make two separate sentences, and (4) rewrite the sentence making one of the independent clauses a dependent clause or another subordinate construction.

1. Climate influences our lives very much we change the styles of our clothes and buildings in different climates.

2. Houses in areas with much snow have steep roofs to keep snow from collecting on them too much snow on the roof may cause it to collapse.

3. Houses in tropical climates do not need steep roofs they need to be built to give more protection from the hot sun.

Sentence Patterns

Sentence pattern or verb pattern means the different grammatical constructions in a clause that are possible with different kinds of verbs.

Patterns with Intransitive Verbs

	Subject	Verb	Adverb (optional)
S + V:	The man	coughed.	
	The students	laughed.	
S + V + Adv:	The children	walked	down the street.
	The waiter	hurried	away from the door.

S

Patterns with Linking Verbs   (see **Predicate Complements**)

	Subject	Verb	Predicate Noun or Adjective	Adverb (required if no complement)
S + V + PN or Adj:	The baby	is	fat. (adj.)	
	The losing team	seems	unhappy. (adj.)	
	This building	is	the library. (noun)	
	The major	has become	a student. (noun)	
S + V + Adv:	My house	is		on River Road.
	The groceries	are		in the kitchen.

Patterns with Active Transitive Verbs   (see **Passive Verb**)

	Subject	Verb	Direct Object	Adverb (required) with certain verbs)
S + V + DO:	The baby	likes	bananas.	
	Dogs	chase	cats.	
S + V + DO + Adv:	The guard	put	the key	in the door.
	The police	treated	the old man	politely.

	Subject	Verb	Direct Object	Objective Complement
S + V + DO + OC:	The child	made	her mother	happy. (adj.)
	The committee	elected	Alan	treasurer. (noun)

	Subject	Verb	Indirect Object	Direct Object	To + Indirect Object
S + V + IO + DO:	The shopper	gave	the clerk	ten dollars.	
	Pearl	sent	Tom	a book.	
S + V + DO + to + IO:	The shopper	gave		ten dollars	to the clerk.
	Pearl	sent		a book	to Tom.

(see also **Indirect Object, Objective Complement,** and **Predicate Complements**)

Sentence patterns can be expanded by modifiers (adjective and adverbs). Many transitive sentences can be changed into passive sentences, and all patterns can be changed into questions and commands.   (see **Commands, Modifiers, Questions, and Verbs, kinds of**)

Inverted word order is used in questions, for emphasis, and with expletives: It is . . . , There is . . . , Here is . . . . (see **Expletives**)

Test Yourself

Underline the verb in the following sentences and identify it. Put *I* for intransitive, *L* for linking, or *T* for transitive in the blank to the left.

_____ 1. New Year's Day is the first day of the calendar.

_____ 2. Nearly every society has a New Year's Day of some kind.

_____ 3. Janus, the Roman god from whom we get the name for January,

_____ 4. looked backward and forward at the same time.

_____ 5. Many people give parties on New Year's Eve.

_____ 6. They celebrate the end of the old year and the beginning of the new one.

_____ 7. New Year's resolutions for a better life in the new year seem important to many people.

_____ 8. People say "Happy New Year" to each other on New Year's Eve

_____ 9. when the clock strikes midnight

_____ 10. and a new year begins.

Sentence Structure

Sentence structure can be *simple, compound, complex,* or *compound-complex* according to the kinds of clauses in the sentence.   (see **Clauses**)

A **simple** *sentence* has one independent or main clause (one subject-main verb combination).

We *were* sorry.
The *car stopped.*

A simple sentence can be expanded into a very long sentence, but adding modifiers does not change its basic structure.

Feeling the disappointment of our friends at our early departure, *we were* sorry to leave before meeting all the guests.

In the sentence above, *feeling, to leave,* and *meeting* are verbals, not finite or main verbs. Although the sentence is long, it still has the structure of a simple sentence: one subject and one main verb or verb phrase.   (see **Verbals**)

A simple sentence can have a compound subject (two or more subjects joined by a coordinating conjunction).   (see **Coordinating Conjunctions**)

Francis and Chris were sorry.
Francis, Chris, and *Joe* were sorry.

A simple sentence can have a compound verb (two or more verb forms joined by a coordinating conjunction).

Francis *ate* some toast and *drank* a cup of coffee.

A simple sentence can have a compound subject and a compound verb.

Francis and *Chris ate* toast and *drank* coffee. (Both parts of the subject performed the action in both parts of the verb.)

The verb in one clause (a simple sentence) can be a verb phrase (more than one word). Verb phrases form most English tenses.

Present Tense:	*Monkeys* often *eat* bananas.
	verb phrase
Future Tense:	*The monkeys will eat* bananas tomorrow.
	verb phrase
Present Perfect Tense:	*The monkeys have been eating bananas* today.

A **compound** *sentence* has two or more independent clauses without any dependent or subordinate clauses. A certain kind of a compound sentence is called a balanced sentence.   (see **Parallel Structure**)

The weather has been good today, and *it will be even better* tomorrow.

The clauses of a compound sentence may be joined either by a semicolon or by a comma and a coordinating conjunction (*and, but, or, for, nor, yet,* and *so.*)   (see **Coordinating Conjunctions**)

    independent clause   + semicolon +   independent clause
    The bus was crowded   ;   I had to stand all the way.

                            coordinating
    independent clause   +,+ conjunction +   independent clause
    The bus was crowded,   *and*/*so*   I had to stand all the way.

                        coordinating
    independent clause   +,+ conjunction +   independent clause
    We had to stand all the way,   *but*/*yet*   we were not very tired.

A **complex** *sentence* has one independent clause and one or more dependent clauses   (see **Clauses, dependent**)

                    dependent clause
    independent clause +   (adverb)
    We were sorry   when *we left* early.

dependent clause
independent clause +   (noun)
Our father *said*   that *he was* very *pleased*.

A **compound-complex** sentence has two or more independent clauses and at least one dependent clause. A compound sentence becomes a compound-complex sentence when one or more dependent clauses are added to it.

independent clause
Many *men* and *women* today *are being trained* on their jobs, and

independent clause
some of them later *study* at colleges and technical schools

dependent clause
where *they improve* their skills.

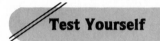

Test Yourself

A. Identify the sentence structure in the following sentences. Put *S* for simple, *CPD* for compound, *CX* for complex, and *C-C* for compound-complex.

_____ 1.   Most people have to write business letters sometimes, and many people have to write them often.

_____ 2.   Knowing the correct format of a business letter is important.

_____ 3.   Business letters should be brief because their readers are busy people.

_____ 4.   Good business letters are courteous; they present their message without being rude even when it is a complaint.

_____ 5.   Business letters have a heading, which may be printed on the stationery of the business or may be typed in; the heading gives the name and address of the business or the address of the writer if the writer is an individual instead of a business.

_____ 6.   A business letter often begins with "Dear" (the salutation) and ends with "Sincerely yours" (the complimentary close).

_____ 7.   Every business has a style and format for its letters.

B. Write a topic sentence that fits the following information. Then combine the following pieces of information into eight to twelve sentences. Then identify the kinds of sentences you have written: simple, compound, complex, or compound-complex. For sentence variety, be sure you have at least one sentence of each type. You may wish to write about a specific product with which you are familiar instead of "goods." You may change the order if you wish.

1. Trade is buying and selling.
2. People exchange goods and services.
3. Products pass through many hands.
4. Brokers sometimes pass goods from the producer to the processor or manufacturer.
5. Brokers sometimes pass goods from the manufacturer to the distributor.
6. Brokers sometimes pass goods from the distributor to the wholesaler.
7. Sometimes products go directly from producer to consumer.
8. Products usually go through brokers at some point.
9. Prices pay for services as well as goods.
10. Prices pay people who have a part in production and transportation.
11. Governments collect taxes on internal trade.
12. Governments collect tariffs on international trade.
13. Storage of goods is expensive.
14. Raw materials must be stored before shipping.
15. Raw materials must be stored before and after manufacturing.
16. Raw materials must be stored in wholesale warehouses.
17. Raw materials must be stored in retail stores.
18. Trade means changing ownership of goods.
19. New owners borrow money to pay for goods.
20. Interest on borrowed money is added to the cost of goods.

Speech, direct, see **Direct Speech**

Speech, indirect, see **Reported Speech**

Spelling

English spelling is difficult and irregular, but some rules work almost all the time.

Adding Endings

Look at the last letter or letters in the base word before adding *-s* to make a noun plural or a simple verb into the third person singular, present tense. Add *-es* if the base word ends in

1 an *s* sound: *-ch, -s, -sh, -tch,* or *-x.*

chur*ch*, chur*ches*	ma*tch*, ma*tches*
lun*ch*, lun*ches*	hi*tch*, hi*tches*
bu*s*, bu*ses*	bo*x*, bo*xes*
fus*s*, fus*ses*	thora*x*, thora*xes* (also thoraces)
ga*s*, ga*ses*	so*x* is an alternate plural for sock, socks
ma*sh*, ma*shes*	
ru*sh*, ru*shes*	

NOTE: Many scientific words have two plural forms: *apex, apexes, apices.* (see **Nouns, foreign words**)

Most words ending in -z already have a double z at the end of the base word or double the z before adding -es: fuzz, fuzzes; whiz, whizzes; quiz, quizzes

2 -o: For words ending in -o add -s or -es. Most add -s, some are correct with either ending, and a few must have -es. Most dictionaries agree that the following words end in -es.

do, does	go, goes	potato, potatoes
echo, echoes	hero, heroes	tomato, tomatoes
embargo, embargoes	Negro, Negroes	torpedo, torpedoes
		veto, vetoes

NOTE: Words relating to music (*alto, piano, solo, trio*) and words in which a vowel comes before the -o (bamboo, patio, stereo, zoo) never add -es.

3 -y: when a consonant comes before a final y, change the y to i and add -es, -ed, or -er. Add -ing without change.

Consonant before -y		*Vowel Before -y*
berry, berries	try, tries, trying	pay, pays, paying
bury, buries, burying	satisfy, satisfies, satisfying	buy, buys, buying, buyer

NOTE: This rule applies to other endings except those beginning in -i and to proper names. Drop the y before -ify and -ize.

glory, glorify

beauty, beautiful

friendly, friendlier,
   friendliest,
   friendliness

happy, happier,
   happiest,
   happiness

lucky, luckily

-ize

agony, agonize

harmony, harmonize

sympathy,
   sympathize

Proper Names

Kelly, Kellys

Murphy, Murphys

Bundy, Bundys

Some Irregular Forms

pay, paid, paying

say, said, saying

shy, shyly, shyer or shier

lady, ladyship, ladylike

day, days, daily

dry, drier, dryness

wry, wryness

busyness (state of being busy;
   business is connected with
   commerce)

Doubling the Final Consonant

4 When the last letter of a word is a consonant, *double* it if you are adding -ed, -er, -est, -ing, and -ish and if (1) it is a single consonant, (2) it has a single vowel before it, (3) it is the last letter of the word, (4) and the word has one syllable or is accented on the last syllable.

One-Syllable Word	Accent on Last Syllable of Base Word
big, bigger, biggest	begín, begínner, begínning
hot, hotter, hottest	omít, omítted, omítting
pit, pitted, pitting	occúr, occúrred, occúrring
win, winner, winning	refér, reférred, but réference (accent changes to first syllable) and referée (accent on last syllable)

fit, fitted, fitting, but bénefit, bénefited (accent on first syllable)

smart, smarter, smartest (two consonants together at end of word—do not double either consonant)

fast, faster, fastest

clean, cleaner, cleanest (two vowels come before the final consonant—do not double the consonant)

soon, sooner, soonest

man, mannish, but manly (ending is -ly—do not double final consonant)

Words Ending in One Final -e

5   Drop a single, final -e before endings beginning with a vowel. (Final -e usually shows that the vowel sound in the last syllable is "long"—that is, the vowel "sounds its name" in English. No final -e usually means that the vowel sound in the last syllable is not the sound of the name of the letter in English. Note the differences in pronunciation of the words listed below.)

Words without Final -e— Double Final Consonant	Words with Final -e—Drop -e Before Adding Ending
hop, hopped, hopping	hope, hoped, hoping
win, winner, winning	wine, wined, wining
sit, sitter, sitting	site, sited, siting
fat, fatter, fattest	fate, fated
mat, matted, matting	mate, mated, mating

NOTE: mow, mower, mowing and whole, wholly. Changeable and singeing keep the final -e because of pronunciation, but in the United States the e is dropped in acknowledgment and judgment. Words ending in -ye keep the -e before -ing: dye, dyeing; eye, eyeing.

Choosing Between ie and ei

Learn this rhyme to decide whether to use ie or ei:

	Examples
I before e	achieve, believe, view, friend, field, relief, siege, thief
Except after c	ceiling, conceit, deceive, perceive, receive, receipt
Or when sounded as a	eight, freight, rein, reign, sleigh, veil, vein
As in neighbor and weigh.	

Additional Exceptions

*Ei*ther, n*ei*ther, l*ei*sure, s*ei*ze.   anc*ie*nt, caff*ei*ne, cod*ei*ne, consc*ie*nce, counter-
Are exceptions; watch for these.   f*ei*t, forf*ei*t, for*ei*gn, h*ei*fer, h*ei*r, prot*ei*n,
    sover*ei*gn, w*ei*rd

NOTE: The rhyming rule does not apply to most words that end in *-r* or to words that have been formed by changing *y* to *i* before adding an ending:

cash*ie*r, caval*ie*r, front*ie*r, p*ie*r, merr*ie*r, prett*ie*r, and so on.

(See **Confusing Choices** for words that are often confused and misspelled; **Nouns** for irregular plurals ending in *-ves,* old plural forms, singular forms with plural meanings, and foreign plurals; **Punctuation, apostrophe** for spelling of possessives; and see also **Contractions, Syllable Division,** and **Word Formation.**)

Homonyms

Homonyms are words that sound alike but are spelled differently and have different meanings. The English language has many homonyms. Using the same-sounding word in different meanings to make a joke or to get attention is common in English. A joke or riddle that depends on words that sound the same is called a *pun.*

Puns

What is black and white and red (read) all over? A newspaper.
What ingredients do newlyweds like in salads? Lettuce alone. (Let us alone.)
War never determines who is right (correct); it only determines who is left (remaining).

Some of the words in the following list are not pronounced exactly alike by native speakers of English, but they are close enough in pronunciation to confuse you. Sometimes it is difficult to tell whether you are hearing one word or two words. In rapid speech most people pronounce pairs such as *meter* and *meet her* very nearly the same. Contractions also often sound very much like other words.

let's and *lets*	*he'll* and *heel*
its' and *its*	*he'd* and *heed*
I'll and *isle* or *aisle*	*we'd* and *weed*

Word processors have spelling programs to check spelling. These programs are helpful, but they cannot tell the difference between two words that both exist in English.

Some Homonyms and Near Homonyms

accept, except	bail, bale	cede, seed
a choir, acquire	bare, bear	choir, quire
air, heir	be, bee	chorale, corral
allowed, aloud	beat, beet	cite, sight, site
a rest, arrest	blew, blue	clothes, close
ate, eight	bough, bow	council, counsel
a way, away, aweigh		
		eyes, *i*'s

Some Homonyms and Near Homonyms

fair, fare
faze, phase
feat, feet
flea, flee
for, four, fore
foreward, forward
freeze, frieze
friar, fryer

grate, great
guise, guys

hail, hale
hair, hare
hear, here
higher, hire
hole, whole
hue, hew, Hugh

knead, need, kneed
knew, new
knight, night
knot, not
know, no

ladder, latter
lead, led
load, lode
loan, lone
lo, low

made, maid
mail, male
meat, meet, mete
medal, metal, meddle
might, mite

one, won
our, hour

pail, pale
pair, pare, pear
pause, paws
peace, piece
peak, peek
pedal, petal, peddle
pleas, please

rain, reign, rein
read, red
read, reed
real, reel

right, rite, write
ring, wring
road, rode
roe, row

sail, sale
scene, seen
seam, seem
seas, sees, seize
sew, so
sighs, size
steal, steel
suite, sweet

tail, tale
there, their, they're
threw, through
to, too, two
toe, tow

wait, weight
way, weigh, whey
who's, whose
wood, would

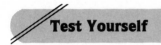

Test Yourself

Find the incorrect homonyms in the following sentences and correct them. (Word-processing spelling checks will find no errors in this paragraph if the words are in its dictionary.)

Many people no the story of the tortoise (turtle) and the hair (rabbit). This story teaches a lessen: slow and steady is batter then fast if the fast won stops every now and than. The slow tortoise and the fast hair had a raise. The hair had grate speed, but whenever he wanted arrest, he stopped. The tortoise kept rite on going without stopping too rest a tall. At the beginning the hair lead, but soon the tortoise past him, and finally was sew for a head that the hair never could ketch up.

Words Often Misspelled

Learn the following words that are often misspelled. Notice which words follow one of the rules given above and which words are irregular. Look up words followed by (*CC*) in "Confusing Choices."

1. accept (CC)
2. accommodate
3. achieve
4. across
5. address
6. advertise
7. advice (CC)
8. advise (CC)
9. affect (CC)
10. almost
11. all right
12. all together (CC)
13. all ways (CC)
14. a lot
15. altar
16. alter
17. although
18. altogether (CC)
19. always (CC)
20. among
21. argument
22. attendance
23. bargain
24. basically
25. beautiful
26. becoming
27. before
28. beginning
29. believe
30. breath
31. breathe
32. brilliance
33. buried
34. business
35. calendar
36. careful
37. category
38. certain
39. changeable
40. chief
41. choose
42. chose
43. color
44. coming
45. committee
46. comparative
47. compatible
48. complement
49. completely
50. compliment
51. conscience
52. conscious
53. controlled
54. convenient
55. council
56. counsel
57. daily
58. deceive
59. decision
60. definitely
61. dependent
62. describe
63. dining
64. disappoint
65. disappear
66. effect
67. eighth
68. embarrassment
69. engineering
70. equipped
71. except (CC)
72. field
73. foreign
74. forty
75. fourth
76. friend
77. government
78. height
79. hoping
80. interest
81. interrupt
82. its (CC)
83. it's (CC)
84. knowledge
85. length
86. live
87. loose (CC)
88. lose (CC)
89. making
90. necessary
91. necessity
92. ninety
93. occasionally
94. occurred
95. offered
96. omitted
97. opinion
98. opposed
99. opposite
100. paid
101. parallel
102. passed (CC)
103. past (CC)
104. perceive
105. perception
106. performance
107. personal
108. personnel
109. physical
110. physician
111. piece
112. possibly
113. procedure
114. professor
115. psychology
116. quiet
117. quietly
118. quit
119. quite
120. really
121. receive
122. receiving
123. recommend
124. recommendation
125. reference
126. referred
127. referring
128. relief
129. relieve
130. repeat
131. repetition
132. satisfied
133. satisfaction
134. satisfy
135. science
136. scientific
137. sentence
138. similar
139. separate
140. spatial
141. special
142. straight
143. studying
144. succeed
145. successful
146. strength
147. sufficient
148. taught
149. technical
150. technique
151. than (CC)
152. then (CC)
153. their (CC)
154. there (CC)
155. they're (CC)
156. thorough
157. thoroughly
158. thought
159. through
160. to (CC)
161. too (CC)
162. two (CC)
163. transferred
164. truly (CC)
165. unnecessary
166. wear
167. weather (CC)
168. were (CC)
169. where (CC)
170. whether (CC)
171. view
172. writing
173. written
174. your (CC)
175. you're (CC)

Stative Verbs

Some verbs are not usually used in the continuous/progressive forms in certain meanings, especially when these verbs have a meaning of knowledge, of sense perception, or of emotion. When these verbs show a state or condition rather than an activity or an event they can be called *stative*.

Knowledge and Mental Activity

Verbs showing that the subject has knowledge are often followed by a noun clause beginning with *that*.

believe (that)	guess (that)	remember to,
doubt (that)	imagine (that)	remember (that)
feel (that)	know (how to)	think (that)
forget to,	recognize (that)	understand (that)
forget (that)		want to

Do not use stative verbs in the continuous/progressive forms except in special meanings.

The doctor *believes* (that) his diagnosis is correct. (not *is believing*)
The student *imagines* (that) she will be a great actress someday. (not *is imagining*)
She *imagines* herself to be more beautiful than she is. (not *is imagining*)
She *wants* a cup of coffee. (not *is wanting*)
Sometimes Dan *forgets* to put gas in his car. (not *is forgetting*)
The tutor *understands* the problems. (not *is understanding*)
The dog *feels* the cold air blowing on him. (not *is feeling*)

but

Pat had a cold last week, but he *is feeling* better now. (change in physical condition)
I *doubt* the truth of that statement. (not *am doubting*)
I *know* how to drive. (not *am knowing*)
The coach *knows* tennis. (not *is knowing*)
We *know* (are acquainted with) our neighbors. (not *are knowing*)
Our dog *knows* when she has disobeyed. (not *is knowing*)

Sometimes these verbs are used with *always* in the continuous/progressive forms in an unfavorable meaning: "You do this all the time, but especially now, and it is a bad thing to do."

Some people *are always imagining* themselves to be more intelligent than they really are.
Dan *is always forgetting* to put gas in his car.
Some students *are always doubting* that they will pass.

NOTE: *Remember* and *forget* can be followed by either the infinitive or *-ing* form, but the meaning of the forms is different.   (see **Infinitive/-*ing* Choice**)

An *-ing* form after *forget* or *remember* shows an action or situation happening *before* the action of the main verb.

Do you *remember* learn*ing* to read?
I had *forgotten* asking you to come to the office today. (that I asked you)

An infinitive form after *forget* means that the action did not happen.

I *forgot to ask* you to come today.
We *forgot to bring* our books.

An infinitive form after *remember* means that the action of the infinitive takes place *after* the action of the main verb.

I *will remember to come* today.
Please *remember to bring* your books.
They *remembered to buy* bread yesterday.

Sense Perception

Verbs of the senses are not usually used in the progressive forms except for special emphasis on the duration of the activity. *Perceive* can be used for all senses. *Listen to, notice, observe,* and *watch* are usually *not* stative.

hear	smell	taste
see	sound	

Tom is deaf; he does not *hear* well.
An eagle *sees* small animals from far above the ground.
The rotten meat *smells* bad.
Your plans *sound* interesting.
My music teacher *notices* every mistake.

but

The coach *was noticing* how the swimmers were making their turns during practice this
    afternoon. (an action over a period of time)

After a verb of the senses, use an *-ing* form to show continuing action, but use a bare infinitive to show a single event.

We *saw* the flags *waving* in front of the United Nations building.
We *saw* the flags *dip* as the color guard passed the reviewing stand.

Condition Rather Than Event

Some verbs are not used in the continuous progressive forms when they mean that the subject is in a state or condition instead of showing that an activity is taking place during a limited time. The following list gives examples of verbs that can be used in stative meanings.

appear (meaning *seem*)	coast	deserve
	consist of	equal
be	contain	fit
belong to	depend on	have (meaning *possess*)

include   need   possess
involve   owe   resemble
lack   own   seem
matter   please   tend

Stative Uses

The brothers *resemble* each other.
New shoes *please* small children.
My cousin *owes* me twenty dollars.
The Parkers *own* a house in the city.
We do not always get what we *deserve*.
Friendly people *have* many friends.
This experiment *seems* easy.
Our lives *are* not always what they *appear* to be.
Two and two *equals* four.

Verb	State or Condition	Activity of Limited Duration
be	Tom *is* tall.	Tom *is being* difficult.
involve	The problem *involves* three steps.	Our present difficulties *are involving* several people.
fit	The coat *fits* well.	The tailor *is fitting the coat.*
depend on	Our plans *depend on* the weather.	I *am depending on* your help to finish the project.

Past and Perfect Tenses

The examples above are all in the present tense. Verbs in stative meanings can be used in the past and perfect tenses.

We *believed* what they told us. (not *were believing*)
John *wanted* a cup of coffee. (not *was wanting*)
I *doubted* the truth of his statement. (not *was doubting*)
Charles *needed* to buy a new coat. (not *was needing*)

Test Yourself

Choose the correct form.

Mary and Paul went to the New Year's Day parade. They had planned to sit on the steps of city hall, but the crowd was so large they couldn't find a place.

"I (1) (believe, am believing) I cannot stand up to watch the whole parade. I (2) (guess, am guessing) I will try to find a place to sit down," Paul said.

"Oh, Paul," Mary said. (3) "(Do you try, Are you trying) to find an excuse to go home early? (4) (Don't you remember, Aren't you remembering) last year's parade? You didn't get too tired watching it. Maybe we still (5) (have, are having) time to find a good place.

"Mary," Paul replied. "I (6) (doubt, am doubting) you (7) (remember, are remembering) what I did last night. I worked all night and I (8) (am, am being) tired. If we cannot find a place to sit down, I (9) (think, am thinking) I will go home to rest."

"I (10) (am, am being) sorry," Mary said. "If you (11) (are, are being) tired, we (12) (need, are needing) to go home now."

"That's all right," returned Paul. "You (13) (were not, were not being) difficult. You just (14) (weren't understanding, didn't understand) how tired I am."

 Subjunctive

The subjunctive is rarely used in spoken English except in a few set phrases such as *if I were you* and *as it were*. Most of the meanings that are shown in other languages by the subjunctive are shown in English by the modals, by *should* (especially by British speakers), and by other constructions shown in the table. Subjunctive forms express *nonfact*: actions or states that *can, may, might, should,* but not necessarily *do* happen or *have* happened.   (see **Modals**)   Subjunctive forms also express contrary-to-fact or impossible states.   (see **Conditional Sentences** for forms after *if.*)

Use the simple verb form (bare infinitive) after verbs that suggest, command, or request or use one of the other constructions given in the table below.

subjunctive

It is *recommended that* our chairman   *be*   given a vote of thanks.

subjunctive

The clerk's employer *suggested that* he *transfer* to another division.

or with a modal

modal

The clerk's employer *suggested that* he *should transfer* to another division.

or

noun

The clerk's employer *suggested* a *transfer* for him.

subjunctive

The report *urged that* the company   *hire*   another accountant.

or, less formal

infinitive

The report urged the company *to hire* another accountant.

Use the past subjunctive (the same form as the plural past tense) after *wish.*

I *wish* I *had* more help. (I wish I *could have* more help.)
The children *wish* they *visited* the zoo every day.
He *wishes* he *were* king.

Use the past perfect form of the verb to show actual past time after *wish*.

The children *wish* they *had visited* the zoo last week.
Both roommates *wish* they *had had* more time to clean their apartment yesterday.

Style

The subjunctive is often very formal. It is used in legal documents, parliamentary proceedings, and bureaucratic communications. Use a simpler construction if you can. (Some writers use this construction with the present indicative—he/she/it comes.)

Common Verbs That Can Be Followed by the Subjunctive

Verb	With Subjunctive	With Another Construction
advise	advise that she come	advise her to come
		her coming
		ask her to come
ask (only in the sense of *request*)	ask that she come	
demand	demand that he come	
desire	desire that he come	desire him to come
		his coming
forbid	forbid that he come	forbid him to come
		his coming
insist	insist that she come	insist on her coming
prefer	prefer that she come	prefer her to come
		her coming (to her going)
plan	plan that she come	plan for her to come
		her coming
propose	propose that he come	propose his coming
recommend	recommend that he come	recommend him to come
		his coming
request	request that he come	request him to come
		his coming
require	require that he come	require him to come
		his coming
suggest	suggest that she come	suggest her to come
		her coming
urge	urge that she come	urge her to come
		her coming

It is + past participles of the verbs above + *that* clause requires the subjunctive.

It is   required   } { that he come.
        suggested } { that he be there.

It is   recommended } { that she come.
        necessary   } { that she be there.

In the "other constructions" listed above, the emphasis may be different from the emphasis when the subjunctive is used. The personal object is emphasized before an infinitive phrase.

We recommend that the secretary $\begin{cases} \text{come.} \\ \text{be there.} \end{cases}$

We $\begin{matrix} \text{recommend} \\ \\ \text{suggest} \end{matrix}$ the secretary to $\begin{cases} \text{come. (emphasis on \textit{the secretary} instead of} \\ \quad \text{someone else)} \\ \text{be there.} \end{cases}$

Test Yourself

Put the correct form of the verb in the sentence, and then copy it in the blank to the left. Then rewrite the sentence two ways: first use a modal, and then use an infinitive.

_____ 1. It is imperative that you _____ at the committee meeting on January 6 at

9:00 A.M. (be)

_____ 2. The executive committee asks that everyone _____ prepared for a full dis-

cussion of our financial difficulties. (come)

_____ 3. Your committee urges that every member _____ prepared to help solve our

problems. (be)

_____ 4. It is recommended strongly that discussion of our problems _____ confiden-

tial at this moment. (remain)

_____ 5. We propose that no one _____ separate negotiations at this time, (try)

_____ 6. but that the entire matter _____ kept confidential. (be)

Subordinating and Reducing

Subordination means putting less important ideas in less important grammatical structures. Put the most important idea in a sentence in the subject and verb of the main clause. Put less important ideas in single-word modifiers, in modifying phrases, and in dependent clauses. (see **Clauses** and **Modifiers**)

Embedded clauses are ideas that could be put in separate clauses, but that are put in subordinate grammatical structures. Sometimes putting several ideas together into one sentence is called *sentence combining* or *reducing*. (see **Wordiness**)

The youngest runner won the hundred-yard dash.
The youngest runner arrived at the stadium late.

Which idea is more important? Put that idea in the independent clause.

dependent clause   independent clause
Although the youngest runner arrived at the stadium late,   she won the hundred-yard dash.

The sentence above can be reduced even more.

dependent participial phrase   independent clause
Although arriving late at the stadium,   the youngest runner won the hundred-yard dash.

By choosing which idea is most important and leaving out all unnecessary words, you will write effective, focused sentences.

The security guard who was watching the parking lot saw a thief who was breaking into my car. The security guard caught the thief.

Which idea is more important? How can the number of words be reduced?

The security guard watching the parking lot caught the thief breaking into my car.

Test Yourself

Combine the following pairs of sentences. Be sure the most important idea is in the independent (main) clause. See also Exercise B, pp. 340–341.

1. The tornado blew the roof off Uncle Ben's barn.
   The tornado struck at 3:00 P.M.
2. Tornadoes have struck three times in the past year near Uncle Ben's farm.
   Uncle Ben's farm is in Kansas.
3. Repairs to Uncle Ben's barn will cost $50,000.
   No one was injured or killed.

Suffixes, see **Word Formation, suffixes**

Syllable Division

In writing, single words can be divided at the right-hand end of a line in order to make the lines even at the right-hand margin. Always divide words between syllables. Syllable division is based on pronunciation, but pronunciation does not always show where the division should be in writing. If you need to divide a word in two parts, put the hyphen after the first part of the word. Do not put a hyphen at the beginning of the following line.   (see **Punctuation, hyphen**)

Look the word up in a dictionary to find out if it can be divided and, if so, where it can be divided. Most dictionaries use dots between syllables instead of hyphens. Dictionaries show hyphens only in words that must always have hyphens in them.

1   Never divide a word of one syllable, even if it is long.

tongue	bought	helped	through	freight	seize
sewed	strength	plague	straight	naught	mowed

2   Never divide a word of more than one syllable so that one letter stands alone on either line. In handwriting do not separate just two letters, especially *-er* and *-ed*. Words such as the following should not be divided.

bury	open	bony	alone	naughty	ebony
awake	opal	army	empty	eclipse	able

3   Divide compound words between their parts.

down-stairs	house-keeper	hair-dresser	sun-burned	light-weight
come-back	drum-beat	money-bag	sand-storm	patch-work

4   Divide most words that contain consonants or consonant combinations that represent different sounds between the two consonants.

hol-low	cancel-lation	tac-tics	sug-ges-tion	caus-tic
mid-dle	cab-bage	crys-tal	ket-tle	mar-ket

EXCEPTION: Never divide two different letters that stand for one sound.

nor*th*-ern	sym-*ph*ony	grap*h*-ics	phos-*ph*ate
psy-*ch*ology	syn-*th*etic	ba*ch*-elor	ca*th*-e-ter

5   Separate most prefixes and suffixes of three letters or more from the root of the word.   (see **Word Formation**)

dis-honest	comfort-*able*	confine-*ment*	year-*long*
sui-cide	number-*less*	thank-*ful*	rough-*age*

EXCEPTION: When prefixes or suffixes result in a doubled consonant, the word is often divided between the doubled consonants following rule 4.

swim-ming   admit-tance

Use rules 4 and 5 as guidelines when you do not have a dictionary at hand. Look up all doubtful words, as there are many exceptions and conflicting rules.

Test Yourself

Put a hyphen or hyphens in the following words in places where they could be divided at the end of a line.

1. paragraph   6. awake

2. through   7. preferred

3. thorax   8. sympathize

4. reduced   9. funniest

5. schoolteacher   10. thorough

Tag Questions, see **Operators**

Tense

Tense is the term used to show relationship between time and other conditions and the form of the verb. Some changes in the verb form are not directly related to time. The way the speaker or writer thinks about the event also affects verb forms. In addition to showing time, different forms show conditions such as certainty, definiteness, and possibility. *Mood* and *aspect* are grammatical terms that show how the verb expresses ideas that go beyond yesterday/today/tomorrow divisions. Did the action ever happen? Is it completed or continuing? You do not need to know all the grammatical terms to express yourself clearly, but you must learn the exact verb forms to use to express your ideas if you want your readers to understand your writing.   (see **Finite Verbs**)

Most of the conjugations in this section are shown using *walk,* a regular intransitive verb that does not need a complement. Sometimes another verb must be used to illustrate differences in meaning. For a complete conjugation of *to be,* see **Be**. See **Passive Verbs** for examples of transitive verbs in active and passive forms. Passive forms are not shown in this section.

Although contractions are common in speech, avoid them in formal writing. See **Contractions** for contracted forms if you need to use them in direct quotations.

The Present Tense

Add *-s* to make the third person singular. Remembering to add *-s* in the present tense is very important in academic and technical writing, since a large part of it is done in the present tense (see pp. 341–342).

	Walk
Singular	*Plural*
I walk	we walk
you walk	you walk
he, she, it walk*s*	they walk

The present tense can be used in several ways. It does not always show what is happening *now,* as you would think from its name. (The present progressive tense more often shows what is actually happening now; see below.)

1   Use the present tense to show **present state** or **condition,** particularly with stative verbs.   (see **Stative Verbs**)

Adverbs:

now	Ben *is* hungry.
at this time/moment	I *believe* (that) you are right.
today	That cake *smells* good.
tonight	Do you *realize* what you are saying?
this minute/morning	Harold *lives* in Rome now.
noon/evening	Caroline *attends* college in Canada.

2   Use the present tense to show an **eternal truth** or **natural law.**

Adverbs:

always/never	The moon *affects* the tides.
inevitably	Parallel lines never *meet.*
without fail	Hydrogen and oxygen *combine* to make water.
at all times	Subjects and verbs *agree* in number.
invariably	Hot air *rises.*

3   Use the present tense to show **habitual action**—repetition or nonrepetition of the same act.

Adverbs:

always/never	Many people *drink* coffee every morning.
usually/seldom	We always *celebrate* my birthday with a family party.
sometimes	The Browns *do* not *wash* their windows every week.
rarely	The Andersons *plant* tomatoes every year.
not ever	Sometimes we *go* to a soccer game on Sunday afternoon.
occasionally	
often/not often	
every	
each	

4   Use the present tense to show the historical present in **criticism** to discuss writing, drama, music, and art, and in **research** that quotes or paraphrases what other people have said or written in the past.

Adverbs of Value Judgment Rather Than Time—A Few of Many Possibilities
skillfully, cleverly (in) correctly clumsily, brilliantly well, poorly, (in)adequately, properly, rightly, wrongly

In the short story "The Lottery," Shirley Jackson *writes* an allegory of the injustices of life.
Darwin *presents* evidence for the development of life from lower to higher forms.
Looking at all the evidence, one *agrees* with the critic who *calls* the play a success.
The author of this textbook *explains* the problems clearly.

5   Use the present tense for **definitions** and **explanations.**

Adverbs:
always/never
then
next
after that

Gross National Product *means* the total value of all goods produced and services performed in one country in one year.
The screw *is* inserted in the lower right-hand corner of the frame.
Plate B *replaces* Plate A in the old model, as shown in Diagram 2.

6   Use the present tense to show **future possibility** in conditional and time clauses.

Uncle Robert will give you fifty dollars *if* he *likes* your work. (condition)
Uncle Robert will give you fifty dollars *when* he *sees* you. (time)

7   Use the present tense to show **future events** that are considered certain to happen.

The plane *leaves* at 9:25 tonight.
The term *is* over on December 16.

Test Yourself

Put the correct verb form in the sentence. Then put the number of the rule that applies in the sentence in the blank to the left.

_____   1.   Early ballooning was based on the principle that hot air _____ (rise).

_____   2.   Principles of physics _____ (explain) how this phenomenon

_____   3.   _____ (occur).

_____   4.   Hydrogen _____ (be) lighter than air.

_____ 5. Some balloons _____ (use) hydrogen, which _____ (explode) under certain

_____ circumstances.

_____ 6. Helium, which _____ (be) safer than hydrogen,

_____ 7. _____ (have) less lifting power than hydrogen.

_____ 8. Helium _____ (be) also more expensive than hydrogen.

_____ 9. Many balloonists today _____ (use) burners to heat the air in their bal-

_____ loons.

_____ 10. Blimps, small nonrigid airships, _____ (contain) helium.

The Present Perfect Tense

Make the present perfect tense from _have_ (_has_ in the third person singular) + past participle (_-ed_ form) of the main verb. (See **Verbs, Irregular** for irregular past participles.)

Walk

Singular	_Plural_
I have walked	we have walked
you have walked	you have walked
he, she, it has	
walked	they have walked

The present perfect tense usually shows an action that began in the past and goes on to the present or to an indefinite time closely related to the present.

1 Use the present perfect tense to show **an action that began in the past and is still going on.**

Do not use _ago_ with any meanings.

Adverbs:
for + period of time
since + specific date or time
in or during the last or past hour, day, week, month, year, decade, century
yet, so far
up to now

Shirley _has lived_ in Chicago for six years. (still living in Chicago)
They _have waited_ since ten o'clock. (still waiting)
During the last century, many people _have moved_ from rural to urban areas. (the movement continues)
I _have_ not _finished_ that problem yet. (still unfinished)

2   Use the present perfect tense to show **an action that began in the past and was finished at an indefinite time but is closely related to the present and/or future.**

Adverbs:

already, not yet   I *have* already *finished* those exercises.

early, late, just   You *have been* absent a great deal lately. (I expect that you will

this minute, today   be absent again.)

this month/year   The players *have come* early.

recently, lately   The players *have* just *arrived*.

                     The chef *has prepared* a delicious meal. (Although the work is

                     finished, it can be done again.)

                     They *have* recently *announced* their engagement. (They are still

                     engaged.)

Test Yourself

A. Put the correct verb form in the blank. Use the present perfect tense.

Farm families (1) _____ (move) away from rural areas for hundreds of years. Indus-

trialization (2) _____ (cause) people to move to cities in many parts of the world. Small

farmers (3) _____ (leave) their land and (4) _____ (have) to look for work in cities or on

larger farms. Farms (5) _____ (become) industrialized also. Farmers and governments

(6) _____ (put) many small plots of land together to make agriculture a more efficient

business.

B. Put the correct verb forms in the blanks. Use the present perfect tense. Which present-perfect verbs show action continuing in the present? Which ones show action already completed but closely related to the present or future?

Now that the time for our vacation is almost here, we (1) _____ (start) to get out the

things we want to take with us. My little brother Carl (2) _____ (decide) he must take his

football. My father (3) _____ already _____ (pack) his fishing rods. The cottage my par-

ents (4) _____ (rent) is right on the ocean, so all of us (5) _____ (look) at our swimming

suits recently to see if we need to buy new ones. Fortunately my parents (6) _____ (see)

the cottage where we will stay so they know exactly what we need to take.

C. Put the correct verb forms in the blanks. Use the present perfect tense.

Scientists (1) _____ (make) exciting advances in medicine recently. Surgeons (2) _____ (begin) to transplant human organs to people who are very sick. Some sick people who (3) _____ (receive) transplanted hearts and kidneys (4) _____ (live) much longer than they would have lived without them. Doctors (5) _____ just _____ (begin) to try to replace some organs such as hearts with mechanical devices. For a number of years they (6) _____ (be) able to help people whose kidneys (7) _____ (fail), but the machines are large, the process is difficult, and the costs are high. Some day certain parts of human bodies may be no more difficult and expensive to replace than parts of automobiles are now.

The Present Progressive Tense (sometimes called **Continuous**)

Make the present progressive from the present tense of *be* and the *-ing* form of the main verb (present participle).   (see **Be**)

Walk

Singular	Plural
I am walking	we are walking
you are walking	you are walking
he, she, it is walking	they are walking

NOTE: Some verbs do not occur in the progressive forms in their usual meanings. (see **Stative Verbs**)

A meaning of repetition similar to that of the progressive tense can be made with *keep on* or *go on* + *-ing* form or by repeating the verb with *and*. These constructions can be used in all tenses.

He *keeps on* walking.	He *goes on* walking.	He *walks* and *walks*.
She *keeps on* talking.	She *goes on* talking.	She *talks* and *talks*.

The present progressive tense shows action as a process that is incomplete now but will end. With an adverb of frequency this tense can show habitual action and in certain situations it can show future action.

    1   Use the present progressive tense to show **action as a process** that is going on now.

Adverbs:

now, today	Our dog *is chasing* your cat.
this minute, this	The children *are playing* outside.
month, this year	It *is raining/snowing/sleeting.*
at the moment	This winter we *are seeing* a weather pattern that is different from last year's pattern.

Test Yourself

A. Put the correct form of the present progressive tense in the blanks.

This year the mountain areas (1) _____ (have) much more rain in September than they had last year. In fact, they (2) _____ (get) too much rain. Some crops (3) _____ (rot) in the fields. Some days the rainstorms are so bad and the winds are so strong that no one (4) _____ out _____ (walk) on the streets. Many people, especially young children and the elderly, (5) _____ (become) ill because of the cold and dampness. Water levels in the dams (6) _____ (rise), however, and all water supplies (7) _____ (improve).

B. Could you use the present perfect tense in any of the blanks in *A*? Would the meaning be any different if you used the present perfect tense?

C. Could you use the present progressive tense in any of the blanks in the exercises on the present perfect (p. 359)? Would the emphasis be any different? Are there any blanks that cannot be filled with the present progressive tense? Why not?

2 Use the present progressive tense to show **habitual action,** often with the idea of showing dislike or disapproval.

Adverbs:

always, usually	The dog *is* usually *chasing* the cat.
most of the time	They *are* always *asking* for special favors.
more often than not	That little girl *is* always *biting* her fingernails.
	Tracy *is* always *eating* too much.

Test Yourself

D. Put the correct form of the present progressive tense in the blanks in the following sentences. *Always* used with this tense in a complaining manner may mean *often, usually,* or *again and again.*

My sister often annoys me. She (1) _____ always _____ (ask) me to help her with her work whether I have time to help her or not. She (2) _____ always _____ (depend) on me to remind her to take her money for lunch and for the bus. Worse still, my mother (3) _____ always _____ (find) excuses for her and (4) _____ (blame) me for her mistakes. I (5) _____ (get) tired of the way everyone (6) _____ (treat) me.

3 Use the present progressive tense to show **future action** that you are looking forward to now.

Adverbs:

Use an adverb of the future appropriate to the time the event will take place, such as this afternoon, tonight, tomorrow, next week, soon, next month.

My father and mother *are arriving* from New York at 2:15 tomorrow night.
A storm *is coming* tonight.
They *are going* to a concert tomorrow night.
We *are repeating* the experiment next month.
Refreshments *are being served* at 5:00 P.M. (passive)

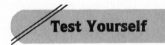

Test Yourself

E. Put the correct form of the present progressive tense in the blanks in the following sentences.

The Rockdale Packaging Company (1) _____ (have) a grand opening of its new plant this afternoon. The mayor (2) _____ (cut) a ribbon to begin the celebration at 2:00 P.M. Refreshments (3) _____ (serve, passive) after the mayor cuts the ribbon. The Rockdale Packaging Company's entire operation (4) _____ (expand, passive) to serve this region better. Additional products (5) _____ (add, passive), and the company (6) _____ (offer) its customers better service than ever before.

The Present Perfect Progressive Tense (sometimes called Continuous)

Make the present perfect progressive from the present tense of *have* + *been* + *-ing* (present participle) form of the main verb.

Walk

Singular
I have been walking
you have been walking
he, she, it has been walking

Plural
we have been walking
you have been walking
they have been walking

Use the present perfect progressive to show **incompleteness or indefiniteness very close to the present time,** often contrasted with *now. Just* shows that the activity is very recent.

Adverbs:

just	The trainer *has been washing* his dog, but he isn't now.
just now	She *has been feeling* ill, but she feels better now.
recently	Our car *has been giving* us trouble recently, but it is running better now.
	He *has been looking* everywhere for you, and he still is.
	She *has* just *been asking* about you.

Test Yourself

F. Put the correct form of the present perfect progressive in the blanks.

(A secretary is speaking on the telephone.) Thank you for returning our call. Mr. Edson (1) _____ (try) to reach you all morning. He (2) _____ (work) on the final bids that will be submitted on Friday. We (3) _____ (have) difficulty getting firm prices for materials to be delivered six months from now. Mr. Edson (4) _____ just _____ (talk) to your competitors to get their prices. He (5) _____ (wait) for your response, but he must have it today. He cannot wait any longer.

G. Combined Exercise on Present, Present Perfect, Present Progressive, and Present Perfect Progressive Tenses

Put the correct verb form in the blanks. Choose from the present tenses.

Lee (1) _____ (live) in Miami. He (2) _____ (live) there for two years, ever since he (3) _____ (be) in the United States. He (4) _____ (study) English every morning and (5) _____ (work) at a restaurant every afternoon and evening. Sometimes he

(6) _____ (have) to work until after midnight. He (7) _____ (try) to find a different job

even though the restaurant owner (8) _____ just _____ (promote) him to night manager.

He (9) _____ (live) with his uncle until he (10) _____ (save) enough money to buy furni-

ture to have his own apartment.

The Past Tense (sometimes called the **simple past**)

Make the past tense in regular verbs by adding *-ed* to the simple present.   (See **Be**
and **Verbs, irregular** for their past forms.)

                    Walk
I, you, he, she, it, we they walked.

1   Use the past tense for **events that happened at a specific time in the
past.** Use the past tense for a single event or for events that took place over a period of
time if that period is finished. Phrases with *ago (two weeks ago, ten years ago, two
thousand years ago)* can be used with all the past tenses. Do not use *already* with past
tenses but only with perfect tenses.

Adverbs:

a minute, hour, day,
   week, year, century
   ago
for + period of time
at + specific time
in + specific year
on + day of week or
   date, yesterday, in
   the morning/evening
last week/month/year/
   century
when . . .

The packages *came* at 2:30 this afternoon.
The children *started* kindergarten two weeks ago.
A storm *came* through here yesterday.
Three sisters *worked* in the same office for two years.
Last year the number of children in school in this city *in-
   creased* two percent.
When we *heard* about the eclipse, we *wanted* to see it.
The moon *was* full last night.

Our neighbor's dog barked at the moon every night last week.

Use the past tense as above to **tell a story**, to **discuss history**, and for **repeated** or
habitual actions that no longer occur.

Test Yourself

A. Put the correct past tense in the blanks in the following sentences.

The Hurston River Dam Project really (1) _____ (begin) in 1957. At that time, the

worst flood in the history of the entire region (2) _____ (cause) several million dollars

worth of damage. Flood waters (3) _____ (kill) livestock, both cattle and sheep. Fortunately no one (4) _____ (die) as a direct result of the flood. The citizens of the area

(5) _____ (try) to get their local government to ask for a study of the watershed, but they

(6) _____ (be) unsuccessful at that time. More than ten years later, however, in 1968, the

policies (7) _____ (change) and engineers (8) _____ (prepare) plans for a dam to control

flooding. The Flood Control Act (9) _____ (set) aside funds to begin the project in 1970.

Completed in 1974, the dam (10) _____ (fill) slowly because it (11) _____ (rain) very little

for several years, but in 1979 the last section of the lake (12) _____ (be) finally full. The

heavy floods of 1981 (13) _____ (show) that construction of the dam (14) _____ (save)

both farms and towns from disaster, for it (15) _____ (hold) back the heavy runoff from a

dangerous combination of heavy rain and melting snow in the mountains.

2   Use the past tense to **change from direct to reported speech** if the verb in the dialogue guide is in the past.   (see **Reported Speech** and "Sequences of Tenses" on p. 376.)

	present		past
Direct Quotation:	"*Is*	Joyce at home?" Susan *asked.*	

	past	present
	Francis *said,* "I *understand* this problem now."	

	past	past
Reported Speech:	Susan *asked* if Joyce *was* at home. (The speaker must come at the beginning of the sentence.)	
	Francis *said* that she *understood* this problem.	

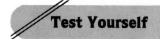

Test Yourself

B. Rewrite (paraphrase) the following direct quotations into reported (indirect) speech.

1. When Winston Churchill became Prime Minister of Britain in 1940, he said, "I have nothing to offer but blood, toil, tears, and sweat."
2. "There is nothing I love as much as a good fight," said Franklin D. Roosevelt at the beginning of his political career.
3. Samuel Johnson, an Englishman who lived at the time of the American Revolution, said, "I am prepared to love all humanity except an American."

3   Use past forms **after *if*** or ***unless*** to write about **events that are not true or that are not likely to happen.** Use *would* in the independent clause.   (see **Conditional Sentences**)

If the driver *ran* the red light, he *would* be to blame for the accident.
If Arthur *wore* a blue tie with that jacket, it *would* look better.
Unless a miracle *happened,* I *would* never make the honor roll.
If you *loved* me, you *would* not leave now.

Test Yourself

C. Put the correct verb forms in the blanks in the following sentences.

1. If Mark _____ (return) his books on time, he would not have to pay a fine. (Mark did

    not return his books on time.)

2. You would know that the library closes at 11:00 P.M. every night if you _____ (look) at

    the schedule. (You have not looked at the schedule.)

3. If you _____ (ask) where the reference section was, someone would tell you. (You

    have not asked.)

4. John would ask for help if he _____ (find) locating the books difficult. (John does not

    find locating books difficult.)

5. John and Mark would not ask us to study with them if they _____ (be) not sure they

    have all the books they need. (John and Mark are sure.)

NOTE: Using the past instead of the present can make a statement very tentative and polite. "I *wanted* to tell you about the problem" can mean "I *want to.* . . ."

The Past Perfect Tense

Make the past perfect tense with *had* + past participle of the main verb.   (See **Verbs, irregular** for irregular past participles).

      Walk
I, you, he, she, it, we, they had walked.

Use the past perfect tense to show **action in the past that happened before some other action in the past** shown by a past tense verb.

Adverbs:	past past perfect

Adverbs:
already and all
adverbs that can be
used with the
past tense

                                    past   past perfect
Before the new French teacher *came* here, she *had studied* in
    Paris for two years.

                           past perfect   past
After the old man *had failed* twice, he finally *passed* the test for
    his driver's license.

past   past perfect
When the old man *found* out that he *had failed* again,

past
he *gave* up.

If the meaning of "past before past" is clear from an adverb in the sentence, such as *before* and *after* in the sentences above or from the context, the past tense is often used for both verbs.

past   past
Before the new French teacher *came* here, she *studied* in Paris for two years.

past   past
After the old man *failed* twice, he finally *passed* his test for his driver's license.

Test Yourself

Fill in the blanks with the past perfect tense.

The Hurston River Dam was finished in 1974, but residents of the area

(1) _____ (begin) to ask for help after the flood of 1957. They (2) _____ (try) to get a

study of the watershed at that time, but they (3) _____ (be) unsuccessful. When funds

later became available, the requests that they (4) _____ (make) earlier were found, and

finally a dam was built. The heavy floods of 1981 did not do as much damage as the flood

of 1957 (5) _____ (do) because the lake behind the dam was able to hold the extra water

from the mountains.

The Past Progressive Tense (sometimes called **Continuous**)

Make the past progressive tense with the past tense of *be* (*was/were*) + *-ing* form (present participle) of the main verb.

Walk

Singular	*Plural*
I was walking	we, you, they were walking
you were walking	
he, she, it was walking	

1   Use the past progressive tense to show **duration, with emphasis on the length of time, of an act that is no longer going on.**

Adverbs:
the same as for the past tense

They *were waiting* to buy a house *for three years* before they found one they could afford.

We *were waiting* for the plane to arrive *for six hours* before it came.

2   Use the past progressive tense for **an action in the past that was not completed in the time period mentioned.**

I *was trying* to clean house last week. (I did not complete the cleaning.)
They *were looking* for an apartment yesterday. (They did not find one.)
We *were doing* a difficult experiment in the lab this morning. (We did not finish it.)

3   Use the past progressive tense for **an action that was going on at a time in the past when something else happened.**

James and I were *were watching* television when lightning *struck* the house.

or

While James and I *were watching* television, lightning *struck* the house.

While means *during the time. While* often introduces the clause showing duration. *When* means *at that time. When* often introduces the clause showing the intervening action. Do not use both *while* and *when* in the same sentence. *After* or *before* can replace *when.*

The driver of the car *was* not *paying* attention *when* he *ran* off the road.
The cook *was* not *watching* the pot *when* the sauce *boiled* over.

Test Yourself

Fill in the blanks with the past or past progressive tense.

While engineers (1) _____ (build) the Hurston River Dam, very little rain (2) _____ (fall). The lake behind the dam (3) _____ (fill) slowly over a period of several years because of the drought. While the lake (4) _____ (come) up to its normal level, trees and stumps just below the water level (5) _____ (make) boating dangerous. After the lake (6) _____ (reach) its normal level, however, Lake Hurston (7) _____ (become) one of the most popular lakes in the country for boating and sailing.

The Past Perfect Progressive Tense (sometimes called **Continuous**)

Use the past perfect progressive tense to show that an **action in the remote past was temporary** or that the **time it lasted is important** or that **an action was going on when something else happened.**

Walk
I, you, he, she, it, they had been walking.

No one knew that Mr. Allen had a wig because he *had been wearing* it secretly. (temporary)

Jane *had been looking* for a new roommate for six weeks before she finally found one. (temporary)

John *had been trying* to meet Mary for three months before he finally succeeded. (the length of time is important)

Women *had been demanding* the right to vote for many years before they finally got it. (the length of time is important)

The Chinese *had been using* gunpowder for centuries before its use *was known* in Europe. (the action was going on when something else happened)

Many people *had been swimming* when the shark *was sighted.* (the action was going on when something else happened)

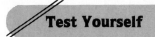

Test Yourself

Fill in the blanks with past or past perfect progressive forms.

The Chinese (1) _____ (invent) printing with movable type long before Gutenberg (2) _____ (develop) it in Europe. The Chinese (3) _____ (use) wood blocks for at least seven hundred years before Europeans (4) _____ (discover) the principles of modern printing. Four hundred years before Gutenberg, Pi Sheng (5) _____ (make) individual ideographs out of clay, but because Chinese has thousands of separate characters, the invention (6) _____ (simplify) printing much less for Chinese than it later (7) _____ (simplify) copying in languages with alphabets based on twenty to thirty sounds. The Chinese (8) _____ (print) with a process that later (9) _____ (change) communications greatly when Gutenberg (10) _____ (reinvent) it in Europe. Because of the nature of the Chinese language, the process (11) _____ (have) a much less revolutionary effect in China even though the Chinese (12) _____ (develop) it for a much longer time.

The Future Tense

Show future time by using *will* or *shall* + the infinitive (simple present) form of the main verb. This way of showing future time is formal. Use it when the decision to do something is newly made or when someone in authority gives an order.

Walk
I, you, he, she, it, we, they will walk.

In the United States, *will* is commonly used in all forms of the future. In England, *shall* is used with *I* and *we,* but the usage is reversed in an emphatic statement. (I, we *will* and he, she, it, they, you *shall* are emphatic in this usage.) For other meanings of *will* and *shall* besides showing future time, see **Modals.**

Avoid the contracted *'ll* and *won't* form in formal writing.

Other verb forms can also show future ideas:

Is Going to as Future

1   Use the present tense of *Be* + *going* + *to* + *base infinitive* (simple present) of the main verb to show planned or intended future.

I *am going to walk* two miles every day.
You (we, they) *are going to walk* two miles every day.
He (she, it) *is going to walk* two miles every day.

The *is going to* future is more informal and wordy than the *will* future. Do not overuse it in academic writing. Both the *will* and *is going to* futures can be used with both personal and inanimate subjects.

The art class *will* visit the museum tomorrow.
The art class *is going to* visit the museum tomorrow.
The weather report predicts that it *will rain* tonight.
The weather report predicts that it *is going to rain* tonight.

Three additional verb constructions can be used to show future events. Use these three constructions mainly with events, states, or statements that are subject to human control.

Present of *Be* + Infinitive as Future

2   See **Be** for conjugation.

New students *are to register* at two o'clock this afternoon.
Our dog *is to get* a rabies shot next week.

This construction shows obligation or regulation. It is similar in meaning to *have to.* It is rather formal.

Present Tense as Future

3   You can use the present tense to show future events that are **fixed or certain,** whether personal or impersonal, after **if, unless,** and **whether** and **after relative adverbs of time.**

If the price *is* reasonable, Steve will buy a new car.
The sun *sets* at 6:05 this evening.
Our train *leaves* at 9:07 A.M. tomorrow.
The cost of first-class mail *increases* after January 1.
When you *find* the answer to that problem, you can go.

The Present Progressive Tense as Future

4 The present progressive tense can show action that will happen in the future. (See "Present Tense" on p. 360 for conjugation.)

We *are having* dinner at seven this evening.
My parents *are coming* to visit me next month.
Our soccer team *is not playing* in the regional championship games this year.

Test Yourself

A. Fill in the blanks in the following sentences in five different ways that give a future meaning.

1. The prices of our entire line of products _____ (rise) by 5 percent on January 1.

2. Professor Hamilton _____ (complete) work on her latest book by the end of July.

3. Harry _____ (finish) law school in May.

4. According to an ad in today's paper, Technomet Company _____ (hire) fifty new

    employees next week.

B. Some of the ways of forming the future are not likely to be used in some of the following sentences. How many ways can you rewrite each sentence? Write the different ways that are likely. Why are they possible? Why are others not likely?

1. The weather forecast says it *will rain* tomorrow.
2. Probably the rain *won't come* in time to keep our tomato plants from dying.
3. John's parents *are coming* to visit him soon, but he is not sure when.
4. Paul thinks he *will understand* chemistry better after he gets a tutor.
5. Ellen's dog *is going to be trained* by a professional handler.

The Future Perfect Tense

Make future perfect forms with *will* + *have* + past participle of the main verb. (see **Verbs, irregular** for irregular past participles) English speakers in the United States use *will* in all persons. (See p. 370, "Future Tense," for more about the *shall/will* distinction.)

Walk

I, you, he, she, it, we, they will have walked.

Use the future perfect to show **an action that will be completed in the future.**

Adverbs:

by phrase	This obedience school *will have trained* fifty dogs *by* the end of
at that time	the year.
(by) tomorrow	*By* the end of the winter season, more tourists *will have visited*
(by) this afternoon	the island than ever before.
(by) tonight	I left several letters unfinished on my desk, but I *will have fin-*
(by) next week,	*ished* them *before* noon tomorrow.
month, year,	
specific time or date in	
the future, *before* . . .	
not later than . . .	

Test Yourself

Fill in the blanks with future perfect forms.

1. Because the year 2000 is a convenient symbol of division, many predictions are made

   about what _____ (happen) by then.

2. Some doctors predict that great advances in prolonging life _____ (occur) by then.

3. Agriculturalists say that hunger _____ (conquer, passive)

4. Many countries _____ (wipe out) illiteracy.

5. The lives of many people _____ (become) more comfortable than they are today.

The Future Progressive Tense (sometimes called **Continuous**)

Make the future with *will + be + -ing* form.   (See "Future Tense" p. 370, for more about the *shall/will* distinction.)

Walk

I, you, he, she, it, we, they will be walking.

Use the future progressive to emphasize **duration, intention, or a temporary condition in the future.**

I will mail that package for you since I *will be walking* by the post office this afternoon.
As long as we live next to you, our dog *will be chasing* your cat.
Sometimes I think I *will be studying* English the rest of my life.
Our salesman *will be calling* you soon to confirm your order.

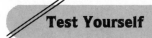 **Test Yourself**

Fill in the blanks with future progressive forms.

1. Futurists study trends that _____ (occur) in the future.

2. They think about how technology _____ (affect) the lives of ordinary people.

3. They also look for inventions that have not yet been fully developed, but that _____ (bring) changes in the future.

4. Has something already been invented that _____ (change) society in the next twenty years the way transistors, for example, have changed it in the recent past?

5. Many people think that biological sciences rather than engineering will be the source of the most radical changes that _____ (alter) our lives in the twenty-first century.

The Future Perfect Progressive Tense (sometimes called Continuous)

Make the future perfect progressive with *will* + *have* + *been* + past participle (*-ed* form) + *-ing* form. (See **Verbs, irregular** for irregular past participles and see "Future Tense" above for more about the *shall/will* distinction.)

Walk
I, you, he, she, it, we, they will have been walking.

Use the future perfect to **combine the ideas of completeness and duration of time in the future.**

By the end of this year, the Anderson family *will have been living* in the same house for a hundred years.
Soon he *will have been studying* here six months.
The hikers started out at sunrise this morning; by eight o'clock they *will have been walking* for three hours.

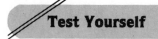 **Test Yourself**

Fill the blanks with the correct forms of the future perfect progressive tense.

1. Looking to the future people like to plan for special anniversaries. In the year 2000 people _____ (think) about anniversaries that will occur that year.

2. By the year 2000 we _____ (lived) in the Atomic Age for fifty-five years.

3. At that time the United States government _____ (be) in operation for 211 years from the time George Washington was inaugurated as President in 1789.

4. The oldest university in the Western Hemisphere, the University of Santo Domingo in the Dominican Republic, was founded in 1538; by the year 2000 it _____ (be) in existence 462 years.

5. Far older than any university in the Western Hemisphere is the University of Al-Azhar in Cairo; founded in 970, by the year 2000, it _____ (functioned) 1030 years.

Future Time in the Past

Several constructions can be used to show future time as viewed from a point in the past.

1 *would* + **bare infinitive**

        past
Finally the time *came* to leave; later he *would remember* how everyone stood waving goodbye.

     past
Sam *bought* new tires so that his car *would pass* the safety inspection.

2 *was/were going to* + **bare infinitive**

  past
We *hurried* because we *were going to be* late.

  past
Jane *was* happy because she *was going to pass* the examination.

3 *was/were* + **infinitive** (Use this construction only for events subject to human control.)

The president *was to open* the new building the next day.
The winner *was to receive* a trophy at the banquet later that night.

4 past progressive (a) with verbs that are not stative   (see **Stative Verbs**) and (b) to replace verbs in the present progressive tense in reported speech if the reporting verb is in the past tense.   (see **Reported Speech**)

Jane hurried because she *was arriving* late.
They *knew* that we *were having* a party the next day. (after *knew*)
Carl *said* that he *was* never *climbing* that mountain again. (after *said*)

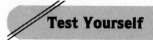
Test Yourself

Complete each of the following sentences in the number of ways shown to indicate future time in the past.

1. It rained a little this morning. It rained very hard this afternoon.
   Use a form of *rain:* It rained a little this morning;

   later it _____ harder.

   later it _____ harder.

   later it _____ harder.

2. Andy studied hard for his test, but he was so nervous when he took it that he forgot some of the things he knew.
   Use a form of *draw:* Andy did not draw the diagram for problem three;

   later he _____ the same diagram easily.

   later he _____ the same diagram easily.

   later he _____ the same diagram easily.

   later he _____ the same diagram easily.

3. Tom failed his test to get his driver's license. He made an appointment to try again the next day.
   Use a form of *try:* Tom failed the test for his driver's license, but

   he _____ again the next day.

   he _____ again the next day.

   he _____ again the next day.

   he _____ again the next day.

Combined Exercise on Present and Future

Fill in the blanks with future or present forms. Then copy the forms in the blanks to the left.

1. _____ The State Transportation Office (1) _____ (give) final approval to the new

   highway project

2. _____ after a final citizens' hearing (2) ____ (be) held.

3. _____ According to law, notices for the hearing (3) ____ (post)

4. _____ thirty days before the hearing (4) ____ (take)

5. _____ place. As soon as the clerk (5) ____ (schedule)

6. _____ the hearing, groups of residents (6) ____ (meet) to decide whether or not

    they will oppose the road.

7. _____ The highway department (7) ____ (not buy) property for the

8. _____ project until all interested people (8) ____ (have) a chance to present their

    opinions.

Sequences of Tenses

Do not make unnecessary shifts in tense in your writing. Often you can choose to use a framework in the present or you can use a framework in the past, but be consistent and do not change back and forth without a reason for the change.

In Reported Speech

You must change from the present to the past tense when you change direct speech to reported speech if the reporting verb is in the past. (See **Reported Speech** for illustrations and exercises.)

Statement: "Literature courses *are* difficult for me," Henry said.
Henry *said* that literature courses *were* difficult for him.

Question: "Why *do* you want to work while you *are* in school?" the interviewer asked Sue.
The interviewer *asked* Sue why she *wanted* to work while she *was* in school.

In Time Clauses

In a sentence that has a dependent clause beginning with one of the following expressions of time, if you use the **future** tense in the independent clause, use the **present** tense in the dependent clause. (See **"Present Tense"** on p. 357.)

when(ever)	before	the day (that)
as soon as	until, till	the week (that)
after	the moment (that)	the year (that)

                                        after
The manager *will read* your report   when   he *comes* in.
                                        as soon as

I *will look* for your book $\begin{smallmatrix} \text{whenever} \\ \text{as soon as} \end{smallmatrix}$ I *have* time.

The doctor *will* not *examine* patients before they *fill* out these forms.

(see also **Conditional Sentences** and **Subjunctive**)

Titles

Books, Magazines, and Newspapers

Capitalize words in titles of books, magazines, and newspapers according to conventional usage. (see **Capitalization**) Underline titles in handwriting and typing to show that these titles would be printed in italics in the style for writing in humanities. If you are writing a paper in another subject, refer to the style sheet for that subject. (see **Punctuation, underlining**)

A Tale of Two Cities (book)
Treasure Island (book)
Science for Today (book)
Newsweek (magazine)
Reader's Digest (magazine)
The New York Times (newspaper)
The Wall Street Journal (newspaper)

Capitalize but do not underline titles of books that are sacred to a religion.

The Bible	The Koran	The New Testament
The Gita	Revelations	The Torah

Put quotation marks around titles of articles in magazines, newspapers, and journals and capitalize them. (see **Punctuation, quotation marks**)

"New Crisis in California" (article in newspaper)
"The Future of Metals" (article in a magazine)
"New Developments in Solar Cells" (article in a journal)

Put quotation marks around chapters of books, short stories, and poems unless a single poem is published as a separate book.

"The Unicorn in the Garden" (short story)
"Patterns" (poem)
"The Expository Paragraph" (chapter in a book)
"A Rose for Emily" (short story)

People

Capitalize but do not underline or put quotation marks around titles of people.

the President
Professor Susan C. Thompson

Doctor Albert Jones
Miss Pamela Rockston

Write titles out in full in formal writing. In business letters and addresses, however, use the abbreviations Mr., Mrs., and Ms. Professional titles are often written out in full in business correspondence. (Miss is not an abbreviation.) Do not use a title both before and after a name.

Ms. Gladys Beckman
Mr. Peter Smith
Doctor Edward Prentiss
Professor Thomas Carlson

Some married women prefer Mrs. to Ms. They may use their own first name for business affairs and their husband's name for social affairs.

Mrs. Elizabeth Jones (business)
Mrs. Arthur Jones (social)

Compositions

Do not underline or put quotation marks around the titles of your own compositions.

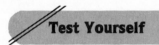 **Test Yourself**

Punctuate and capitalize the following sentences correctly.

1. When a student asked "professor" Jones for some information on the history of mathematics, the professor told her to start by looking at the famous book on geometry, the elements, which was written by euclid, a mathematician in ancient times.

2. To find information about euclid's life, the student looked for an article called euclid of alexandria in the encyclopaedia britannica.

3. Another article entitled relativity was in another encyclopedia.

4. The student finally decided to write about recent mathematical discoveries; she called her paper mathematics of the twentieth century.

Two-Word Verbs

Two-word verbs are formed from a verb and a preposition or an adverb (sometimes called a particle). These verbs are sometimes called phrasal verbs or idioms. Two-word verbs are used more often in speech and informal writing than in formal writing, but they may be used in formal writing also.

Meaning

A two-word verb often has a one-word synonym, a single word which has the same meaning. The one-word form is generally more formal.   (see **Style**)

call up	telephone/summon
catch on	understand
cry out	exclaim
give in/up	surrender
go/come along	accompany/agree
keep on	continue
leave out	omit
pay back	repay
pick out	choose
put off	postpone
turn off	appear/find

The meanings of many two-word verbs are idiomatic; that is, you cannot easily figure out their meanings from the meanings of the separate parts. Many slang expressions that are vulgar or taboo are two-word verbs. United States and British meanings of two-word verbs are not always the same. *Call on,* for example, means *ask for help* in both usages. People in the United States also use *call on* in the sense of *visit,* but the British do not. In the United States people *call* others *up* on the telephone, but the British *ring* them *up.* Look in dictionaries and books of idioms for the meanings of two-word verbs. Many of the two-word combinations have more than one meaning, and some fit in more than one of the constructions explained below. *The Longman Dictionary of Contemporary English* lists two-word verbs as separate entries. *The Oxford Advanced Learner's Dictionary* and some dictionaries written for native English speakers list two-word verbs in the listing for the first word.

Inseparable Two-Word Verbs

Always keep the parts of inseparable two-word verbs together. If there is a direct object, it follows the second word.

(These two-word verbs are sometimes called *prepositional verbs.*)

	direct object
You must *account for*	the *money.*
You must *account for*	*it.*
Shirley *got over*	her *cold.*
She *got over*	*it.*
Look after	your *brother.*
Look after	*him.*

Some Inseparable Two-Word Verbs and Idiomatic Phrases

The nouns in parentheses are possible objects for the verbs listed. If no noun follows the verb, the verb is intransitive (is not followed by an object). Other meanings are possible for some of the combinations given.

account for (the money)

ask for (help)

bear up

boil over

break in

    into (the house)

    out

call for (a decision)

  on (friends)

care for (a person)

carry on

clean up (with a direct object, *clean up* is separable; see below)

clear up (with a direct object, *clear up* is separable; see below)

come away

come into (the house)

    out

get over (the illness)—*get it over with* means *be finished with*

give in

    out

go ahead

    back

    up

grow up

hold off

    up

look after (my family)

    ahead

    away

    for (help)

pull up

run over (a nail)

see through (the curtain) (*see it through* means *continue to the end*)

send for (a friend)

stand by (a friend)

stand for (something)

stay up

talk back

turn up

wear away

Separable Two-Word Verbs

Like inseparable two-word verbs, separable two-word verbs have idiomatic meanings. The object, however, is movable. A pronoun object comes between the first and second part of a separable two-word verb. A short noun object can come between the two parts, or can follow the second part. Separable two-word verbs are transitive (they have an object). (see **Passive Verbs**) Separable two-word verbs are sometimes called *phrasal verbs.*

               object

The rescue squad *turned on* the *light.*

object

They *turned* the *light on*.

object

They *turned*   *it*   *on*.

If the direct object is long, especially if it is modified by a phrase or a clause, put it after the second part of the two-word verb.

object

The rescue squad *turned on* the *light* by the door.

object

The rescue squad *turned on* the *light* that had just been fixed.

Some two-word verbs can be either separable or inseparable according to their meanings in a certain context.

The workmen *cleaned* the rugs. (removed dirt)
          cleaned up the building site. (removed dirt and trash)—*cleaned* it *up*.
The gambler *cleaned up* at the casino. (won a lot of money)

The soldier *passed out* after standing for four hours in the hot sun. (fainted)
The leader *passed out* the tickets. (distributed)—*passed* them *out*.

The car *broke down*. (stopped operating)
The police *broke down* the door. (opened by force)—*broke* it *down*.

He *showed up* late. (arrived)
The supervisor *showed* him *up* as a fool. (exposed)

Right as an adverb meaning *immediately* or *completely* may come between the two parts of both separable and inseparable two-word verbs. With separable two-word verbs, *right* comes just before the second part of the verb. *Right* is informal; do not use it in very formal writing.

The new buildings are going *right* up.
The flight attendant turned the light *right* on.
The flight attendant turned it *right* on.

Some Separable Two-Word Verbs

Use a pronoun or a noun object. Never use both. Many other nouns are possible; these are given as examples.

back	(it)	up	(the car)
blow	(it)	out	(the candle)
	(it)	up	(the balloon)
break	(them)	down	(the statistics)
	(them)	off	(the negotiations)
bring	(it)	about	(change)
	(it)	up	(the subject)
burn	(it)	down	(the building)
	(them)	up	(the papers)

clear	(them)	away	(the dishes)
	(it)	up	(the misunderstanding)
close	(it)	down	(the business)
draw	(it)	up	(an agreement)
fill	(it)	in/out	(a form)
	(it)	up	(the cup)
find	(it)	out	(the answer)
give	(it)	away	(this old coat)
	(it)	up	(eating candy)
	(it)	out	(the news)
hand	(it)	in/out	(the news, the work)
keep	(them)	down	(expenses)
	(it)	on	(the radio)
leave	(it)	out	(the question)
let	(them)	in/out	(our friends)
lock	(them)	up	(the prisoners)
look	(them)	up	(our friends in Detroit)
make	(it)	out	(the handwriting)
	(it)	up	(a story)

NOTE: *Make it up to* someone, if there is no antecedent for *it,* means *repay.*

mix	(it)	up	(a story, food being prepared)
	(them)	up	(people—confuse them or make them acquainted with each other)
pass	(it)	on	(the responsibility)
pay	(it)	back	(the money)
	(them)	back	(my enemies)
pick	(it)	out	(a new coat)
point	(it)	out	(the problem)
put	(it)	across	(an idea)
	(it)	away	(the laundry)
	(it)	off	(the work)
	(them)	out	(the cats)
round	(them)	off	(the numbers)
	(them)	up	(the cattle)
set	(it)	up	(the appointment)
take	(them)	in	(people)
	(it)	up, over	(a project)
talk	(it)	over	(the problem)
think	(it)	over	(the offer)
throw	(it)	away	(the trash)
try	(it)	on	(the coat)
turn	(them)	away	(the demonstrators)
	(it)	down	(the radio)
	(it)	off	(the light)
	(it)	over	(the mattress)
	(it)	up	(the volume)

wear	(them)	out	(the shoes)
wind	(it)	up	(the clock, the business)
wipe	(it)	off, out, up	(the dirt)
work	(it)	out	(the problem)

Many nouns are formed from two-word verbs. Some are spelled with hyphens.

backup   cleanup   lockout   shake-up   tryout

Many of these are informal rather than formal in usage. Look in a dictionary to be certain of the usage of each meaning. (see **Word Formation,** p. 405, for more examples)

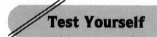

Test Yourself

Writers using formal academic style often replace two-word verbs with single-word verbs that come from Latin roots. Business writers often prefer two-word verbs because they are more informal and are easier for native speakers to understand. Which words in the two lists below can have the same meaning? (Some of the two-word verbs have more than one meaning.) Write the more formal synonym in the blank. A dictionary written for nonnative speakers of English will help you find the answers.

A.   1. _____ blow out   observe
     2. _____ live through   retreat
     3. _____ look at   remove
     4. _____ stand against   endure
     5. _____ count in   display
     6. _____ take off   extinguish
     7. _____ beef up   oppose
     8. _____ show off   illuminate
     9. _____ turn back   include
    10. _____ light up   strengthen

B.   1. _____ sell out   equalize
     2. _____ cut out   disappoint
     3. _____ let down   encounter
     4. _____ come between   discard
     5. _____ run into   intervene
     6. _____ talk into   remove
     7. _____ take out   conceal
     8. _____ hush up   eliminate
     9. _____ even up   persuade
    10. _____ throw away   betray

C. Which of the two-word verbs in A and B can be separable? Write a sentence with each one using a noun object. Then rewrite the sentence using a pronoun object.

Three-Word Verbs

A verb that must be followed by two words, an adverb and a preposition, is sometimes called a three-word verb. These verbs are common in speech, but avoid using them in formal writing, especially if one of the particles comes at the end of the sentence. Do not put any other words between the parts of a three-word verb.

Informal: Some discomfort has to be *put up with*. (endured)
I won't *put up with* that. (endure)
That's what he's *holding out for*. (demanding, refusing to compromise)
The old lady's daughter *looks in on* her every day. (visits, checks)
When you cross the street, *watch / look out for* cars. (watch for, be careful of)

Some Three-Word Verbs

break in on	get down to	put up with
catch up on	go back on	stand up for
catch up with	go through with	stand up to
check up on	live up to	try out for
come down with	look in on	tune in to
cut down on	look out for	turn out for
do away with	look up to	walk off with
face up to	make up for	walk out on

Test Yourself

Which three-word verb in the list above can mean the same as the following?

(1) reduce, (2) visit, (3) admire, (4) win, (5) leave, (6) renege, (7) interrupt, (8) catch (a disease), (9) investigate, (10) audition

Verb Patterns, see **Sentence Patterns**

Verb Phrases, see **Phrases**

Verbals

Verbals are verb forms that are used as nouns or modifiers in a clause rather than as the main verb or as part of a verb phrase that is the main verb. (see **Infinitives, Gerunds,** and **Participles**)

 Infinitive phrases are made of *to* + the *infinitive* form of the verb.

 Gerunds are *-ing* forms of the verb used as nouns.

 Present participles are *-ing* forms of the verb used as adjectives and in verb phrases to form the progressive tenses.

 Past participles are *-ed* forms of regular verbs. (see **Verbs, irregular** for past participles with other endings) Past participles are used as adjectives and in verb phrases to form the perfect tenses. Some grammar books call past participles *-en* forms to distinguish them from the simple past forms, which are called the *-ed* forms.

385

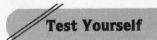

Test Yourself

Use the correct verbal in the following sentences, and then write it in the blank to the left.

1. _____ (1) _____ (Find) out about far-away places interests most people.

2. _____ Explorers try (2) _____ (find) places that are not well known as well as the highest mountains and deepest parts of the ocean.

3. _____ Some brave people spend the winter in the Antarctic, (3) _____ (live)

4. _____ in isolation during months of darkness in order (4) _____ (learn)

5. _____ about (5) _____ (survive) in a very cold and lonely place.

6. _____ Many mountain climbers dream of (6) _____ (climb) Mount Everest, the world's highest mountain.

7. _____ Divers use Scuba gear and rubber suits in shallow and medium depths and scientists use special submarines (7) _____ (explore) as deeply as possible in the ocean.

8. _____ (8) _____ (Live) things are found deep in the ocean and at high altitudes on mountains.

9. _____ (9) _____ (Explore) the sky began with balloons.

10. _____ Now rockets make it possible (10) _____ (explore) space.

Verbs

Many sections of this book deal with verbs. These sections are listed alphabetically here and in the book.

Agreement of Subject and Verb	Auxiliary Verbs	Complements
	Be	Direct Object
Aspect	Clauses	*Do*

Finite Verbs
Gerunds
Have
Indirect Object
Infinitive
Infinitive/-*ing*
  Choice
Modals
Negation
Number, Singular
  and Plural

Operators
Participles
Passive Verbs
Predicate
Principal Parts of
  Verbs
Questions
Reported Speech
Sentence Structure

Stative Verbs
Subjunctive
Tense
Two-Word Verbs
Verbs, irregular
Word Formation

If you are having difficulty with *subject-verb agreement,* look up

Agreement of Subject and Verb
Auxiliary Verb
Finite Verb (main verb in the
  sentence)

Operators
Number, Singular and Plural
Questions

If you are having difficulty with the verb *to be,* look up

Be
Mood
Operators

Passive Verbs
Tense

If you are having difficulty using the right *verb form,* look up

Agreement of Subject and Verb
Finite Verbs
Infinitive/-*ing* Choice
Modals
Negation

Operators
Principal Parts of Verbs
Subjunctive
Tense
Verbs, Irregular

If you are having difficulty using the right *tense,* look up

Conditional Sentences
Modals

Reported Speech
Tense

If you are having difficulty with the *word order* of verb forms, look up

Finite Verbs
Operators

Questions
Reported Speech

Classifications of Verbs

Aspect
  Simple
  Perfect
  Progressive (Continuous)

Mood
  Indicative
  Interrogative

Imperative
Subjunctive

Number
  Singular
  Plural

Person (see Point of View)
  First

Second	Present Perfect
Third	Past Perfect
Tense	Future Perfect
Present	Progressive Aspects of these
Past	tenses
Future	*Voice (transitive verbs only)*
	Active
	Passive

Complementation (words that must follow verbs)

Linking (predicate nominative or adverb)
Intransitive (no noun or adjective complement)
Transitive
  Active (direct object required, indirect object and objective complement possible with some
    verbs)
  Passive (no complement required)

Verbs, Irregular

Many of the most common verbs in English are irregular; that is, their past and past participle forms are not made by adding *-ed* to the present form. Most irregular verb forms were regular forms hundreds of years ago. They represent ways of making tenses that we do not use anymore. This list *does not include* (1) modals   (see **Modals**); (2) irregular verbs that you see in reading but that you are not likely to use in writing—look them up in a dictionary when necessary (lists of all irregular verbs in alphabetical order are in the *Oxford Advanced Learner's Dictionary* and in the *Longman Dictionary of Contemporary English*); (3) irregular verbs that have a common regular form that means the same thing (*proved, proven* and *sowed, sown,* for example)—you will always be correct if you use the regular form; and (4) *-ing* forms, since they are regular in all verbs.   (see **Spelling**).

Examples of Use of the Principal Parts (see also **Principal Parts of Verbs**)

Present:	We *eat* breakfast every day.
Past:	We *ate* breakfast yesterday.
Past Participle:	We *have* already *eaten* breakfast today.
-ing Form (Simple Present + -ing):	We *are* not *eating* breakfast now.

Group I

Irregular verbs in which the past participle ends in *-n* or *-ne* usually have different forms for the past and the past participle. (Exceptions in this list are *shine, spin,* and *win.*) Most of the verbs that end in *-ne* have a spelling change in the vowel from the past to the past participle, also.

Simple Present	Past (-ed form)	Past Participle (-en form)
be	was/were	been
bear	bore	born
bear (forbear)	bore	borne
beat	beat	beaten
begin	began	begun
bite	bit	bitten
blow	blew	blown
break	broke	broken
choose	chose	chosen
do	did	done
draw	drew	drawn
drive	drove	driven
fall	fell	fallen
fly	flew	flown
forget	forgot	forgot, forgotten
forgive	forgave	forgiven
freeze	froze	frozen
get	got	got, gotten
give	gave	given
go	went	gone
grow	grew	grown
hide	hid	hidden
know	knew	known
lie (see p. 117)	lay	lain
ride	rode	ridden
rise	rose	risen
run	ran	run
see	saw	seen
shake	shook	shaken
shine (see p. 122)	shone	shone
speak	spoke	spoken
spin	spun	spun
steal	stole	stolen
strike	struck	stricken (see p. 124)
swear	swore	sworn
take	took	taken
tear	tore	torn
throw	threw	thrown
wear	wore	worn
weave	wove	woven
win	won	won
write	wrote	written

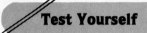

Test Yourself

A. Put the correct verb forms in the blanks.

1. When the club _____ (go) on a picnic everyone was _____ (bite) by mosquitoes.

2. The members all _____ (forget) to get insect repellent to keep the mosquitoes off.

3. The mosquitoes _____ (bite) almost everyone at the picnic.

4. Have you been _____ (bite) by mosquitoes at the lake?

5. What a picnic! Ned _____ (fall) in the lake, and Penny _____ (break) her glasses.

6. If Ned hadn't _____ (fell) in the lake, he would have had a good time, but he had _____ (forget) to bring extra clothes with him.

7. As soon as it _____ (grow) dark, we _____ (drive) home because the mosquitoes _____ (get) even worse. Didn't they _____ (bite) fiercely!

8. But we didn't leave before the moon _____ (rise).

9. The area that was _____ (choose) by the committee

10. _____ (give) us some problems.

Group II
Irregular verbs in which the past participle ends in -t have the same forms for the past and the part participle.

Simple Present	Past (-ed form)	Past Participle
bend	bent	bent
bring	brought	brought
build	built	built
buy	bought	bought
catch	caught	caught
deal	dealt	dealt
feel	felt	felt
fight	fought	fought
keep	kept	kept
kneel	knelt	knelt
leave	left	left
lend	lent	lent

Simple Present	Past (-ed form)	Past Participle
lose	lost	lost
mean	meant	meant
meet	met	met
seek	sought	sought
send	sent	sent
sit	sat	sat
shoot	shot	shot
sleep	slept	slept
spend	spent	spent
sweep	swept	swept
teach	taught	taught
think	thought	thought

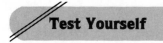

Test Yourself

B. Fill in the blanks with the correct forms.

1. Many new houses have been _____ (build) in Westown in the last six months.

2. A new electronics factory has _____ (bring) many new people into the area.

3. Many people who had _____ (feel) they could never work on an assembly line have

    been _____ (teach) how to assemble parts for the equipment made there.

4. Some people in Westown _____ (think) the new plant would not _____ (bring) many

    jobs here.

5. But the management has hired many local people and has _____ (send) some to

    Boston for training.

6. The people of Westown _____ (fight) to _____ (keep) their steel mill, but

    they _____ (lose) it anyway.

7. Getting a new industry has _____ (mean) a lot to the town.

8. People have _____ (feel) much more optimistic since the new factory opened and

    have _____ (spend) more money too.

9. Few people have _____ (leave) Westown in the last six months.

Group III

Irregular verbs in which the past participle ends in -*d* have the same form for the past and the past participle.

Simple Present	Past (-ed form)	Past Participle
bind	bound	bound
bleed	bled	bled
breed	bred	bred
feed	fed	fed
find	found	found
grind	ground	ground
have	had	had
hear	heard	heard
hold	held	held
lay	laid	laid
lead	led	led
make	made	made
pay	paid	paid
say	said	said
sell	sold	sold
slide	slid	slid
stand	stood	stood
tell	told	told
understand	understood	understood
† wind	wound	wound

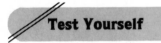 **Test Yourself**

C. Fill in the blanks with the correct forms.

1. Many years ago bakers _____ (sell) bread in their own small shops.

2. Today the bakery industry has _____ (find) that huge bakeries with deliveries to supermarkets are more profitable.

3. Many things connected with food have become part of the huge food industry; for example, cattle are _____ (feed) in huge feed lots before they go to market.

4. New kinds of chickens have been _____ (breed) that have more meat on their bodies.

5. Consumers have always _____ (pay) extra for fancy packages even though they were sometimes _____ (tell) there was no extra charge.

† A regular form that means *to be out of breath* has a different pronunciation.

6. Most coffee is _____ (sell) after it has been _____ (grind) and put in cans or packages.

7. The food industry has _____ (say) that large-scale operations have _____ (make) the cost of food go down.

Group IV

Irregular verbs in this group have a vowel change from the simple present to the past and past participle, which are usually the same form. This vowel change is clear in both pronunciation and spelling.

Simple Present	Past	Past Participle
cling	clung	clung
†come	came	come
dig	dug	dug
fling	flung	flung
††hang	hung	hung
ring	rang	rung
shrink	shrunk, shrank	shrunk
sing	sang	sung
spring	sprung, sprang	sprung
stick	stuck	stuck
sting	stung	stung
stink	stunk, stank	stunk
strike	struck	struck (see p. 124)
string	strung	strung
swim	swam	swum
swing	swung	swung
†††wake	woke, waked	woke, waked

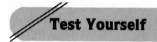 **Test Yourself**

D. Fill in the blanks with the correct forms.

1. Mike's last vacation was a disaster; his car got _____ (stick) when he was unloading his boat.

2. After he _____ (dig) his car out of the mud, he was _____ (sting) by a hornet.

3. When he took his boat out on the lake, it _____ (sink); and when he _____ (swim) to shore, he almost didn't make it.

† *welcome* is regular.
†† *hang* (regular) means to die or cause to die with a rope around the neck.
††† *awake* has similar forms; *awaken* is regular.

4. A skunk came near his tent and _____ (stink) up the place.

5. He got caught in the rain and his new shirt _____ (shrink).

6. Lightning _____ (strike) so near his camp that he felt the electricity in his legs.

7. When he _____ (wake) the last morning and thought about all that had happened to

 him, he decided he hadn't had a very good vacation.

Group V
 These irregular verbs have only one form for the present, the past, and the past participle. Notice that all of them end in *-d* or *-t*.

bet	cut	put	shed	spread
†bid	fit	quit	shut	thrust
burst	hit	††read	slit	†††wet
cast	hurt	rid	spit	
cost	let	set	split	

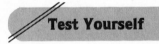

Test Yourself

E. Correct the errors in the following sentences. (NOTE: Some of the words are misspelled.)

1. The clown blew the balloons up until they bursted.

2. He payed for the balloons when he bout them.

3. Did they told him the balloons could be blew up very big when he buyed them?

4. The clown blowed them too hard.

5. He could made funny animals out of balloons that he twisted together.

6. His dogs, cats, monkeys, and giraffes maded everyone laugh.

7. He always brung his own balloons.

8. The children always thought he had a special kind of balloons that costed extra.

---

† *Bid, bade, bid* or *bidden* (tr.) *means give a greeting, order, or command; bid, bid, bid* (intr.) *means to offer a price* or *to seek something.*
†† All three forms are spelled the same, but the past and past participle are pronounced differently (rhymes with feed, fed, fed).
††† Regular endings are sometimes used in certain meanings.

F. Put the correct verb forms in the blanks.

The Monkey Who Left His Heart in a Tree

1. _____   Once there was a monkey living in a large tree. Its branches

2. _____ (1) _____ (hang) half over the town and half over the sea.

3. _____ Every day the monkey (2) _____ (eat) the fruit from the

4. _____ tree. Some of the fruit (3) _____ (fall) into the sea,

5. _____ and a shark (4) _____ (come) and (5) _____ (get) some

6. _____ of it. The shark (6) _____ (do) this for

7. _____ many months.

8. _____   One day the shark (7) _____ (say), "You (8) _____ (be)

9. _____ my friend. I want to (9) _____ (do) something kind for you.

10. _____ (10) _____ (come) with me to my home." The

11. _____ shark (11) _____ (tell) the monkey not to worry about

12. _____ swimming; he could (12) _____ (keep) dry on the shark's

13. _____ back. The shark would (13) _____ (let) the monkey

14. _____ (14) _____ (ride) on his back. When the shark

15. _____ (15) _____ (know) they (16) _____ (be) far at sea,

16. _____ he (17) _____ (begin) to explain what was really

17. _____ happening.

18. _____   "Look, I will (18) _____ (tell) you the truth. My king

19. _____ has (19) _____ (be) very sick and he has been

20. _____ (20) _____ (tell) that the only medicine that can cure him

21. _____ is the heart of a monkey." Then the monkey (21) _____ (feel)

22. _____ very frightened. He (22) _____ (think) fast and finally

23. _____ (23) _____ (see) a way to save himself.

24. _____   He (24) _____ (speak) to the shark, "If

25. _____ I had only (25) _____ (understand) before we

26. _____ (26) _____ (leave) my tree, I could

27. _____ have (27) _____ (bring) my heart with

28. _____ me. I (28) _____ (be) terribly sorry to say

29. _____ I (29) _____ (put) it at the very top of the tree so

30. _____ it could be (30) _____ (keep) safe.

31. _____ Don't you (31) _____ (know) that from the

32. _____ beginning monkeys have always (32) _____ (leave) their

33. _____ hearts behind when they (33) _____ (take)

34. _____ trips?" The monkey (34) _____ (think) perhaps

35. _____ the shark didn't believe him, so he continued, "We'll (35) _____ (go)

36. _____ on to your place. You may (36) _____ (beat)

37. _____ me when we (37) _____ (get) there if

38. _____ you (38) _____ (find) my heart. I really don't have it with me."

39. _____   Then the shark (39) _____ (know) he wanted to go back for

40. _____ the monkey's heart. But the monkey (40) _____ (shake) his head,

41. _____ saying, "Don't go back now. That would be a terrible mistake."

42. _____   Finally the shark (41) _____ (make) the monkey agree and they

(42) _____ (go) back to the tree for the heart. At the

43. _____ tree, the monkey jumped off the shark's back and (43) _____ (run) up in

the highest branches of the tree. "Wait

44. _____ for me here, shark, until I (44) _____ (bring) you my heart," he shouted.

Then the shark (45) _____ (swim) around in

45. _____ the sea under the tree, but the monkey stayed up high in the top.

"Come down," called the shark. But the monkey still stayed in the top

of the tree.

46. _____ "Our friendship is (46) _____ (break)," shouted the monkey

47. _____ as he (47) _____ (cling) to the top of the tree. "Goodbye."

48. _____ When the shark (48) _____ (hear) this, he realized he had

49. _____ (49) _____ (lose) and that he couldn't fool the monkey any

50. _____ longer, so he quit trying and (50) _____ (steal) away to look for another

monkey in another tree.

—Swahili story

WH-Words

WH-words can begin direct questions that are complete sentences or indirect questions that are dependent clauses in statements. (see **Questions, Infinitive/-*ing* Choice,** and **Clauses, adjective** and **noun**) *How, however* in certain meanings, and *if* (when it means *whether*) are usually included as WH-words (see **Pronouns,** pp. 288–291).

    1 *who, whose, whom,* and *whoever, whomever*

Statements and Questions: Use for People
Alan knows *who* is going.
Who is going?
Whoever (anyone who, the person who) goes out last should lock the door.

    2 *what, whatever*

Statements: Use for Things, Including Abstract Ideas, and Choice
Rose knows *what* she found.
Rose knows *what* she believes.
Rose knows *what* she has decided to do. or . . . *what* to do.
Whatever (anything that) Rose has decided to do will be fine.

398

Questions: Use to Find Out Actions or Conditions (*whatever* has the idea of "anything at all" in a yes-no question: Did she find anything at all?)
What (whatever) did Rose find? (thing)
What (whatever) does Rose believe? (idea)
What (whatever) will Rose do? (choice)

3   *which, whichever*

Statements: Use for Things in Statements (U. S. usage for things that are already identified—see **Punctuation, Commas, Rule 9**)
Understanding Chemistry, which is the textbook I bought yesterday, is expensive.
You may borrow *whichever* book you want. (any one—it doesn't matter)

Questions: Use to Find Out Choice or Identity
Which book did you buy? *Which* one did you want?

4   *when, whenever*

Statements and Questions: Use for Time but Not for Frequency
They came *when* they could.
When did they come? *When* it was time. *When* they were ready. At 10:00 P.M.

5   *where, wherever*

Statements and Questions: Use for Place
Rose put the money *where* it would be safe.
Rose put the money *wherever* it would be safe. (indefinite—anywhere at all)
Where did Rose put the money?

6   *how, however* (*however* is usually used as an adverb meaning *nevertheless*)

Statements and Questions: Use for Manner: what way, means, condition, or degree (often combined with another word, as in *how much, how many, how often*)
Alan learned *how* to fly. *How* is often left out before *to* + verb in a statement: see **Infinitive/ -ing Choice**
Alan learned *how* the instructor wanted him to land.
How did Alan learn to fly? (The answer is a *method* or an adverb such as *easily, quickly,* with *difficulty.* Use *who taught* to find out the name of the instructor and *where* to find out the place.)
What did Alan learn? (The answer is a kind of knowledge: *how* to fly.)
How long did it take him to learn? (The answer is a *period of time.*)
How much did it cost? (The answer is a *sum of money.*)
How many times has he flown? (The answer is a *number.*)
How often has he flown? (The answer is a *statement that shows frequency.*)
How high has he flown? (The answer is a *distance.*)
How far did he go on his last flight? (The answer is a *distance.*)
How do you account for his interest in flying? (The answer is an *explanation.*)

7   *why* (*how come* means *why* but is used only in very informal speech.)

Statements and Questions: Use for Cause, Reason, Explanation
Rose wants to know *why* the book cost so much.
Why did the book cost so much?

8   *whether* (and *if* when used as a less formal word for *whether*)

Statements: Use for Choice Between Alternatives, for Reporting Yes-No Questions. (For direct questions use *yes-no* questions.)
Rose wants to know *whether* (or not) she can buy a used book. (*or not* is formal)
Rose wants to know *if* she can buy a used book.

Questions: Use Yes-No Questions
Can Rose buy a used book?

See **Operators** for word order in a clause that follows a WH-word.

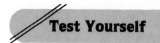
Test Yourself

A. Janet wants to get a certificate in early childhood development from Gorder Community College. Write some WH-questions she must ask to find out about courses.

1. the location of the college
2. the building the classes are held in
3. the method of transportation most students use
4. bus routes that go to the college
5. time of classes
6. frequency of class meetings
7. names of teachers
8. courses that are required to get a certificate
9. subjects Janet must study in the required courses
10. distance from Janet's apartment to the college campus
11. cost of each class
12. cost of the whole course

Write each of the following questions at least two different ways using two different WH-words.

13. explanation of the low cost of the classes
14. length of time usually needed to get a certificate

B. Choose the correct WH-words and put them in the blanks in the following sentences.

Ed doesn't know (1) _____ (what, how) to do. He knows (2) _____ (what, how) to

apply for the job he wants with the electric company, but he is not sure (3) _____ (what,

how) to fill out the application. He is not sure (4) _____ (which, how) blanks to fill in.

(5) _____ (Who, Whom, Which) should he put down as references? He is not sure

(6) _____ (which, what) to put down about his education. (7) _____ (what, which) about

schools he went to in his own country? (8) _____ (what, how) should he do? (9) _____ (what, how) should he put down for his answers? (10) _____ (when, how often) can he make an appointment for an interview? One question says, "How did you come to apply for a job here?" He asked the woman at the desk (11) _____ (how, why) they wanted to know if he came on the bus, and she laughed. She said that question means, "Why do you want a job here?" (12) _____ (Why, What) don't they say (13) _____ (how, what) they mean? Ed decided to take the application home with him so he can find a friend (14) _____ (who, which) can help him fill it out.

Wishes, see **Subjunctive**

Women, Terms Referring to

Speech and writing that make unnecessary distinctions based on sex are called *sexist language.* Many people today object to some features of English usage that do not treat men and women in the same way.

    Ms. does not show whether or not a woman is married. The traditional terms *Mrs.* for a married woman and *Miss* for a single woman make this distinction. Since *Mr.* does not show whether or not a man is married, many people feel that women need a title that does not give this information.

    He, him, and *his* have often been used to refer to a male or a female or to some one whose sex is not known.

A child has thrown *his* ball. (*Child* can refer to a male or female.)
A student lost *his* book. (*Student* can refer to a female or male.)

To avoid the problem of using a masculine pronoun for someone who may be feminine, you can often use an article or determiner in place of the pronoun.

A child has thrown *the* ball.
A student lost *this* book.

Sometimes *his/her, she/he* or *(s)he* is used.

Every student must pay *his/her* fees by Wednesday.

Avoid the awkward *his/her* by putting the sentence into the plural.

All students must pay *their* fees by Wednesday.

or avoid the problem by rewriting the sentence without pronouns.

All student fees must be paid by Wednesday.

Some people object to occupational terms that show the sex of the person who is doing the work.

Traditional	*Nonsexist*
stewardess	flight attendant
postman	postal worker, letter carrier
chairman	chairperson or chair
saleslady	salesperson or salesclerk
policeman	police officer

Avoid using *man* or *mankind* to refer to people of both sexes.

Traditional	*Nonsexist*
mankind	human beings
man and wife	man and woman or husband and wife (Do not identify one person by sex and the other by marital status. Use the same categories for both.)
all men everywhere	all people everywhere

lady, woman, female—*Lady* has traditionally meant a woman of high station and breeding and *woman* has been a more general term that means an adult female. Some people today dislike *lady* because of its connection with class distinctions. Some people like it because it has a connotation of good manners. *Female* means a person, plant, or animal of the sex that bears young.

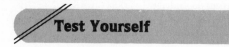

Test Yourself

Rewrite the following paragraph in nonsexist language.

Every child should learn the history of his country. His country has heroes that he should learn about and imitate. A child should feel proud of his country and of the contributions that his own family or group has made to his country. Because of the importance of heroes, a committee has been appointed to write a new textbook that will teach every child his heritage. He will learn about people in his country who have done important things. Professor Smith has been appointed chairman of the committee to develop new materials.

Word Formation

Many English words are formed by adding to the *base word* or *root*. A base word is a form that exists as a word in English; a root or stem is a form that is not used by itself but joins with other word parts. Sometimes the addition comes at the beginning of the base word or root and sometimes it comes at the end. These additions can be called *affixes.* An affix at the beginning of the word is a *prefix.* An affix at the end of a word is a *suffix* or an *ending.* Prefixes change or add to the *meaning* of the base word or root, but most suffixes change the *part of speech* of the word; sometimes they change the meaning also.

Compound Words

Compound words are two words put together. Knowing when to use a hyphen and when to spell them as one word is difficult. British and U. S. usages do not always agree, and different dictionaries published in the same country do not always agree. In U. S. usage fewer hyphens are used than in British usage. Today more compound words are written as one word. Compound adjectives are two separate words that together modify a noun. They are usually written with a hyphen if they come before the word they modify, but sometimes usage changes and they become one word. (see **Punctuation, hyphen**)

Written as One Word	*Written with a Hyphen*	*Written as Two Separate Words*
firsthand	first-degree (adjective)	first aid
landholder	land-poor (adjective)	land office
steamboat		steam engine
postgraduate	post-Victorian post-mortem	*post meridiem* (P.M.)

NOTE: After prefixes such as *post,* a hyphen is usually used if the word that follows is a proper name or a Latin form.

Some Examples of Prefixes and Suffixes

BASE WORD:	beauty (n)	self (n)	harmony (n)	hand (n and v)
Suffix				
noun to adjective	beauti*ful* beaut*eous*	self*ish*	harmoni*ous* harmon*ic*	hand*y* left-hand*ed* (verb to adjective)
adjective to noun		selfish*ness*	harmonious*ness*	hand*iness*
adjective or noun to adverb	beautiful*ly*	selfish*ly*	harmonious*ly*	hand*ily*
noun or adjective to verb	beaut*ify*		harmon*ize*	
verb to verb				two-word verbs: hand *in,* hand *over,* hand *down,* and so on.

verb to noun	beautifi*cation* beautifi*er*		harmoni*zation* harmoni*zer*	hand*ful*
noun to noun	beauti*cian*	self*hood*		compound nouns: hand*book*, hand*gun*, hand*out*, and so on.
negation (without)		self*less* (adj) self*less*ly (adv) self*less*ness (n)		hand*less* (adj)

Prefix

negation *un*		*un*selfish (adj) *un*selfishly (adv) *un*selfishness (n)		*un*hand (v)

dis
in
			*dis*harmony
			*in*harmonious
			  (adj)
			*in*harmoniously
			  (adv)
			*in*harmoniousness
			  (n)	

self	*self*-beautifi- cation			

NOTE: *Self* as a prefix is always followed by a hyphen except in *selfhood*.

Blends

Some words are made by combining two words, but using only parts of them in the new word. Advertisers and journalists form many words in this way. Some of them are forgotten almost at once, but a few of them become part of the general vocabulary.

agriculture + business	becomes	agribusiness
electro + execution	becomes	electrocution
helicopter + airport	becomes	heliport
motor + hotel	becomes	motel
news + broadcast	becomes	newscast
smoke + fog	becomes	smog
stagnation + inflation	becomes	stagflation
television + marathon	becomes	telethon
transfer + resistor	becomes	transistor

Acronyms

Acronyms are made from the first letters of a group of words. They are often written in capital letters without periods between them and pronounced as words instead of initials. A few acronyms have become common nouns, particularly some words connected with science and technology.

laser	comes from	*l*ightwave *a*mplification by *s*imulated *e*mission of *r*adiation
loran	comes from	*lo*ng *ra*nging *n*avigation
radar	comes from	*ra*dio *d*etection *a*nd *r*anging
scuba	comes from	*s*elf-*c*ontained *u*nderwater *b*reathing *a*pparatus
sonar	comes from	*so*und *na*vigation *r*anging

Two-Word Verbs

Many two-word verbs become nouns. Some of these nouns are written as one word with no hyphen, and others are written with a hyphen between the two words. Many of these nouns are slang.

Noun Formed from a Two-Word Verb	*Meaning*
a blowout	bursting of a tire
	uncontrolled activity of an oil or gas well
a blow-up	a photographic enlargement
	an explosion
	sudden anger
a buildup	an increase
a callup	an order to report for military service
a cutback	a reduction
a cutoff	an endpoint
a cutout	something cut out, usually from paper or wood
a payoff	a payment
a rip-off (slang)	a theft or an overcharge
a runaway	a person who leaves for another place without permission
a run-down	a summary
a run-in	a quarrel
a run-off	an overflow
	a competition to decide the winner of heats or to break a tie
a run-through	a rapid review
a show-off	a person who tries to get attention
a slowdown	a decrease in speed, especially in work

A few nouns have the verb last: *downbeat, input, intake, outbreak, outcome, outlet, output, outreach, upbringing,* and *upkeep,* for example.

A few verbs have the verb last: *overdo, overlook, overturn, update, upgrade,* and *uphold,* for example.

Prefixes

Prefixes are one- or two-syllable additions at the beginning of a word that change its meaning but do not change its part of speech. In this list nouns are indicated by an article in front of them, *a* or *an* for a countable noun and *the* for an uncountable noun.

Verbs are indicated by *to*. All other words in the list are adjectives. Some adjectives can also be used as adverbs.

Today most prefixes are not followed by a hyphen, but always look in a dictionary if you are not sure whether to use one or not.

Test Yourself

Look up the following words in a recent standard dictionary. Correct any that are spelled incorrectly.

1. passport (n)
2. patch work (n)
3. postscript (n)
4. pot hole (n)
5. pre-historic (adj)
6. present day (adj)
7. push-over (n)
8. push-up (n)

Some Common Prefixes

Notice the large number of prefixes that are negative: *a-, anti-, counter-, dis-, in-, mal-, non-,* and *un-*. Different negative forms on the same base word can have different connotations and meanings. If an example has *a* or *an* before it, it is a countable noun. If it has *to,* it is a verb. If it has *the,* it is an uncountable noun. Other words are adjectives.

Prefix	Meaning	Example
a-	not	*a*moral
		an *a*theist
ante-	before	to *ante*date
anti-	against	an *anti*body
		the *anti*freeze
arch-	highest	an *arch*bishop
auto-	self	an *auto*biography
bi-	two	a *bi*cycle
		to *bi*sect
		a *bi*centennial
co-	with	to *co*ordinate
		a *co*pilot
counter-	against,	*counter*clockwise
	opposite to	a *counter*revolution
de-	reverse action	to *de*frost
dis-	not	*dis*loyal
	reverse action	to *dis*connect
ex-	former	an *ex*-president
	out of	an *ex*patriate

Prefix	Meaning	Example
exo-	outside	an *exo*-skeleton
fore-	before	to *fore*tell
hyper-	too much	*hyper*sensitive
in- (il-, im-, ir-)	not	*in*sensitive
		*il*logical
		*im*moral
		*ir*religious
inter-	between, among	*inter*national
mal-	bad, badly	*mal*formed
maxi-	most, large	a *maxi*skirt
mini-	least, small	a *mini*computer
mis-	wrong, wrongly	a *mis*print
		to *mis*print
mono-	one	a *mono*rail
multi-	many	*multi*racial
neo-	new, revived	the *neo*colonialism
non-	not, without	*non*stop
out-	to do something to a greater degree	to *out*do
	away from	an *out*patient
over-	too much	to *over*eat
	above	an *over*pass
para-	alongside, resembling	a *para*phrase
poly-	many, much	*poly*gamous
post-	after	*post*war
pre-	before	*pre*war
pro-	on the side of, in favor of	*pro*-communist
proto-	first, original	a *proto*type
pseudo-	false, imitation	*pseudo*-classic
quad-	four	a *quad*rangle
re-	again, renew	to *re*start
semi-	half, partly	*semi*private
		a *semi*circle
sub-	beneath, less, lower than	a *sub*way
		*sub*normal
trans-	from one place to another, across	to *trans*port
		*trans*atlantic
tri-	three	a *tri*cycle
ultra-	extremely, beyond	the *ultra*nationalism
		*ultra*sonic
un-	reverse action	to *un*cover
	not	*un*broken
under-	too little	to *under*expose
uni-	one	a *uni*form
vice-	deputy, one who acts in place of	a *vice*-president

NOTE: A few prefixes change their spelling before roots beginning with certain consonants. An example of a prefix that does this in the table above is *in,* which becomes *il-* before a root beginning with *l, im-* before a root beginning with *m,* and *ir-* before a root beginning with *r.*

Test Yourself

Fill in the blanks with the correct words in the sentences that follow. Choose answers from the words in parentheses at the end of each section.

1. Land that has no crops on it is _____ ; land that produces small crops is _____ .

   Hindering the production of crops by allowing cattle to graze on the same land that is

   cultivated is _____ . (nonproductive, counterproductive, unproductive)

2. If you are brought before a court of law, you hope the judge will be _____ but

   not _____ . (disinterested, uninterested)

3. Actions that have no connection with moral beliefs, such as those of animals,

   are _____ . Actions against moral beliefs are _____ . A person who claims to have no

   moral beliefs is called _____ . (amoral, immoral, nonmoral)

4. Behavior that is not related to that of human beings, such as behavior of animals,

   is _____ , but human behavior that does not follow the normal standards of human-

   ity is _____ . (nonhuman, inhuman)

5. A _____ believes in one God, a _____ believes in many gods, a _____ equates God or

   gods with nature and in the forces of nature, and an _____ believes there is no

   supreme being. (atheist, monotheist, pantheist, polytheist)

6. Bus drivers who do not have special training for driving large vehicles may be _____ .

   Licensed drivers may be _____ if they have accidents due to carelessness. (disquali-

   fied, unqualified)

7. Sometimes furniture can be bought more cheaply if it is _____ . Later after it has been assembled it can be _____ in order to be moved easily. (unassembled, disassembled)

8. To _____ the influence of a strong political party, several small parties may make an alliance so that their total influence will be the same as that of the strong party. After an election, agreements may change to correct a new _____ in power resulting from the new election results. An _____ person is mentally deranged. (counterbalance, imbalance, unbalanced)

9. A deformed plant or animal does not have its natural form: it is _____ . Something that has not yet been created but is still undeveloped is _____ . But to be _____ usually means to be aware of facts or news. (informed, malformed, unformed)

10. A _____ job does not require professional qualifications; _____ behavior does not follow the standards of a particular profession. (nonprofessional, unprofessional)

Suffixes

A suffix is an ending added to a word that usually changes the part of speech of the word and may also change the meaning of the word. Look up forms that are new to you in a dictionary, as not all suffixes can be added to all words. In some cases, more than one suffix can be added to the same word: nation, nation*al,* nation*ality,* nation*alism.*

The endings -*s* and -*ed* on regular verbs and -*s* and -*es* on nouns do not change the part of speech.   (see **Nouns** and **Spelling, Adding endings**)

Adjectives
The following suffixes change other words into adjectives.

Suffix	*Meaning*	*Example*
-able, -ible	able to be, having the quality of	teach, teach*able* reduce, redu*cible*
-al	having the quality of, related to	nation, nation*al* person, perso*nal*

Suffix	Meaning	Example
-ant	having the quality to	tolerate, toler*ant*
		dominate, domin*ant*
-arian	having the quality of	authority, authorit*arian*
-ative	connected with	argument, argument*ative*
-ed	past participle of regular	wall, wall*ed*
	verbs (see **Partici-**	please, pleas*ed*
	ples)	
-ese	showing national origin	Lebanon, Leban*ese*
		China, Chin*ese*
-esque	in the style of	picture, pictur*esque*
		Roman, Roman*esque*
-ful	having, full of	meaning, meaning*ful*
		thank, thank*ful*
-ic	having the quality of	democracy, democrat*ic*
-ical	having the quality of	theory, theoret*ical*
-ing	present participle (see	swing, swing*ing*
	Participles)	fall, fall*ing*
-ish	belonging to (national	Swede, Swed*ish*
	origin)	Ireland, Ir*ish*
-ish	somewhat, approximately,	red, redd*ish*
	having the quality of	young, young*ish*
-ive	having the quality of	explode, explos*ive*
		collect, collect*ive*
-less	without, lacking in	child, child*less*
-like	having the quality of	child, child*like*
-ly	having the quality of	father, father*ly*
-ous, -eous, -ious	having the quality of	virtue, virtu*ous*
		courtesy, court*eous*
		ambition, ambit*ious*
-some	full of	burden, burden*some*
		bother, bother*some*
-worthy	deserving	praise, praise*worthy*
-y	full of, covered with,	hair, hair*y*
	having the quality of	sand, sand*y*
		brain, brain*y*

(See **Adjectives, comparison of,** for *-er* and *-est* endings on gradable adjectives.)

Test Yourself

A. Add an ending to make an adjective form that does not end in *ed*. Use a dictionary to find the correct forms.

1. Portugal	6. fear (2)	11. stone	16. marriage	21. mother
2. educate	7. weary	12. statue	17. risk	22. workman
3. scholar	8. gene	13. leaf	18. universe	23. glory
4. mind	9. addition	14. Poland	19. nerve	24. humanity
5. storm	10. innovate	15. magic	20. fiend	25. news

Nouns

The following suffixes change other words into nouns or change the meaning of a noun.

Nouns Referring to People

Suffix	Meaning	Example
-an	member of, belonging to, favoring	Atlanta, Atlan*tan* republic, republi*can*
-ant, -ent	agent, a person who does, makes	inhabit, inhabit*ant* correspond, correspond*ent*
-arian	belonging to a group, favoring	vegetables, veget*arian* discipline, disciplin*arian*
-crat	a person connected with	democracy, demo*crat* bureaucracy, bureau*crat*
-ee	variation of *-er,* a person who does, makes	absent, absent*ee* employ, employ*ee*
-eer	a person who does, makes, is connected with	auction, auction*eer* engine, engin*eer*
-er	a person who does, makes, operates, comes from	bake, bak*er* dream, dream*er*
-ese	national origin	Portugal, Portugu*ese* China, Chin*ese*
-ess	feminine form	waiter, wait*ress*
-ette	feminine form	usher, usher*ette*
-ian	connected with	Paris, Paris*ian*
-ite	member of a group	social, socia*lite*
-let	small, unimportant	star, star*let*
-ling	unimportant (small, sometimes derogatory)	weak, weak*ling* found, found*ling*
-or	variation of *-er,* a person who . . .	survive, surviv*or* advise, advis*or*
-ster	a person making or doing something, a member of	trick, trick*ster* gang, gang*ster*
-y	familiar form (usually used in family, with children)	dad, dadd*y* Bill, Bill*y*

Test Yourself

B. Add the correct ending to change the following words into nouns that refer to people, or, if the noun already refers to a person, to a different person.

1. library	5. steward	9. son	13. London	17. major
2. mountain	6. retire	10. Asia	14. reside	18. drive
3. direct	7. command (2)	11. aristocracy	15. mob	19. hire
4. immigrate	8. republic	12. address	16. soil	20. write

Nouns That Do Not Refer to People (Impersonal)

Suffix	Meaning	Example
-age	extent, amount	drain, drain*age*
		sink, sink*age*
		store, stor*age*
-ant	agent, impersonal: the thing that . . .	lubricate, lubric*ant*
		disinfect, disinfect*ant*
-ation, -ition	institution, condition of being done	organize, organiz*ation*
		educate, educ*ation*
		nourish, nutr*ition*
		note, no*tation*
-er	agent, the thing that . . . , something having	silence, silenc*er*
		two wheels, two-wheel*er*
-ery	place of activity	refine, refin*ery*
		surgeon, surg*ery*
-ery	collective, uncountable	machine, machin*ery*
		baskets, basket*ry*
-ess	female form	lion, lion*ess*
-ette	small, compact	kitchen, kitchen*ette*
		room, room*ette*
	imitation	leather, leather*ette*
-ful	the amount contained	mouth, mouth*ful*
		cup, cup*ful*
-ing	turns countable nouns into uncountable nouns indicating material	pipe, pip*ing*
		wire, wir*ing*
		panel, panell*ing*
	activity from action of the verb (see **Gerunds**)	walk, walk*ing*
-let	small or unimportant	pig, pig*let*
		isle, is*let*
-or	thing that . . .	conduct, conduct*or*
-y (sometimes -ie)	familiar, small	nightgown, night*ie*
		dog, dog*gy*
		bird, bird*ie*

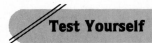

Test Yourself

C. Add the correct endings to make the following words into impersonal nouns or to change to another noun.

1. plant	5. deposit	9. refrigerate	13. carpet	17. statue
2. acre	6. irritate	10. hand	14. roof	18. modernize
3. communicate	7. prepare	11. move	15. bake	19. hatch
4. arm (2)	8. ignite	12. grind	16. heat	20. swim

Abstract Nouns

Suffix	Meaning	Example
-age	act of, extent	marry, marri*age*
		cover, cover*age*
		shrink, shrink*age*
-ance, -ence	activity, condition	guide, guid*ance*
		attend, attend*ance*
		independent, independ*ence*
-ancy, -ency	activity, condition of being	constant, const*ancy*
-ation	state of doing something	dominate, domin*ation*
		communicate, communic*ation*
-dom	condition	free, free*dom*
-ery	domain, condition	brave, brav*ery*
		slave, slav*ery*
-hood	status	false, false*hood*
		mother, mother*hood*
-ion	act of doing something	confess, confess*ion*
-ism	doctrine, belief, condition	commun*ism*, absentee*ism*
-ity	state, quality	complex, complex*ity*
		curious, curios*ity*
		sane, san*ity*
-ment	state, action	arrange, arrange*ment*
		govern, govern*ment*
-ness	state, condition	ill, ill*ness*
		selfish, selfish*ness*
-ocracy	system of government, organization	democrat, dem*ocracy*
		autocrat, aut*ocracy*
-ship	status, condition	friend, friend*ship*
		hard, hard*ship*

Test Yourself

D. Add the correct endings to make the following words into abstract nouns. Use a dictionary.

1. parent	4. ready	7. diplomat	10. adult	13. intend
2. brother	5. align	8. authentic	11. different	14. hero
3. measure	6. helpless	9. decisive	12. intervene	15. bore

Adverbs

Suffix	Meaning	Example
-ly (-*ally* after -*ic* and -*ment*)	in the manner of	strange, strange*ly* happy, happi*ly* comic, comical*ly* basic, basical*ly* fundamental*ly*
-ward	manner, direction of movement	home, home*ward* on, on*ward* after, after*ward*(s) back, back*ward*(s)
-wise	in the manner of	clock, clock*wise*

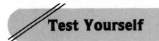

Test Yourself

E. Add the correct endings to make the following words into adverbs or into another form of an adverb.

1. down   3. bare   5. east   7. fundamental   9. like

2. other   4. easy   6. automatic   8. up   10. energetic

Verbs

The following suffixes change adjectives and nouns into verbs.

Suffix	Meaning	Example
-ate	cause to become	regular, regul*ate* active, activ*ate*
-en	cause to become	tight, tight*en* deaf, deaf*en*
-ify	cause to become	beauty, beaut*ify* simple, simpl*ify*
-ize	cause to become	popular, popular*ize* regular, regular*ize*
	cause to enter	hospital, hospital*ize* institutional, institutional*ize* (can also mean *cause to become*)

Test Yourself

F. Add the correct endings to make the following words into verbs or into another form of a verb.

1. length   3. emphasis   5. modern   7. ripe   9. light

2. different   4. philosophy   6. equal   8. pure   10. international

Roots

You can improve your vocabulary by learning Latin and Greek roots. Over half of all English words come from them. The roots in this list are common and easy to see in English words. They are marked (L) if they come from Latin and (G) if they come from Greek, but you do not need to learn this to use them. Most scientific terms are made from Greek roots, and many literary words are made from Latin roots. A few of these roots are English words without prefixes or suffixes added to them.

Root	*Meaning*	*English Words*
alien (L)	another, foreign	*alien*ate, in*alien*able, *alien*ation
am (L)	love	*am*iable, *am*ity, *am*icable
anim (L)	mind, life	*anim*al, *anim*ate, *anim*ism
ann (L)	year	*ann*als, *ann*ual, *ann*uity
anthrop (G)	human being	*anthrop*ology, *anthrop*omorphic, mis*anthrope*
arch (G)	rule, chief	an*arch*y, mon*arch*y, *arch*itect
aud (L)	hear	*aud*io, *aud*itorium, *aud*ible
auto (G)	self	*auto*mobile, *auto*matic, *auto*biography
bene (L)	good, well	*bene*ficial, *bene*factor, *bene*volent
bio (G)	life	*bio*logy, *bio*sphere, *bio*graphy
caust (L)	burn	*caust*ic, *caut*erize, holo*caust*
cent (L)	hundred	*cent*ury, *cent*ipede, *cent*igrade
chron (G)	time	*chron*ic, *chron*ology, ana*chron*ism
cide (L)	kill	sui*cide,* insecti*cide,* geno*cide*
cosm (G)	order, world	*cosm*ic, *cosm*etic, *cosm*opolitan
cred (L)	believe	*cred*it, *creed*, dis*cred*it
crit (L)	judge	*crit*ic, *crit*erion, *crit*icism
dem (G)	people	*dem*ocracy, epi*dem*ic, en*dem*ic
derm (G)	skin	*derm*atitis, *derm*atology, epi*derm*is
domin (L)	master, lord	*domin*ion, *domin*ate, pre*domin*ate
dynam (G)	power, force	*dynam*ic, *dynam*o, *dynam*ite
fac (L)	make	*fac*tory, manu*fac*ture, *fac*simile
fin (L)	end, limit	*fin*ish, *fin*ite, de*fin*e
fort (L)	strong	*fort*ress, *fort*ify, ef*fort*
frat (L)	brother	*frat*ernity, *frat*ernal, *frat*ernize
geo (G)	earth	*geo*graphy, *geo*logy, *geo*de
graph (G)	write	*graph*ic, mono*graph,* demo*graph*y
hydra (G)	water	*hydra*nt, *hydra*ulic, de*hydra*te
litera (L)	letter	*litera*ture, il*litera*te, *litera*l
log (G),	word,	*log*o, dia*log*ue, ana*log*ous
-logy	science of	bio*logy,* astro*logy,* physio*logy*
magn (L)	great	*magn*ify, *magn*ate, *magn*animous
manu (L)	hand	*manu*al, *manu*script, *man*ipulate
mater (L)	mother	*mat*ron, *mater*nal, *mater*nity
meter (L)	measure	kilo*meter,* thermo*meter,* *met*ric
micro (G)	small	*micro*scope, *micro*be, *micro*cosm
multi (L)	much, many	*multi*ply, *multi*tude, *multi*form
mon (G)	alone	*mon*opoly, *mon*otone, *mon*otonous
mut (L)	change	*mut*ant, com*mut*e, im*mut*able
neo (G)	new	*neo*natal, *neo*classical, *neo*colonialism

Root	Meaning	English Words
nom (G)	law	astronomy, agronomy, economy
nomin, nomen (L)	name	nominate, nominal, misnomer
nym (G)	name	anonymous, pseudonym, synonym
op, oper (L)	work	operate, cooperate, inoperable
pan (G)	all, whole	panorama, panacea, pantheism
pater, patr (L)	father	paternal, paternity, patriotic
path (G)	feeling	apathy, pathetic, pathos
ped (G)	child	pediatrics, pederast, pedagogy
ped (L)	foot	pedal, pedestrian, biped
phil (G)	love	philosophy, philanthropy, philharmonic
phys (G)	body, nature	physical, physician, physics
phon (G)	sound, voice	telephone, phonetic, phonograph
phos, phot (G)	light	photograph, photocopier, phosphorescent
plen (L)	full	plenty, plenary, replenish
poli (G)	city	politics, cosmopolitan, metropolis
port (L)	carry	portable, export, import
prim (L)	first, original	prime, primitive, primer
psych (G)	soul, mind	psychology, psychotic, psychic
rupt (L)	break	rupture, interrupt, bankrupt
scop (G)	look at	scope, microscope, telescope
scrib, script (L)	write	script, describe, inscription
sect (L)	cut	section, dissect, bisect
simil (L)	alike	similar, simile, simulate
soph (G)	wisdom	philosophy, sophistry, sophisticated
tele (G)	far away	television, telegraph, telephone
tempor (L)	time	temporary, temporal, contemporary
theo (G)	God	theology, theocracy, atheist
therm (G)	heat	thermal, thermometer, thermodynamics
uni (L)	one	unit, union, unite
vac (L)	empty	vacuum, vacant, evacuation
verb (L)	word	verbal, verbose, adverb
vol (L)	wish, willing	volunteer, volition, benevolent
volv (L)	roll	evolve, volume, involve

NOTE: Common roots *nom* and *ped* each have different meanings depending on the origin, Greek or Latin.

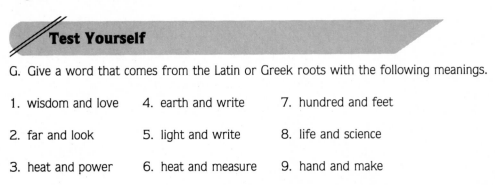

Test Yourself

G. Give a word that comes from the Latin or Greek roots with the following meanings.

1. wisdom and love   4. earth and write   7. hundred and feet

2. far and look   5. light and write   8. life and science

3. heat and power   6. heat and measure   9. hand and make

Word Order

Normal word order is the subject before the verb with most adverbs following the verb. *Inverted* word order is the verb before the subject. Since English words do not always change their forms when their grammatical use changes, word order is very important in English. Special problems of word order are found in the following sections.

Absolutes	Determiners	Parallel Structure
Adverbs, word order	Direct Speech	Participles, as adjectives
Adjectives, order of	Indirect object	Questions, Passive Verbs
Agreement of Subject and Verb	Interrupters	Reported speech
Appositives	Modifiers	Sentence variety
Complements	Operators	Two-word verbs

Wordiness

To develop a good style of writing in English, use as few words as possible, but choose them carefully. Do not use more words than you need. (In speaking, repetition can be helpful for explanation and emphasis.) Look at your writing for the following kinds of wordiness and *reduce* unnecessary words (see **Subordinating and Reducing**).

1 Do not use more words than you need to make your ideas clear.

a **Take out words** that do not add meaning to your writing. The words in parentheses can be taken out without changing the meaning. (Many other examples are not listed.)

return (back)	combine (together)
repeat (again)	(personal) friend
(past) history	cooperate (together)
proposed (new)	(mistaken) error
each (and every) one	(final) outcome
many (in number)	(necessary) essentials
large (in size)	(optional) choice
early (in time)	(end) result
(new) innovation	the reason (why)

b Do not use prepositional phrases that do not add meaning. **Use one word** in place of a phrase if you can.

	Wordy		*Improved*
Reduce	the house of the Johnsons	to	the Johnsons' house
	one of the purposes		one purpose
	one of the results		one result

Wordy	*Improved*
two of the reasons	two reasons
several of the students	several students
height of five feet	five feet high
weight of ten pounds	ten pounds
the potatoes are ten pounds in weight	the potatoes weigh ten pounds
with the exception of	except for
in this day and age	today, now
at the present time	today, now
at this point in time	today, now
at that point in time	then
in regard to	about
by the time (that)	when
subsequent to	after
before long	soon
during the time (that)	while
as a result of	because of
in the event (that)	if
on condition (that)	if
provided, providing (that)	if
due to the fact (that)	since
inasmuch as	since
in view of the fact (that)	since
prior to	before

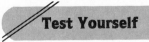

Test Yourself

A. Rewrite and reduce the wordiness in the following sentences.

1. This morning at 10:00 A.M. each and every request for transfer to another position will be combined together for review and consideration.
2. One of the reasons why the requests that have been made may not be granted or given is the present and current uncertainty about the final outcome of projected plant expansion in the future.
3. With the exception of workers who have been hired in the last month or thirty days, however, every effort will be made to ensure and be certain that all jobs and employment of workers are protected and saved.
4. During the time that management is making decisions about what to do in the future in regard to the construction of the projected new plant, workers and employees are asked to continue to keep on with their regular duties.
5. At that point in time when a final decision has been made, management will inform workers and employees of the decision in a published written newsletter.

2 Avoid using the expletives *there* and *it*.   (see **Expletives**)

Wordy: There are four books that art students need to read in the library this week. It is known that . . .

Improved: Art students need to read four books in the library this week.

Wordy: There are several buses that are waiting in the parking lot.
         It is known that . . .

Improved: Several buses are waiting in the parking lot.

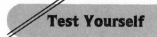

Test Yourself

B. Reduce wordiness in the following sentences.

1. There is always great uncertainty when two businesses combine.
2. There is a feeling of helplessness among employees because they may lose their jobs through reorganization.
3. It is true that many employers make work for their employees when business is bad.
4. However, there is no business that can continue to pay workers when there is no work for them to do.
5. It is a known fact that people are afraid of the unknown.

    3 Reduce wordiness by changing grammatical structure.
    a **Reduce clauses and phrases to single words.**

Wordy: The brown smoke *that was polluting the air* could be seen from far away.

Improved: The *polluting* brown smoke could be seen from far away.

Wordy: The birds *that were destroying the fruit* settled *in the trees of the orchard.*

Improved: The *destructive* birds settled in the orchard.

Test Yourself

C. Reduce the underlined clauses in the following sentences to a word or a phrase.

1. The tornado <u>that caused great destruction</u> touched the ground in only one place.

2. The <u>people who owned the property</u> were heartbroken when they saw <u>the roof that was on their barn</u> fly off.

3. The rain <u>that accompanied the tornado</u> ruined all the feed <u>that was stored in the barn</u>.

4. The rain <u>that accompanied the tornado</u> ruined the feed. (use a pronoun to replace a clause that repeats information in a previous sentence.

5. The feed was ruined <u>when the tornado hit</u>. (Use a single-word adverb to replace a clause that repeats information in a previous sentence.)

b Reduce wordiness by **changing a compound sentence to a complex or a simple sentence.**

Wordy: Robert has been studying agriculture for three-and-a-half years, and he will soon graduate.

Improved
(simple sentence):   After studying / Having studied agriculture for three-and-a-half years, Robert will soon graduate.

Wordy: Eleanor's car has been giving her a great deal of trouble by breaking down recently, so she thinks perhaps she should buy a new one.

Improved
(complex):   Eleanor is considering buying a new car since her old one has often been breaking down.

 **Test Yourself**

D. Reduce one of the independent clauses to a dependent clause, phrase, or word.

1. Everyone watching the tornado was afraid; tornadoes are dangerous.

2. Tornadoes sometimes occur at sea; such tornadoes are called waterspouts.

3. Tornadoes have very strong winds; these winds may cause buildings to explode.

4. Tornadoes occur in many parts of the world, but the worst area on earth for tornadoes is the great plains of the United States.

c Reduce wordiness by **reducing clauses to phrases.**

Wordy: The windstorm blew down the trees *that line the road* along the lake.

Improved: The windstorm blew down the trees *lining the road* along the lake.

Wordy: Very cold weather killed the flowers *that bloom early in the spring* weather.

Improved: Very cold weather killed the *early-blooming spring* flowers.

d If a form of *be* follows the relative pronoun in an adjective clause, the clause can often be reduced to make the sentence less wordy. Take out the relative pronoun and the form of *be* that follows it. Be sure to use the correct form of the participle. If the meaning is active, use the *-ing* form. If the meaning is passive, use the past participle, sometimes called the *-en* form.

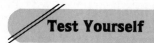

Test Yourself

E. Cross out the relative pronouns and forms of *be* that make the following sentences wordy.

1. Several employees who are concerned about the operation of the office have been gathering facts to present to the management.

2. The information that was put in some files is incorrect.

3. A new file that will be corrected with updated materials needs to be opened.

4. Some mail that was sent to the main office never arrived.

5. The papers that were returned for correction have been misplaced.

6. The candidate who was chosen for an interview today has called to say he is no longer interested in the job because of the delay in making him an offer.

7. The plan that has been outlined to improve profits this year has been delayed.

8. No building engineer who is acquainted with the original installation of the heating and air conditioning system can be found.

9. Contracts that have been prepared for signatures are not always delivered promptly.

10. The workers who are leaving are the ones who are the most experienced.

   e   Reduce wordiness by **leaving out a repeated verb or by replacing it with an operator.**   (see **Operators**)   Leave out a repeated verb after an operator that follows another verb or after *so*.

Wordy:	The reporter has written as much as he *can write* tonight. (Leave out *write.*)
Improved:	The reporter has written as much as he *can* tonight.
Wordy:	The cook is not working as hard as the waiter *is working.* (Leave out the second *working.*)
Improved:	The cook is not working as hard as the waiter.
Wordy:	The detective will do all the paperwork that she *must do* before tomorrow. (Leave out the second *do.*)

Improved: The detective will do all the paperwork that she *must* before tomorrow.

Sometimes *do so, does so, so do,* or *so does,* replaces part of the sentence, especially in formal writing.

The clerk works three hours every night, and *so does* the supervisor. (Do not repeat *three hours every night.*)

The crowd began to leave as soon as the dean asked them to *do so.* (leave)

The children got ready to board the bus as soon as their teacher asked them to *do so.* (get ready to board the bus)

Fill out these forms. As soon as you *do so,* we can process your application. (*Do so* replaces a repetition of *fill out these forms.*)

Test Yourself

F. *a.* Reduce the verb of the second clause by leaving out the verb or replacing it with an operator. Do not repeat complements after the verb in the second clause.

1. A hurricane covers a much larger area than a tornado covers.

2. Winds in a hurricane do not blow as hard as winds in a tornado blow.

3. Hurricanes last much longer than tornadoes last.

4. Hurricanes have very strong winds, and tornadoes have very strong winds too.

5. Hurricanes cause a great deal of damage, and tornadoes cause a great deal of damage too.

6. Hurricanes destroy lives of human beings and animals, crops, and buildings; and tornadoes destroy lives, crops, and buildings too.

7. The winds in hurricanes are not as strong as those in tornadoes are strong.

8. A gale-force wind is strong (32–63 miles per hour), but it is not as strong as a hurricane is strong (above 75 miles per hour).

b. Rewrite sentences 4–6 using *so do* at the beginning of the second clause.

G. Combine the following sets of sentences, reducing wordiness in every way you can.

1. Marilyn plans to be an engineer. She will enter a technical college this fall. She had no trouble getting in because she has good grades.

2. Engineering has several branches. There are chemical engineering, electrical engineering, nuclear engineering, textile engineering, and ceramic engineering, for example. Students must decide which branch they want to study.
3. Civil engineers are engineers who usually work for governments or for large firms that do business with governments. The projects that civil engineers design and build are usually too large and too expensive to be built by anyone or any group except a government body of some sort.
4. Civil engineers design the plans and oversee the building of roads, streets, highways, freeways, bridges, and sometimes they work on projects such as canals and flood control near rivers, lakes, and bays.
5. Another thing that civil engineers do is design and build dams across rivers and tunnels under things such as rivers and bays. In addition to all the other things mentioned, civil engineers also work in flood control projects. Civil engineers work on erosion control along beaches that face the ocean.
6. Engineering students must study physics courses and chemistry courses and many math courses. These courses are difficult and students must study hard. Many people think that physics courses and chemistry courses and math courses are not at all easy.

Key to Exercises

Abbreviations (Humanities)

1. about 551 B.C.
2. yesterday morning, . . . Mrs. Smith (or Mrs. Harriet Smith or Mrs. Emerson Smith)
3. dyes, and other substances. (*or* dyes, etc.)
4. WHO . . . United Nations . . . communicable diseases: for example, against
5. European history . . . Roman Empire in A.D. 476 to the fifteenth or (15th) century.
6. John James Audobon . . . American birds. . . . to the United States . . . Philadelphia, Pennsylvania. . . . in Kentucky . . . Mississippi River. . . . New Orleans, Louisiana. . . . in several different parts in Great Britain. . . .

Abbreviations (Scientific)

1. Absolute zero is $-273.16°C$ or $-459.69°F$.
2. One hectare $= 10,000$ m^2, but one acre $=$ only 4047 m^2.

Abbreviations (Business)

1. . . . Pennsylvania, . . . Massachusetts.
2. . . . Virgin Islands . . . Mr. *or* Mister . . . Equitable Building.
3. Mr. Peter J. Wilson
   1015 East Grand Boulevard
   Atlanta, Georgia 30308

Absolute

1. Every evening Jim watched television, his dog sitting on the floor at his feet.
2. Two hours having passed, I tried to call my mother again. *or,* I tried to call my mother again, two hours having passed.
3. The rain having stopped, we walked from the library to the car. *or,* We walked from the library to the car, the rain having stopped.
4. The wind having died, Mary and Paul lowered the sails of their boat and tied up at the dock. *or,* Mary and Paul lowered the sails of their boat and tied it up at the dock, the wind having died.

Abstract and Concrete

1. move
2. clothing
3. weather
4. transportation
5. animal
6. correspondence

Adjective/Adverb Choice

1. change *brightly* to *bright*
2. change *strongly* to *strong*
3. correct—see *Adverbs, Formation*
4. change *hardly* to *hard*—see *Adverbs, Formation*
5. change *good* to *well*

Adjectives, Forms

1. Imaginative
2. Clever . . . technological
3. imaginative
4. unnatural . . . strange
5. fiction
6. mental powers . . . these
7. different
8. male character . . . stronger . . . his . . . his *or* female character . . . stronger
9. her . . . her *or* a male character
10. strange . . . different

Adjectives, Order

1. ancient Greek foot races
2. modern professional horse racing
3. interscholastic doubles tennis matches
4. This year's Miss Universe beauty contest
5. three or four low-slung, powerful racing cars *or* three or four powerful, low-slung racing cars

Adjectives, A-Word

1. A burning building *or* a building that is ablaze
2. sleeping people *or* people who are asleep

3. correct
4. correct
5. a door (that is) ajar
6. Elderly people (who are) alone
7. correct
8. separate smoke detectors *or* smoke detectors located apart

Adjectives, Comparison of

1. tallest
2. taller
3. tallest
4. tall
5. Tall
6. lower
7. high

Adjectives, Comparison of

1. most famous
2. highest
3. most
4. high
5. most beautiful
6. higher
7. flatter

Adjectives, Structures of Comparison

1. *broadcasts of* any other sport or *those of* any other sport
2. do *better* than
3. *the* best
4. *the* greatest heroes *or* great heroes
5. a *young* age
6. than *that of* its neighbor or *than its neighbor's team* or *than its neighbor does*
7. correct
8. be different *from*
9. as difficult as *that* required
10. *great* honor *or the greatest* honor

Adjectives Used as Nouns

1. The well-off and comfortable can help the less fortunate.
2. The elderly often need special care.
3. The middle-aged often have to help care for the elderly.
4. The young and strong should help the less fortunate.
5. The rich can help the hungry.
6. The weak sometimes need help from the strong.

Adjectives Followed by Prepositions

1. for	3. in	5. for
2. of	4. of	6. of

7. to   10. for   13. with
8. for   11. about   14. in
9. for   12. at   15. of

Adverbs, Word Order

1. often have
2. not called
3. carefully builds . . . may be used for the homes of animals and people.
4. cleverly enlarge
5. safely rests and hides its food *or* rests and hides its food safely
6. often overpopulate . . . sometimes called
7. a large one . . . ; people easily associate
8. often live . . . homes of wild animals are never called *or* never are homes of wild animals called
9. defend their young with great fierceness *or* fiercely defend
10. can be left alone by themselves in the nest.
11. the fathers hunt for food during the day
12. run alongside their mothers as soon as they are born.

Adverbs, Formation

1. deep
2. likely
3. Low
4. deep
5. low
6. hard

Adverbs, Comparison

1. change *more fast* to *faster*
2. change *most fast* to *fastest*
3. change *than a rabbit runs fast* to *than a rabbit does.*
4. *less swift* could be changed to *slower;* change *the very most high* to *the very highest*
5. change *most speedy* to *speediest* (in two places)
6. change *most tiny* to *tiniest* . . . change *most fast* to *fastest*
7. change *than smaller animals find it* to *than smaller animals do.*

Adverbs, Combined

1. change *hardly never* to *hardly ever*
2. change *more accurately measure* to *measure more accurately*
3. change *only recently have been developed* to *have been developed only recently.*
4. change *in Africa in game parks* to *in game parks in Africa*
5. change to *many human beings have become more concerned about preserving wild animals in the latter part of the twentieth century.* Or, *many human beings in the latter part of the twentieth century have become more concerned* . . . (Note the difference in meaning in the two versions.)
6. change to *the park was established March 1, 1872, by an act of Congress.*
7. change *have now* to *now have;* change *can observe and study easily* to *can easily observe and study;* change *scientists can in their native habitats study them* to *scientists can study them in their native habitats.*

Agreement of Subject and Verb (A)

All subjects and verbs are given; changes are underlined.

1. Lightning . . . <u>causes</u>
2. A hurricane . . . results; tides that <u>accompany</u>
3. forecasting . . . <u>allows</u>
4. Storms . . . <u>do</u>; that have been sighted; those that arrive
5. part . . . <u>is</u>;
6. <u>are</u> certain times . . . (times) . . . that are
7. sun <u>crosses</u> . . . weather is
8. danger . . . <u>comes</u>
9. <u>are</u> dangers . . . people build . . . places that are
10. is no part . . . that never <u>faces</u>

Agreement of Subject and Verb (B)

Subjects and verbs are given; changes are underlined.

1. Either the wind or the lightning <u>has</u>
2. Neither . . . crew nor the residents <u>have</u> been able . . . tree that has fallen
3. Either our dog or your cat <u>has</u>

Agreement of Subject and Verb (C)

Subjects and verbs are given; changes are underlined.

1. child . . . <u>learns</u> . . . they are
2. *Profiles in Courage* <u>is</u> . . . ; reading . . . teaches
3. The Confederate States of America <u>was</u> . . . soldiers are honored
4. Remembering . . . who died . . . <u>is</u>
5. A medical researcher who has helped . . . <u>is</u>
6. Nobel prizes . . . <u>are</u> given
7. Teaching . . . and training . . . <u>are</u>
8. advice . . . <u>is</u>

Agreement of Subject and Verb (D)

Subjects and verbs are given; changes are underlined.

1. Snow, rain, and sun <u>affect</u>
2. Snow and ice <u>cause</u>
3. snowfall . . . <u>makes</u>
4. weather and rain <u>seem</u> . . . doctors say germs and viruses are
5. Hats and . . . clothing <u>are</u>
6. kind . . . <u>is</u>
7. costs . . . <u>are</u> (correct)
8. cost . . . <u>is</u>

Agreement of Subject and Verb (E)

Subjects and verbs are given; changes are underlined.

1. Problems . . . <u>seem</u>
2. distribution . . . <u>is</u>
3. Technologies . . . <u>exist</u>
4. food . . . <u>was</u>
5. All . . . <u>were</u>
6. Most . . . <u>was</u>
7. All . . . <u>brings</u> . . . it is
8. people . . . <u>have</u>
9. Cattle <u>are</u> . . . meat will be sold . . . beef can be transported
10. team . . . <u>makes</u>

Agreement of Subject and Verb (F)

The beginning and end of the dependent clauses are shown; the correct verb is underlined.

1. that <u>have</u> . . . bed
2. who <u>work</u> . . . time
3. that <u>operates</u> underwater
4. that <u>develops</u> . . . bed
5. who <u>have</u> . . . problems

Agreement of Subject and Verb (G)

Combined exercises

1.	have	6.	has	11.	is
2.	C	7.	has	12.	C
3.	has	8.	has	13.	are
4.	C	9.	comes	14.	are
5.	C	10.	is	15.	C

Alphabetizing

1. Anthony, Mary   Moore, Marvin
   Arnett, Paul   Nelsen, Roseanna
   Arnold, Susan   Nelson, Anne
   Brown, Ernest   Smith, Abner
   Dempsey, Margaret   Smith, Annabelle
   Hampstead, Arnold   Smith, Peter
2. Albee, Peter, "Musical Visions"
   Aronson, Aaron, *A Look at the Moon*
   Aronson, Aaron, *The New Majority* (the author's name might not be repeated in some kinds of writing)
   Mitchell, Martha, "Talking Back"
   Paul, Jerome H., "The Importance of Being"
   Prentiss, Gerald, "Interpreting the Facts"

_____ , *Many Mansions*

_____ , *A Point in Space* (the solid line means the author is the same as the author of the previous entry—the name could be repeated)

Smith, P. T., *Beside the Waterfall*

Smith, Paulding, *The Ten*

3. *Beside the Waterfall*

"The Importance of Being"

"Interpreting the Facts"

A Look at the Moon

Many Mansions

"Musical Visions"

The New Majority

A Point in Space

"Talking Back"

The Ten

Appositives

1. correct
2. Jupiter, the largest of the planets, has . . . .
3. Mars, a planet that is . . . .
4. . . . from Sirius, a star.
5. correct
6. Our galaxy, the Milky Way, is one of . . . .

Articles (A)

1.	an apple	6.	an escape	11.	an honored guest
2.	a university	7.	a lucky escape	12.	an invitation
3.	a tree	8.	an uncle	13.	a jaw
4.	an apple tree	9.	a history test	14.	an operation
5.	a windy day	10.	an ounce	15.	a yearly review

Articles (B)

1.	the United States	11.	the Cherokee.
2.	the settlers	12.	an idea
3.	The early log cabins	13.	the fact
4.	The colonists	14.	a log cabin
5.	the skill	15.	the most famous
6.	The first	16.	the United States.
7.	A different	17.	a few
8.	the Scotch-Irish	18.	The few
9.	the frontier.	19.	the pioneers
10.	the eastern part	20.	the old ways

Articles (C)

1. people, cabins,
2. cabins, North America, Scandinavia, Germany
3. houses, labor, money
4. forests, Europe
5. shelters, logs

6. America, settlers, Delaware, 1638
7. colonists, Britain,
8. skills
9. none
10. Indians, North America, cabins
11. tribe, Indians, cabins
12. pioneers, cabins
13. Politicians, cabins, origins
14. campaigns.
15. Abraham Lincoln
16. Presidents
17. idea
18. none
19. generations
20. Visitors, Norway, Sweden, examples, cabins, parks, life.

   Reasons for not having an article: the noun is part of a generalization in the plural; the noun is a geographical name that does not have an article; the noun has another determiner with it, as in "this idea"; or the noun follows the possessive form of a proper noun, such as "Abraham Lincoln's."

Articles (D)

People everywhere in the world might say, "When strangers do not understand the customs that we follow, they are confused and do not understand what is happening."

Good manners are different in different parts of the world. In many places, for example, accepting gifts or anything important with the left hand shows bad manners and even rudeness. People with good manners accept important things with both hands or at least with the right hand. Using the left hand to accept important things shows not only discourtesy but also shows that the person who is accepting thinks the thing being given is worthless. In Europe and North America, however, people do not follow this custom and give and receive with either hand without thinking about the meaning of what they are doing.

Articles (E)

1. some
2. any
3. some
4. any
5. some

Articles (F)

1. the	6. 0	11. the
2. 0	7. 0	12. 0
3. the	8. 0	13. the
4. 0	9. the	14. 0
5. the	10. the	15. the

Be (A)

1. is	3. was	5. to be
2. has been	4. have been	6. were

7.	were	10.	is	13.	be
8.	are	11.	be	14.	is
9.	are	12.	is		

Be (B)

1. are
2. is
3. have been
4. were
5. are
6. is
7. is

Capitalization

1. Alexander Graham Bell
2. Bell . . . Edinburgh, Scotland,
3. Later Bell . . . London
4. After Bell's
5. The Bell . . . Atlantic Ocean . . . Brantford, Ontario, Canada,
6. After Alexander Graham Bell . . . Boston . . . Boston University.
7. Helped by Thomas A. Watson, . . . Bell
8. In . . . Bell's
9. On March . . . Watson heard Bell say, "Mr. Watson, . . . ; I . . ." . . . Bell
10. Bell
11. Because . . . Bell's . . . National Geographic Society
12. Although . . . United States . . . Bell . . . Canada . . . Nova Scotia

Clauses, Independent and Dependent (A)

1.
     ind   dep
Mary ran up the steps | that lead to her classroom. (2)

2.
     dep   ind
Because Mary was late, | she ran up the steps. (2)

3.
               ind
Late to class, Mary ran up the steps. (1)

4.
     dep   ind   dep
As Mary ran up the steps, | she realized | that she would be late to class. (3)

5.
     ind   dep
Mary worried | that she would be late to class.

6.
        ind   ind
Mary had to get off the bus far from the classroom, | but she ran

        dep
as fast as she could to get to class on time. (2)

7.
     ind   dep
She dropped her books | when she ran up the steps. (2)

  ind

8.   Mary got off the bus and ran to the classroom building. (1)

                         ind

9.   She got off the bus far from her class; |

                              dep

     because she was running so fast to get to class on time, |

                     ind

     she fell while running up the steps. (3)

Clauses, Adjective (B)

The relative pronouns (clause markers) are underlined and the last word in the dependent clause is given.

1. <u>that</u> . . . world.
2. <u>who</u> . . . batter and <u>who</u>
3. <u>which</u> . . . scoring
4. <u>who</u> . . . British and <u>who</u> . . . world <u>that</u> . . . Empire
5. <u>where</u> . . . popular.
6. <u>that</u> . . . Caribbean
7. <u>that</u> . . . popular
8. <u>who</u> . . . world
9. <u>who</u> . . . Canada
10. <u>who</u> . . . league
11. <u>that</u> . . . Commonwealth

Clauses, Reducing (C)

1. Diseases diagnosed
2. Patients feeling
3. Medicine given
4. A nurse or family member giving
5. drugs taken
6. Patients taking
7. Doctors prescribing
8. patients taking
9. Patients following
10. Patients recovered

Clauses, Adverb (D)

1. The work is divided into separate units when businesses expand beyond a few workers.
2. Production and marketing are separated as the business grows.
3. Because many employees are needed to keep accounts, bill customers, collect bills, pay taxes, and arrange for credit, finance may become a separate unit.
4. As the business develops, a separate marketing division will advertise, take orders, and sell the product.

5. So that large businesses can develop new products and improve old ones without sharing their secrets with the competition, they have their own research and development divisions.

Clauses, Noun (E)

1. *What some people say* is confusing.
    ^subject

2. Some people confuse others because they do not think about *what they are going to say* before they speak.
    ^object of preposition

3. Friends know *who these people are* and *how they usually act.*
    ^direct object   ^direct object

4. Friends know, therefore, *that their actions are more important than their words.*
    ^direct object

5. Strangers, however, may be insulted by *what such people say.*
    ^object of preposition

6. Thinking ahead before speaking is *what everyone should do.*
    ^predicate nominative

Clauses, Combined Exercises (F)

A. 1. adjective
   2. adverb
   3. no dependent clause
   4. adverb, independent, noun
   5. noun
   6. adverb
   7. adverb
   8. no dependent clause
   9. adverb

B. 1. that exists only informally in highly developed societies—adjective
   2. whatever one has of value—noun used as subject
   3. When people barter—adverb
   4. because such a system makes collecting taxes difficult.—adverb
   5. so that people can avoid taxes and governmental control of their activities.—adverb
   6. that do not use money—adjective

Clauses, Meanings of Connecting Words (G)

Some possible answers follow.
1. The farmer's wife cut off the mice's tails, for they chased her.
2. The mice chased the farmer's wife, so she cut off their tails.
3. The mice chased the farmer's wife; therefore, she cut off their tails.
4. The farmer's wife could run, or she could attack the mice.
5. The mice got into trouble; indeed, they got into terrible trouble.
6. The mice got into trouble; in fact, they lost their tails.
7. The farmer's wife could attack with a knife, but the mice could not.
8. The farmer's wife was large; on the other hand, the mice were very small.

Clauses, Errors with Connecting Words (H)

1. Even though baseball is played in many countries in the world, association football (soccer) is played in even more countries.

    Baseball is played in many countries in the world, but association football (soccer) is played in even more countries.

2. Because soccer is probably the world's most popular game, more people watch the World Cup on television than any other sporting event.

    Soccer is the world's most popular game, so more people watch the World Cup on television than any other sporting event.

3. Although long-distance running, especially the marathon, has become very popular, running is not as easy for spectators to watch as stadium sports are.

    Long-distance running, especially the marathon, has become very popular, but running is not as easy for spectators to watch as stadium sports are.

4. Though the spectators do not have places to sit while they watch road races, they do not have to pay admission charges to stand by the road.

    The spectators do not have places to sit while they watch road races, yet they do not have to pay admission charges to stand by the road.

5. Granted that many countries have special sports that are not popular in other places, some form of individual combat and some kind of running are popular worldwide.

    Many countries have special sports that are not popular in other places, yet some form of individual combat and some kind of running are popular worldwide.

Colloquialisms

1. When I was younger, I did not study very hard for my examination, *or,* When I was a child, ...
2. Since I was not very good at math (or mathematics), I did not want to study for math tests at all because I thought I would fail them anyway.
3. I thought I was never going to be (*or* I never would be) smart enough to pass anyway.
4. Why did I think that?
5. I thought I was dumb (stupid) because I had never studied hard enough to learn anything.
6. Now I have learned whom to ask to get help with things I do not understand.

Comma Splices (Some answers—other answers are also possible.)

1. Ignatius; it caused *or* Ignatius, and it caused *or* Ignatius. It *or,* When in 1985 . . . Ignatius, it
2. killed; however, *or* killed. However,
3. correct
4. struck; as a result, some *or* struck, and as a result some *or* struck. As a result *or* Because high tides came . . . struck, some
5. drink; contaminated *or* drink, for contaminated *or* drink. Contaminated *or* drink because contaminated
6. correct
7. days; food *or* days; then food *or* days. Food *or* days, and food *or* days until food.
8. correct
9. developed; then *or* developed. Then *or* developed, and then
10. windows; they *or* windows, and they *or* windows. They *or* windows. In addition, they
11. easier; residents *or* easier, and residents *or* easier. Residents *or* Since early warnings . . . easier *or* easier; as a result, residents . . .

Commands (Other answers are possible.)

1. Can you tell me how to get to the bus stop?
   Would you (please) tell me how to get to the bus stop?
   (Please) how can I get to the bus stop?
2. Excuse me, please.
   Coming out, please.
   May I get through, please.
3. Would you help me with this package, please.
   Can you give me a hand with this package? (*give me a hand* means *help*)
   Will you help me with this package?

Complements

1. direct object
2. predicate noun
3. objective complement
4. direct object
5. predicate adjective
6. direct object

Concession

1. Although the rains came at the right time, the crops failed because of the insects. *or* The rains came at the right time but the crops failed because of the insects.
2. Even though *or* Though farmers planted more rice than ever before, dry weather caused a poor crop.
3. Farmers have bad years sometimes, yet most farmers want to stay on the land rather than move to a city. *or* Farmers have bad years sometimes; nevertheless, most farmers . . . .
4. Some young people leave the farm because . . . ; in spite of that, a few plan to stay and farm like their parents. *or* Some young people leave the farm because . . . ; still a few plan to stay and farm like their parents.
5. Although problems of weather, debt, and falling prices make farming difficult; some farmers say they will never leave their land. *or* Problems . . . make farming difficult; however, some farmers say they will never leave their land.

Conditional Sentences, Real (A)

1. activities will be affected
2. people will lose property . . . will even be injured
3. they might be injured
4. Hurricanes will cause great damage
5. Unless people had prepared . . . their property would probably have been damaged.

Conditional Sentences, Combined Real and Contrary-to-Fact (unreal) (B)

1. were, would finish
2. asked, would explain
3. help, do
4. help, will have
5. is, will be
6. will be posted, will be required
7. would be.
8. plan

9. are, will find
10. have, are

Conditional Sentences, Short Forms (C)
1. laws; if not, they may be fined.
2. If not, she shops on Thursday.
3. If so, she will have to wait . . . .

Conditional Sentences, Combined (D)
1. activities will be affected.
2. a tornado struck.
3. they might be injured
4. did not cover (*will cover* is possible to show a real condition)
5. had prepared . . . would probably have been or . . . was damaged.

Confusing Choices, Part I (*affect* to *choice*) (A)
1. change *in* to *at* and *besides* to *beside*
2. change *Ever since* to *For* and take out *before;* change *because of* to *because*
3. change *from* to *between* or *and* to *to* and *all ready* to *already*
4. change *already* to *yet* and *number* to *amount*
5. change *excepted* to *accepted* and *after* to *later*
6. change *other* to *others* and *like* to *as if* or *as though*
7. change *at* to *on* and *besides* to *beside*
8. change *some* to *any* and *someone* to *anyone*
9. change *all together* to *altogether* and *at* to *after*
10. change *another houses* to *another house* or *other houses* and *on* to *at*

Confusing Choices, Part II (B)
1. change *do* to *make* and *everyone* to *every one*
2. change *do* to *make* and *loose* to *lose*
3. change *little* to *a little* and *everyday* to *every day*
4. change *a few* to *few* and *rejoiced* to *rejoice*
5. change *its* to *it's* and *every one* to *everyone*
6. change *chooses* to *choices* and *do* to *make*
7. change *few* to *a few* and take out *of.*
8. change *Everyday* to *Every day* and *hundreds* to *hundred*
9. change *device* to *devise* and *do* to *make*
10. change *every other* to *one another* and *a few* to *few*

Confusing Choices, Part III (C)
1. change *remind* to *remember* and *rose* to *raised*
2. change *number* to *a number* and *there* to *their*
3. change *some time* to *sometime* and *passed* to *past*
4. change *from* to *in* and *the number* to *a number*
5. change *principle* to *principal* and *there* to *their*
6. change *This* to *These* and *that* to *those*
7. change *Their* to *They're* and *there* to *their*
8. change *wear* to *were* and *there* to *their*
9. change *were* to *where* and *too* to *to*
10. change *which* to *who* and *whether* to *weather*

Conjunctions

1. cr
2. ca
3. sb
4. cd
5. cr

Contractions

1. We are; did not
2. we had; we would
3. Let us; we will
4. We are; will not
5. there is; what has

Coordinating Conjunctions

1. and
2. but
3. for
4. so
5. nor
6. and

Countable and Uncountable Nouns (Other answers are possible.)

A.
1. a pound, kilo, cup, measure of rice
2. tablets, capsules, or cubic centimeters of penicillin
3. bushels, bags, or tons of wheat
4. acres, square miles, or hectares of land
5. necklaces, bracelets, grams, bars, or ounces of gold
6. cups, glasses, litres, quarts, or gallons of milk
7. replace with a unit of measurement of a country: dollars, pounds, francs, pesos, etc.
8. a piece of machinery, or the name of the machine
9. ingot, bar, ton or other measure of weight of iron
10. a piece of luggage
11. replace with a course or class
12. replace with an example of beauty—a beautiful person, sunset, action, piece of art
13. cubic centimeters, cubic feet of air
14. a piece of publicity
15. a piece of equipment—or the name of the specific piece
16. a stroke of lightning

B.
1. machinery
2. machinery
3. usefulness
4. equipment
5. traffic
6. transportation
7. Inequalities

Determiners

1. take out *of*
2. take out *a or* change *a* to *an* and take out *one or not one*
3. change *A distances* to *A distance*
4. change *This* to *These*
5. take out *amount of*
6. change *no one* to *none*

Direct Speech (Other answers are possible.)

1. When Jane found the clerk who had sold her the television set, she said, "The television set I bought here yesterday doesn't work. I can't get a picture on it at all."

   The clerk said, "Bring it back and we will either repair it for you or give you a new one in exchange."

   "Thank you," Jane said. "I'll bring it back this afternoon."
2. "I need some change to make a phone call at a pay phone. Do you have change for a dollar?" Joe asked Sally.

   "Yes, I do; here is your change," Sally said.

   Joe took the change from Sally. He said, "Thank you for helping me out," and gave Sally a dollar bill.

Expletives

1. Nothing is more frightening than an earthquake.
2. The feeling of helplessness upsets people . . . .
3. Certain belts across the earth's surface . . . .
4. Landslides, tidal waves, and cracks in the earth are possible . . . .
5. Shock waves go in all directions . . . .
6. Thinking of (or to think of) the earth shaking, rolling, or moving under one's feet is frightening.
7. No place is more dangerous than inside a building . . . .
8. . . . no one knows for sure what triggers them.

Finite Verbs

1. have
2. dry
3. smoke, dry
4. use
5. learn
6. invented
7. use
8. develop
9. given
10. shown
11. going to have
12. grows *or* is grown

Fragments

1. C
2. F
3. F
4. C
5. F
6. F
7. C
8. F
9. C
10. F
11. C
12. F
13. C
14. F
15. F
16. C
17. F
18. F

A Revision of the Entire Passage (Other versions are possible.)

Comfort is an idea of very modern times in Europe although the technical knowledge for being comfortable has been around for thousands of years. People in earlier times knew a great deal about comfort. Nearly four thousand years ago, the inhabitants of ancient Crete had sanitary plumbing, which can be seen today in the ruins at Knossos. The ancient Romans had central hot-air heating to use during cold weather and incredibly luxurious baths. People in Europe during the Middle Ages lost the knowledge of how to be comfortable, no longer thinking that comfort or what we think of as common cleanliness was necessary. Dignity and prestige were more important to the upper classes, who could have had comfort. Hard, straight chairs were preferred to padded chairs that caused the person sitting in them to relax and thus lose dignity and respect. More important, the chair was reserved for those in power, for in the Middle Ages only the great had chairs. Even today "the chair" shows the person in charge of a meeting, the president or chairperson who directs the proceedings. Large buildings with great halls and huge rooms were necessary to impress the lower classes but such rooms were impossible to heat comfortably. Modern houses that are smaller than the great palaces of earlier times are much easier to heat during cold weather. While Europeans were cold, uncomfortable, and dirty, people in other parts of the world knew a great deal about cleanliness and comfort that was later rediscovered in Europe.

Gender

1. her cousin
2. his sister
3. his mother
4. her niece or nephew
5. her uncle or aunt
6. her grandson
7. her granddaughter
8. her own children

Gerunds

1. The following words should be underlined: making, rubbing, striking, rubbing, making, guarding, keeping, borrowing, starting, making, caring, changing
2. a hunting dog   a sleeping bag
   building licenses   running shoes
   a racing car   lighting fixtures
   a cutting board   training courses

3. (1) camping place
   (2) camping gear
   (3) sleeping tents
   (4) sleeping bags
   (5) cooking utensils
   (6) cooking pots
   (7) frying pans
   (8) dining tent
   (9) hiking boots
   (10) fishing gear

Indirect Object

A. 1. others (*possibly* them) (indirect object)
   2. them *or* throw them Frisbees (indirect object)
   3. them (indirect object)

4. them (direct object); it (direct object)
5. it (direct object); them (indirect object)
6. them (indirect object); it (direct object)
7. them (indirect object)
8. them (indirect object) *or* give them points (improved)
9. them (direct object)
10. them (indirect object)

B. 1. The boys playing in the street threw a ball to their brother Jim, who was walking with his arms full of groceries.
2. The boys threw it to him.
3. . . . and threw it back to them.
4. . . . and finally threw them the ball that he had caught with one hand.
5. The boys explained to him that they were only joking.
6. Jim suggested to them a better place to play ball. *or,* Jim suggested a better place to play ball to them.
7. Jim gave them directions to the park.

Infinitives

A. 1. I
2. I
3. I
4. P
5. P
6. P
7. P
8. P (a gerund follows the preposition)
9. I
10. I
11. P (a gerund follows the preposition)
12. I

B. 1. to measure
2. to measure
3. measure
4. to measure
5. measuring
6. measure
7. to measure
8. measure

Measurement or measurements could be used in 5.

Infinitive/-*ing* Choice

A. 1. to live, a
2. leave, bare
3. to keep, b
4. to leave, a
5. to save, a
6. to stay, a

7. to leave, b
8. to leave, b
9. stay, bare
10. to resume, a

B. Follow directions

C. 1. are difficult to protect
2. are necessary to warn
3. are not easy to make
4. is likely to help

D. 1. where to build
2. what to do
3. how to protect
4. what to do

E. 1. building
2. flooding
3. planting
4. controlling
5. paving
6. planning
7. avoiding

F. 1. overflow
2. ignore
3. building
4. living
5. to living
6. moving
7. deciding
8. moving
9. staying
10. to predict
11. to control
12. bring

G. 1. change *moving* to *to move*
2. change *to damage* to *damaging*
3. add *to* before *build*
4. change *to decide* to *deciding*
5. change *give up* to *giving up*
6. change *having* to *have*
7. change *move* to *moving*
8. add *to* before *develop*
9. change *move* to *moving*
10. change *working* to *to work*

H. 1. to go
2. making
3. thinking
4. to write

    5. to write
    6. to look
    7. to go
    8. looking

I. 1. watched grazing (continuing act)
    2. noticed struggle (completed act)
    3. saw waiting (continuing act)
    4. Hearing calling (continuing act)

Interjections
1. change *O* to *Oh*
2. change *Oh* to *O*
3. correct
4. change *o* to *oh*
5. change *Oh* to *O*

Interrupters
1. . . . seeds: in addition, in common use . . . .
2. Vegetables, however, ...
3. . . . plant; for example, they . . . .
4. . . . vegetables; however, they . . . .
5. Furthermore, the . . . .
6. . . . they grow; that is, some . . . .

It, Impersonal Use (Other sentences are possible.)
1. Your writing us about your problems . . . is a good thing. *or,* is good.
2. Our offices will be closed for the Columbus Day weekend.
3. However, you will be able to reach . . . before the holiday.
4. If you call our Chicago office today, we can arrange a service call Friday morning.
5. When customers tell us about their problems, we can correct them more easily.

Markers

		noun	verb
A.	1.		Peach*es,*	originat*ed*
	2.		Travelers	carri*ed*
	3.	Alexander	the Great*'s armies*	introduc*ed*
	4.		Span*ish* ships,	transport*ed*
			peach*es,* Americas	

B. 1. that, who, which, who
    2. Since
    3. that, who, because

Modals: can and could
A. 1. Paul will be able to swim better when . . . .
    2. Last summer he thought he could swim well, but . . . .
    3. . . . if he could.
    4. He can go to the first class . . . if he can buy a new swimsuit by then.

B. 1. . . . we believe we can win . . . .
   2. . . . we could have won last year too.
   3. . . . we could have misinterpreted . . . . *or* unless we complete . . . we can
   4. The rain yesterday could not have flooded the basement . . . .

C. 1. could
   2. can
   3. will not be able to
   4. will be able to *or* can
   5. can
   6. can

D. 1. could, would the doctor be able to
   2. could have kept, would have been able to keep
   3. could have kept, would have been able to keep
   4. could not have kept, would not have been able to keep
   5. could not have kept, would not have been able to keep
   6. cannot, will not be able to
   7. be able to

Modals: may and might

1. may
2. may
3. may, might (more doubtful)
4. may, might (more doubtful); be able to
5. may, might (more doubtful)
6. might, may
7. might

Modals: will and would

A. 1. . . . but would the doctor see me?
   2. would have kept
   3. would have kept
   4. would not have kept
   5. would not have kept
   6. *would* not possible
   7. *would* not possible

Using *would* emphasizes the intention of a person; using *can, could,* or *be able* emphasizes outside influences beyond a person's control.

B. 1. Will (agreement); would (doubtful possibility)
   2. will (*are* makes *would* impossible in this sentence)
   3. would
   4. would
   5. would
   6. will

Modals: shall and should

1. shall
2. should

3. should
4. should

Modals: shall, should, ought to

1. should/ought to
2. should/ought to
3. should/ought to
4. should/ought to
5. should
6. should/ought to

Modals: should, ought to, must, have to, had to

1. must
2. have to
3. should, ought to
4. must
5. had to
6. have to
7. must, should
8. must, should
9. must, have to
10. should
11. must, should, have to, ought to
12. must
13. must
14. must (*should* and *ought to* are not strong enough here)

Modals: had better, used to, be used to, get used to

A. 1. is not used to
   2. used to
   3. had better
   4. used to
   5. get used to
   6. get used to
   7. had better

B. 1. is not accustomed to
   2. once employed
   3. must
   4. once thought
   5. get accustomed to
   6. get accustomed to
   7. should, must

Other answers are possible for 1, 2, 4, 5, and 6.

Modifiers of Nouns

1.	A	4.	H	7.	I
2.	J	5.	A	8.	G
3.	A	6.	E	9.	C

10.	D	12.	B	14.	F
11.	F	13.	A	15.	A (determiner)

Additional modifiers: Polar, A; large, A; arctic, A; their, C; strong, A; their, C; ice, H; their, C; white, A; difficult, A; Polar, A; good, A; small, A; long, A; also *the* before *mainstay,* an appositive, and *bears* after bears has already been identified.

Negation

1. . . . do not always
2. Fog is no different
3. . . . are not always the same . . . .
4. Why are clouds not the same . . . ?
5. . . . winds are not the same . . . .
6. . . . winds in the upper atmosphere do not blow or winds in the upper atmosphere rarely blow . . . .

Negation, Answers to Negative and Positive Questions

1. No, I haven't.
2. No, she didn't.
3. Yes, he has.
4. No, they haven't.
5. Yes, they will.

Negation, Common Errors

1. not the highest
2. Nowhere in the Andes . . . .
3. . . . are not much lower than . . . .
4. . . . not uncommon . . . .
5. . . . not so high as those in the central area anywhere. *or* are nowhere so high as . . .
6. Although not as high as . . . .

Negation, Substitutions

1. absent
2. away/out
3. optional, voluntary
4. mandatory, required (by law)

Nouns

A.
1. lives
2. feet
3. babies
4. teeth
5. mice
6. wheat
7. beliefs
8. luck
9. thieves
10. proofs

B.
1. hypotheses
2. criteria.
3. analyses
4. data
5. symposia, symposiums

6. indexes, indices
7. Synopses

C. archives, credentials, premises, particulars, materials, proceeds, misgivings, means, news

D. 1. predicate nominative
   2. subject
   3. indirect object
   4. appositive
   5. objective complement
   6. object of a preposition

Numbers

1. The height of Mount Kilimanjaro is 19,340 feet . . . .
2. . . . Mount Kenya, which is 17,040 feet high.
3. The five highest . . . .
4. La Paz, Bolivia, 12,795 feet above sea level, is . . . .

Objective Complements

1. blue
2. open
3. unsafe
4. *Sis*

Operators: The King and the Spider

A. 1. Was Robert the Bruce a king of Scotland in the fourteenth century?
   2. Had he been defeated six times by his enemies?
   3. Was he hiding from them in a cave?
   4. Did he watch a spider . . . ?
   5. Did he notice that . . . ?
   6. Did it fail six times?
   7. Did the king decide that . . . ?
   8. Did the spider attach its thread on the seventh try?
   9. Was Robert encouraged?
   10. Did he go out and defeat his enemies?

B. Many answers are possible. Some correct ones are:
   1. Why was the king discouraged?
   2. How did the king get new courage?
   3. How many times did the spider try to attach its web?
   4. Where was Robert the Bruce hiding? Where did Robert the Bruce live?
   5. When did Robert the Bruce live?
   6. How often had Robert been defeated?
   7. What was the spider trying to do?
   8. Who won in the end? Who was Robert the Bruce?
   9. Which side won the battle in the end?
   10. From whom was Robert the Bruce hiding?

C. Answers will vary.

D. 1. , wasn't he?
    2. , hadn't he?
    3. , wasn't he?
    4. , didn't he?
    5. , didn't he?
    6. , didn't it?
    7. , didn't he?
    8. , didn't it?
    9. , wasn't he?
    10. , didn't he?

E. 1. John did not want to buy . . . .
    2. He did not like . . . .
    3. He did not enjoy cold weather because he was not used to it.
    4. The rest of his family would not have liked to live in Florida.
    5. They did not want to compromise . . . .

F. Tag questions for positive sentences
    1. , didn't he?
    2. , didn't he?
    3. , didn't he? (tag question refers to main clause, not dependent clause)
    4. , wouldn't they?
    5. , didn't they?

    Tag questions for negative sentences
    1. , did he?
    2. , did he?
    3. , did he?
    4. , would they?
    5. , did they?

G. 1. is
    2. was
    3. did
    4. were
    5. isn't, is not
    6. was
    7. does

H. 1. did
    2. was

Parallel Structure (Other answers are possible.)

1. Some sports such as running, wrestling, and fishing are popular in many parts of the world.
2. People like to watch sports they understand, such as bicycle and auto races.
3. A sport that is popular in many parts of the world is horse racing; another that is popular is soccer. *Or,* less wordy: A popular sport in many parts of the world is horse racing; another is soccer.
4. Games of strategy and skill have been played for thousands of years: board games have been found in the ancient pyramids of Egypt (by archaeologists).

5. Many games are played with a ball, which may be stuffed with rubber, cork, yarn, animal hair, string, or twine.
6. The outer covering of a ball may be leather, rubber, or plastic.
7. In sports such as basketball, volleyball, and football, players use an inflated ball made of leather; but golfers use a ball filled with rubber thread wound tightly around a small core filled with liquid.
8. A ball for a game may be hard or soft, solid or filled with air.
9. Most games are played with round balls, but American football and rugby are played with oblong balls.
10. Bowling balls, made of hard rubber or plastic, may weigh as much as sixteen pounds; but table tennis balls, made of celluloid, weigh only one-tenth of an ounce.

Participles

A. 1. having
   2. built
   3. limited
   4. living
   5. providing
   6. seen
   7. lying
   8. warming
   9. hunting
   10. related
   11. curving
   12. pressing
   13. staying
   14. observed
   15. imported
   16. freed
   17. causing
   18. surviving

B. 1. modifies *reptiles*
   2. modifies *controls*
   3. part of passive verb
   4. object of *to*
   5. modifies *areas*
   6. part of passive verb
   7. modifies *lizards*
   8. modifies *lizards*
   9. modifies *lizards*
   10. modifies *snakes*
   11. object of *by*
   12. object of *by*
   13. modifies *snakes*
   14. part of a passive verb
   15. part of a passive verb
   16. part of a passive verb
   17. part of a progressive verb
   18. part of a progressive verb

C. 1. acquainted
   2. given
   3. made
   4. Broken
   5. bitten
   6. discharged
   7. set

D. 1. *vf,* change *showed* to *shown*
   2. *fr,* change *being* to *were*
   3. *c*

4. c
5. *inf,* change *to be eaten* to *being eaten*
6. *fr,* change *attacking* to *attacked*
7. *dp,* change the sentence to: Having been found almost complete in some cases, skeletons can be reconstructed by scientists from fossil bones. Or, Scientists can reconstruct skeletons from fossil bones that have been found almost complete in some places.
8. *dp,* Weighing up to fifty tons, dinosaurs were the largest land animals that ever lived, evidence shows. *or* Evidence shows dinosaurs, weighing up to fifty tons, were the largest land animals that ever lived.
9. *vf,* change *founded* to *found*
10. *fr,* change *believing* to *believe*

E. 1. embarrassing
    2. Amused
    3. Helped
    4. interesting
    5. interested
    6. said
    7. Encouraging
    8. Encouraged
    9. rewarding
    10. tiring

F. Present participle and adjective pairs are given; many sentences are possible. All words in the list have at least two forms.
    1. advising, advisable. Advising his daughter, Mr. Adams told her to continue her education. Mrs. Adams told her daughter that more education was advisable.
    2. defending, defensible, defensive. Defending her young, the mother bird attacked the cat. Birds build their nests in places that are defensible. Birds have many defensive tactics to protect their young.
    3. dreading, dreadful. Dreading the test, the students entered the classroom slowly. The test was dreadful.
    4. exploding, explosive. Exploding in the sky, the fireworks made a beautiful display. Increasing taxes is an explosive issue.
    5. favoring, favorable, favorite. Favoring parents, some governments provide special family allowances. Some laws give parents favorable treatment. Ice cream is Harry's favorite food.
    6. imagining, imaginary, imaginative. Imagining a monster in the dark, the child called out. The monster was imaginary, not real. An imaginative child may invent friends that do not exist.
    7. learning, learned. Learning a new trick, the dog walked on its hind legs. Scholarly articles are published in learned journals. (Note pronunciation of *learned* as an adjective.)
    8. loving, lovely. Loving his mother, the boy gave her a hug. We had a lovely party.
    9. resting, restive, restless. Resting on the beach, the students enjoyed their vacation. Restless from the long wait, the people in the line at the bank began to grumble. Restive before the race, the horse was difficult to control.

Parts of Speech

	adj	n	prep	n	v	v	adj	prep	n	prep	n
A. 1.	Printed	communication	on	paper	has	been	important	for	hundreds	of	years.

adj   n   adv v adv   v   prep   n prep   n   adj   n
Most education today is still based on the use of books and handwritten materials

prep   n
in the classroom.

2.
           adj   n   prep   n   v   adj   n   v   v   adv
The exact origin of the alphabet is unknown. Scholars believe it was probably

       v   prep n   adv adv   n   prep   adj   n   v   adv   v   prep n
invented in Asia long ago. Paper of vegetable fibers was also invented in Asia.

        adj   n   adv   v   adj   n   adv   v   v   adv   prep
Chinese people first developed movable type. Later it was reinvented separately   in

    n   prep   adj n prep   adj   n
Europe in   the first half of the fifteenth century.

3.
        adj   n   prep   n   v   adv   v   v   prep   n   n
Two kinds   of   alphabets exist today: those that are based on sounds (English

        adj   adj   n   v   v   prep n   n
and other European languages) and those that are based on ideas (Chinese).

	Word	*Part of Speech*
B. a.	1. right	adjective
	2. right	adjective
	3. right	verb
	4. Righteous	adjective
	5. rightful	adjective
	6. righteousness	noun
	7. righteous	adjective
	8. rightfully	adverb
b.	1. organ	noun
	2. organism	noun
	3. Organic	adjective
	4. organism	noun
	5. organically	adverb
	6. organization	noun
	7. Organic	adjective
	8. organize	verb
c.	1. memory	noun
	2. memorize	verb
	3. memorable	adjective
	4. memorabilia	noun
	5. memorably	adverb
	6. memory	noun

Passive and Active Verbs

1. tea is drunk
2. It is prepared
3. tea is made
4. the leaves are pounded

5. it (or the powder) is mixed
6. the English are often associated
7. tea was considered
8. milk was added by both the English and the French
9. Iced tea was developed by a tea salesman in the United States.
10. It was invented
11. The tea bag was also invented in the United States.
12. a strong essence of tea is made
13. it is poured into a glass and thinned
14. Very strong tea is made in Tibet, *or* by Tibetans
15. In Tibet tea is boiled *or* Tea there is boiled

Phrases

1. is called
2. between producers and users
3. large wholesale lots, smaller units
4. very often
5. offering services to customers
6. Some large department store chains
7. to attract customers
8. have begun
9. Understanding the needs of customers

Point of View

Change to second person: You visit the Falls from either the Canadian or the U. S. side. You can cross a bridge and go to the other side after you get there.

Change to third person: . . . are interesting places to visit because one of the world's great waterfalls is between them. Tourists visit . . . . They can cross . . . . They can go into the caverns . . . . *The Maid of the Mist,* . . . takes visitors. . . . Visitors . . .

Possessives

1. Bicycle riders
2. bicycle seat
3. their needs
4. everyday use

Predicate Complements

A. 1. strange, adjective
   2. different, adjective
   3. solid, adjective
   4. brighter, adjective
   5. curved, adjective
   6. illusions, noun

B. 1. change *beautifuls* to *beautiful*
   2. change *differents* to *different*
   3. *blind,* change *inconveniently* to *inconvenient* or *an inconvenience*
   4. change *more bad* to *worse*
   5. change *difficulty* to *difficult* or to *a difficulty*
   6. *factors* (*around us* is an adverb of place)

Prepositions

A.
1.	around	11.	at	21.	From
2.	in/from	12.	in	22.	to
3.	to	13.	in	23.	at
4.	in, at	14.	in	24.	across, through, around
5.	on	15.	on	25.	from
6.	to	16.	to	26.	to
7.	in	17.	From/In	27.	at
8.	From	18.	through/across	28.	to
9.	to	19.	to	29.	on
10.	In	20.	on	30.	in

B. Answers will vary.

C.
1.	on	6.	at	11.	before
2.	on	7.	in	12.	for
3.	by	8.	for	13.	After, In
4.	at	9.	before, until	14.	During
5.	in	10.	since	15.	Up to
				16.	Before

D.
1. for
2. of
3. of
4. on
5. for
6. for
7. but/except
8. of

E.
1. add *of* after *account*
2. take out *of*
3. take out *any* or change to *without a penalty.*
4. change *method* to *methods*
5. change *beside* to *besides*
6. add *of* after *spite*
7. change *problem* to *problems*
8. take out *of*
9. change *like* to *that* or leave out *like*
10. change *with no some* to *with no* or to *without*

F.
1. The Watsons planned to buy their son a new bicycle at the end of the month.
2. They looked at bicycles of several different makes *or* at several different makes of . . .
3. They took several bicycles out for test rides.
4. Their son really did not like the first bicycle because it didn't have enough gears for him.
5. They finally found a bicycle their son liked, but they did not see the price tag on it.
6. They wanted to pay cash for the new bicycle.
7. They had to apply for credit, however.

G.
1. Concerning
2. Barring
3. behind

    4. beyond

    5. Pending

Principal Parts of Verbs

A. 1. change *gets* to *get*

    2. change *returned* to *return*

    3. change *asked* to *ask*

    4. change *asked* to *ask*

B. 1. change *seen* to *saw*

    2. change *driven* to *drove*

    3. change *come* to *came*

    4. change *payed* to *paid*

    5. change *rised* to *rose*

C. 1. change *decide* to *decided*

    2. change *take* to *taken*

    3. change *fix* to *fixed*

    4. change *did* to *done*

    5. change *took* to *taken*

D. 1. change *taken* to *taking*

    2. change *driven* to *driving*

    3. change *seen* to *seeing*

    4. change *get* to *getting*

    5. change *written* to *writing or* leave out *been.*

Pronouns

A. 1. his   6. her

    2. she   7. he

    3. she   8. her

    4. her   9. him

    5. His   10. them

B. 1. my

    2. me

    3. our

    4. us

    5. us

C. 1. At the circus with his father, the little boy laughed at the clown.

    2. Clowns always try to make people laugh.

    3. If you get there early, you can go into the circus tent as soon as the gates are opened and you can get a good seat. *or,* People who get there early can go into the circus tent as soon as the gates are opened to get a good seat.

    4. We like to go to the circus whenever we hear it is coming to town.

    5. Sometimes getting seats to the circus is hard.

D. 1. them   5. her

    2. the   6. herself

    3. the   7. themselves

    4. the   8. the

9. one another
10. his
11. the
12. me
13. his
14. the
15. she
16. her
17. her.
18. herself.
19. her
20. herself.

Additional pronouns:
4. they, subject
5. she, subject
6. her, possessive
12. he, subject
13. he, subject
18. She, subject
19. She, subject; she, subject
20. she, subject; him, object of *taught*

E.
1. this
2. Those
3. these
4. those
5. this
6. that
7. those
8. Those

F.
1. another
2. other
3. others
4. other
5. another
6. others

G.
1. any
2. Some
3. any
4. Some
5. some
6. any
7. some

H.
1. no one
2. Not one
3. someone
4. anywhere
5. anyone
6. anything
7. None
8. everything
9. anyone
10. another one
11. something else
12. everywhere
13. anything else
14. everything
15. a
16. everything possible
17. everyone's
18. anything else

I.
1. who
2. whom
3. which
4. that
5. whose
6. who

J.
1. whom
2. who
3. whom
4. whom
5. whoever
6. who

K. Cross out the following pronouns
1. it
2. them
3. it
4. it
5. they
6. it.

L. 1. because ~~that~~ she wants to know
2. since ~~that~~ we have been here
3. After ~~that~~ we have
4. before ~~that~~ we leave

M. 1. know
2. are
3. is
4. take
5. makes

Combined Exercise on Pronoun Reference
1. they, them
2. that
3. this
4. who
5. it
6. its
7. They
8. This
9. You
10. It

Revision (Other versions are possible.)
1. . . . wild animals to look at and kept them in captivity.
2. The first collection of animals that was made for scientific study was in Paris.
3. . . . in their natural places; seeing the animals helps everyone understand . . . . *or* . . . zoos help everyone understand
4. . . . animals that are kept in zoos.
5. . . . which they like to feed and see it use its trunk to eat.
6. change *its head* to *their heads*
7. change *They* to *zoos*
8. Living out of cages is better . . . *or* Places like their natural homes are better . . . .
9. Visitors can watch . . . .
10. Zoos try . . . .

Punctuation, Apostrophe
A. 1. Elizabeth's book
2. a table leg
3. a day's wages
4. Charles' ideas
5. Chris' shoes
6. Professor Martin's class
7. a college requirement
8. Mr. and Mrs. Roberts' house
9. a bicycle tire
10. Pat's shoes

B. 1. It's difficult . . . .
2. no apostrophe
3. correct, ...
4. It's barking because it thinks it's lost its master.
5. no apostrophe

6. They'll be here by ten o'clock . . . .
7. . . . Mrs. Jones' sister-in-law's house . . . .
8. She's the one who's been . . . .
9. She wouldn't . . . , but she'll . . . .

Punctuation, Colon
1. . . . services: lending . . . .
2. no colon is needed
3. no colon is needed
4. . . . disciplines: art, ...
5. . . . places: hospitals, ...
6. . . . 8:30 . . . 9:30 . . . .

Punctuation, Comma (Rules 1–6 combined)
1. . . . twenty-one years old, his family moved again, settling . . . .
2. . . . another year, he helped . . . cabin, plant a crop, and split . . . .
3. . . . 1831, . . . New Orleans Lousiana, . . . River, the farthest . . . .
4. no commas needed
5. . . . Illinois, . . . Salem, . . . store, . . . jobs, . . .
6. . . . fighting, ...
7. . . . states, wasn't . . . .
8. . . . president, not . . . .

Commas (Rules 1–7)
1. . . . nicknames, among . . . honest, upright . . . .
2. no commas needed
3. Lincoln's energetic, hard work . . . .

Commas (Rule 8)
1. . . . historians doubt, however, that . . . .
2. no commas
3. Nevertheless, Lincoln . . . .
4. . . . his proposal, however; after that, he . . . .

Commas (Rule 9)
1. no commas needed
2. . . . Sarah, a widow . . . .
3. Sarah, Lincoln's stepmother
4. . . . "the three R's," which stands for "reading, "riting, and "rithmetic."
5. no commas needed
6. . . . *Washington,* which . . . .
7. . . . family, who . . . frontier, moved . . . .
8. . . . Illinois, a state that was . . . .
9. . . . New Salem, a town

10. . . . education, which . . . Indiana, ...
11. no commas needed
12. no commas needed

Combined Comma Exercises
1. . . . origins, that were not uncommon, however, in his own time.
2. . . . standards, ...
3. . . . life, Lincoln himself said, ...
4. Nevertheless, deaths of family members, lack of schools, and . . . .
5. . . . child, but he . . . United States, a country . . . .
6. . . . March 4, 1861, to his death on April 14, 1865, the . . . .
7. . . . Springfield, Illinois, for burial; his tomb there, which . . . year, is . . . .

Punctuation, Dash
A. 1. Lawyers—also called attorneys, counsel, or counselors—give . . . .
   2. . . . people—someone . . . .
   3. . . . others—teachers, professors, instructors—must . . . .

B. Parentheses can replace dashes in all the sentences above.

C. A colon can be used in sentence 2: . . . people: someone . . . .

Punctuation, Ellipsis
" . . . you may fool all the people some of the time; . . . but you can't fool all of the people all the time." (other answers are possible)

Punctuation, Exclamation Point
1. Help! The building is on fire!
2. The man is drowning! Come help us!
3. "No!" he shouted. "I positively will not take you with me!"

Punctuation, Hyphen
1. vice-president, opti-
2. one-third, twenty-six
3. April-June, fast-food
4. Atlanta-Paris, January-March

Punctuation, Parentheses
1. writing (scientific, technical, and business) than in others (humanities).
2. the 1800's (1800–1899) but it means the 1700's (1700–1799).
3. *disinterested* (*impartial*) does not mean the same as *uninterested* (*not interested*).

Punctuation, Period
1. Mr. and Mrs. . . . tomorrow.
2. . . . U.S., . . . year.
3. Put a period at the end of the sentence.

Punctuation, Quotation Marks

1. "The desire to take medicine is perhaps the greatest feature that distinguishes man from animals," said a famous doctor, Sir William Osler.
2. "Take your medicine," Mrs. Penney said to her little boy; "it will make you feel better."
3. A famous proverb says, "A merry heart does good like a medicine."
4. no quotation marks needed

Punctuation, Periods and Question Marks

1. Did Mr. Sharp lecture on the history of mathematics at 8:00 P.M.?
2. Put a period at the end of the sentence.
3. B.C. . . . accurate.
4. 3.14159.

Punctuation, Semicolon

1. . . . recently; many people . . . .
2. . . . running; and a serious . . . .

Punctuation, Underlining and Quotation Marks

1. . . . <u>Pilgrim's Progress</u> and <u>Robinson Crusoe</u>.
2. . . . <u>Citizen of New Salem</u>, <u>The Great Proclamation</u>, and <u>Lincoln as They Saw Him</u>.
3. Sections called "Lincoln, Abraham" in encyclopedias . . .
4. . . . say about them, "They dot all their i's and cross all their t's."
5. The sinking of the <u>Titanic</u> . . .

Quantity and Measure

1. . . . a dozen pencils
2. . . . one of the laboratory workbooks. Or, a laboratory workbook.
3. . . . aspirin tablets, a box of one hundred.
4. . . . three cabbages
5. . . . six pounds of cabbage.

Questions, Direct

Yes-No Questions

A. Many answers are possible. The following are some possibilities.
1. Did two women claim the same baby?
2. Was Solomon able to know at first who the real mother was?
3. Did the first woman say the baby was hers?
4. Were both women claiming the same baby?
5. Did Solomon say he would cut the baby in half?
6. Was one woman going to let Solomon kill the baby?
7. Did the real mother ask to give the baby up rather than let it be killed?

B. Answers vary based on answers given above. These answers are possible:

1. Both women claimed the same baby.
2. Solomon was able to know at first who the real mother was.

3. The first woman said the baby was hers.
4. Both women were claiming the same baby.
5. Solomon said he would cut the baby in half.
6. One woman was going to let Solomon kill the baby.
7. The real mother asked to give the baby up rather than let it be killed.

WH-Questions

A. 1. what (time is it?)
    2. where (do I go to get to . . . ?) *or* how (do I get to the courthouse?)
    3. where (is the courthouse?)
    4. how (do you feel)
    5. where (are you going?)
    6. when (is she getting married?)
    7. what (do I have to do?)
    8. what (is the answer?)
    9. what (will the weather be tomorrow?)
   10. what (should I do?)
   11. how (do you spell . . . ?)
   12. how much (rice do we need?)
   13. how many (players are on a soccer team?)
   14. how often (do you go the library?)
   15. why (do you go to the library every day?)

B. Use phrases given as answers to A.

C. Many answers are possible. Following are some possibilities.

    1. Where did the women take the baby?
    2. Why did the women go to King Solomon?
    3. How did Solomon solve the problem?
    4. How many women claimed the same baby?
    5. Which woman wanted to save the baby's life?
    6. Who was King Solomon?
    7. To whom did Solomon give the baby?
    8. Whose baby was it?
    9. What kind of person was King Solomon?
   10. What did King Solomon decide?

Indirect Questions

A. Many answers are possible. The following are some possibilities.
    1. they had come to him.
    2. he should cut the baby in half and give half to each one.
    3. she agreed.
    4. she was crying.

B. Many answers are possible. Such as:
    1. the restaurant was going to *or* would open.
    2. the restaurant was going to *or* would be.
    3. the restaurant was going to *or* would be open.
    4. the restaurant was going to *or* would open.

5. they were going to hire many people.
6. food they were planning to serve.
7. the restaurant would be managed.
8. want to eat there.
9. their restaurant would succeed.
10. they would make a lot of money.

C. The answers given are for the indirect questions above. Other answers are possible.
1. George asked Sarah, "Do you know when the restaurant will open?" *or* "When will the restaurant open?"
2. George also asked, "Do you know where the restaurant will be?"
3. Sarah asked George, "Do you know how many hours a day the restaurant will be open?"
4. George asked, "How soon will it open?"
5. George and Sarah asked their parents, "Are you going to hire many people?"
6. They also asked, "What kind of food will you serve?"
7. They asked, "Who will be the manager? Who will buy the groceries and supplies? How will you advertise? Who will clean up at night?"
8. Their parents asked Sarah and George, "Who do you think will want to eat in our restaurant?"
9. The whole family wondered, "Will our restaurant be successful?"
10. They also wondered, "Will we make a lot of money?"

Reported Speech, Verbs
1. . . . told us (her, him, them) to wear gloves.
2. . . . asked for gloves. or asked to wear gloves.
3. . . . insisted on our wearing . . . .
4. . . . asked to go to the nurse.
5. . . . permission to go to the nurse . . . .

Reported Speech
1. Mrs. Mason said that their city tried to keep its pay scales similar to those of industry. She also said that they had good health insurance.
2. The personnel manager also asked Peter where he got his training.
3. Peter replied that he had an associate in science degree from Ephraim College and that he had finished the course the May before.
4. Mrs. Mason asked Peter if he had any experience.
5. Peter answered that he had been working full-time all summer for Heatling Construction Company, and that he also had worked afternoons and Saturdays while he was taking his college courses.
6. The personnel manager asked Peter if he could start work the next day.
7. Peter said he was ready to start any time. Tomorrow would be fine.
8. Mrs. Mason told Peter to be there the next morning at eight o'clock to see how he would do for two weeks.

Run-on Sentences
1. . . . much; we change . . . .
    much, for we change
    much. We change
Because climate influences our lives very much, we change . . . .

2.   . . . on them; too much snow . . . .
          on them, for too much snow . . . .
          on them. Too much snow
   Houses in areas with much snow have steep roofs to keep snow from collecting on them since too much snow . . . .
3.   . . . steep roofs; they need . . . .
          steep roofs, but they need
          steep roofs. But they need
   Although houses in tropical climates do not need steep roofs, they need to be built . . . .

Sentence Patterns

1. is, L
2. has, T
3. get, T
4. looked, I (*backward* and *forward* are adverbs)
5. give, T
6. celebrate, T
7. seem, L
8. say, T
9. strikes, T
10. begins, I.

Sentence Structure

A. 1. cpd
   2. s
   3. cx
   4. c-c
   5. c-c
   6. s
   7. s

B. Many answers are possible. The first sentence in the following paragraph is the topic sentence.

   Many factors increase the value and cost of goods in trade (s). Products and goods pass through many hands as they are bought and sold (cx). Although occasionally goods go directly from the producer to the consumer, at some point they usually go through a broker (cx). Brokers pass goods from the producer to the processor or manufacturer and then to the distributor and the wholesaler (s). Every transaction increases the price, which pays for services as well as goods (cpd). Prices pay for production, manufacturing, and shipping; prices also pay for government taxes inside a country and tariffs in international trade (cpd). Storage of goods at each step also increases the price: at the place of origin before shipping, before and after manufacturing, and at the wholesale and retail levels (s). As ownership of goods changes, new owners often borrow money to pay for goods, adding even more to the final cost (cpd).

Spelling

   Many people *know* the story of the tortoise (turtle) and the *hare* (rabbit). This story teaches a *lesson:* slow and steady is better than fast if the fast *one* stops every now and *then*. The slow tortoise and the fast *hare* had a *race*. The *hare* had *great* speed, but whenever he wanted *a rest,* he stopped. The tortoise kept *right* on going without stopping *to* rest *at all*. At the beginning the *hare led,* but soon the tortoise *passed* him, and finally was *so far ahead* that the *hare* never could *catch* up.

Stative Verbs
1. believe
2. guess
3. Are you trying
4. Don't you remember
5. have
6. doubt
7. remember
8. am
9. think
10. am
11. are
12. need
13. were not being
14. didn't understand

Subjunctive
1. should be, be
2. should come, come
3. should be, be
4. should remain, remain
5. should try, try
6. should be, be

Subordinating and Reducing (Other answers are possible.)
1. The tornado that struck at 3:00 P.M. blew the roof off Uncle Ben's barn. *or* When the tornado struck at 3:00 P.M., it blew the roof off Uncle Ben's barn.
2. Tornadoes have struck . . . Uncle Ben's farm in Kansas.
3. Although repairs to . . . $50,000, no one was injured or killed. *or,* No one was . . . although repairs . . . $50,000.

Syllable Division
1. par-a-graph
2. no division
3. tho-rax
4. re-duced
5. school-teacher
6. no division
7. pre-ferred
8. sym-pa-thize
9. fun-ni-est
10. thor-ough

Tense, Present
1. rises
2. explain
3. occurs
4. is
5. use, explodes
6. is
7. has
8. is
9. use
10. contain

Tense, Present Perfect
A. 1. have moved
2. has caused
3. have left
4. have had
5. have become
6. have put

B. 1. have started (continuing)
   2. has decided (completed)
   3. has packed (completed)
   4. have rented (completed)
   5. have looked (completed)
   6. have seen (completed)

C. 1. have made (continuing)
   2. have begun (continuing)
   3. have received (completed)
   4. have lived (continuing)
   5. have begun (continuing)
   6. have been (continuing)
   7. have failed (completed)

Present Progressive

A. 1. are having
   2. are getting
   3. are rotting
   4. is out walking
   5. are becoming
   6. are rising
   7. are improving

B. The present perfect tense is possible. It does not necessarily imply that what is happening will continue.

C. Yes. The emphasis is slightly different as the present progressive implies that what is happening will continue. The present progressive could *not* be used in the following blanks in the exercises on use of the present perfect on p. 359:
   A. 1. because of "for hundreds of years"
   B. 2. "must" implies that the decision has already been made
      6. action is completed
   C. 6. stative verb

D. 1. is always asking
   2. is always depending
   3. is always finding
   4. blaming
   5. am getting
   6. is treating

E. 1. is having
   2. is cutting
   3. are being served
   4. is being expanded
   5. are being added
   6. is offering

Tense, Present Perfect Progressive

F. 1. has been trying
   2. has been working

3. have been having
4. has just been talking
5. has been waiting

Tense, Combined Exercise on Present, Present Perfect, Present Progressive, and Present Perfect Progressive

G. 1. has been living
    2. has lived
    3. has been
    4. studies
    5. works

    6. has
    7. has tried
    8. has just promoted
    9. is living
  10. saves

Tense, Past (A)

1. began
2. caused
3. killed
4. died
5. tried

6. were
7. changed
8. prepared
9. set
10. filled

11. rained
12. was
13. showed
14. saved
15. held

Past Tense in Reported Speech (*that* may be left out) (B)

1. . . . he said (that) he had nothing to offer but . . . .
2. At the beginning of his political career Franklin D. Roosevelt said (that) there was nothing he loved as much as a good fight.
3. Samuel Johnson, . . . , said (that) he was prepared to love all humanity except an American.

Past Tense in Unreal Conditions (C)

1. returned
2. looked
3. asked
4. found
5. were

Tense, Past Perfect

1. had begun
2. had tried
3. had been *or* were
4. had made
5. had done

Tense, Past Progressive

1. were building
2. fell
3. was filling *or* filled
4. was coming
5. made
6. reached
7. became

Tense, Past Perfect Progressive

1. had invented
2. developed
3. had used
4. discovered
5. had made
6. had simplified
7. simplified
8. printed, had printed also possible
9. changed
10. reinvented
11. had
12. had developed (developed also possible)

Tense, Future

A. 1. will rise, are going to rise, are to rise, rises, are rising
   2. will complete, is going to complete, is to complete, completes, is completing
   3. will finish, is going to finish, is to finish, finishes, is finishing
   4. will hire, is going to hire, is to hire, hires, is hiring

B. 1. is going to rain; no obligation; not certain; *is raining* would mean *now*; present tense would change the meaning in this sentence
   2. isn't going to come; reasons for not using the other forms—see *1* above
   3. will come, are going to come; no obligation; not certain; present and present progressive forms cannot be used with *soon*
   4. is going to understand, no obligation; not certain; present and present progressive forms cannot be used with *after he gets a tutor*
   5. will be trained, is to be trained, is being trained

Tense, Future Perfect

1. will have happened
2. will have occurred
3. will have been conquered
4. will have wiped out
5. will have become

Tense, Future Progressive

1. will be occurring
2. will be affecting
3. will be bringing
4. will be changing
5. will be altering

Tense, Future Perfect Progressive

1. will have been thinking
2. will have been living
3. will have been
4. will have been
5. will have been functioning

Tense, Future Time in the Past
1. would rain, was to rain, was going to rain,
2. would draw, was going to draw, was to draw, was drawing,
3. would try, was going to try, was to try, was trying

Tense, Present and Future Combined
1. will give, is giving, is going to give, will be giving
2. is
3. will be posted, are to be posted
4. takes
5. schedules
6. will meet, are going to meet, will be meeting
7. will not buy, is not going to buy (less formal), will not be buying,
8. have

Titles
1. . . . Professor Jones . . . book on geometry, <u>The Elements</u>, which was written by Euclid, a mathematician . . . .
2. . . . Euclid's life, . . . "Euclid of Alexandria" in the <u>Encyclopaedia Brittanica</u>.
3. . . . "Relativity" . . . .
4. . . . she called her paper "Mathematics of the Twentieth Century."

Two-Word Verbs
A. 1. extinguish
   2. uphold
   3. observe
   4. oppose
   5. include
   6. remove
   7. strengthen
   8. display
   9. attend
  10. illuminate

B. 1. betray
   2. remove
   3. disappoint
   4. intervene
   5. encounter
   6. persuade
   7. eliminate
   8. conceal
   9. equalize
  10. discard

C. Some possible answers follow:
  (A) 1. Blow out the candle; blow it out.
       5. Count our friends in; count them in.
       6. Take off your hat; take it off.
       7. Beef up the defenses; beef them up.
       8. Show off your new furniture; show it off.
     10. The fireworks light up the sky; light it up.
  (B) 1. Sell out your friends; sell them out.
       2. Cut out a pattern; cut it out.
       3. Let down your teammates; let them down.
       6. Talk your brother into helping us; talk him into it.
       7. Take out the opposition; take it out.
       8. Hush up the scandal; hush it up.
       9. Even up the score; even it up.
     10. Throw away the broken cup; throw it away.

Verbs, Three-Word

1.	cut down on	6.	go back on
2.	look in on	7.	break in on
3.	look up to	8.	come down with
4.	walk off with	9.	check up on
5.	walk out on	10.	try out for

Verbals

1. gerund—Finding
2. infinitive—to find
3. participle—living
4. infinitive—to learn
5. gerund—surviving
6. gerund—climbing
7. infinitive—to explore
8. participle—Living
9. gerund—Exploring
10. infinitive—to explore

Verbs, Irregular

A.
1. went, bitten
2. forgot *or* forgotten
3. bit
4. bitten
5. fell, broke
6. fallen, forgot or forgotten
7. grew, drove, got, bite
8. rose
9. chosen
10. gave

B.
1. built
2. brought
3. felt, taught
4. thought, bring
5. sent
6. fought, keep, lost
7. meant
8. felt, spent
9. left

C.
1. sold
2. found
3. fed
4. bred
5. paid, told
6. sold, ground
7. said, made

D. 1. stuck
   2. dug, stung
   3. sank, swam
   4. stunk
   5. shrank
   6. struck
   7. woke

E. 1. burst
   2. paid, bought
   3. tell, could be blown, bought
   4. blew
   5. could make
   6. made
   7. brought
   8. cost

F.
1.	hung	11.	told	21.	felt	31.	know	41.	made
2.	ate	12.	keep	22.	thought	32.	left	42.	went
3.	fell	13.	let	23.	saw	33.	take	43.	ran
4.	came	14.	ride	24.	spoke	34.	thought	44.	bring
5.	got	15.	knew	25.	understood	35.	go	45.	swam
6.	did	16.	were	26.	left	36.	beat	46.	broken
7.	said	17.	began	27.	brought	37.	get	47.	clung
8.	are	18.	tell	28.	am	38.	find	48.	heard
9.	do	19.	been	29.	put	39.	knew	49.	lost
10.	Come	20.	told	30.	kept	40.	shook	50.	stole

WH-Words

A. (Other answers are possible.)
   1. Where is the college (located)?
   2. Which building are the classes held in? *or,* What building . . . ?
   3. How do students get to the college?
   4. Which buses go to the college? *or,* What buses . . . ?
   5. When are the classes?
   6. How often do classes meet?
   7. Who are the teachers? *or,* What are the names of the teachers?
   8. What courses are required to get a certificate?
   9. What subjects are required for my course?
   10. How far is the college from my apartment?
   11. How much does each class cost?
   12. How much does the whole course cost?
   13. Why are the classes so cheap? *or,* What is the reason for the classes being so cheap?
   14. How long does it usually take to get a certificate? *or,* What is the usual time to get a certificate?

B. 1. what   4. which
   2. how   5. Whom
   3. how   6. what

7.	What	11.	why
8.	What	12.	Why
9.	What	13.	what
10.	When	14.	who

Women, Terms Referring to (Other answers are possible.)

All children should learn the history of their countries. Their countries have heroes that they should learn about and imitate. Children should feel proud of their country and of the contributions that their own families or groups have made to their country. Because of the importance of heroes, a committee has been appointed to write a new textbook that will teach all children their heritage. They will learn about people in the country who have done important things. Professor Smith has been appointed chairperson of the committee to develop new materials.

Word Formation, Prefixes

The following spelling corrections should be made: patchwork, pothole, prehistoric, present-day, pushover.

Word Formation, Prefixes

1. nonproductive, unproductive, counterproductive
2. disinterested, uninterested
3. nonmoral, immoral, amoral
4. nonhuman, inhuman
5. theist, polytheist, pantheist, atheist
6. unqualified, disqualified
7. unassembled, disassembled
8. counterbalance, imbalance, unbalanced
9. malformed, unformed, informed
10. nonprofessional, unprofessional

Word Formation, Suffixes

A.
1. Portuguese
2. educable
3. scholarly
4. mindful
5. stormy
6. fearful, fearsome
7. wearisome
8. genetic
9. additional
10. innovative
11. stony
12. statuesque
13. leafy
14. Polish
15. magical
16. marriageable
17. risky
18. universal
19. nervous
20. fiendish
21. motherly
22. workmanlike
23. glorious
24. humanitarian
25. newsworthy

B.
1. librarian
2. mountaineer
3. director
4. immigrant
5. stewardess
6. retiree
7. commandant, commander
8. republican
9. son-in-law
10. Asian
11. aristocrat
12. addressee
13. Londoner
14. resident
15. mobster
16. sailor
17. majorette
18. driver
19. hireling
20. writer

C. 1. planting
   2. acreage
   3. communication
   4. arms, army, armament
   5. depository, also deposition
   6. irritation
   7. preparation

   8. ignition
   9. refrigeration
   10. handful
   11. movement
   12. grinder
   13. carpeting
   14. roofing

   15. bakery
   16. heater, heating
   17. statuary
   18. modernization
   19. hatchery
   20. swimming

D. 1. parentage
   2. brotherhood
   3. measurement
   4. readiness
   5. alignment

   6. helplessness
   7. diplomacy
   8. authenticity
   9. decisiveness
   10. adulthood

   11. difference
   12. intervention
   13. intention
   14. heroism
   15. boredom

E. 1. downward
   2. otherwise
   3. barely
   4. easily
   5. eastward, eastwardly
   6. automatically
   7. fundamentally
   8. upward
   9. likewise (*likely* is an adjective)
   10. energetically

F. 1. lengthen
   2. differentiate (*differ* is the base form)
   3. emphasize
   4. philosophize
   5. modernize
   6. equalize
   7. ripen
   8. purify
   9. lighten
   10. internationalize

G. 1. philosophy
   2. television
   3. thermodynamics
   4. geography
   5. photography
   6. thermometer
   7. centipede
   8. biology
   9. manufacture

Wordiness

A. (Other answers are possible.)
   1. At 10: A.M. all requests for transfers will be reviewed together.
   2. One reason for not granting (refusing) requests is uncertainty about projected plant expansion.

3. Except for workers hired in the last month, however, every effort will be made to protect all jobs.
4. While management is deciding whether or not to construct a new plant, employees are asked to carry on regular duties.
5. When a final decision has been made, management will inform employees in a newsletter.

B. (Other answers are possible.)
1. Uncertainty always follows mergers.
2. Many employees feel helpless because they may lose their jobs through reorganization.
3. Many employers make work for their employees when business is bad.
4. However, no business can continue to pay workers who have nothing to do.
5. People fear the unknown.

C. 1. The destructive tornado
2. The property owners . . . their barn roof fly off.
3. The rain accompanying the tornado . . . stored feed/feed stored in the barn.
4. That rain ruined the feed.
5. The feed was ruined then.

D. 1. Everyone watching the dangerous tornado was afraid.
2. Tornadoes at sea are called waterspouts.
3. Strong winds in tornadoes may cause buildings to explode.
4. The worst place on earth for tornadoes is the great plains of the United States.

E. 1. employees concerned
2. information put
3. file corrected
4. mail sent
5. papers returned
6. candidate chosen
7. plan outlined
8. engineer acquainted
9. contracts prepared
10. workers leaving are the most experienced.

F. *a.* 1. . . . a tornado does.
2. . . . a tornado do.
3. . . . tornadoes do.
4. . . . and tornadoes do too.
5. . . . and tornadoes do too.
6. . . . and tornadoes do too.
7. . . . as those in tornadoes (are).
8. . . . as a hurricane is (above 75 miles per hour).

F. *b.* 4. . . . , and so do tornadoes.
5. . . . , and so do tornadoes.
6. . . . , and so do tornadoes.

G. (Other sentences are possible.)
1. Marilyn, planning to be an engineer, can easily get in a technical college this fall because her grades are good.

2. Students must decide which branch of engineering to study: chemical, electrical, nuclear, textile, or ceramic, for example.
3. Civil engineers usually work on government projects that are too large and expensive to be built privately.
4. Civil engineers design and build roads, streets, highways, freeways, bridges, canals, and flood-control projects.
5. Civil engineers also design and build dams, tunnels, and flood and erosion control projects.
6. Engineering students must study difficult physics, chemistry, and math courses.

Index